Historical Dictionaries of Asia, Oceania, and the Middle East
Edited by Jon Woronoff

Asia

1. *Vietnam*, by William J. Duiker. 1989. *Out of print. See No. 27.*
2. *Bangladesh*, 2nd ed., by Craig Baxter and Syedur Rahman. 1996. *Out of print. See No. 48.*
3. *Pakistan*, by Shahid Javed Burki. 1991. *Out of print. See No. 33.*
4. *Jordan*, by Peter Gubser. 1991
5. *Afghanistan*, by Ludwig W. Adamec. 1991. *Out of print. See No. 47.*
6. *Laos*, by Martin Stuart-Fox and Mary Kooyman. 1992. *Out of print. See No. 35.*
7. *Singapore*, by K. Mulliner and Lian The-Mulliner. 1991
8. *Israel*, by Bernard Reich. 1992
9. *Indonesia*, by Robert Cribb. 1992. *Out of print. See No. 51.*
10. *Hong Kong and Macau*, by Elfed Vaughan Roberts, Sum Ngai Ling, and Peter Bradshaw. 1992
11. *Korea*, by Andrew C. Nahm. 1993
12. *Taiwan*, by John F. Copper. 1993. *Out of print. See No. 34.*
13. *Malaysia*, by Amarjit Kaur. 1993. *Out of print. See No. 36.*
14. *Saudi Arabia*, by J. E. Peterson. 1993. *Out of print. See No. 45.*
15. *Myanmar*, by Jan Becka. 1995
16. *Iran*, by John H. Lorentz. 1995
17. *Yemen*, by Robert D. Burrowes. 1995
18. *Thailand*, by May Kyi Win and Harold Smith. 1995
19. *Mongolia*, by Alan J. K. Sanders. 1996. *Out of print. See No. 42.*
20. *India*, by Surjit Mansingh. 1996
21. *Gulf Arab States*, by Malcolm C. Peck. 1996
22. *Syria*, by David Commins. 1996. *Out of print. See No. 50.*
23. *Palestine*, by Nafez Y. Nazzal and Laila A. Nazzal. 1997
24. *Philippines*, by Artemio R. Guillermo and May Kyi Win. 1997

Oceania

1. *Australia*, by James C. Docherty. 1992. *Out of print. See No. 32.*
2. *Polynesia*, by Robert D. Craig. 1993. *Out of print. See No. 39.*
3. *Guam and Micronesia*, by William Wuerch and Dirk Ballendorf. 1994

Historical Dictionary of Syria

Second Edition

David Commins

Historical Dictionaries of Asia,
Oceania, and the Middle East, No. 50

The Scarecrow Press, Inc.
Lanham, Maryland • Toronto • Oxford
2004

SCARECROW PRESS, INC.

Published in the United States of America
by Scarecrow Press, Inc.
A wholly owned subsidary of
The Rowman & Littlefield Publishing Group, Inc.
4501 Forbes Boulevard, Suite 200, Lanham, Maryland 20706
www.scarecrowpress.com

PO Box 317
Oxford
OX2 9RU, UK

British Library Cataloguing in Publication Information Available

Library of Congress Cataloging-in-Publication Data
Commins, David Dean.
  Historical dictionary of Syria / David Commins. — 2nd ed.
    p. cm. — (Historical dictionaries of Asia, Oceania, and the Middle East ;
50)
  Includes bibliographical references.
  ISBN 0-8108-4934-8 (cloth : alk. paper)
  1. Syria–History–Dictionaries. I. Title. II. Series.
  DS94.9.C66 2004
  956.91'003–dc22   2003028317

For Marcia Faye Swanson Commins

CONTENTS

EDITOR'S FOREWORD

For some three decades, Syria has remained largely in the background, despite its acknowledged strategic importance. This was partly because it was overshadowed by Saddam Husayn's Iraq, but even more so because its president Hafiz al-Asad was considerably more cautious and balanced in his policies. This brought relative stability and even modest economic and social progress yet ultimately resulted in stagnation and dissatisfaction, especially among the younger generation. The time had come for change and reform, which was promised by Bashar al-Asad, but that has not amounted to much so far. Thus, Syria is now a much greater focus of attention than before. It must meet some of the domestic expectations and also international ones, given its evident influence over events in the surrounding region, especially Lebanon, Palestine, and Israel. That is why it is particularly fortunate that a second edition of the *Historical Dictionary of Syria* is appearing at this juncture.

Despite renewed interest in present-day Syria, events could hardly be understood without a good look at the whole period of Ba`th Party rule and the ineffectual regimes that preceded it, to say nothing of the period of the French Mandate, or of Ottoman domination, or the many kingdoms and empires that preceded that. This book takes a very long view, with a chronology stretching back to the first settlements, an introduction that provides a broad sketch of the country and its history, and a dictionary section which looks more closely at the details. This includes information on significant persons, not only political and military but also literary and religious, major events, the various institutions which emerged, and even aspects of ordinary life for ordinary people. This is capped by a substantial bibliography.

David Commins, who is a professor of history at Dickinson College, spends much of his time teaching students and others about the Middle East, especially Syria. Ever since his stay there in the early 1980s, he has followed current events, but also delved into the past, particularly the Ottoman era. This has resulted in various articles and a book, *Islamic Reform: Politics and Social Change in Late Ottoman Syria*. At present, he is concentrating more on modern Islamic thought; yet his range of interests is amazingly wide, to judge by the entries in this volume, and he is willing to be sufficiently frank when necessary to explain the actual situation. That is a virtue rare enough in writing on the Middle East to be highly appreciated.

Jon Woronoff, Series Editor

ACKNOWLEDGMENTS

It is with pleasure that I reflect on the many scholarly and personal debts that I have accumulated in the course of studying Syria for 20 years. Many Syrians have taught me meanings of hospitality and graciousness that no foreign scholar could ever deserve, for they are truly gifts. These Syrians include the young men who befriended me at Damascus University's "*wahdat ula*," the families of Muhammad Sa`id al-Qasimi and Sa`id al-Ghabra, my dear friend Atallah Hoshan, the much-beloved Ibrahim family of culinary fame, and the Virginian branch of the Naanou family.

I am most fortunate to have found a niche within the close-knit community of scholars who dedicate themselves to understanding Syria's past and its present. I am especially grateful to a few individuals whose knowledge and judgment I value, and whose friendship has been the true reward for working in the same field: Randi Deguilhem, James Gelvin, Joshua Landis, and Najwa al-Qattan. For providing me details on a number of modern personalities, I thank Sami Moubayed.

Dickinson College has provided a stimulating and supportive environment. Interactions and collaborations with students, colleagues, staff, and even administrators make the college a special place to work. For this particular project, I have benefitted from the resources of Dickinson's Waidner-Spahr Library, and most especially the interlibrary loan department, so splendidly managed by Tina Maresco and Sandra Gority that I have come to believe that the rarest monographs and articles are readily at hand. Producing a camera-ready manuscript is never as straightforward as I imagine it will be, but I know I can rely on Elaine Mellen to quickly penetrate the mysteries of word processing with her amazing acumen. Most authors know the risk of taking their work, and themselves, far too seriously. Few are fortunate to have a friend so ready to guard against that risk as Steve Weinberger.

Most of the writing for this new edition took place at home, on a desktop computer shared with my teenage daughter Marcia. I owe her—not so much for the practical aspect of scheduling times on the computer, but for taking it easy on me while she negotiates the journey through adolescence. Thank you for making it easy to be a father. Finally, I want to thank my mother, Marcia Faye Swanson Commins, for her abiding confidence and cheerful encouragement of my first ventures overseas, travels that led to many adventures and to an abiding passion for Syria.

READER'S NOTE

Because this work is intended for a general audience, I transliterate Arabic names and terms without the diacritics that specialists often prefer and that mean nothing to others. There are two Arabic consonants, *hamza* and *ayn*, that cannot be represented by any letters in the English alphabet. The conventional designations are ' for *hamza* and ` for *ayn*. I have transliterated these two letters when they occur in the middle and end of a word. For example, "Ba`th party" or "Faruq al-Shara`" show the ayn but "Ali" does not.

In Arabic, the definite article is "al-" and I have included it only when a name is first mentioned. To look up al-Quwwatli, for example, the reader will find it under "Q" and not under "A."

The Arabic word "*mamluk*" is used in two related but distinct senses. In the general sense, indicated by the lower case, it refers to a slave soldier. It may also refer to a sultanate that ruled Syria for 250 years, and in that sense it is capitalized.

A note on using the dictionary: Cross-references are indicated by the use of **bold** type at the first mention of a name or term in an entry.

ACRONYMS AND ABBREVIATIONS

CUP	Committee of Union and Progress
DMZ	Demilitarized Zones
EU	European Union
ICARDA	International Center for Agricultural Research in Dry Areas
NRCC	National Revolutionary Command Council
PKK	Kurdistan Workers' Party (Partiya Karkeren Kurdistan)
PLO	Palestine Liberation Organization
SCP	Syrian Communist Party
SSNP	Syrian Social National Party
UAE	United Arab Emirates
UAR	United Arab Republic
UN	United Nations
UNDOF	United Nations Disengagement Observer Force
UNESCO	United Nations Educational, Scientific, and Cultural Organization
UNRWA	United Nations Relief and Works Agency
US	United States
USSR	Union of Soviet Socialist Republics

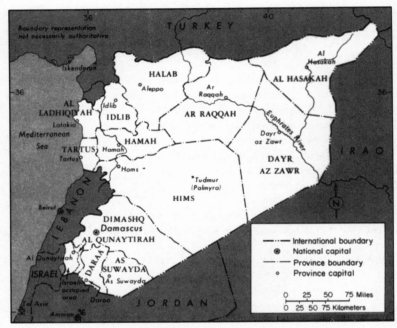

Figure 1. Administrative Divisions of Syria
Used by permission of the American University Press

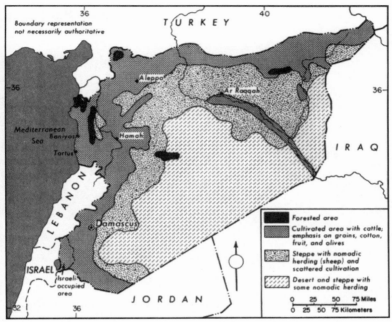

Figure 2. Land Use
Used by permission of the American University Press

CHRONOLOGY

B.C.

3500   Early settlement at Ebla

2450-2350   Ebla flourishes in northern Syria

2200-2000   Amorite migration into northern Syria

2000-1800   Amorite domination in the north; emergence of Ugarit and Aleppo

1800-1650   Amorite kingdom of Yamkhad at Aleppo

1650-1350   Mitanni domination in the north; Egyptian domination in the south

1590   Hittite invasion of the north

1350-1200   Hittites supplant Mitanni rule; Carchemish emerges as major Hittite kingdom; Egyptians continue to dominate the south

1200-1000   Early Iron Age; Aramaean immigration; raids by Sea Peoples along the coast; Assyrian military expeditions

c. 1180   Destruction of Ugarit

1000-732   Aramaean kingdom of Aram with capital at Damascus; rise of Aramaean kingdom at Hama in central Syria

732-612   Assyrian rule

612-538   Babylonian and Neo-Babylonian rule

538-333   Persian Achaemenid rule

333-332   Alexander the Great conquers Syria

312-A.D. 106   Arab Nabataean dynasty in southern Syria

301-240   Era of Seleucid rule

240-198   Ptolemies of Egypt annex Syria

198-64   Era of Seleucid decline

64 B.C.-
A.D. 334   Roman rule

A.D.

106-272   Semiautonomous kingdom at Palmyra

334-634   Capital of Roman Empire moves to Byzantium; Syria ruled
                       by Christian emperors

632-661   Rightly guided caliphs

634-641   Arab Muslim conquests

661-750   Umayyad caliphate

750-1258   Abbasid caliphate

868-905   Tulunid rule

905-935   Restoration of Abbasid rule

935-969   Ikhshidid rule

944-1016   Hamdanid dynasty (northern Syria)

978-1078   Fatimid dynasty (southern Syria)

1016-1023   Fatimids rule northern Syria

1023-1079   Mirdasid dynasty (northern Syria)

1079-1104	Saljuk rule in Damascus
1086-1113	Saljuk rule in Aleppo
1098-1303	Crusades
1104-1171	Atabegs in Damascus
1128-1171	Atabegs in Aleppo
1171-1260	Ayyubid dynasty
1260-1516	Mamluk sultanate
1516-1918	Ottoman dynasty
1725-1783	Azm governors
1775-1804	Ahmad al-Jazzar
1831-1840	Egyptian occupation
1839-1876	Tanzimat era
1850	Communal massacre in Aleppo
1860	Communal massacre in Damascus
1876	**December:** Ottoman constitution promulgated
1876-1909	Reign of Sultan Abdulhamid II
1878	**February:** Abdulhamid suspends constitution
1908	**July:** Military mutiny to restore constitution
1908-1918	Constitutional era
1914	Ottoman Empire enters World War I on side of Entente

1914-1915	Husayn-McMahon Correspondence: Britain pledges to support an independent Arab kingdom in exchange for a revolt against Ottoman rule in Arabia
1916	**May:** Sykes-Picot Accord between France and Britain to partition Arab lands of the Ottoman Empire into spheres of influence. **June:** Arab Revolt against Ottoman rule
1918	**October:** Allies defeat Ottomans and end Ottoman rule in Syria; Amir Faysal forms an Arab government
1920	**April:** San Remo Agreement assigns France the League of Nations mandate for Syria. **July:** French army occupies Aleppo; battle of Maysalun; French occupation of Damascus. **September:** France creates Greater Lebanon by detaching portions of Syrian territory and incorporating them into Lebanon; divides Syria into separate states centered on Damascus and Aleppo; establishes separate regime for the Alawis
1920-1946	French Mandate
1922	France establishes separate regime for Jabal Druze
1925	France combines Damascus, Aleppo, Homs, and Hama into a single administrative unit
1925-1927	The Great Revolt
1928	**April-June:** Elections to constituent assembly; National Bloc minority dominates proceedings. **July:** Constituent Assembly publishes draft constitution. **August:** France rejects draft constitution, adjourns the assembly
1929	**February:** France prorogues constituent assembly
1930	**May:** France approves modified version of constituent assembly's constitution as basis for national elections to parliament

1931-1932   **December-January:** National elections to parliament; National Bloc wins 17 of 69 seats

1933   **November:** France temporarily suspends parliament for rejecting France's proposal for a treaty

1936   **January-March:** General strike throughout Syria in response to French crackdown on the National Bloc; strike ends in victory for the Bloc when the French invite its leaders to Paris to negotiate a treaty. **April-September:** Negotiations on Franco-Syrian Treaty to define mechanisms for Syria's eventual independence and admittance to the League of Nations. **November:** National elections to parliament, huge victory for National Bloc. **December:** Parliament elects Hashim al-Atasi to be president of the republic; Jamil Mardam appointed prime minister; parliament ratifies treaty with France; Jabal Druze and Territory of the Alawis are incorporated into Syria

1937   **November:** The League of Nations places Alexandretta Province under a special autonomous regime with tenuous formal links to Syria

1938   **July:** Franco-Turkish Friendship Treaty guarantees Turkey's neutrality in the event of aggression against France; Turkey allowed to send troops into Alexandretta. **December:** French parliament refuses to act on the Franco-Syrian Treaty, effectively killing it

1939   **February:** Mardam government resigns. **June:** Turkey formally annexes Alexandretta. **July:** High Commissioner suspends constitution, dissolves parliament, restores separate administration for Jabal Druze, Latakia, and Jazira

1939-1945   World War II

1940   **December:** Vichy administration established in Syria

1941   **June-July:** Allied invasion of Syria and Lebanon to remove Vichy administration; Britain becomes dominant military power in Syria. **October:** Free French restore constitutiona! government

1942   **February:** France reunites Jabal Druze and Latakia to the rest of Syria

1943   **July:** National elections result in huge victory for National Party; Shukri al-Quwwatli becomes president

1945   **May:** Anti-French demonstrations by crowds seeking independence. **29-30 May:** French bombardment of Damascus kills 400 Syrians; British forces wrest control from the French

1946   **17 April:** France withdraws troops

1946-1958   Syrian Republic

1947   Founding of Ba`th Party by Michel Aflaq and Salah al-Din al-Bitar

1948   War with Israel

1949   **30 March:** Military coup by Husni al-Za`im. **20 July:** Armistice with Israel. **14 August:** Military coup by Sami al-Hinnawi. **15-16 November:** Election of constituent assembly. **19 December:** Military coup by Adib al-Shishakli

1950   **February:** Akram al-Hawrani forms Arab Socialist Party. **September:** New constitution promulgated

1951   **November:** Shishakli dismisses civilian government

1952   **April:** Shishakli bans all political parties

1953   **July:** Shishakli elected president in plebiscite

1954   **February:** Shishakli overthrown; civilian democratic regime and 1950 constitution restored. **September:** National elections increase strength of neutralist and leftist trends

1955   **February:** Formation of the Baghdad Pact, a pro-Western military alliance between Iraq and Turkey; political pressures on Syria to join the alliance. **April:** Assassination of Col. Adnan al-Malki, leader of neutralist faction in officer corps, bolsters popular anti-Western sentiment. **October:** Security pact with Egypt and Saudi Arabia formed to keep Syria out of Baghdad Pact

1956   **February:** Arms deal with Czechoslovakia

1957   **August-October:** Crisis in relations with US, Turkish troops mass near border

1958   **February:** Formation of United Arab Republic between Syria and Egypt

1959   **December:** Resignation of Ba'thist ministers from UAR government

1961   **July:** Socialist decrees nationalize banks and other large firms. **22 September:** Syria secedes from UAR

1962   **28 March-2 April:** Abortive military coups against conservative civilian government

1963   **8 March:** Military coup by Ba'thist and Nasirist officers. **18 July:** Nasirist uprising suppressed; Ba'thist officers take power

1964   **April:** Antigovernment demonstrations in Hama forcibly repressed; provisional constitution promulgated

1965   **January:** Nationalization of industry and foreign trade. **May:** Struggle for power within the Ba'th Party leads to Aflaq's resignation as secretary-general

1966   **23 February:** Power struggle within Ba'th Party leads to coup by radical "neo-Ba'thist" faction

1967   **5-10 June:** War between Israel and Syria, Egypt, and

Jordan; Israeli forces seize Golan Heights; relations with United States severed. **November:** United Nations passes Resolution 242 calling for negotiations to end the Arab-Israeli conflict and the return of Arab territory seized in June

1968-1969   Development of power struggle between Salah al-Jadid and Hafiz al-Asad

1970   **12 November:** Hafiz al-Asad comes to power in the corrective movement, a coup d'état against the Ba`th Party's radical wing

1971   **February:** Hafiz al-Asad becomes president of Syria

1973   **12 March:** Promulgation of a new permanent constitution. **6-24 October:** Syria and Egypt fight war with Israel

1974   **May:** Syria and Israel sign disengagement accord to separate armed forces on the Golan Heights. **June:** US-Syrian diplomatic relations reestablished

1975   **April:** Civil war erupts in Lebanon

1976   **June:** Syrian forces intervene in Lebanese Civil War against leftist Lebanese and Palestinian militias. **October:** Cease-fire in Lebanese Civil War

1979   **June:** Muslim Brothers carry out massacre of military cadets in Aleppo

1980   Islamist and secular opponents launch campaign of demon-strations, protests, and assassinations against the Asad regime; government responds with draconian measures

1981   **December:** Israel extends its law to Golan Heights

1982   **February:** Uprising by Islamist forces in Hama brutally quelled by the Syrian army. **June-August:** Israel invades Lebanon, skirmishes with Syrian troops, forces Palestine

Liberation Organization to leave Lebanon, and engineers election of Bashir Gemayel as president of Lebanon. **September:** Gemayel assassinated; his brother Amin Gemayel succeeds him; United States, France, and Italy dispatch a multinational force to stabilize Beirut after Christian militia massacres Palestinian civilians

1983   **May:** Lebanese and Israeli negotiators agree on a security accord; Syria announces its opposition to it and rallies Lebanese parties and militias to undermine it. **13 November:** President Asad falls ill and disappears from public view. **27 November:** Asad makes his first public appearance in two weeks. **December:** Escalation in confrontation between Syria and US and Israel over Lebanon; Syria supports Palestinian factions attacking groups loyal to PLO chairman Yasir Arafat; they expel Arafat from the northern Lebanese city of Tripoli

1984   **February:** US withdraws its forces from Lebanon. **29 February:** Lebanese President Gemayel formally renounces the May 17 agreement with Israel. **March:** Power struggle between Rif at al-Asad and rival officers threatens to destabilize the regime. **May:** Rif at al-Asad leaves Syria on "diplomatic" trip that turns into a six-month exile. **November:** Rif at returns to Syria but much of his power base is dismantled

1985   **January:** Asad issues presidential amnesty to certain members of the Muslim Brothers, invites several exiles to return to Syria. **June:** Israel withdraws its forces to a strip of Lebanese territory along the border that it declares a security zone. **December:** Rif at al-Asad again leaves the country for an extended period

1986   **10 October:** Great Britain severs ties with Syria because of its role in an abortive terrorist operation at London's Heathrow airport. **24 October:** US and Canada recall ambassadors from Damascus. **November:** West Germany downgrades relations with Syria over its role in a March bombing of a German-American Friendship Club in West Berlin

1987   **February:** Syrian troops enter West Beirut to end several months of incessant strife among rival militias. **June:** Syria closes offices of terrorist Abu Nidal organization to improve ties with Europe and the United States

1988   **August:** War between Iran and Iraq ends in a victory for Iraq, defeat for Asad's pro-Iranian foreign policy. **September:** Lebanese President Gemayel's term expires without election of a successor; he appoints General Michel Aoun head of a caretaker government; Lebanese cabinet rejects Aoun; anti-Syrian groups rally behind Aoun

1989   **March-August:** Clashes between General Aoun and pro-Syrian forces prompt intense Arab diplomatic efforts. **12 October:** Lebanese parliament convenes at Ta'if in Saudi Arabia and agrees to modestly redistribute political power and calls on Syrian forces to withdraw from the Beirut area to the Bekaa valley within two years. **27 December:** Syria and Egypt restore relations that were broken off when Egypt signed a peace treaty with Israel in 1979

1990   **2 August:** Iraq invades Kuwait. **20 August:** Syria sends 1,200 troops to Saudi Arabia. **13 October:** Syrian warplanes bomb Michel Aoun's presidential palace; he flees to the French embassy and clears the way for implementing the Ta'if Accord

1991   **January-March:** Desert Storm evicts Iraqi army from Kuwait; 15,000 Syrian troops are part of the coalition but do not participate in combat. **22 May:** Syria and Lebanon sign Treaty of Brotherhood, Cooperation, and Coordination to regulate bilateral relations. **30 October-4 November:** Syria attends international peace conference at Madrid and agrees to start bilateral talks with Israel but boycotts multilateral talks. **10 December:** Syria and Israel begin talks in Washington, D.C.

1992   **June-September:** Lebanese hold popular demonstrations calling for Syria to withdraw its forces from much of the country to the Bekaa valley. Lebanese elections take place amid a general strike in East Beirut and widespread Maronite boycott. **December:** Israel expels 400 Palestinian militants to Lebanon; Arabs suspend peace talks in protest

1993   **April:** Peace talks resume. **August:** Oslo Accords between Israel and the PLO weaken Syria's negotiating position

1994   **16 January:** American President Bill Clinton meets Hafiz al-Asad in Damascus to push peace talks forward. **21 January:** President Asad's 32-year-old son, Basil, dies in an automobile accident. He had recently emerged as a possible successor to his father. **April:** Russia and Syria sign first military and technical agreement since the fall of the Soviet Union. **26 October:** Jordan and Israel sign a peace treaty

1995   **November:** Israeli Prime Minister Yitzhak Rabin assassinated by a Jewish zealot. **December:** New Israeli Prime Minister Shimon Peres initiates resumption of peace talks at Wye River Plantation in the United States

1996   **January:** Wye River talks continue. Turkish government presses Syria to cease support for separatist Kurdish movement. **February:** Palestinian suicide bombers kill dozens of Israelis in less than two weeks. Syria refuses to condemn the terrorist attacks and Israel breaks off peace talks. Israel and Turkey sign a strategic security pact, creating a sense of encirclement in Damascus. **March:** Syria joins dialogue on expanding free trade between the European Union and southern Mediterranean countries launched at Barcelona the previous year. **April:** Israel launches "Grapes of Wrath" military campaign in Lebanon to retaliate for Hizballah attacks on its patrols in south Lebanon. **May:** A series of explosions in several Syrian cities go unclaimed by any group. Israeli national elections bring Likud leader Benjamin Netanyahu to office. His rejection of "land for peace" formula leads to a three-year freeze in peace talks. **June:** Arab summit in Cairo marks Syrian bid to forge a new regional alliance to counter Netanyahu's policies. **December:** An Islamic fundamentalist group bombs a bus in Damascus, killing about 10 people

1997   **June:** Border with Iraq reopens for trade. The government permits businessmen to travel to Iraq and closes Radio Voice of Iraq, an anti-Saddam station

1998   **February:** Hafiz al-Asad officially dismisses his brother Rif'at as vice president. **August:** Oil pipeline from Iraq reopens for the first time since 1982. **October:** Crisis with Turkey over Syrian support for the Kurdistan Workers Party (PKK), an organization that had fought a guerrilla war for Kurdish secession since 1984. The crisis ends when Syria agrees to Turkish demands that it expel PKK leaders and shut down PKK camps in Lebanon and offices in Damascus

1999   **February:** Jordan's King Husayn dies and his son Abdallah succeeds to the throne. National referendum reelects Hafiz al-Asad for a fifth seven-year term as president. **April:** Jordan's King Abdallah II visits Damascus and talks with President Asad result in a notable thaw in relations that had turned cold when Jordan made peace with Israel five years before. The two leaders agree to revive commercial ties. **May:** New spirit of friendship with Jordan affirmed with formal agreement to build a dam on the Yarmuk River. Israeli national elections result in victory of Labor Party leader Ehud Barak over Likud Prime Minister Benjamin Netanyahu. Barak's victory creates a mood of optimism that the three-year stalemate in Syrian-Israeli peace talks could end. **June:** President Asad and Prime Minister Barak publicly declare their willingness to strive for a peace agreement and express cautious optimism about one another. While substantial obstacles remain, the leaders' remarks foster a more positive climate for peace talks. **July:** Asad visits Moscow for first time since 1991 to confer with Russian President Boris Yeltsin on the peace process and Syria's bid to purchase arms. **September:** American efforts to restart Israeli-Syrian peace talks pick up with visits to Damascus by Secretary of State Madeleine Albright and to Washington by Syrian Foreign Minister Faruq al-Shara`. **October:** Government forces seize a compound belonging to Rif'at al-Asad in Latakia to shut down an illegal port and to diminish his ability to challenge Bashar al-Asad's anticipated succession. **November:** Bashar al-Asad visits France, his first official mission to a European country and a further sign that his father intends him to follow him as president. **December:** A new intensive American diplomatic effort results in the resumption of Syrian-Israeli peace talks at Shepherdstown, West Virginia, the following month

2000

2-10 January: Peace talks at Shepherdstown make some progress but Syria's insistence on an Israeli commitment to full withdrawal from the Golan Heights before further talks creates a new stalemate. **February:** Regional climate worsens as Hizballah mounts new attacks on Israeli positions in southern Lebanon and Israel retaliates. **5 March:** Israel declares intention to unconditionally withdraw from Lebanon in four months. **14 March:** Asad forms a new cabinet, ostensibly to smooth the succession of his son Bashar. Other than the prime minister, the most powerful figures in key ministries keep their posts. **26 March:** The meeting between Asad and Clinton at Geneva fails to revive Syrian-Israeli peace talks, souring relations between Washington and Damascus and ending Barak's bid for an agreement with Asad. **13 April:** Israel declares an end to suspension of settlement construction on the Golan Heights, signaling Barak's view that talks had reached a dead end. **10 May:** Bashar al-Asad's anticorruption drive targets Mahmud al-Zu'bi, recently dismissed as prime minister, for undefined abuses. **24 May:** Israel withdraws its forces from Lebanon after a 22-year occupation. **10 June:** President Hafiz al-Asad dies after a long illness one week before a planned Ba'th Party Congress that was to elect Bashar to a seat on the Regional Command. **11 June:** Parliament amends the constitution's provision on the minimum age for head of state to legalize Bashar al-Asad's succession. **27 June:** Parliament ratifies Bashar al-Asad as the sole candidate in a presidential referendum. **10 July:** Bashar al-Asad wins 97 percent of the vote in the referendum. **11-25 July:** Palestinian-Israeli talks at Camp David fail to resolve disputes over refugees, borders, Jerusalem, and Israeli settlements. Bill Clinton joins Ehud Barak in denouncing Yasir Arafat for refusing to compromise. **August:** Proponents of reform hold public meetings, organize voluntary associations, and call for the end of authoritarian regulations on political expression. **28-29 September:** Palestinian uprising against Israel erupts in the West Bank and jeopardizes seven years of Israeli-Palestinian diplomacy. **1 October:** Bashar al-Asad goes to Cairo for his first official visit to an Arab capital to discuss the regional crisis caused by renewed Palestinian-Israeli fighting. **5 November:** Eruption of fighting between Druze villagers and bedouins in Suwayda governorate results in 20 deaths and dispatch of army forces to restore quiet. **16 November:** Release of 600 political prisoners raises hopes that Bashar al-Asad will fulfill promise to relax restrictions on civil liberties

2001   **6 February:** Likud Party leader Ariel Sharon elected prime minister of Israel. Ali Farzat publishes a weekly satirical magazine, *The Lamplighter (al-Dumari)*, the first independent periodical since 1963. **8 February:** Bashar al-Asad announces limits to freedom of expression, marking the beginning of a crackdown on the budding political reform movement. **27-28 March:** Arab summit in Amman to devise a common front against Israel's Ariel Sharon includes a meeting between Asad and Arafat to bring PLO and Syrian positions into alignment. **5-8 May:** Pope John Paul II visits Damascus and his tour of the Umayyad Mosque is the first time a pope enters a mosque. **11 September:** Terrorist attacks on the United States kill 3,000 people and mark a watershed in American relations with the Muslim world. **8 October:** The government attacks the political reform movement by charging two independent members of the People's Assembly with undermining the constitution. **November:** The regime balances its crackdown on liberal dissidents with the release of about 120 political prisoners. **December:** Bashar al-Asad forms a new cabinet that retains the prime minister and veteran ministers of defense and foreign relations

2002   **8 March:** Bashar al-Asad goes to Beirut on the eve of an

Arab summit and is the first Syrian head of state to visit Lebanon's presidential palace. **June:** United States accuses Syria of supporting terrorist actions carried out by Hizballah and Palestinian organizations. **August:** Political trials of eight democracy activists conclude with guilty verdicts and sentences ranging from three to 10 years. **8 November:** UN Security Council passes Resolution 1441 requiring Iraq to dismantle weapons of mass destruction. Syria votes for the resolution with the rest of the Council members

2003   **19 March:** United States launches war to overthrow Saddam Husayn's Ba`thist regime in Iraq. Syrian demonstrators protest American invasion. **9 April:** Baghdad falls to American troops. **May:** US Secretary of State Colin Powell visits Damascus to persuade Syrians to shut down the offices of militant Palestinian groups on the US list of terrorist organizations. **5 October:** Israeli warplanes attack a Palestinian training camp near Damascus in retaliation for an Islamic Jihad suicide bombing in Haifa. It is the first Israeli attack on Syrian soil since the October 1973 War. **24 October:** Bashar al-Asad shuffles the cabinet for the first time since June 2000, but apart from appointing a new prime minister, the other major ministers stay in place. **5 December:** American President George W. Bush signs into law the Syrian Accountability and Lebanese Sovereignty Restoration Act, threatening new trade sanctions if Syria does not withdraw from Lebanon, abandon its non-conventional weapons program, and end support for insurgents in Iraq and Palestinian and Lebanese groups on the US list of terrorist organizations

2004   **January:** Bashar al-Asad visits Turkey to discuss mutual concerns over the prospect of an autonomous regime emerging in Iraqi Kurdistan

INTRODUCTION

In the first years of the new millennium, it appears that Syria is cautiously embarking on a path of economic liberalization and technical modernization while resisting pressures for substantial political change. Observers had believed it possible that the dramatic political and economic transformations attendant upon the fall of the Soviet Union might nudge the Syrian leadership to embrace new policies. Indeed, the realm of foreign affairs witnessed Syria's willingness to enter direct negotiations with Israel as well as attempts to cooperate with the United States in regional policy. Nonetheless, the regime took rather timid steps toward economic reform and left the political arena in the grip of the Ba'th Party and intelligence services.

In 2000, the country had its first change of leadership in 30 years when President Hafiz al-Asad died and was succeeded by his son Bashar. The younger Asad inherited a portfolio that had changed little in nearly 20 years: fitful economic growth, a demographic bulge of youth, a political elite accustomed to authoritarianism, Israeli occupation of Syrian territory, chilly if not hostile relations with other neighbors, and a large military presence in Lebanon. Most accounts of Bashar al-Asad portray him as lacking the experience and personal authority necessary to institute dramatic change, if he wished to. He relies on many of the same military, intelligence, and political advisers who surrounded his father. They in turn represent an entrenched, powerful network with much to lose and little to gain from any kind of reform. The durability of comparable regimes in the Arab world suggests that they have mastered the art of governance as far as regime survival is concerned. Political scientists debate the primacy of economic or cultural causes for the resilience of authoritarianism in Arab lands. For Syrians, it is a moot question until "something gives." In the meantime, they deploy their justly renowned ingenuity to squeeze the most out of the economy as it is in the pursuit of the "good life."

LAND AND PEOPLE

The modern nation of Syria lies between Turkey in the north, Iraq in the east, Jordan in the south, Israel in the southwest, and Lebanon in the west. Before the 20th century, it was rarely independent; rather, larger empires often ruled the country. The term Syria, or its Arabic equivalent, *bilad al-sham*, referred to a broad region encompassing the modern nations of Jordan, Israel, Lebanon, Syria, and the Turkish province of Hatay. Writers refer to Syria in the broader sense as geographical, historical, or greater Syria. Unless otherwise noted, this work restricts itself to Syria in its contemporary dimensions.

Syria's land area measures 185,170 square kilometers (71,500 square miles), roughly the size of North Dakota. The country can be divided into five major geographical zones that run from north to south. First is a narrow strip along the Mediterranean. The coastal plain varies in width from nearly 30 kilometers to a few hundred meters. This area's climate consists of mild winters with fairly abundant rainfall and hot humid summers. The greatest amount of precipitation falls in the north and decreases farther south. The second major zone consists of three mountain ranges that abruptly rise above the coastal plain. In the north the Amanus Mountains have peaks over 1,600 meters. The Baylan Pass through the Amanus range is the main route between Aleppo and its historical port Antioch. South of that pass is the Aqra range, which stretches from Antioch through Latakia province to Tripoli in Lebanon. Within this range is the Jabal al-Ansariyya, a mostly Alawi and Christian region. The Aqra range ends at the Homs Gap, the major land route between Homs and Tripoli. The southernmost range is the Anti-Lebanon Mountains, which run through Syria and Lebanon and have peaks as high as 3,600 meters. These mountain ranges are marked by their own particular climate. They have cold winters with frequent snowfall and the heaviest rainfall in the country. During the summer, the days are hot and the nights cool. The third major zone is a broad interior plain on the eastern side of the mountains. It stretches from Aleppo in the north to the Hawran in the south and is the site of the country's major towns and cities: Aleppo, Hama, Homs, and Damascus. Some parts of this zone receive a fair amount of rainfall, which decreases as one moves farther inland. Winters are mild and summers are hot and dry. The last main region is the Syrian Desert, which is really an extension of the huge Arabian desert and occupies the largest portion of the country in the east and south. The desert receives little rain and has cold winters and very hot, dry summers. In the north, the desert is bisected by the Euphrates River, the waters of which have been used to irrigate fields since ancient times. As one approaches the Turkish border, there is higher and more regular rainfall and the desert merges with a semiarid steppe in the region known as Jazira.

Syria's main river is the Euphrates, which flows southwest from Turkey through Syria into Iraq. Two important tributaries of the Euphrates are the Khabur and Balikh Rivers. The Orontes River courses in a northerly direction through central Syria beneath the eastern slopes of Jabal Ansariyya. The Barada River, although relatively small, has been of great importance in Syria's history because it provides water to one of the country's two major cities, Damascus. The other major city, Aleppo, lies near the Quwayk River.

The current population is approaching 18 million and increasing at an annual rate of 2.5 percent. About 85 percent of the population is Arab, roughly 10 percent is Kurdish, many of whom are Arabized or can speak Arabic, and about four percent are Armenians. In religious terms, close to 75 percent of Syrians are Sunni Muslims; the Alawis, an offshoot of Shi`i Islam, constitute about 12 percent of the population. Christians count for perhaps 10 percent and Druzes for three percent of the total population. Isma`ilis, Twelver or Imami Shi`is, Yazidis, and Jews comprise a tiny minority. The distribution of different language and religious groups is quite varied. The Druzes and Alawis, for instance, both Arabic speakers, each comprise the overwhelming majority in particular regions, while Christians and Sunnis are dispersed throughout various towns and rural districts. The Kurds have been concentrated in the Jazira in the northeast, while most Armenians live in Aleppo and Damascus. For much of Syrian history, remote areas provided refuges for members of religious minorities. Occasionally, Sunni rulers would try to impose their authority, but in general it was not until the 20th century that the Druzes, the Alawis, and the Arab and Kurdish inhabitants of the Jazira lost their communal autonomy. The political integration of Syria's diverse population under urban Sunni domination occurred during the French Mandate and early independence years. Since the 1960s, provincial Sunnis and members of minorities have turned the tables by seizing power through control over the military and the Ba`th Party. Forging a common Syrian identity is an ongoing project that the government fosters through education and the media. Social interaction among Syrians of different religious backgrounds has certainly become more frequent, and a secular culture has made inroads, but communal boundaries remain firm when it comes to marriage.

Syria has a long record of economic integration and cultural coherence rooted in its ancient cities. The major cities—Aleppo, Hama, Homs, and Damascus—have perennially serviced long-distance trade along two distinct axes: a north-south axis from the Indian Ocean, Yemen, and Arabia to Asia Minor and the Mediterranean; and an east-west axis from Iran and Iraq to Egypt and the Mediterranean. Urban merchants organized, financed, and conducted long-distance trade and used the wealth it generated to develop a thriving urban culture. In addition to the cities' role in trade, they served as the centers of political power over the surrounding countryside. The rulers resided in the main towns and extracted the agricultural surplus from the numerically dominant yet politically subordinate peasantry of surrounding villages. This surplus fed the inhabitants of Syria's main cities and supplied raw materials for artisanal manufactures, particularly textiles and leather goods. It also provided the chief source of rulers' wealth, which they lavished on monumental construction, more modest but necessary urban infrastructure (aqueducts, roads, defenses), and conspicuous consumption, which stimulated manufacturing. The cultural coherence, if not unity, of the Syrian polity and economy is evident in the mobility of rulers, soldiers, traders, artisans, laborers, and peasants, who would find similar conditions wherever they went.

In addition to townsmen and villagers, the nomadic bedouin of the desert formed yet another component of Syria's population. While the various tribes preserved their distinctive way of life—reliance on livestock, seasonal migration, and independence of outside political authority—they also formed a part of Syrian society and culture since at least early Islamic times. In the first century of Muslim rule bedouin tribesmen formed the shock troops of conquest and consolidation of Arab authority. Throughout history they supplied animal products (hides, dairy products, meat) to townsmen and villagers, and transported merchandise in long-distance caravans. In the domain of culture, the bedouin embodied the ideals of honor, bravery, and independence, the notion of an Arab way of life inherited from the pre-Islamic past that was diluted in the Muslim empires' effete cities. Moreover, bedouin were considered the bearers and preservers of "pure" Arabic language, uncontaminated by contact with non-Arabic speakers, and for centuries their classical poetry stood as the model to which later creative efforts would be compared. In contrast to this romanticized concept of the bedouin, settled folk held them in contempt for the threat they posed to village and town, for another pattern in Syrian history is the fluctuation of the boundary between the desert and the sown, a flux that has occurred under both natural and political pressures. When central authority was weak or a series of droughts made marginal lands unproductive, the bedouin would advance with their herds to graze at the walls of the towns, forcing peasants to abandon villages. But at times of strong dynasties or abundant rains, the boundary would creep eastward and the bedouin would retreat.

ANCIENT HISTORY

Current archaeological research shows that Syria's history stretches back 4,500 years during which the country has witnessed the rise and fall of many kingdoms, empires, and dynasties as well as numerous invasions. Nonetheless, certain patterns are evident that distinguish Syria from other parts of the Middle East. Its location at the crossroads of western Asia, northern Africa, Arabia, and the eastern Mediterranean and its lack of protective topography have made the country vulnerable to invasion and open to more peaceful migration. Movements of different peoples over the centuries have resulted in the formation of a diverse population. This diversity has been further accentuated by the presence of several physically isolated regions, the lack of a unifying river system, such as the Nile in Egypt or the Tigris-Euphrates in Iraq, and barriers to travel: mountains, desert, and great distances between towns. Such internal diversity has contributed to a history marked by swings between periods of political unification and fragmentation. In addition, Syria has been the object of domination by more powerful neighbors in Egypt, Iraq, and Asia Minor (present-day Turkey) from ancient times to the present. Consequently, periods of Syrian unity and independence have been the historical exception rather than the rule. Since the Arab conquest in the seventh century, there have been only three unified, independent polities: the Umayyad dynasty from 661 to 750; the regime of the Nur al-Din Mahmud in the 12th century; and in modern times since 1946. Otherwise, Syria was politically fragmented or ruled from Baghdad (c. 750-908), Cairo (1171-1516), Istanbul (1516-1918), and Paris (1920-1946).

The earliest Syrian civilization flourished in the vicinity of Aleppo at the ancient city of Ebla, in Arabic, Tell Mardikh. Archaeologists discovered this ancient city in 1974 and have uncovered 15,000 tablets from the Ebla archives that date to around 2400 B.C. The tablets, inscribed in Sumerian cuneiform, mostly pertain to economic and administrative matters and attest to a flourishing trade with Egypt and Mesopotamia as well as textile and agricultural production. The tablets' language, Eblaite, is the oldest Semitic language of western Syria.

Another early center of civilization was founded in the third millennium B.C. by a Mesopotamian people, the Akkadians, at Mari, located on the middle Euphrates River. Mari thus initially represented an extension of Mesopotamian civilization, but around 2100 B.C. the Amorites took it over. These people were nomads of the Syrian desert who gradually shifted to settled life and established a number of city-states between 2100 and 1800 B.C. In 1933, archaeologists discovered the Mari archives, which contain 20,000 clay tablets inscribed in Akkadian cuneiform dating from an 18th-century B.C.

kingdom. During the first centuries of the second millennium B.C., other Amorite kingdoms flourished in northern Syria, the most eminent one being the Yamkhad kingdom that ruled from Aleppo between 1800 and 1650. That period coincides with the greatest activity at Ugarit, in Arabic, Ras Shamra, a commercial center on the northern Syrian coast. Its good harbor and proximity to Crete and Cyprus made it an entrepôt for trade between the Mediterranean and Mesopotamia. There followed more than four centuries of domination by outside powers that established tributary relations with several regional polities. Pharaonic Egypt dominated the southern half of Syria from 1650 until 1200. The northern parts came under the hegemony of the Mitanni kingdom, a northern Mesopotamian power, and then from 1350 the Anatolian Hittite kingdom held sway.

Between 1200 and 1000, Syrian history is more obscure because of the change in writing materials from durable tablets to perishable papyrus and skins. At the beginning of the period, Ugarit was destroyed, either by raiding Sea Peoples or by earthquake. The key development in these dark ages was the gradual migration of the Aramaeans from the south. Beginning around 1000, their city-states dominated Syria for nearly three centuries. The most important Aramaean centers were at Damascus, Hama, and Aleppo, where they built the renowned citadel that still rises above the town. In Damascus the Aramaeans constructed a temple for their deity Baal-Haddad on a site that would later become the church of John the Baptist and for the last 1,300 years the Umayyad mosque. The greatest contribution of the Aramaeans to the ancient world was their language, Aramaic, which became a cosmopolitan language for trade throughout the ancient Middle East and Mediterranean. The Aramaeans also spread the Phoenician alphabet of 30 letters, which other peoples borrowed and adapted to write Hebrew, Arabic, Persian, and Sanskrit. The Syriac dialect of Aramaic spoken at the northern town of Edessa became the liturgical language of Christians, and the term Syrian first referred to speakers of the Syriac language. To this day the Syrian Orthodox Christian church uses Syriac in its liturgy, and an Aramaic dialect is still spoken in a few Syrian towns.

In 732, the Assyrians conquered the Aramaean city-states and ruled Syria until 612, when Babylonian and then Neo-Babylonian invaders established their rule. In 538, Cyrus the Great, founder of the Persian Achaemenid dynasty, absorbed Syria into the first empire to rule the entire Middle East from Egypt to the eastern borders of Iran. Persian rule lasted until Alexander the Great's conquest in 333-332. After Alexander's death in 323, his general Antigonus ruled Syria from Asia Minor, but in 301, his rivals, the Seleucids, took over the province. Seleucus established towns named for his father Antiochus (Antioch), his mother Laodicea (Latakia), and his wife Apamia.

The Seleucids made Damascus their western capital and presided over an era of commercial expansion and Greek colonization, which gave rise to Hellenistic culture, a mixture of Greek, North African, and western Asian cultures. Greek urban colonies had baths, theaters, as well as other Hellenic institutions; yet the Aramaic language and culture persisted among most Syrians throughout this period. In 312, the Seleucids established an outpost on the Euphrates River called Dura Europos. The town was later ruled by the Persians, then the Romans, and finally destroyed by the Persians in A.D. 256; discovered in 1920, Dura Europos is now famous for its Jewish synagogue and Christian chapel. During the Seleucid era, the Nabataeans created the first major Arab polity around 312 B.C., based on the towns of Bosra in southern Syria, and Petra in present-day Jordan.

Seleucid power rapidly declined until the Ptolemies of Egypt seized Syria. Between 240 and 198, Syria was a province of Egypt. The Romans conquered Syria in 64 B.C., and they converted the temple of Baal in Damascus into a temple for Jupiter. In the Roman period, another independent Arab kingdom of the desert appeared at Palmyra, which gained importance after the fall of the Nabataeans in A.D. 106. Known as the "Bride of the Desert" and located 230 kilometers northeast of Damascus, Palmyra prospered as the center of trade between Mesopotamia and the Mediterranean. Although the Romans declared it part of their Syrian province in 64 B.C., Palmyrenes maintained a semiautonomous status and developed one of the region's wealthiest cities. Palmyra's most famous ruler, Queen Zenobia, launched a revolt against Roman rule from 268 to 272, when her armies occupied Egypt and Asia Minor. A Roman counterattack put down the Palmyrene queen and ended up destroying much of the city.

The next major political development was the fourth-century establishment of Byzantium as the successor to Rome. For 300 years the Christian Byzantines ruled Syria from Constantinople. They destroyed Jupiter's temple and made it a church for John the Baptist. In the sixth century, the Byzantines supported an Arab vassal state under the Ghassanids, Arab Christians living on the southern fringes of Syria.

ISLAMIC PERIOD

The first Muslim ventures into Syria were minor raids during the Prophet Muhammad's lifetime and under the first caliph, Abu Bakr. An organized invasion (634-641) to conquer Syria took place under the second caliph, Umar, with the main battles between Byzantine and Arab forces taking place between 634 and 637. On the heels of military triumphs came large-scale immigration from Arabia and consolidation of control over Syria. For the next quarter century, the nascent Arab empire based in the western Arabian town of Medina ruled Syria, Egypt, and Iraq, then the Umayyad dynasty established itself in Damascus and ruled the Arab empire for 90 years, the only time that Syria was the center of an empire. In 750, the Abbasid dynasty supplanted the Umayyads and transferred the imperial center to Iraq. Syria remained under firm Abbasid control for about a century until provincial governors in Egypt asserted control over the country and their autonomy from Baghdad intermittently between 868 and 971.

During the later 10th and 11th centuries, Syria underwent one of its periods of fragmentation as the Fatimid dynasty in Egypt, the Saljuk sultans, who attained ascendance over the Abbasids in Baghdad, the Hamdanids in Aleppo, and a resurgent Byzantine Empire contended for control over Syria. In the closing years of the 11th century, Saljuk princes and vassals were ruling several petty states and feuding with one another when the Crusaders invaded, determined to regain the Holy Land for Christendom. In the early 12th century, the Crusaders set up four Latin kingdoms, while in the Muslim arena power passed from Saljuk princes to their regents, called atabegs. For 50 years, the atabegs warred with one another as often as with the Franks until Nur al-Din Mahmud consolidated power over most of Muslim Syria in 1154. His vassal, Saladin, later established the Ayyubid dynasty, which ruled Egypt and Syria from Cairo. This Muslim hero of Kurdish background stabilized the Muslim-Christian balance of power, but the political foundations he laid dissolved 70 years after his death, and in 1260 the Ayyubids gave way to the Mamluk sultanate, a unique polity based on the creation of households of slave soldiers loyal to the sultan, who himself had to rise from the ranks of former slaves.

In a sense, the Mamluks came on the scene in the nick of time, as Syria faced a threat far more potent and destructive than the Crusaders ever posed. Two years earlier, Mongol invaders from Central Asia had sacked Baghdad and exterminated the Abbasid caliphate; in 1260, a Mongol army invaded Syria, swept away the Ayyubid principalities, and marched into Palestine. That same year, however, a Mamluk force ventured from Egypt to confront the Mongols and dealt them their first military defeat. In repulsing the Mongols, the Mamluks spared Syria the destructive consequences of Mongol rule that would plague Iraq and Iran for centuries. The Mamluks also uprooted the last stronghold of the Crusaders in 1303. Two centuries later, in 1516, the Mamluks fell to a different northern invader, the Ottoman dynasty, which had also vanquished the last vestiges of Byzantine power in 1453, when it seized Constantinople (Istanbul). For the next 400 years, Syria was part of a vast empire that ruled over much of southeastern Europe, the central Arab lands down to the Indian Ocean, Egypt, and North Africa to the frontier of Morocco.

In the context of Syrian history the Ottoman era is conspicuous for bringing security from invasion and a long period of uninterrupted dynastic rule. Under these conditions Syria enjoyed stability and prosperity reflected in population growth, urban dynamism, and expansion of the margins of cultivation. The Ottomans initially divided Syria into three provinces, each with a governor and garrison of janissaries to represent central authority. The northern one had its center at Aleppo; the southern one at Damascus; and a coastal one at Sidon. The Ottomans further divided these provinces into districts. Syria's distance from Istanbul and the strength of local forces compelled the Ottomans to rule in cooperation with urban notables and rural magnates. In the 18th century, the balance of power shifted in favor of local forces, and the Ottomans appointed Syrian Arabs as governors of the province of Damascus. Ottoman vulnerability increased in the early 19th century, and the ambitious governor of Egypt, Muhammad Ali, exploited the situation when he had his army invade at the end of 1831. Egyptian rule lasted until the European powers forcibly imposed an Ottoman restoration in 1840. There followed a lengthy period of administrative and legal reform punctuated by outbreaks of communal violence in Aleppo (1850) and Damascus (1860). By 1900, however, Syria was more firmly tied to Istanbul because of faster transport and communications as well as more effective administration.

MODERN ERA

In November 1914, the Ottoman Empire entered World War I on the side of the Entente, and Syria became exposed to a possible British invasion from Egypt. Around the same time, British diplomats struck an alliance with the Hashemite sharif of Mecca, Husayn ibn Ali, and incited him to launch an Arab revolt against Ottoman rule in exchange for a promise to support the establishment of an independent Arab kingdom. The war concluded with the complete withdrawal of Ottoman forces from Syria. Husayn's son Faysal asserted Syrian independence in the name of a recently developed political ideology, Arab nationalism, but the fragile state was snuffed out by a French invasion in July 1920. There followed a quarter century of French rule under a mandate from the League of Nations and a struggle for Syrian unity and independence.

The unity of greater Syria was shattered in 1920 when Great Britain assumed a separate mandate over Palestine and Transjordan (southern Syria), and France detached portions of Syria and annexed them to Lebanon. The French then further divided Syria by creating separate administrations for the southern Druze and the northwestern Alawi regions. A great uprising broke out in 1925, sparked by a Druze revolt, and the French took nearly two years to suppress it. There followed a decade of political struggle between France and Syrian nationalists, who formed the National Bloc to pursue their aims. The first contentious issue was the drafting of a constitution. France rejected a draft proposed by an elected constituent assembly dominated by the National Bloc, but in 1930 promulgated a constitution largely based on the Bloc's proposal. The next task was the negotiation of a treaty to govern relations between an independent Syria and France. The nationalists and the French could not reach agreement on terms until France agreed to reincorporate the Druze and Alawi regions with the rest of the country in 1936, a watershed year for the mandate. That same year national elections to parliament brought the National Bloc to power for the first time, but the nationalists were to savor their triumph briefly as they encountered difficulties in governing the Druze and Alawi districts as well as the restive Jazira province. To make matters worse, Turkey asserted its claim to Alexandretta, and in 1939, France allowed its annexation to Turkey in yet another blow to Syrian unity. Moreover, at the end of 1938, the French parliament refused to ratify the Franco-Syrian Treaty of 1936. As World War II approached, the National Bloc fell from power and political stalemate resumed.

The fall of France to Germany in 1940, however, fundamentally weakened its position in Syria, where a pro-Vichy administration assumed authority. The British regarded this regime as a threat to their positions in Iraq and Palestine, so they cooperated with Free French forces under Charles de Gaulle in invading Syria in the summer of 1941. Before and after the invasion, Free French leaders declared their commitment to immediate independence for Syria, but once in control again they temporized. It took a combination of nationalist pressure and British intervention to get the French to allow national elections in preparation for independence in July 1943. But even then, the French stalled on withdrawing their forces before they obtained a treaty to guarantee their special status in an independent Syria. The nationalists' refusal to buckle under French pressure led to a new crisis in May 1945 when French warplanes bombed Damascus. At that point, Great Britain, whose troops vastly outnumbered the French forces, forcibly intervened to wrest a commitment from France to evacuate the country. On 17 April 1946, the last French troops left, and Syria was free and independent under an elected government.

The nation had been independent barely two years when events in Palestine plunged Syria into its first war. The creation of the Jewish state of Israel in what was still a predominantly Arab country precipitated military intervention by nearby Arab states. The newly created Syrian army fought the

Israelis, but like the armies of Egypt and Transjordan, failed to establish Arab control over Palestine. At the end of the war, Syrian and Israeli representatives met under United Nations auspices and negotiated an armistice that provided for the creation of demilitarized zones in disputed territory along the frontier. Another consequence of the war was the flight of 100,000 Palestinian refugees to Syria. The government tried to make the army a scapegoat for the military failure, and in March 1949 the army struck back with a military coup against the elected government. This event marked the beginning of military intervention in Syrian politics. By the end of the year, two more military coups would occur.

The mastermind of 1949's third coup, Adib al-Shishakli, managed to remain in power from December 1949 until February 1954. Following his overthrow, Syria saw the rise and fall of seven cabinets in four years. Internally, the major issue was social reform, particularly in rural areas where most of the peasantry lived under landlord domination. In foreign relations, the major questions were Syria's alignment in the Arab world and in the Cold War between the superpowers. Egypt and Iraq were the leading Arab powers and each country sought advantage by strengthening ties with Syria. Some Syrian politicians favored unity with Iraq, while Egypt and Saudi Arabia supported politicians who opposed alignment with Iraq. Superpower rivalries were imposed on these regional contests, as Great Britain and the United States favored pro-Western politicians who tended to look to Iraq for support, while the Soviet Union encouraged neutralist Syrians relying on Egypt to fend off Iraqi bids for union. In the arena of popular opinion, the neutralists, spearheaded by the Arab nationalist Ba'th party, were gaining in popularity, and in the fractious officer corps neutralist sentiment was predominant. Western pressures mounted throughout the period. First, there was a campaign in 1955 to enlist Syria's adherence to the Baghdad Pact, an alliance of Turkey, Iraq, and Great Britain, but Egyptian support and American hesitation allowed Syria to abstain from joining. Then, in 1956, Iraq and Britain tried to organize a pro-Western coup, but the plot was uncovered and its organizers arrested. Syria then turned to the Soviet Union for diplomatic and economic support as well as military supplies, but this alarmed the United States, whose leadership became convinced that Syria was on the verge of becoming a satellite of Moscow. A full-blown crisis between the United States and Syria erupted in August 1957, when the Syrians expelled three American diplomats for conspiring with politicians and army officers against the government. Washington then persuaded Turkey to mass its troops along the border, a move to which the Soviets responded by threatening Turkey should it attack Syria.

The crisis strengthened the position of those Syrian politicians and army officers who looked to Egypt as a shield against Western threats, and in February 1958 a Syrian delegation to Cairo negotiated a merger with Egyptian president Gamal Abd al-Nasir, forming the United Arab Republic. This experiment in Arab unity lasted three-and-a-half years. It foundered on Syrian resentment of Egyptian political and economic domination, and in September 1961, a secessionist coup took Syria out of the union. In the next 18 months, three successive civilian politicians governed a restive country and confronted constant interference from army officers and subversion inspired by the Egyptians. Attempts to curb the military's influence on politics led to the March 1963 coup d'état by Nasirist and Ba`thist officers. By August, the Ba`thists had purged Nasirist officers and suppressed a Nasirist uprising, thereby inaugurating the era of Ba`th Party domination of Syrian politics.

The 1963 "Ba`thist revolution" fundamentally reshaped Syrian politics in that it marked the definitive defeat of the elite political class that had emerged in late Ottoman times, led the struggle for independence, and headed civilian governments since 1946. Power now shifted to men of more humble social origins, many of whom were members of religious minorities. The concentration of power in the Ba`th did not spell the end of political turmoil, for a new phase of struggle within and for control of the Ba`th commenced and sectors of urban society revolted against its rule. Meanwhile, the new regime pursued an ambitious policy of social and economic reform, including land reform and nationalization of industries and businesses. In February 1966, the intra-party conflict resulted in yet another coup, the expulsion from Syria of the party's founders, and the ascendance of its radical wing, dubbed the neo-Ba`th. This regime marked the farthest swing to the left Syria would see. It deepened the state's control over the economy in the name of socialism, advocated the overthrow of Arab regimes in the name of revolution, and backed Palestinian guerrilla raids against Israel; in fact, the neo-Ba`th's provocations of Israel played a key role in precipitating the June 1967 War in which Syria lost territory, the Golan Heights, to Israeli forces. After the war new strains appeared within the regime, and in November 1970, yet another coup d'état resolved intra-party struggle in favor of Hafiz al-Asad, the Syrian president for nearly 30 years.

The Asad regime backed away from its predecessor's unbridled radicalism in the domestic arena and foreign relations. Asad adopted slightly more liberal economic policies to soften urban middle-class resentment, while maintaining the state's domination of the economy. He also broadened the spectrum of allowable political discourse, yet retained a monopoly on power, and he mended ties with Arab governments. His handling of foreign policy bore fruit in the military cooperation he forged with Egyptian President

Anwar Sadat. The two leaders planned a successful surprise attack on Israel in the October 1973 War with the aim of recovering territories lost in the 1967 conflict. The military performance gained Asad credibility in Syria, but it did not succeed in recovering the Golan Heights. Two years later his attention would be absorbed by the civil war in Lebanon, and he decided to send in a large portion of the Syrian army in June 1976 to prevent the rout of conservative, mostly Christian, forces. Asad's Lebanon policy and his reliance on repressive means to stay in power fueled Sunni resentment that exploded in the Islamist uprising of 1978 to 1982. This revolt posed a serious threat to Asad's rule, but he suppressed it by thoroughly destroying its armed partisans in Hama in February 1982. No sooner had Syria passed through its worst internal crisis than Israel invaded Lebanon four months later in order to expel the Palestine Liberation Organization from that country and to install a government friendly to the Jewish state. Syrian forces fought the Israelis for a few days, then accepted a cease-fire and watched the Israeli siege of Beirut force a Palestinian evacuation. In the long run, however, Asad reversed the military verdict through constant pressure on Israel via his Lebanese allies, and by early 1986, Syria again exercised the dominant role in Lebanon.

Throughout the Ba'thist era, Syria was closely aligned with the Soviet Union and on shaky ground with the United States because of the latter's massive military, political, and economic support for Israel. As the Cold War entered its denouement and Soviet support for Syria slackened, it appeared that the Asad regime might be fatally weakened in a manner similar to the Soviets' East European satellites. This calculation turned out to be mistaken; indeed, Asad improved relations with Washington in 1990 when he supported American intervention against the Iraqi invasion of Kuwait. After the Gulf War, Asad furthered the rehabilitation of relations with the United States when he agreed to attend the Madrid Conference, an international peace conference to begin a negotiated settlement of the Arab-Israeli conflict in all its dimensions. While this diplomatic process did not bear fruit on the Syrian-Israeli track, Asad demonstrated his commitment to it and prepared his country for the day it would peacefully coexist with its perennial enemy. In spite of concentrated American diplomatic efforts and extensive Syrian and Israeli negotiations during the 1990s, the two sides failed to reach agreement before Asad died in June 2000.

The vicissitudes of negotiations with the United States and Israel dominated the headlines in the 1990s, but within Syria the more fundamental issue was how to address endemic and urgent economic difficulties. The country had embraced five-year plans and government domination of major sectors in the 1960s to advance the economy and to more equally spread the fruits of growth. Syria was able to offset the intrinsic flaws of centrally planned economies because it had access to two significant sources of financial support. The Soviet bloc provided military, technical, and economic assistance, and oil-producing Arab countries offered billions of dollars in direct aid to Syria because of its role in confronting Israel, especially after Egypt signed a separate peace with Israel in 1979. These external streams of funds dried up in the 1980s when an oil glut depressed petroleum prices and when the Soviet Union entered its last years of crisis. The collapse of the Soviet bloc removed an important bulwark for Syria's centrally planned economy, and many Syrians hoped the government would adopt not only market reforms, but even steps toward a liberal political system. The Asad regime, however, remained intent on keeping its grip on power. Therefore, its economic policies in the 1990s amounted to applying stopgap solutions to immediate crises in foreign exchange and energy supplies and stopped far short of structural adjustment along the lines recommended by the International Monetary Fund. The political situation changed even less—the state of emergency imposed in 1963 persisted with its restrictions on civil liberties and the apparatus of security forces to ensure citizens' acquiescence.

Some observers believed that the economic and political stalemate might loosen after Hafiz al-Asad's death on 10 June 2000. Since his first brush with serious illness in 1983, Syria-watchers speculated on what would happen at the moment of succession. Nobody knew who would succeed Asad or how the transfer of power would take place: in a smooth legal fashion, or by violent means. Most analysts predicted a tumultuous period of internal struggle, but Bashar al-Asad succeeded his father without incident. In his first three years, he has taken timid, and so far ineffective, steps to reform the economy. In the political sphere, a brief spell of freer expression quickly ended when the old guard flexed its muscles to block any movement toward deeper change that might imperil its grip on power. The prospect of reviving peace talks with Israel vanished upon the eruption of violence between Israel and Palestinians after the failure of their own efforts to reach a final peace settlement. On the regional scene, Syria's position suffered a blow in March-April 2003, when the United States invaded Iraq and overthrew the regime of Saddam Husayn. The long-term effects of that sudden and forceful demonstration of American might not become clear for some time. Official Syria regards Washington's recent assertiveness with apprehension that it might result in a fatal blow to Ba'th Party rule in Damascus. Conversely, ordinary Syrians view the deeper involvement of the United States with ambivalence between the hope that it will bring about political and economic shifts that improve their daily lives and the fear that it will translate into a new era of Western domination.

ECONOMIC AND SOCIAL DEVELOPMENT

Before the advent of modernity, Syria's range of economic activities remained stable for millennia. The vast majority of Syrians resided in villages, where they cultivated cereals and legumes, tended orchards, and raised livestock. Annual rainfall normally sufficed to produce crops for subsistence use and a surplus to either sell or cover tax obligations to political authorities. The size of harvests depended more on rain than variation in technical means. Centuries of tinkering and adaptation of tools to the natural environment led to a conservative approach that satisfied needs in most years. Experimentation might threaten yields and was not common. With respect to energy, cultivation depended on human and animal power to plow fields and transport harvests from fields to home and urban markets. Pastoral nomadism was another perennial feature of rural life. The lines between nomad and villager were not hard and fast. Villagers might till fields belonging to nomadic chiefs and send their livestock to graze pastures with animals belonging to nomads. Furthermore, the variable local effects of periodic droughts could parch the steppe and force nomads to take up cultivation in villages, or, conversely, they could result in disastrous harvests and compel cultivators to seek their livelihood as clients of nomadic tribes.

While most Syrians lived in the countryside, a significant portion, perhaps 15 percent during periods of political stability, resided in towns and cities. The urban economy had a vibrant manufacturing sector devoted to processing agricultural products into commodities, most especially textiles from cotton and wool, but also animal products into leather. The artisans of Aleppo and Damascus in particular enjoyed a widespread reputation for the skill they applied to their work. Townsmen also worked in local and long-distance trade via caravans to other parts of the Middle East and to African and Asian lands on the rim of the Indian Ocean. Commerce offered the best opportunities for accumulating wealth, and the urban elite tended to come from or have investments in that sector. It was common for traders to act as moneylenders to peasants in need of assistance to pay taxes or buy seed and to small artisans seeking an advance to buy raw materials.

In the 19th century, Syria and the rest of the Middle East underwent momentous economic changes. The major shifts stemmed from incorporation into the capitalist economic networks emanating from Western Europe that created a new structure of global wealth and power. Trade with Europe became a more important facet of Syria's economy, and that led to the cultivation of more crops for export, the decline of traditional artisanal production in the face of competition from European manufactures, and the rise of European investment in transportation and communications. By the early 20th century, the major cities had amenities like electricity, streetlights, and trams.

During the period of French rule, Syria's economy showed the first signs of industrialization and the introduction of mechanical technology to agriculture. In addition, France's efforts to quell unrest extended to remote regions and the nomads, who for the first time were effectively brought under central political authority. The extension of railroads and the introduction of motor vehicles meant that nomads lost their customary economic role of providing freight-bearing animals to the caravan trade. This combination of factors, then, spelled the end of an ancient way of life. Some nomads continue to raise livestock in the steppe but they frequently use pickup trucks to move their animals from one pasture to another.

The major transformation in economy and society, however, occurred after independence. Improvements in sanitation, transportation, and city services spurred migration from villages to towns and cities. By the end of the 20th century, the concentration of population had shifted from rural to urban areas. Even in rural areas, the disappearance of the nomads, land reforms, and technical advances permanently altered the agricultural sector even though it still employs a large share of Syrian labor. Perhaps the most notable change in the last 40 years is the government's assumption of a central role in financing and marketing crops, providing technical assistance to cultivators, and constructing dams and canals to increase the amount of land under irrigation.

The urban landscape has undergone even more dramatic transformation, most clearly in sheer size as city dwellers burst out of medieval quarters in late Ottoman times and have since sprawled into what had been adjacent orchards and gardens. The modern urban economy spawned large factories employing an industrial labor force and socialist policies spurred the creation of a vast network of public sector companies to complement the numerous government ministries, agencies, and bodies that provide low-paying but steady employment for a large portion of the labor force.

It is quite natural that Syrian society has undergone substantial change in tandem with economic change. One of the most conspicuous areas of social change is in the area of education. Throughout the Islamic period, it was common for townsmen to teach their children to memorize the Qur'an and to learn the rudiments of writing and arithmetic to serve the needs of commerce. More advanced learning in Islamic jurisprudence and theology was available in schools known as madrasas. Christians and Jews would pursue studies at their respective religious institutions. Starting in the 18th century, European and American missionaries founded schools that attracted Syrian Christian pupils. While such schools represented closer interaction with Europe, the first institutions resembling modern public schools created by the Ottomans in the 19th century were designed to meet the modern need for skilled administrators and loyal subjects. The next major change came in the 1960s, when the government placed all schools under the Ministry of Education to inculcate in young citizens a uniform national identity and political outlook. Apart from the development of a national education system for all children regardless of religion, the other major change in education is the creation of universities to train specialists in medical, scientific, educational, and administrative fields. Syria's national education system has done fairly well at raising literacy rates but the higher education system is hampered by outdated equipment, crowding, and the intrusion of politics into administrative and faculty affairs.

Along with urbanization, technical modernization, and national education, the role of religion in society has also changed from a conspicuous element of political authority under Muslim dynasties to a complicated and contested feature of public life in a secular republic. There is no question that religious observance remains important to millions of Muslims and Christians, and that religious principles continue to govern common ideas of morality and justice. There has been a rupture, however, in the historical centrality and supremacy of Islam in a republic that promises to treat all citizens equally regardless of religion. Some conservative Muslims would argue that it is possible to restore Islam to a central place in politics and law without harming the rights of non-Muslim compatriots. They go so far as to assert that the excesses of authoritarian regimes would not occur under rulers answerable to Islam's ethical and legal requirements. In the contest between religious and secular forces, the latter triumphed in the early 1980s. Since that time, Syria has offered one of the most hospitable climates for religious minorities in the Middle East notwithstanding the repressive political atmosphere.

PROSPECTS AND CHALLENGES

In recent years, pressures have been mounting for fundamental economic and political change in a regime that is now 40 years old. The sources of pressure range from the internal need for thousands of new jobs each year for the growing population and frustration with the repressive political climate to external factors like the impact of America's invasion of Iraq to depose Saddam Husayn. Exactly how Syria's leaders and people will respond to these challenges is impossible to predict. In the longer historical perspective, one might see the Ba'th Party regimes as a phase of national economic, social, and political consolidation after the early years of instability and vulnerability to external powers. The Ba`th Party regimes realized some achievements in the realms of education, rural development, and increased regional stature. The price for these achievements included decades of political repression and a ramshackle technical infrastructure that started to crumble in the 1980s. For 20 years, the economy has mostly limped along, sustained by occasional injections of Arab financial aid and foreign exchange from petroleum exports at a level that Syria may not be able to sustain for much longer. For just as long, many Syrians and outside experts have maintained that the only true solution to the country's economic problems, which are typical of countries that embraced planned economies, is to embark on a new path that would open political life and liberalize markets and trade. Such a choice is fraught with its own risks of severe political instability and economic inequality. The regime is not likely to choose that path in the absence of irresistible pressure to do so. As the country's leaders look around the global landscape, they see few examples of smooth transition from controlled economies and single-party regimes that did not result in the collapse of entrenched rulers. In Syria's immediate region, there are no such models.

Of course, looming over the scene is the unsettled conflict with Israel. One cannot completely dismiss the possibility of war in the future however much that prospect has receded since the late 1980s. But the condition of no war, no peace is a factor in Syria's economic stagnation as it dedicates a large portion of national resources to unfruitful military equipment. It is also an element in the national security mentality that justifies—in the minds of the leaders—the suspension of political liberties. The problem with the current situation, then, is that it appears to contain forces that will inevitably over-whelm Syria's economic and political structures, but such an assessment would have been even more apt 20 years ago. Therefore, it seems entirely possible that the near future holds more of the same. The Ba`th Party regime has proven adept at tactical maneuvering, but clumsy at envisioning and enacting bolder initiatives that might more fully tap the country's potential and realize its people's aspirations for greater prosperity and freedom.

THE DICTIONARY

-A-

ABBASID DYNASTY. The greatest of the classical Islamic dynasties, the Abbasids overthrew the **Umayyad** dynasty and held the **caliphate** from 750 to 1258. On coming to power, they moved the political center of early Islamic civilization from Syria to **Iraq**, where they founded a new city, Baghdad, as the imperial capital in 754. During the first century of Abbasid rule, a number of revolts erupted in Syria. These represented resentment against Syria's reduction from imperial center to provincial status and attempts by Umayyad loyalists to regain power. Syria began to move out of the Abbasid orbit during the time of Ahmad ibn Tulun (d. 884), a Turkish soldier assigned the task of collecting revenue and keeping order in **Egypt** on behalf of the caliph. He quelled a number of revolts in Syria, extended his authority there, and made a show of loyalty to the caliph, but in fact he ruled as an autonomous governor and established the short-lived Tulunid dynasty (868-905) over Egypt and Syria.

The Abbasids regained control over Syria in 905 and ruled it directly for 30 years. Then a military commander named Muhammad ibn Tughj (d. 945), whose ancestors came from eastern **Iran**, established another autonomous line of governors known as the Ikhshidids. Ibn Tughj first arrived in Syria in 910 as a deputy governor. He governed Syria effectively and cultivated allies at the Abbasid court in Baghdad in order to secure appointment as governor of Egypt and Syria with the pre-Islamic Persian title of *ikhshid*. In the next decade Ibn Tughj consolidated control over Egypt and southern Syria (**Damascus** and **Palestine**) while he acknowledged **Hamdanid** supremacy in the north. After his death, his successors governed much of Syria for another quarter century until the **Qarmatis** dislodged them in 969. While the Abbasid caliphate endured in Baghdad for three more centuries, its effective rule over Syria was over.

ABD AL-MALIK IBN MARWAN (c. 646-705). The fourth **Umayyad** caliph (r. 685-705). He consolidated power for the Marwanid branch (named for his father) of the Umayyad dynasty. His first achievement was to reestablish authority over **Iraq**, which had thrown off Umayyad rule two years earlier. Abd al-Malik prepared an assault on Iraq by arranging a truce with the **Byzantines** on his northern flank. He then led Syrian forces into Iraq and defeated his rivals in 691.

The following year, his army overcame the forces of a rival claimant to the **caliphate** in Mecca. After suppressing challenges to the Umayyad dynasty, Abd al-Malik placed its rule on firmer footing with a series of centralizing administrative reforms. First he introduced Arabic as the language of administration, whereas previous caliphs had employed Greek and Persian scribes. Second, he ordered the minting of a new Islamic coinage to replace Byzantine gold and Persian silver coins. Abd al-Malik's most enduring legacy stems from his order to construct the Dome of the Rock, Jerusalem's chief Islamic religious complex, long considered the third holiest site in the Muslim world after the western Arabian shrines at Mecca and Medina.

ABDULHAMID II (1842-1918). Ottoman ruler from 1876 to 1909. He gained the throne on 1 September 1876 by agreeing with a powerful clique of military and civilian officials to promulgate a **constitution** for the Ottoman Empire. Abdulhamid indeed proclaimed the constitution on 23 December 1876, but he then dismissed from office the same men who had made him sultan. He did, however, proceed with constitutional government for a brief time. An elected bicameral parliament, which included nine deputies from Syria, convened in March 1877. Less than a year later, on 14 February 1878, Abdulhamid dissolved parliament and suspended the constitution.

For most of Abdulhamid's reign, Syria saw little unrest, largely because of his strategy of combining a conservative religious policy of supporting popular Muslim institutions with technical modernization, which had commenced during the **Tanzimat** era. In pursuit of his religious policy, the sultan paid for the construction of many new mosques and patronized popular **sufi** orders by funding the construction of new lodges, the repair of older ones, and the renovation of holy men's tombs. He also granted members of the Rifa`iyya sufi order exemption from military service.

In the realm of modernization, provincial governors presided over the construction and, where needed, renovation of government offices, courts, and barracks. Urban renewal was another object of imperial attention as rickety bazaars were demolished and reconstructed and rectilinear street systems were installed. Projects to develop the network of carriage roads, initiated by **Midhat Pasha**, continued throughout the 1880s. The sultan also granted concessions to European companies to construct railways and ports, and these projects gave a boost to trade by vastly reducing transport costs and time. Other modernizing ventures included the introduction of electricity to **Damascus** and the construction of a tramway in the city. Abdulhamid also oversaw the expansion of government schools throughout the province, including teacher training schools and a military preparatory school. The purpose of expanding state **education** was to discourage attendance at foreign mission schools, which did not inculcate loyalty to the sultan; in fact, **Christian** mission schools frequently encouraged allegiance to European nations.

Abdulhamid's reign was also important for Syria because he reorganized the provincial administration. He detached southern **Palestine** from Damascus in 1887 when he created a special district with its capital at Jerusalem. The following year he created a coastal province extending from **Latakia** to Acre, with Beirut as the capital. This left a southern province centered on Damascus, stretching from **Hama** to Maan in present-day **Jordan**, and a northern province with **Aleppo** as its capital.

In the later years of Sultan Abdulhamid's reign, the Ottoman constitutional movement was revived by the **Committee of Union and Progress** (CUP). This organization infiltrated the officer corps and recruited widely among younger men who believed in constitutional rule as the solution to the empire's many problems. In June 1908, the CUP inspired a number of mutinies in the Balkans, and on 24 July 1908 the rebellious officers forced the sultan to restore the 1876 constitution. The following April, a conservative coup bent on restoring absolute power to Abdulhamid ousted the constitutional government in Istanbul and provincial centers, but ultimately the bid for an absolutist restoration failed when officers loyal to the constitution marched on Istanbul. On 28 April 1909 the parliament deposed Sultan Abdulhamid, the last Ottoman sultan to effectively wield power, and exiled him, first to Salonika, then in 1912 to a palace near Istanbul, where he died in February 1918. *See also* SAYYADI, ABU AL-HUDA AL-; TRANSPORTATION.

ABID, AHMAD IZZAT AL- (1851-1924). Syrian adviser to **Ottoman** Sultan **Abdulhamid II**. Before his acquaintance with the sultan, Abid worked in the bureau of Turkish and Arabic correspondence and published the first private newspaper in **Damascus** from 1879 to 1887.

He was serving as a judge on the central court of appeals in Istanbul when he entered the entourage of the sultan in 1894 through a connection with **Abu al-Huda al-Sayyadi**, another Syrian adviser at the imperial court. Abid became the most powerful figure in distributing posts, especially in the judicial administration, in the Syrian provinces. He counseled the sultan to adopt pro-German and pan-Islamic policies, but he is best known for developing the idea of a rail link between Damascus and Mecca to be constructed entirely with donations from Muslims. Known as the Hijaz Railway, this project was completed as far as Medina when the project was terminated in 1908. After the 1908 constitutional revolution, Abid fled to **Egypt**, but he returned to the center stage of Ottoman political life at the end of **World War I** when he became the grand vizier and negotiated the armistice.

ABID, MUHAMMAD ALI AL- (1868-1939). Son of **Ahmad Izzat al-Abid** and first president of the Syrian republic from 1932-1936. In the late **Ottoman** era he served in a number of high government positions, including Ottoman minister to the **United States**, and he was closely associated with Sultan **Abdulhamid**. From the time of the 1908 Ottoman constitutional revolution until 1919, Abid lived in Europe. He played little role in politics during the early years of the **French Mandate**. In November 1931, French High Commissioner Henri Ponsot announced that national elections would be held in December 1931-January 1932. The **National Bloc** won 17 out of 69 seats, the remainder going to independents and figures willing to collaborate with the French. Under the **constitution** of 1930, the parliament elected the president of the republic. The National Bloc and the French authorities agreed on Muhammad Ali al-Abid as a compromise candidate in June 1932. The major political issue during his four-year term was the negotiation of a **Franco-Syrian Treaty** to regulate relations in the event of Syria attaining independence. In September 1936, preliminary agreement on terms of the treaty was reached. National elections to parliament, which would have to ratify the treaty, were held in November, and the National Bloc won a huge victory. When the nationalist parliament convened in December, Abid resigned the presidency to make way for Bloc leader **Hashim al-Atasi**.

ABU FIRAS AL-HAMDANI (932-968). A renowned poet and member of the **Hamdanid** dynasty that ruled northern Syria from **Aleppo**. His poetry celebrated the accomplishments of his kinsman Sayf al-Dawla, ruler of Aleppo from 945 to 967, and whose entourage included the great poet **al-Mutanabbi**. Sayf al-Dawla appointed Abu Firas governor of Manbij, a district close to the frontier with the **Byzantines**. In the course of fighting these perennial enemies of the Muslims, the Hamdanid prince-poet was captured in 962. During his four-year captivity, Abu Firas composed some of his finest verse, much of which clearly shows al-Mutanabbi's influence. In 966, Sayf al-Dawla paid the Byzantines a ransom to free his cousin. Two years later the ruler died and his son Abu al-Ma'ali took over Aleppo. Abu Firas quarreled with him and raised a revolt in **Homs**, but the ruler's troops captured and killed him.

ADONIS (1930-). Pen name of Ali Ahmad Sa'id, a leading poet and literary critic. He was born in a small village near **Latakia** and studied philosophy and **literature** at the University of **Damascus**. In 1956, Adonis moved to **Lebanon** to found a poetry journal. He soon gained a wide reputation for his free verse, symbolist poetry that explores political, social, and metaphysical concerns. In 1977, he published a landmark three-volume work on Arab culture entitled *The Permanent and the Changing: A Study of Arab Conformity and Creativity*. Since 1986, Adonis has been living in Paris. His poetry has been translated into more than a dozen languages. He is also one of the Arab world's leading literary critics, and his work *Arab Poetics* has been translated into English and French.

AFLAQ, MICHEL (1910-1989). The cofounder of the **Ba'th Party**. This **Greek Orthodox Christian** native of **Damascus** studied at the Sorbonne in Paris from 1929 to 1934. On his return to Damascus to teach history at a public secondary school, he attracted pupils to his call for Arab unity, liberation from colonial rule, and social justice. In 1947, he and fellow schoolteacher **Salah al-Din al-Bitar** turned their movement into the Arab Renaissance (Ba'th) Party.

During the party's first two decades, Aflaq held the position of secretary-general and remained its intellectual inspiration while staying out of the main political arena. He never ran for parliament and served only briefly as minister of **education** in 1949. In the **United Arab Republic** era, when the Syrian branch of the party voluntarily dissolved itself, Aflaq spent most of his time in Beirut guiding the party's National Command and holding aloof from UAR policies. The Syrian Ba'th reemerged after the breakup of the UAR, but Aflaq no longer enjoyed the authority of the party's senior statesman because a younger generation of party members, including the secret **Military Committee**, resented his earlier dissolution of the party and clove to more radical social ideas. These younger members would challenge Aflaq and Bitar's leadership after the party seized power in the wake of the **March 8, 1963 coup**. For instance, the Syrian Regional Command was reconstituted in 1963, but Aflaq was not included, and in May 1965 Aflaq resigned as secretary-general of the party's National Command. When his allies tried to restore the supremacy of the old guard, the Military Committee and its allies struck in the **February 23, 1966 coup**, creating a permanent split in the party. The **neo-Ba`th** rulers imprisoned many of their former comrades, but they allowed Aflaq to leave the country, never to return. His exile began in Beirut and continued in Brazil until the **Iraqi** branch of the Ba`th seized power in 1968. Its leaders invited him to Baghdad and named him secretary-general of the party. Aflaq spent most of the next seven years in Beirut and moved to Iraq when the **Lebanese Civil War** erupted in 1975. Baghdad's Ba`thist rulers treated him as an honored guest for the remainder of his life.

Aflaq's writings show traces of both Marxist and German romantic nationalist influences. According to Aflaq, Arab unity had to come about through a fundamental reform of the personality of Arabs that would occur if they could transcend their divisive loyalties (to **religion**, clan, or region). Arab freedom means both national independence and personal political freedoms of speech, assembly, and belief. As for socialism, it comprises an intrinsic element of Arab nationalism, but Arabs must adapt socialist ideas to their own particular circumstances. The party's 1947 **constitution** included articles calling for equitable distribution of wealth, state control over foreign trade, and limits on rural landholdings, yet it also recognized the legitimacy of private property.

AFRIN RIVER. This is a small but strategically situated tributary of the **Orontes River** in northwestern Syria. The Afrin flows into Syria from **Turkey**'s Taurus range and then flows back into Turkey's Hatay (**Alexandretta**) province. It cuts a valley that historically served as an east-west artery between the coastal city of Antioch and the **Euphrates River** and as a north-south route from southern Turkey to **Aleppo**. In the early Islamic centuries, the Afrin River valley formed part of the military frontier with the **Byzantine Empire**, and during the **Crusades**, the Franks held it for several decades.

AGHA. This Turkish term refers to a chief or master. In Syrian usage, it denoted the leader of a local **janissary** unit or other urban militia from the 17th to early 19th centuries. Aghas emerged when imperial janissaries blended with provincial urban populations during the 17th century.

In Syrian towns the aghas' command of military power gave them political influence and the means to control economic resources. In **Damascus**, for instance, the aghas came to dominate the grain trade that fed the city. Their local power became evident in the aftermath of an August 1831 uprising against an **Ottoman** initiative to impose a new tax. The city's aghas murdered the Ottoman governor and formed a local government. They then exploited their control over grain storehouses to create artificial shortages and drive up food prices. Long lines at bakeries led to bread riots. The aghas' extortionate reign came to an end in June 1832 when Egyptian troops commanded by **Ibrahim Pasha** occupied the city. During the **Tanzimat** era (1839-1876), the Ottomans gradually reduced the aghas' power and slowly assimilated them into the empire's new administrative structures. By the end of the century, they no longer constituted a distinct social category.

AGRICULTURE. Until recent decades most Syrians throughout history worked in agriculture as small landowners, tenants, sharecroppers, and laborers, and the bulk of the country's wealth came from agricultural production. About 80 percent of Syrian agriculture depends on annually variable rainfall, so production fluctuates from year to year. For example, a bumper grain crop of 2.8 million tons in 1988 was followed by a year of drought and a crop of only one million tons in 1989. There are two main zones of rain-fed agriculture. One is a narrow band that runs northward from the **Hawran** along the foothills of the Anti-Lebanon range to central Syria in the vicinities of **Homs**, **Hama**, and **Aleppo** and then spreads eastward into **Jazira**. This large region includes **Damascus** and its **Ghuta** oasis; the **Orontes River** valley and a vast lowland of drained marshes called the **Ghab**; and Jazira in the northeast. The second zone, which runs between the borders of **Lebanon** and **Turkey**, is the thin coastal strip and the western slopes of mountains rising above the sea. This region produces cotton, tobacco, fruits, and olives. A small proportion of cultivated land has been irrigated by Syria's major rivers since ancient times, and since **World War II** that proportion has increased, particularly along the **Euphrates** and **Khabur Rivers** and in the Ghab.

Wheat is the most widely grown crop, particularly in the region from Homs to Aleppo and in Jazira along the Euphrates and Khabur Rivers. Barley is the next most widely cultivated cereal, usually grown in drier areas. The second major crop and one of Syria's chief exports is cotton, two-thirds of which is grown on irrigated lands along the Euphrates and Khabur Rivers and on rain-fed lands between Aleppo and Hama. In

1965, cotton accounted for 43 percent of Syria's exports. Even though the value of cotton exports continued to grow in the 1970s, its significance in exports diminished, falling in 1972 to one-third of exports, largely because of the development of **petroleum**. Tobacco, grown in the mountains around **Latakia**, is another export crop. Olives are grown primarily in the hills near Aleppo and Idlib. Other crops include millet, lentils, and sugar beets, the latter of which are processed into sugar.

After World War II the amount of land under cultivation increased from 1.75 million hectares in 1953, to 5.9 million in 1969, and to 6.2 million in 1980. Most of this expansion took place in the first decade of independence when private landowners in Homs, Hama, and Aleppo invested in agricultural machinery to open the northeast. The investments of these "tractor capitalists" resulted in larger grain and cotton harvests.

Whereas the expansion of cultivation during the 1940s and 1950s occurred at the initiative of private landowners, in recent decades the government has assumed a more decisive role, beginning with the **United Arab Republic**'s legislation on **land reform** and labor relations. To implement these laws, the UAR created two ministries–the Ministry of Agriculture and the Ministry of Agrarian Reform. The UAR also extended government authority over the **economy**'s most significant export and raw material for domestic manufacturers by establishing the Syrian Cotton Board. The **Ba`th Party** regime deepened the state's role in 1965 by taking over large cotton ginning concerns and creating a public agency to handle grain exports. Two years later the regime created the General Federation of Agricultural Cooperatives, designed to manage the hundreds of privately operated cooperative farms on land that peasants had obtained as a result of land reform. Through these cooperatives, the government took over agricultural credit, marketing, and processing crops in a blend of public and private sectors. By 1970, the Syrian government had consolidated a new hybrid of public and private enterprise in agriculture, where most cultivators worked private holdings and the state dominated credit, marketing, and inputs.

One of the areas under close government supervision has been the extension of irrigation. This is a critical area for economic development because of the higher productivity of irrigated lands. It is estimated that more than half the value of agricultural output comes from irrigated crops even though they cover less than 20 percent of the land. Key crops for food and industrial use like wheat, cotton, and sugar beets depend on irrigation. Government planners aspire to expand the proportion of irrigated fields to 25 percent with a variety of projects. In addition to large-scale projects on the Euphrates and Orontes Rivers, less conspicuous projects will contribute to meeting this goal. They include a series of small dams along the Snobar River in Latakia governorate and efforts to irrigate lands along **Yarmuk River** by installing pumps and digging an extensive canal network.

Another facet of squeezing more out of Syria's scarce **water** supply is conservation. The customary technique of "basin" irrigation inundated orchards and fields cultivated for grains and vegetables. A small but increasing proportion of land now has sprinkler irrigation to use water more sparingly. Nonetheless, irrigation is a mixed blessing for Syrian agriculture because in many parts of the country the soil is vulnerable to salinization due to inadequate drainage, and unless highly saline soil is remedied, the amount of cultivable land will decline. Given the natural limits on the total supply of surface water and the **environmental** hazards of intensive irrigation, agrarian experts look to an international research center on dry area farming at Aleppo (ICARDA) to identify new ways to increase productivity in rain-fed regions.

Even though Syrian agriculture has expanded in recent decades, its overall part in the Syrian economy has fallen from 35 percent of gross domestic product in 1953-1959, to 26 percent in 1960-1973, to 20 percent in 1974-1980 before rising in recent years to about 25 percent. This relative decline is due to increases in the commercial, mining, and manufacturing sectors. In 1972, agricultural goods made up half of Syria's exports, but after 1974, oil surpassed agriculture, which in 1980 comprised just 13 percent of exports. Another measure of the relative decline in agriculture's role in the Syrian economy is the proportion of labor engaged in this sector. Before 1960, 60 percent of the labor force worked in agriculture; by 1979, that figure had fallen to 31 percent. In the early 1990s, agriculture engaged only 23 percent of the labor force. *See also* LABOR MOVEMENT.

AHMAD PASHA "AL-JAZZAR" (?-1804). Ottoman governor of southern Syria in the late 18th and early 19th centuries. His brutal methods of extracting revenues, extorting wealth, and keeping order gained him the nickname "*al-jazzar*," the butcher. Born in Bosnia, he began his rise to prominence in Istanbul by attracting the notice of an Ottoman official. He later entered the company of the **mamluks** in **Egypt**, but in 1768 he fell out with his patron and went to Syria, where the Ottomans appointed him governor of the coastal province of Sidon in 1775. Various circumstances allowed Ahmad Pasha to become the dominant figure in southern Syria for nearly three decades. One was the increase in trade to Europe in **agricultural** products. His control over

Syrian ports enabled him to skim a rich revenue in customs taxes, which he used to enlarge the military resources at his disposal. He also benefited from Istanbul's declining ability to exercise authority over the provinces. In the face of challenges from the insubordinate mamluks in Egypt, **Wahhabi** raids from Arabia, wars with Russia, and **Napoleon Bonaparte**'s invasion, the Ottomans experimented with different administrative solutions to the problem of keeping order in Syria. One option was to place the usually separate provinces of Sidon and **Damascus** under a single governor. Thus, Ahmad Pasha was governor of southern Syria from 1785 to 1786, 1790 to 1795, and 1801 to 1804. He established himself at the port of Acre and built up its fortifications to make it a formidable stronghold. In the 1790s he maneuvered to extend his authority over **Lebanon**, but his endeavors were interrupted by Napoleon's 1799 invasion. Following his successful defense of Acre against a French siege, in 1801 the Ottomans again appointed him governor of Damascus, which he remained until his death in 1804.

AJNADAYN, BATTLE OF. This was the first major battle between Arab Muslim and **Byzantine** forces. Although the Arab chroniclers give different dates, most historians assign the battle to July 634, at a site 35 kilometers southwest of Jerusalem. Byzantine forces included the brother of the emperor and other dignitaries, but the Arabs decisively defeated them. The Arab victory opened the way for their conquest of **Palestine** and Syria.

ALAWI. Syria's largest heterodox Muslim sect. They currently account for roughly 12 percent of the population. Around 75 percent of the Alawis live in **Latakia** province, where they comprise 60 percent of the population. There are also Alawi communities in the Akkar region of northern **Lebanon** and in southeastern **Turkey**. In Syria they are divided into four tribal confederations: the Kalbiyya, the Khayatin, the Haddadin, and the Matawira. Members of this sect call themselves followers of **Ali**, but **Sunnis** and **Shi`is**, who consider them heretics, call them Nusayris, followers of Muhammad ibn Nusayr, a ninth-century Shi`i propagandist.

Muhammad ibn Nusayr (d. 883), a Persian who spent most of his life in **Iraq**, claimed to be the "door," or means of access, to the eleventh Shi`i **imam**, who, Twelver Shi`is believe, had gone into occultation in 873. Later followers brought the sect to northern Syria in the 10th century. Al-Husayn ibn Hamdan al-Khasibi (d. 957) was the key figure in spreading the sect in Syria after he settled in **Hamdanid Aleppo**. In 1031, a later Alawi leader moved from Aleppo to Latakia, whence the sect spread into the mountains behind the city that have since become known as Jabal Nusayri or **Jabal Ansariyya**.

Alawi texts reveal a heterodox version of Shi`ism that is distinguished by belief in a trinity of Ali as the divine incarnation, Muhammad as the Prophet, and Salman al-Farsi as the propagator of **religion**. Alawi interpretation of the Qur'an posits an esoteric meaning of certain verses, which in their reading establish the special status of Ali and his descendants. Moreover, they believe in cycles of revelation that began with Adam, continued with Noah, Abraham, Moses, and Jesus, and ended with Muhammad. According to the Alawis, each cycle represented an advance over the previous one to correspond with advances in human society. They explain their differences from other Muslims by claiming that they possess secret knowledge of religion that others are not fit to receive. Like the **Druzes**, the Alawis recognize a spiritual hierarchy that possesses and transmits esoteric knowledge, while ordinary believers are familiar with simpler aspects of the religion. Unlike Muslims, the Alawis do not observe prayer in mosques, fast during Ramadan, or perform the pilgrimage to Mecca.

For centuries the Alawis fended off attempts by Sunni rulers to impose their authority. In the early 20th century they rallied to **Shaykh Salih al-Ali**'s revolt against French rule. After **France** suppressed his movement in 1921, the **French Mandate** authorities created a separate Territory of the Alawites, thereby perpetuating their traditional political separation from the rest of Syria. Under this regime, the French created religious law courts that were supposed to apply Twelver Shi`i jurisprudence on the grounds that Alawis were part of that branch of Shi`ism. In 1936, France dissolved the separate administration for the Alawis and united their region, as the province of Latakia, with the rest of Syria under the terms of the **Franco-Syrian Treaty**. When the **National Bloc** government appointed a Sunni Muslim as governor of the province, there were protests by Alawis, and a revolt erupted under the leadership of **Sulayman al-Murshid**. In July 1939, the National Bloc government resigned, and France reestablished an autonomous regime for the Alawis, but the region was permanently reunited with the rest of Syria in February 1942. In independent Syria, the Alawis obtained formal recognition in the **legal system** for their Twelver Shi`i courts in 1952.

Since the early 1960s Alawi members of the **armed forces** and the **Ba`th Party** have played a dominant role in Syrian politics. In 1971 **Hafiz al-Asad** became the first Alawi head of state. He has attempted to gain recognition as a full-fledged Muslim, but conservative Sunni opponents continue to regard him and his coreligionists as heretics determined to destroy **Islam**. The Alawi composition of Asad's entourage offered him a reliable circle of advisers at the same time it proved a liability in gaining the trust and support of Sunni Muslims. Observers have long disagreed as to whether Asad turned Syria into an Alawi regime or merely depends on close relatives and associates to handle the most sensitive matters and distributes power more broadly to members of other religious communities. The situation has not changed under Asad's son **Bashar al-Asad**. *See also* MUSLIM BROTHERS.

ALEPPO. *Halab* in Arabic. This northern city is on the banks of the **Quwayk River,** a minor stream that flows from the Taurus Mountains of nearby **Turkey**. It lies in a semiarid region that receives enough rainfall to grow wheat, cotton, olives, vines, and its famous pistachios. Aleppo's proximity to the northern reaches of the Syrian desert has made it a market town for **bedouin** for centuries.

Aleppo is one of the world's most ancient cities, being mentioned in 20th-century B.C. Egyptian texts. It is famous for its citadel, which dominates the area from a rocky height and has provided a defensive stronghold for townsfolk and garrisons many times over the centuries. In the second millennium B.C., Aleppo came under Mitanni and then Hittite rule. An Aramaean city-state flourished in the early first millennium, but it was conquered by Assyrian invaders in the ninth century and the city did not regain prominence until the Seleucid era.

The Arabs conquered Aleppo in 636, but its Muslim population grew more slowly than in other Syrian towns. For a time, Aleppo was the capital of a northern Syrian dynasty, the **Hamdanids** in the 10th century, but it then entered an era of strife and violence because of warfare between the **Byzantines** and Muslim dynasties and among local factions. The city did not recover until the middle of the 12th century under the **atabegs**. Sultan **Nur al-Din Mahmud** established the city's first six **madrasas** as well as **sufi** convents and a hospital. The city enjoyed a period of great prosperity and expansion during **Ayyubid** rule in the 13th century, when the citadel was completely rebuilt and repaired and various markets were renovated. This era abruptly ended with a **Mongol** attack at the beginning of 1260. In the next several years, Aleppo passed between the hands of the **Mamluks** and Mongols, and during their wars the citadel again was destroyed.

Aleppo received a new boost under **Ottoman** rule when it became the center of its own province and a nexus for **trade** between the Orient and Europe. During the 16th and 17th centuries, Venetian, French, British, and Dutch consulates and trading stations were established.

Aleppo's role as a transit center for international trade declined in the last quarter of the 18th century. In the **Tanzimat** era, Aleppo was the scene of a major uprising against local Christians in 1850. When **France** and Great Britain drew the boundaries of modern Syria at the end of **World War I** they severed Aleppo from its natural hinterland of southern Turkey and northern **Iraq**; the city received a further blow with the 1939 cession of **Alexandretta** to Turkey, thereby losing its traditional Mediterranean port. Since independence, the city has developed into a major industrial center, especially its private sector firms in textiles, food processing, pharmaceuticals, and glass. The city population has grown from 300,000 in 1945 to around three million by 2000. The city has a large **Christian minority**, including many **Armenians**.

ALEPPO MASSACRE OF 1850. On 17-18 October 1850, Muslim crowds attacked a **Christian** suburb of Aleppo in the city's only instance of communal riots in the **Ottoman** era. The Ottoman authorities had recently completed the first census of Aleppo's adult males and there was widespread apprehension that conscription would follow. A crowd of Muslims gathered before the governor's building to protest, but the governor refused to deal with them, and they proceeded to Judayda, the prosperous quarter of **Uniate** Christian merchants. There the mob entered homes and churches, plundered and looted, and murdered between 10 and 70 Christians. As word of the atrocities spread, Christians living in other quarters took refuge in the homes of Muslim neighbors and in the commercial district. On 19 October, the leader of the local **janissary** faction headed off further violence by promising to present the Ottoman governor with the crowd's demands, including a promise not to carry out conscription and to prohibit public processions by Christians. A brief calm was broken by a second round of violence in the first days of November when fighting erupted between janissary and **ashraf** factions. By that time Ottoman reinforcements had arrived and they forcibly repressed the quarreling factions. The authorities arrested around 600 men for their part in the riots and punished them by drafting some and exiling the others. They also demanded the restoration of stolen property, but little of it was recovered. In the months after the massacre, several hundred Christians emigrated from the city to settle in Beirut and Izmir.

Historians explain the unusual communal outbreak as a consequence of Ottoman reform and **Tanzimat** policies, including the 1826 abolition of the janissaries that damaged the economic and social standing of Aleppo's deeply entrenched janissary faction; and the imposition of a capital tax on Muslims, who perceived the measure as signaling a threat to their customary superiority to Christians, who always paid such a tax. Economic tendencies may also have played a role. The city's Uniate Christians prospered from the growing trade with Europe in the 1840s, and their good fortune may have incited the envy of the city's Muslims.

ALEXANDRETTA. *Iskandarun* in Arabic; *Hatay* in Turkish. All three terms refer to both the city and the province, or *sanjak*, currently located in southeastern **Turkey**. The port city of Alexandretta historically served as **Aleppo**'s outlet to the Mediterranean. By the early 20th century, the Sanjak's population consisted of Turks, **Sunni** Arabs, **Alawis**, **Christian Arabs**, and **Armenians**. After the destruction of the **Ottoman Empire**, both the Turkish Republic and Syria under the **French Mandate** claimed the territory. As part of the **Franklin-Bouillon Agreement** of 1921, **France** pledged to safeguard the status of the Sanjak's Turks. By the 1923 Treaty of Lausanne, Turkey recognized the international boundary that assigned Alexandretta to Syria. In the various administrative arrangements of the early French Mandate, the Sanjak was part of the Syrian state and did not have a special autonomous status like that in **Jabal Druze** or **Jabal Ansariyya**.

Controversy over Alexandretta's status erupted following the negotiation of the **Franco-Syrian Treaty of 1936**, which alarmed the Turkish government because it appeared to portend the permanent absorption of the Sanjak into an independent Arab country and made no provision for continuing its special status. Popular sentiment in Turkey favored its annexation, a view the government eventually adopted. The League of Nations approved a new independent regime for Alexandretta in November 1937. Several months later, France's alarm at Italy's expansionist ambitions led to the conclusion of the July 1938 Franco-Turkish Friendship Treaty by which France agreed to the introduction of Turkish troops into the Sanjak. There followed the opening of a local parliament with the Turkish majority that France had promised to Turkey. Over the next several months, the parliament gradually merged the province with Turkey through economic and judicial legislation. In June 1939, France completely withdrew from the province, paving the way for Turkey to annex it. Syrian nationalists vehemently condemned France's surrender of the territory, and the episode became a lasting point of friction between Turkey and Syria.

Since Syria gained its independence seven years after Turkey's annexation of the region, **Damascus** governments have never made a serious bid to recapture it, but they have not been reconciled to Turkish sovereignty either. It still rankles many Syrians, especially refugees from the territory and their descendants. Moreover, the loss of Alexandretta has played a role in the politics of independent Syria in two specific respects. First, a faction of the **Ba`th Party** inspired by **Zaki al-Arsuzi**, himself a refugee, represented recidivist feelings about the region. Second, the Syrian government supported the separatist Kurdistan Workers' Party's (PKK) anti-Turkish activities there in the 1990s.

ALI IBN ABI TALIB (c. 600-661). The cousin and son-in-law of the Prophet Muhammad, Ali emerged in the years after Muhammad's death as a leader in Muslim affairs. His later followers claimed that he was the rightful successor to Muhammad's supreme leadership, but that others usurped his legitimate claim to the **caliphate**. After the murder of the third caliph Uthman in 656, Ali became the fourth caliph, but the slain caliph's kinsmen, the **Umayyads**, demanded that Ali bring Uthman's assassins to justice before they would recognize his authority. Ultimately, Ali led an army against the Umayyads at the 657 Battle of Siffin, but the engagement reached an inconclusive end when the parties agreed to arbitration. A number of Ali's followers seceded from his movement and became his enemies because they condemned his willingness to compromise. This group became known as the **Kharijis**, and one of them assassinated Ali in 661. Nonetheless, a large section of Muslims remained loyal to Ali and claimed that legitimate religious and political authority continued to reside in his descendants, the **imams**, or rightful leaders of Muslims. This following became known as *shi`at Ali*, or the party of Ali, hence the term **Shi`i** for those Muslims who uphold Alid legitimism. *See also* ALAWI; DRUZES; ISMA`ILI; NIZARI; QAR-MATI.

ALI, SHAYKH SALIH AL- (1884-1926). An **Alawi** landowner in **Jabal Ansariyya**, Shaykh Salih led Alawi resistance to the establishment of the **French Mandate** in order to preserve his community's customary autonomy. In 1919, Shaykh Salih forced a French garrison to abandon its post in the Jabal Ansariyya. With support from regional notables, Amir **Faysal**'s government, and Turkish nationalists fighting the French in southeastern **Turkey**, the revolt held off the French for two years. Once the French defeated Faysal's forces in July 1920 and occupied **Damascus**, they concentrated their resources on subduing revolts in various parts of the country, including Shaykh Salih's. The Alawi leader then gained the support of a revolt that erupted west of **Aleppo** under the leadership of **Ibrahim Hananu**. But in October 1921 the French ended

Turkish support for Shaykh Salih by reaching the **Franklin-Bouillon Agreement**. With the arrival of French reinforcements in Jabal Ansariyya and outside help no longer available, the revolt fizzled and its leader went into hiding until he was pardoned. He spent the remainder of his life in his home village in Jabal Ansariyya.

ARAB NATIONALISM. The idea that Arabs comprise a political community distinct from other peoples arose in modern times. It first appeared in **Ottoman** Syria during the early 20th century among a handful of intellectuals and a faction of the urban political elites of **Damascus** and Beirut. The contribution of intellectuals, both secular and religious, was to emphasize the unique role of Arabs and the Arabic language in the history of Islamic civilization. They argued that this role indicated a special status for Arabs in the world, although they did not initially draw the conclusion that the Arabs should secede from the Ottoman Empire. As for the protonationalist politicians, whom historians refer to as Arabists, their identification of particular Arab grievances in the empire had as much to do with intra-elite competition for office as ideological conviction. Before **World War I** the Arabists sought a greater degree of autonomy for Arab provinces and the exclusive use of Arabic in law courts, government offices, and schools. Prewar Arab nationalist societies included **al-Fatat** and al-Ahd. The latter group was established in 1913 among Arab military officers, mostly Syrian and Iraqi. Their program was to obtain political autonomy for the Arab provinces of the Ottoman Empire.

During World War I Arab nationalist activity increased because of the uncertainties surrounding the war's outcome and the prospect that a European power, namely Great Britain, might provide material support for the establishment of an independent Arab kingdom. At a 1915 meeting with Amir **Faysal** in Damascus, Arab nationalists formulated the Damascus Protocol, stating their goals to be British recognition of Arab independence and the end of commercial and fiscal privileges for foreigners and their local protégés. Nonetheless, during the war most Syrians remained loyal to the empire. The Ottoman defeat and occupation of Syria by the forces of Great Britain, **France**, and Amir Faysal transformed the political landscape and Arab nationalism gained greater popularity. When France occupied Syria two years later, Arab nationalism became a rallying point for resistance to European rule.

During the **French Mandate** a number of Arab nationalist parties and groups formed, including the **League of National Action** and the **Ba`th Party**. In the 1950s, the scope of Arab nationalism broadened beyond the original focus on the Ottoman Arab lands of historical Syria and **Iraq** to include all Arabic-speaking countries from the Atlantic Ocean to the Persian Gulf. The movement attained its greatest moment in 1958 when Syria merged with **Egypt** to form the **United Arab Republic**, but the failure of this union dealt Arab nationalism a severe blow. Later developments in Syria and the region that further weakened the ideology included the 1966 split within the Ba`th Party and the defeat of Arab nationalist regimes in the **June 1967 War**. Since 1970, the consolidation of durable Arab regimes pursuing disparate policies has further enervated the early vigor of Arab nationalism, although the sentiment can still be tapped, as was demonstrated in popular Arab reaction against the American-led military assault on Iraq's occupation of Kuwait in 1991. Syria still officially adheres to an Arab nationalist ideology, but in the 1990s it appeared to be spent as a dynamic force in history. *See also* ARAB REVOLT; HUSAYN-MCMAHON CORRESPONDENCE.

ARAB REVOLT. In June 1916, forces loyal to the sharif of Mecca, **Husayn ibn Ali**, launched a revolt against **Ottoman** rule in western Arabia and seized Mecca. Great Britain had been at war with the Ottoman Empire since November 1914, and British military planners were concerned about the effect of pan-Islamic propaganda on the loyalty of the British Empire's Muslim subjects in **Egypt** and India. A political-military alliance with the Meccan sharif could only strengthen Britain's war effort. After the exchange of correspondence between Husayn and Sir Henry McMahon, the British high commissioner in Egypt, the sharif plotted his anti-Ottoman revolt.

Funded and supplied by British agents, the revolt immediately succeeded in seizing control of Mecca, but encountered determined Ottoman resistance at Medina, so Arab forces bypassed that city and marched toward Syria. Husayn's son **Faysal** played a significant part in leading Arab forces to the capture of Ottoman positions in northern Arabia and southern Syria. In the fall of 1918, Arab forces advanced toward **Damascus** via Dar`a while British troops pushed the Ottomans out of **Palestine**. The campaign culminated when Arab forces occupied Damascus on 1 October 1918. *See also* HUSAYN-MCMAHON CORRESPONDENCE.

ARAB SOCIALIST PARTY. Created by **Akram al-Hawrani** in January 1950 to promote the confiscation of feudal estates and the distribution of land to poor peasants. The party also advocated a neutral **foreign policy**, secularism, universal **education**, and the emancipation of **women** from traditional constraints. The base of this party lay in **Hama** and surrounding towns among peasants, workers, and shopkeepers. Hawrani's backers seized lands and fought off landlords' attempts to regain them. The party received the backing of **Adib al-Shishakli** when he first came to power in 1949, thus further encouraging the burgeoning peasant movement to take over the land they worked, but in 1952 he dissolved the party. Later that year or in early 1953, Hawrani merged the Arab Socialists with the **Ba'th Party**, thus creating the Arab Socialist Renaissance Party and ending the independent existence of the Arab Socialist Party.

ARCHAEOLOGY. European interest in studying the artifacts of the Middle East's ancient civilizations is commonly said to have begun with **Napoleon Bonaparte**'s 1798 invasion of **Egypt**. While that event may have marked an intense phase of field investigation, it was not truly the beginning. In the case of Syria, European travelers had previously reported on the splendid ruins at **Palmyra**, and the first published study of its inscriptions came out in 1753. Organized archaeological exploration came in the wake of **France**'s military intervention after the 1860 communal conflict in **Lebanon**. A team of French scholars led by Ernest Renan scoured the Levantine coast for Phoenician artifacts and conducted the first surveys of ancient sites at Arwad, **Tartus**, and Amrit. In the next several decades, European and American attention focused on the Holy Land in an effort to uncover the material remains of sites associated with biblical events. Consequently, Syria was neglected until the **French Mandate** authorities created a special Antiquities Service to organize digs at Ra's Shamra (Ugarit) and Mari and to restore some of the country's more striking late classical (Palmyra) and medieval (Crac des Chevalliers/**Hisn al-Akrad**) sites. The independent government of Syria created a Directorate of Antiquities and Museums to oversee all aspects of archaeological activity, from approving a growing program of European and American excavation to exhibits at the major museums in **Aleppo** and **Damascus**.

Perhaps the country's two most famous ancient sites are Ebla (Tell Mardikh) and Ugarit. An Italian dig at Ebla, located 50 kilometers south of Aleppo, uncovered a huge store of clay tablets inscribed in cuneiform and dating from around 2300 B.C. The Ebla archives have shed new light on the early history of Semitic languages. A French team working at Ugarit, located near **Latakia**, unearthed an ancient Mediterranean port containing temples, palaces, and residential areas. Texts and artifacts from Ugarit provide insight into early Hebrew culture. Archaeologists also continue to work on remains from the Hellenistic, Roman, and **Byzantine** eras at several sites that attract many Western tourists. Apamea (north of **Hama**) is renowned for its two-kilometer long thoroughfare along which the facades and columns of buildings still stand. Along the **Euphrates River**, Dura Europos (southeast of **Dayr al-Zur**) is famous for its **Christian** and **Jewish architecture** and **art**, especially an intact third-century synagogue painted with frescoes. One of the best-preserved Roman theaters in the world is at Bosra (south of Damascus). A remarkable Byzantine-era site is St. Simeon (northwest of Aleppo), one of the most important Christian sites in the eastern Mediterranean. Its fame rests on a cruciform church built to commemorate St. Simeon the Stylite (d. 459), renowned for spending the last 34 years of his life atop a pillar near a monastery. There are literally dozens of lesser sites from different eras scattered around the country. In the 1990s more than 400 foreign archaeological projects were in progress in addition to Syrian digs under the Directorate of Antiquities.

ARCHITECTURE. When the Arabs conquered Syria, they encountered an architectural tradition that blended Hellenistic, Roman and **Byzantine** styles. Early Muslim architecture in the **Umayyad** period took a religious form as mosques and a secular form as **desert palaces**. The caliph al-Walid (r. 705-715) ordered the construction of royal mosques at Medina, Jerusalem, and **Damascus**. Certain features of the last one—the concave prayer niche (*mihrab*), the elevated pulpit (*minbar*), and the axial nave crossing the prayer aisles—became typical for other mosques. The desert palaces were built on the sites of agricultural estates and combine Roman, Byzantine, and Sassanid Persian forms.

Urban construction flourished in the late **Saljuk**, **Zangid**, and **Ayyubid** eras (roughly 1070 to 1260), especially at Damascus and **Aleppo**. Rulers and wealthy patrons created endowments (sing. **waqf**) to erect and maintain **madrasas**, **sufi** hospices, institutes for instruction in Prophetic tradition (*dar al-hadith*), and hospitals (**bimaristans**). During the **Crusades**, the need for effective defense spurred rulers to put up new walls to fortify the cities and to build bulky but functional strongholds such as Aleppo's 13th-century citadel that towers over the town and is a distinctive landmark to this day. **Mamluk** governors of Damascus and Aleppo put their mark on the urban landscape with massive tomb complexes that followed the example of sultans in Cairo. The Mamluk era also saw the construction of ordinary public buildings like baths, caravanserais, sufi hospices, and mosques. The trademark feature of Mamluk buildings was the "*ablaq*" pattern of alternating layers of light (white or pale yellow) and dark (black or grey) stone. That same distinctive appearance is evident in one of the finest specimens of **Ottoman** architecture in Damascus, the Sulaymaniyya Complex designed by master architect Sinan and completed in the 1550s. Its purpose was to demonstrate Ottoman support for the annual pilgrimage caravan with a mosque, caravanserai, lodging, eating area, and shops. Since the Ottoman era, architectural design in Syria has not assumed a distinctive form.

ARMED FORCES. When Syria became independent its armed forces consisted of the **Troupes Spéciales** created under the **French Mandate**. At first **Sunni** Arabs were underrepresented in the army while **Alawis** and **Christians** along with **Kurds** and **Circassians** had numbers greater than their share in the overall population. In a few years, that imbalance shifted with the admittance of more Sunni Arabs to the military academy at **Homs**. Under **Adib al-Shishakli**, universal conscription for two-year service was instituted. While the Syrian army grew during the next 10 years, political strife within the officer corps and seemingly perpetual purges, especially between 1955 and 1966, undermined any attempt at instilling professionalism in the armed forces. In the same period, however, the armed forces acquired substantial amounts of weaponry from the **Soviet Union**. On the eve of the **June 1967 War**, the army had about 50,000 troops, 500 tanks, and 100 Soviet warplanes. Minister of Defense **Hafiz al-Asad** then embarked on an ambitious strengthening of the armed forces. At the time of the **October 1973 War**, Syria had more than 130,000 men under arms with better professional training and command than a few years earlier. Although Israeli forces withstood Syria's assault and drove its forces back, the Syrians proved themselves far more formidable foes than they had been just six years before.

When **Egypt** embarked on its path toward a separate peace with **Israel** in 1978, it meant that Israel could concentrate its military resources against Syria. President Hafiz al-Asad then embarked on a massive buildup of the armed forces and extended military service to 30 months. In the 1970s and 1980s, Syria spent about 30 percent of its gross domestic product on the armed forces, a total of $51 billion from 1977 to 1988. From the late 1970s to 1985, Syria doubled the size of its army to about 400,000 men. During the same period, its stock of tanks nearly doubled from 2,300 to 4,050. Syria paid for this with $22 billion in military aid from oil-rich Arab countries and $20 billion in civilian aid between 1977 and 1988. This immense amount of Arab aid followed the 1978 Baghdad Summit, which was held to formulate a policy in response to Egypt's peace treaty with Israel. The Arab countries pledged $1.8

billion per year to Syria for 10 years. Between 1978 and 1981, actual aid came close to that target, but then began to diminish because of Syria's support for **Iran** against **Iraq** in the first Gulf War and falling oil revenues. The decline in actual aid and the high military spending contributed to a foreign exchange crisis at the end of 1985. From 1986 to 1988 Syria received only $500 million per year, mostly from **Saudi Arabia**.

Syria's support for Kuwait in the second Gulf War reopened the channels of financial aid, again making it possible to pay for large arms deals. A portion of the nearly $2 billion that came from Saudi Arabia was spent from 1991 to 1992 on arms deals with Bulgaria, Czechoslovakia, and Russia. The Syrians bolstered their ground forces with new tanks and antitank weapons. Budget constraints, however, forced the regime to reduce the size of the armed forces to 300,000, and prompted the adoption of a different approach that focuses on deterrence rather than parity. As a deterrent against Israeli air power, the Syrians have obtained surface-to-surface missiles from North Korea and developed chemical warheads. The **nonconventional weapons** program reportedly includes work on biological agents as well. When foreign observers criticize Syria's work in those fields, the government points out that Israel is a nuclear power, so **Damascus** needs a deterrent force. Moreover, Israel's military cooperation with the **United States** enabled it to increase its technological advantage during the 1990s while Syria lost its superpower patron when the Soviet Union collapsed. Any regime in Damascus will strive to augment its military power as long as it does not reach a peace agreement with Israel.

In addition to national defense, the Syrian armed forces have political and economic roles to reinforce the **Ba'th Party** regime. Recruits are routinely subject to ideological "education" and the Ministry of Defense has special **radio and television** broadcasts to publicize its achievements in supporting national goals. The armed forces also control sizable economic enterprises, the most important of which is the Military Housing Establishment, which has employed as many as 45,000 men. Not only does this virtual business erect military structures and housing for officers, but it also constructs public works like bridges, hospitals, and schools. A substantial portion of construction workers in the **public sector** work for various military enterprises. The political and economic roles assumed by the armed forces stem from the regime's reliance on them for maintaining internal stability. The economic enterprises in particular provide abundant opportunities for top rank career officers to accumulate tremendous wealth.

ARMÉE DU LEVANT. The French military force stationed in Syria and **Lebanon** during the **French Mandate** era. Some 1,000 French officers commanded troops recruited from colonies in Africa: Senegal, Madagascar, and Morocco. Initially, the Armée du Levant had 70,000 men, but budget constraints forced its reduction to 15,000 in 1924. It remained at that size for most of the mandate period, except for increases during the **Great Revolt** and **World War II**.

ARMENIANS. A non-Arab **minority** whose ancestral homeland is in present-day **Turkey** and the Caucasus. There have been small numbers of Armenians in Syria since ancient times, and in the early Islamic period educated Armenians served the **Umayyad** caliphs as secretaries and administrators. In the **Mamluk** era, a thriving Armenian community grew in **Aleppo**, which has remained their main center in Syria to the present. Large numbers of Armenians fled wartime atrocities in **Ottoman** Turkey during **World War I**, and a second wave followed in the early 1920s when **France** withdrew from southeastern Turkey (Cilicia). By 1925, approximately 50,000 refugees had settled in Aleppo, while others had migrated to towns in **Jazira**, such as **Dayr al-Zur**, **al-Hasaka**, and **Qamishli**. In the **French Mandate** era Armenians encountered animosity from Syrian Arabs because of the willingness of some Armenians to enlist in the **Troupes Spéciales**, which were used to suppress nationalist demonstrations. More recently, the **United Arab Republic** and **Ba`th Party** regimes banned Armenian-language newspapers and cultural associations, although **Hafiz al-Asad**'s regime adopted a more tolerant attitude toward Armenian self-expression. Today the Armenians comprise about four percent of Syria's population and mostly belong to the Armenian Orthodox Church (also called the Gregorian church), although a small number, perhaps 15 percent of the Armenians, adhere to the **Uniate** Armenian Catholic Church.

ARMISTICE OF 1949. At the end of the **Palestine War of 1948**, **Egypt**, **Lebanon**, and **Jordan** negotiated armistice agreements with **Israel** under **United Nations** supervision at Rhodes. Syria, however, did not attend those negotiations, but it did agree in March 1949 to hold talks with Israel. The talks were conducted under the newly installed regime of **Husni al-Za`im**, who had seized power on 30 March. Representatives met near the Syrian-Israeli cease-fire lines on 5 April. Israel wanted the Syrians to evacuate land they had occupied in the fighting because this land lay inside the borders of **Palestine** agreed upon by Great Britain and **France** in the early 1920s. Behind the scenes, Za`im made some

surprising offers to the Israelis. He told them that Syria would permanently absorb 300,000 **Palestinian** refugees and settle them in the
northeastern region of **Jazira**, far from the border with Israel. In return
he sought border adjustments and financial support to integrate the
refugees. He also offered to begin direct negotiations at the highest level
of representation to conclude a peace treaty, not just an armistice.
Israel's leaders, however, insisted on a Syrian withdrawal before any
further steps, so the talks stalled. In the end Syria and Israel signed an
agreement on 20 July 1949. Its terms provided for the creation of
demilitarized zones in areas occupied by Syrian forces during the war
and for the formation of a Mixed Armistice Commission with two
representatives from each country and a United Nations chairman. The
two parties maintained their claims to sovereignty over the zones, so the
armistice agreement deferred a final settlement to later negotiations.
Such talks did not take place, and Israel eventually asserted its control
over those lands by force.

ARSLAN, ADIL (1882-1954). Arslan came from a family of Lebanese
Druze notables. He remained loyal to the **Ottoman Empire** during
World War I and served Amir **Faysal** as governor of Mount Lebanon
and political adviser between 1918 and 1920. A leading figure in the
Istiqlal Party, he left Syria at the beginning of the **French Mandate** and
went to **Transjordan**, where he became a close adviser to Amir Abdallah. In 1923, the British pressured Abdallah to expel him, and he
moved to the Hijaz. He then became active in the **Syrian-Palestine
Congress**, particularly its radical pan-Arab wing that maintained a keen
interest in **Palestine**'s fate as well as that of Syria. During the **Great
Revolt** of 1925-1927 against French rule, Arslan went to Jerusalem to
raise funds for the nationalist cause. In the 1930s, he joined the **National
Bloc** and became Syria's envoy to Ankara under the government of
1936-1939. He held a number of high government offices in the early
years of independence, including foreign minister under **Husni al-Za`im**
in 1949. Soon after taking power, Za`im had Arslan approach the Iraqis
about the possibility of a Syrian-Iraqi union, but Za`im suddenly
switched to an anti-**Hashemite** stance. Arslan's early pan-Arabism also
manifested itself when he refused to support Za`im's secret diplomacy
with **Israel**.

ARSLAN, SHAKIB (1869-1946). Perhaps the most prominent activist for
Muslim political causes between the world wars. Born into a prominent
Druze family in **Lebanon**, Shakib Arslan's upbringing and aspirations

led him to become a **Sunni** Muslim. His high birth entitled him to important offices in the Druze districts of Lebanon during the late **Ottoman** era, when he also gained a reputation as the "prince of eloquence" for his masterly prose. In 1911 Arslan volunteered to join Ottoman forces resisting the Italian invasion of Libya. When he arrived there, he developed a close relationship with Ottoman officers, especially Enver Pasha, who soon after became a member of the **Committee of Union and Progress** triumvirate, which ruled the empire from 1913 to 1918. During **World War I** Arslan staunchly supported the empire against **Arab nationalists** and bitterly opposed the **Arab Revolt** and its **Hashemite** leadership. He believed that a strong Ottoman Empire was the Arabs' only hope for preventing direct European rule and he condemned the Arab Revolt as a betrayal of Arabs and **Islam**. Arslan's earlier acquaintance with Enver Pasha put him in good stead with **Jamal Pasha**, another member of the CUP triumvirate and military governor of Syria for much of the war. His loyalty to the empire and association with Jamal Pasha caused many Syrians to blame him for the governor's harsh policies, including deportations and executions of suspected nationalists.

The end of the war found Arslan in Germany, and for the next few years he roamed restlessly between Europe and **Turkey** in search of a viable political cause. During the **French Mandate** era he made his first commitment to an Arab cause by joining the **Syrian-Palestine Congress** and eventually became one of its representatives to the League of Nations, in large part because he had settled down in Switzerland. When the **Great Revolt** erupted in 1925, Arslan publicized the Syrian cause in European newspapers and petitioned the League of Nations' body responsible for mandates, the Permanent Mandates Commission. In November 1925, though, Arslan aroused anger and jealousy in other leaders of the Syrian-Palestine Congress when he agreed to meet with French High Commissioner Henry de Jouvenel. Their talks resulted in an agreement wherein Arslan insisted on the unity and independence of Syria and **Palestine**, but conceded the permanence of Greater Lebanon, a French monopoly on military assistance to Syria, and a 30-year military alliance. This accord never developed into an official French offer, but it did deepen divisions within the Congress between Arslan's pro-Saudi faction and **Abd al-Rahman Shahbandar**'s pro-Hashemite group.

After the suppression of the Great Revolt, Arslan continued to argue Syria's case before the League of Nations, but he also widened his concerns and became an active inspiration to Arab nationalist movements in North Africa. He returned briefly to Syria in 1937 when the French authorities sought his support for the **Franco-Syrian Treaty**, but his public statements on Palestine and other Arab causes made him unwelcome, and the French asked him to leave before the end of the year.

During **World War II** Arslan again sided with Germany, this time in the belief that its victory would bring independence to Arabs struggling against French and British imperialism, but he was no longer the effective spokesmen of earlier years. Indeed, he spent most of the war in Switzerland fretting over financial difficulties. In October 1946, Arslan left Switzerland for Beirut, where he died two months later.

ARSUZI, ZAKI AL- (1901-1968). Alawi teacher and political activist from **Alexandretta**. After his studies at the Sorbonne in **France**, Arsuzi resided in Antioch and worked as a schoolteacher. From 1938 to 1939, he led the pan-Arab **League of National Action**'s efforts to oppose **Turkey**'s annexation of Alexandretta. After several arrests, Arsuzi left his home province and resettled in **Damascus**. There he emerged as a leading figure among intellectuals and students in favor of Arab unity and revival. He used the term *ba`th*, or rebirth, when speaking of Arab revival, and his followers claim that **Michel Aflaq** stole the term from Arsuzi. Their ideas had a certain affinity, but the two men never worked together because of personal differences. Consequently, many of Arsuzi's followers, mostly young Alawi students, would join the **Ba`th Party**, while Arsuzi himself never again became active in politics. He spent his later years in poverty, devoting his energies to a work on the Arabic language. The **neo-Ba`th** regime, which included many Alawis who had entered the party as his followers, elevated him to the standing of founding party ideologue and erased Aflaq from official party literature. His loyal admirers in the regime granted him a pension to lift him from poverty.

ART. The heritage of classical Islamic art ranges from the Arabic calligraphy adorning public buildings to miniature paintings illustrating books to the design of everyday utensils like vases and bowls. The best-known aspect is the arabesque, a nonfigurative, intricate repetitive design that frequently decorates public buildings in tiles and carved stucco. Only a small number of objects survive from the **Umayyad** and early **Abbasid** eras, but the much richer artistic record from the **Zangid** era onward testifies to the refined skills of craftsmen creating objects for royal patrons and public use. Wood-carvers turned out exquisite doors, pulpits, and screens for prayer niches, including some of the most complicated geometric patterns ever seen in that medium. Metalworkers crafted brass candleholders, incense burners, ewers, and washing basins inlaid with gold and silver, composed of horizontal bands adorned with either human figures in hunting and combat scenes or calligraphy and vegetal patterns. Other media for artistic creation included ceramic vessels and colored glass lamps to illuminate mosques. Painters and calligraphers embellished manuscript copies of scientific texts, popular tales, and of course, the Qur'an. During the Islamic era, **Christians** continued to produce **Byzantine**-style icons for churches and homes. In the 18th and 19th centuries, a distinctive local style emerged in **Aleppo** and **Homs**.

The repertoire of modern art in the 20th century has incorporated the historical Christian and Islamic legacies as well as European movements from impressionism onward. The first paintings on canvas were done in the late **Ottoman** period under the influence of Turkish artists. In the **French Mandate** era, a number of prominent French painters visited and produced works based on urban settings and rural landscapes. Syrians in turn began to study European art in Rome and Paris. Artists' associations appeared in the major cities during the 1940s and 1950s, when realism was the most common style. Impressionist renditions of landscapes and traditional urban quarters would become popular as well until the 1960s, when artists turned to Expressionist and Abstract styles to convey political and social themes. The **June 1967 War** affected the art scene just as it did **literature** and **theater**. A number of exhibits concentrated on **Israeli** belligerence and **Palestinian** displacement, portraying them as part of a biblical narrative of suffering and victimization.

Not all artistic production is an effect of political currents and European influences, or perhaps more exactly for recent decades, of postmodern cosmopolitan trends. Syrian artists have striven to create a local identity by drawing on the country's ancient heritage for motifs and by turning to nonrepresentational art. For centuries before **Islam**, Syria had a rich legacy of sculpture, but the Muslim taboo on idols spelled the end of that art form until recently. Public sculptures of national heroes like **Saladin** or the martyrs of **Maysalun** contribute to the visual construction of a Syrian national identity. The visual arts resemble the country's literary and theatrical scenes in that all depend on government support for school **education** and subsidies for publications and exhibitions.

ASAD, BASHAR AL- (1965-). Syria's president since July 2000 following the death of his father **Hafiz al-Asad**. In the early 1990s, Hafiz al-Asad was preparing his oldest son Basil to succeed him, but upon his death in a 1994 automobile accident, he turned to Bashar, who had been in London studying ophthalmology at the time. During the next six years,

Hafiz al-Asad groomed Bashar by entrusting him with various tasks, particularly related to an anticorruption campaign, introducing computer technology, foreign investment, privatization, and relations with **Lebanon**. Powerful military and **security** chiefs proved their loyalty to the late president with support for Bashar's succession. More formal roles were played by the People's Assembly, which amended the **constitution**'s provision on the president's minimum age, and by the **Ba`th Party** Regional Command, which made Bashar its secretary-general. His uncle **Rif`at** declared the succession unconstitutional but had no way to block the transition from his exile in Spain. A referendum in July gave Bashar over 97 percent of the vote and he was installed as president on 17 July. The succession occurred smoothly, contrary to the prognostications of observers who had expected a period of instability and perhaps even collapse of the regime.

For many Syrians, relief at the orderly transfer of power was mixed with hopes that as the representative of a new generation Bashar might guide the country toward liberal political and economic policies. Political activists publicly called on him to take the first steps toward democracy, including the establishment of a free press and the release of all political prisoners. A handful of activists held salons at their homes to discuss ways to advance **civil society** and democracy. In November 2000, Bashar released 600 men from different opposition groups—**Muslim Brothers**, pro-**Iraqi** Ba`thists, and communists. He also permitted the publication of a private periodical for the first time since 1963. This brief spell of political relaxation lasted from fall 2000 until early 2001, when Bashar imposed regulations on private political salons. It seems the political establishment surrounding the new president feared that even a limited amount of political criticism could snowball into an uncontrollable movement. The crackdown even affected two members of the People's Assembly, who launched a hunger strike on behalf of guarantees for the rule of law, an independent judiciary, and limits on the power of the security services.

When Bashar succeeded, the economic situation was manageable but in a chronically difficult condition, with unemployment in the range of 20-25 percent, the population annually growing at 3.1 percent, and per capita annual income around $1,000. Most observers predicted that he would follow the "Chinese model" of liberalizing the **economy** while preserving single-party rule, but in his first three years, even steps to open the economy to foreign capital and **trade** have been timid.

Bashar al-Asad has faced particularly challenging regional circumstances because of the failure of **Syrian-Israeli peace talks** in January

2000 and the **Israeli** withdrawal from Lebanon in May. He has followed his father's practice of seeking a broad basis for a strong posture against Israel. This has meant, for instance, the continuation of Syria's military presence in Lebanon in the face of popular demands that Syria withdraw its troops and release Lebanese political prisoners detained in Syria. Bashar made a conciliatory gesture in June 2001 by redeploying troops out of Beirut, but otherwise he keeps a firm grip. Like his father, he considers **Hizballah** a military asset for the confrontation with Israel and as insurance against the prospect of a separate Israeli-Lebanese peace treaty. Economic factors also come into consideration because tens of thousands of Syrians work in Lebanon, thereby easing unemployment in Syria and offering opportunities to powerful figures in the regime to profit from smuggling. In other regional relations, Bashar pursued the thaw in relations with **Jordan** that his father had initiated and maintained cordial ties with **Egypt** and **Saudi Arabia** while furthering the process of reconciliation with Iraq until the American invasion deposed Saddam Husayn's regime in spring 2003. The prospect of a long American occupation in a neighboring country at a time when the United States is reconsidering its traditional policy of engagement with Damascus will create new pressures and uncertainties for the untested Syrian leader. *See also* FARZAT, ALI; FOREIGN POLICY.

ASAD, HAFIZ AL- (1930-2000). President of Syria from February 1971 until June 2000. He came to power in the **corrective movement** of November 1970. Asad was born in Qurdaha, a village in **Jabal Ansariyya**, the historical home of the **Alawis**. Asad got his education in the nearby city of **Latakia**, where he met the Ba'thist teacher **Wahib al-Ghanim**, who imparted the ideas of **Zaki al-Arsuzi** and recruited Asad to the **Ba'th Party**. In 1951, Asad entered the Military Academy at **Homs** and enrolled in a special training course for pilots in Syria's nascent air force. For the next several years, he remained active in Ba'thist politics and continued his career as an air force pilot. During the **United Arab Republic** era, Asad's unit was transferred to **Egypt**, where he and other Ba'thist officers shared their resentment of party leaders **Michel Aflaq** and **Salah al-Din al-Bitar** for betraying the party when they agreed to its dissolution as a condition for creating the UAR. Asad and four other officers stationed in Cairo founded the **Military Committee**, which was dedicated to rebuilding the Ba'th and gaining power in Syria.

At the breakup of the UAR, Asad returned to Syria, but the new regime distrusted Ba'thists and removed him from the air force, assigning him to a desk job in the ministry of **economy**. For the next 18 months, Asad and his colleagues on the Military Committee plotted a coup. An attempt in April 1962 failed, but the **March 8, 1963 coup** succeeded. In the new regime Asad was promoted from captain to lieutenant-colonel and appointed commander of an air base near **Damascus**. Later that year, he was elected to the party's Regional Command. His chief task, however, was to make the **armed forces** a bastion of the Ba'th Party. Asad purged the officer corps, promoted men loyal to the party, and invited Zaki al-Arsuzi to lecture on party ideals before the troops. When strife within the Military Committee surfaced in 1964, Asad sided with **Salah al-Jadid**, and he was rewarded with promotion to commander of the Syrian air force. After the **February 23, 1966 coup**, which brought the **neo-Ba'th** to power, Asad became minister of defense. In that capacity he helped organize **Palestinian** commando raids against **Israel** that triggered retaliations against Syrian forces in the **Golan Heights**. From these skirmishes erupted the crisis of May 1967 that led to the **June 1967 War**, in which Syria lost the Golan Heights. Many blamed Asad for Syria's miserable military performance during the war, but he argued that it was the fault of policies pursued by dogmatic radicals in the neo-Ba'th. He further argued that the time had come for the regime to back away from its revolutionary program in order to concentrate the country's resources on the military confrontation with Israel. His comrade from the Military Committee and the regime's strongman, Salah al-Jadid, took the side of the radicals. Asad then consolidated his power base in the armed forces by getting rid of men loyal to Jadid. In February 1969, Asad dispatched units to take over the party newspapers and the national radio stations, and in so doing proved his mastery of the armed forces.

In September 1970, civil war broke out in **Jordan** between the government and Palestinian guerrillas. Asad sent Syrian armor into northern Jordan to support the Palestinians but withheld the air force, thereby making possible an effective Jordanian counterattack that drove out the Syrian tanks. At the end of October, Jadid made a bid to dismiss Asad, but in the trial of strength between the last two members of the Military Committee on the political scene, Asad easily prevailed. His men arrested his opponents, including Jadid, in a bloodless coup that Asad dubbed the corrective movement. At first he designated a **Sunni**, Ahmad al-Khatib, to serve as head of state, but in February 1971, Asad restored the presidency, which the neo-Ba'th had abolished, and occupied the office himself. This was a bold move because it was the first time that a non-Sunni was president of Syria.

On taking power Asad "corrected" what he considered the excesses of the previous regime. He eased restraints on travel and **trade**, made overtures to the urban Sunni bourgeoisie by announcing plans to liberalize the economy, and reined in the **security forces**. He further broadened the regime's base in March 1972 by forming the National Progressive Front, a coalition of political parties dominated by the Ba`th (the other parties were the **Syrian Communist Party**, the Arab Socialist Movement, the Socialist Unity Party, and the Arab Socialist Union). He also reshuffled the Ba`th Party's Regional Command, installing men loyal to him and assuming the position of secretary-general. For the most part, these moves gained popular backing from Syrians opposed to the neo-Ba`th's strict exclusion of other political forces and its dogmatic socialism. He also altered Syria's **foreign policy**, which under his predecessors' radicalism had isolated Syria in the Arab world. Asad mended relations with **Egypt, Saudi Arabia**, and other Arab countries. He was particularly eager to develop a close working relationship with Egyptian President Anwar Sadat in order to forge an Arab military capability to confront Israel. As for the superpowers, Asad cultivated a steady relationship with the **Soviet Union** because of Syria's dependence on Moscow for arms, while he continued the break in relations with the **United States** that had occurred following the June 1967 War.

Asad's priority was the retrieval of the Golan Heights and in pursuit of that end he and Sadat made secret plans for a surprise attack on Israel. In April 1973, the two leaders agreed on plans for the **October 1973 War**. A few weeks before the war, Syria restored relations with Jordan in a move to shore up Arab solidarity. Although the war resulted in additional territorial losses, the armed forces' initial success and ability to stop Israel's counterattack further bolstered Asad's standing in Syria. After the war American Secretary of State Henry Kissinger engaged in "shuttle diplomacy," traveling back and forth among Israel, Egypt, Syria, Moscow, and Washington. His first achievement was an agreement between Egypt and Israel to disengage their forces in Sinai in January 1974. Kissinger then managed to mediate a disengagement accord between Syria and Israel on the Golan front in May 1974. This accord stipulated the stationing of the **United Nations Disengagement Observer Force** in a buffer zone between Syrian and Israeli forces. But that was as far as American mediation between Syria and Israel would go, and a new stalemate ensued, albeit stabilized by the buffer zone. When Sadat embarked on his solitary endeavor to reach peace with Israel, Asad's position became more vulnerable, but he was able to convince the Soviet Union to assist his massive buildup of the armed forces and he gained access to the deep pockets of Arab Gulf states to pay for new military equipment.

In the mid-1970s, Asad was preoccupied by the **Lebanese Civil War**, in which he ordered the Syrian army to intervene in June 1976. When Syrian troops fought against Palestinian and Lebanese Sunni forces, much of Syrian popular opinion was outraged and some believed that Asad was motivated by Alawi prejudice against Sunnis. This perception fueled smoldering resentment among Syrian Sunnis not reconciled to having an Alawi president. Conditions for unrest were augmented by deteriorating economic conditions in 1976 and 1977. Furthermore, morale among Syrian **Islamic fundamentalists** such as the **Muslim Brothers** shot up with the triumph of the Islamic Revolution in **Iran** in 1979. This combination of factors contributed to the uprising of Islamist and secular forces that threatened to topple the Asad regime from 1979 to 1982. The government weathered the storm by relying on fierce repression and strong support from the Ba`th Party's partisans. At the same time, the regime buttressed its standing among the large number of public sector employees by raising salaries in 1980. In order to take some steam out of urban middle-class frustrations, the regime also eased constraints on imports. The Islamist revolt peaked in the first week of February 1982 when the Muslim Brothers took over **Hama** and called on Syrian Muslims to rise up in the rest of the country. No other uprisings occurred and Asad sent army units and special forces to regain control of the city. In two weeks of fighting, between 5,000 and 20,000 people were killed. The suppression of the revolt in Hama marked the defeat of the Islamist revolt.

No sooner had Asad survived that strong challenge than Israel invaded **Lebanon** in June 1982, beginning the **Lebanese War of 1982**. Syria suffered initial reverses and had to endure the specter of Israeli domination over much of Lebanon, thereby posing a new threat to Syria. But by mobilizing Lebanese opposed to Israel and its Lebanese allies, Asad managed to turn the tables so that by the end of 1985 Israeli forces withdrew to a narrow strip of territory along the Israel-Lebanon border. His achievement in Lebanon was made more difficult by his isolation in the Arab world because he supported Iran against **Iraq** in the war that broke out between them in 1980.

Questions about Asad's durability arose in November 1983, when he disappeared from public view for several days, prompting rumors of serious illness and anxieties over the unsettled issue of succession. The specific nature of Asad's illness was never made public and when he reemerged he had to overcome a bid for power by his younger brother

Rif'at al-Asad. The president decisively won the showdown and forced Rif'at to spend most of the next several years abroad in the Soviet Union and **France**. By the late 1980s, Asad's regime was on a sounder footing than it had been since 1974, its worst problems stemming from a prolonged period of difficulty in the economy, in particular a shortage of foreign exchange. Beginning in 1986, the government took measures to reform the economy by encouraging a larger role for the private sector and these measures succeeded in stimulating a mild economic recovery.

When Iraq invaded Kuwait in August 1990, Asad decided to support the United States' initiative for defending Saudi Arabia against a possible Iraqi attack. Syria's participation in the anti-Iraq alliance paid handsome dividends: large cash payments from Saudi Arabia, a free hand to reconstitute Lebanon according to the **Ta'if Accord**, and better relations with Washington at a time when the Soviet Union was coming unraveled. After the war, the United States urged Syria to attend an international peace conference to resolve the Arab-Israeli dispute, and in July 1991 Asad agreed to send a delegation to the **Madrid Conference**. Bilateral talks between Syria and Israel sputtered along for the next eight years but failed to reach an agreement in which Syria would regain all of the Golan Heights and Israel would feel secure in a new era of normalized relations with its longtime adversary.

The last five years of his presidency were eventful in the realm of foreign policy but perhaps most notable for the way he orchestrated his son **Bashar**'s succession as Syria's leader. As was the case for most of his rule, Asad focused on regional affairs, especially the efforts to bring **Syrian-Israeli peace talks** to a successful conclusion. While Syria and Israel made strides toward an agreement when the Labor Party's Yitzhak Rabin and Shimon Peres held office (1992-1996), the talks were suddenly suspended in March 1996 after Damascus refused to condemn a wave of Palestinian suicide bombings. Two months later Likud Party leader Benjamin Netanyahu was elected, and for the next three years the peace process was frozen because of his refusal to meet Syrian demands that he resume talks where his predecessors had left off. During Netanyahu's tenure, Asad tried to forge a regional coalition including Egypt, Saudi Arabia, and Iran to counter the newly formed Israeli-Turkish relationship aligned with Washington. He also seized the opportunity offered by the **United Nations** oil-for-food program for Iraq to revive bilateral trade and reopen the oil pipeline. The regional situation changed with the May 1999 election of Labor leader Ehud Barak, whose bold pronouncements injected new hope for the peace process. In January 2000 Barak met with Foreign Minister **Faruq al-Shara'** in **Shepherds-**

town, West Virginia, to pave the way for a final deal. This initiative foundered as well, and Barak pulled Israeli forces out of Lebanon in May.

On the domestic front, Asad groomed his son Bashar for succession by gradually increasing his "portfolio" to include the sensitive matter of relations with Lebanon and an anticorruption drive to bolster his legitimacy. When it came to the fundamental distribution of political power and state control over the economy, however, Asad chose to stand pat with the formula that had kept him in power and maintained stability for 30 years. The steps to elevate Bashar included the dismissal of the powerful military intelligence chief **Ali Duba** in February and a cabinet reshuffle in March. A Ba'th Party Congress was scheduled to take place in mid-June, when it was anticipated that Bashar would be given a seat on the Regional Command, but Hafiz al-Asad died on 10 June, one week before the Congress was due to open.

Assessments of his regime tend to acknowledge that he brought internal political stability to a country that had been arguably the most unstable in the Arab world. He also consolidated a secular political order during a period when Islamic fundamentalism threatened governments and religious minorities like Arab **Christians** and non-Sunni Muslims. On the other hand, his stern rule stifled dissent by imposing a security apparatus that routinely and arbitrarily violated **human rights**. Moreover, his intervention in Lebanese and Palestinian affairs to harness them to his vision of Syrian, if not Arab, interests aggravated regional political divisions. Furthermore, his refusal to liberalize the economy may have spared Syrians the difficulties of structural adjustment, but most observers believe that since the mid-1980s he merely delayed the inevitable for political ends and at high economic cost.

ASAD, RIF'AT AL- (1937-). Younger brother of **Hafiz al-Asad** and from 1984 to 1998 one of Syria's three vice presidents. Under his older brother's influence, Rif at joined the **Ba'th Party** as a youth and entered the Military Academy at **Homs**. During the first Ba'thist regime, Rif at took over command of a special armed unit charged with defending the **Military Committee** and its allies in the party. After Hafiz al-Asad seized power in November 1970, he enlarged Rif at's armed force, named it the Defense Companies, and assigned it the task of protecting the regime against any internal enemies. By the late 1970s, Rif at wielded considerable power as the president's brother and commander of the country's most powerful elite armed force. At its height, the Defense Companies numbered more than 50,000 men and had its own air, armor, and artillery units. As Rif at became more influential, he also gained notoriety for leading an extravagant and debauched personal life, and thus turned into a magnet for animosity toward the regime.

Rif at reached his greatest influence during the Islamist uprising spearheaded by the **Muslim Brothers**. He advocated ruthless repression as the answer to the guerrillas' armed struggle. His Defense Companies participated in the April 1980 suppression of dissent in **Aleppo**. After an assassination attempt against the president in June, Rif at's men massacred several hundred Muslim Brothers held at a prison at Tadmur (**Palmyra**). The younger Asad, however, misplayed his hand when the president fell ill in November 1983. Rif at took steps to seize control in the event of his brother's demise, and in doing so contradicted the president's express orders for the formation of a collective authority to govern in his absence. After the president recovered in late November, he took several steps to break Rif at's power, including the transfer of command over the Defense Companies. The president also designated three vice presidents, including Rif at, who correctly figured that the appointment actually meant demotion to a purely titular role. The younger Asad responded at the end of March 1984 with a bold bid to take over the regime, but the president made him climb down by sheer force of his personality. Two months later Hafiz al-Asad sent Rif at to Moscow on a "diplomatic" mission that ended in a prolonged exile to first Switzerland, then France. In his absence, the president defanged the Defense Companies and reassigned some of its men to other units. Asad then allowed Rif at to return in November, still one of three vice presidents but unable to rebuild his power base.

Since falling afoul of his older brother, Rif at has mainly played the role of a spoiler. Even though he officially remained a vice president, he spent about eight years in Europe before Hafiz al-Asad allowed him to return in 1992 for their mother's funeral. Rif at's souring on the regime became public in 1997, when his son Sumar started a satellite television channel called Arab News Network that aired criticism of the regime. The next two years, however, saw his final fall from any vestige of official influence. First, in February 1998, Hafiz al-Asad dismissed him as vice president. Then in fall 1999, the government launched a campaign to arrest his backers and shut down an illegal private port he operated in **Latakia**, where fighting erupted between his men and government forces before the latter overwhelmed the renegades. He nevertheless refused to cease his insistence on keeping a high profile in his quest for power. For example, he attended the funeral of Morocco's King Hassan II and consulted with Yasir Arafat. When Hafiz al-Asad died in June 2000, his brother was actually barred from entering the country for the funeral, and he declared in turn that **Bashar al-Asad**'s succession was illegal. In view of his long exile and the government's dispersal of his once-feared paramilitary force, Rif at al-Asad was in no position to do more than annoy his nephew, the new president.

ASALI, SABRI AL- (1903-1976). Three-time prime minister of Syria in the 1950s. His political activism dated to his participation in the **Great Revolt** of 1925-1927 for which the **French Mandate** authorities exiled him. In Cairo he joined the **Syrian-Palestine Congress** and developed a close association with **Shukri al-Quwwatli**. He returned to Syria in 1928 and opened a law practice in **Damascus**. In 1935, Asali became the head of the **League of National Action**, but the following year the League expelled him for joining the **National Bloc**. As a member of the Bloc and its successor the **National Party**, Asali won parliamentary seats in 1936, 1943, and 1947. In the early independence era he served in several cabinets.

Following **Husni al-Za`im**'s March 1949 coup and National Party leader Shukri al-Quwwatli's flight to Egypt, Asali took over the party's leadership. He achieved his greatest influence from 1954 to 1958 when he was prime minister a number of times. From 1 March until 11 June 1954, he headed a pro-Western cabinet inclined to pursue unity with **Iraq**. A few days before his fall he secretly met with an Iraqi representative to discuss ways to implement the **Fertile Crescent Plan**. Asali again assumed the office on 13 February 1955, this time with the support of neutralist forces opposed to Syria's adherence to the **Baghdad Pact**, and he aligned the country with **Egypt** and **Saudi Arabia**, but this government fell in September. Asali would become prime minister one last time in June 1956, when he headed a cabinet that allotted two key portfolios (Foreign Relations and Economy) to the **Ba`th Party**. It was this government that negotiated Syria's merger with Egypt in the **United Arab Republic**. Asali became a vice president in the UAR, but Nasir made him resign in October 1958. In March 1963, Asali was one of several prominent politicians whom the Ba`thist regime formally stripped of their civil rights.

ASHRAF. Hereditary body in Muslim societies that claims descent from the Prophet Muhammad. In Syrian history, the ashraf of **Aleppo** became organized as a distinct political-military body in the 18th century and contended for power with the **janissaries** stationed in the city. Conflict was particularly sharp during the last three decades of the century, until a janissary massacre of ashraf in 1798.

ASSASSIN. *See* **NIZARI.**

ASSYRIANS. Nestorian Christians who speak a dialect of Syriac, they were once widely spread throughout the Middle East, but in the early 20th century they mostly lived in eastern **Turkey**, northern **Iraq**, and northwestern **Iran** near Lake Urmiyah. During **World War I**, they enlisted Russian support in a revolt against the **Ottomans**, but were defeated and forced to flee into Iran. The British then sent 25,000 Assyrians gathered at Hamadan in western Iran to a refugee camp near Baghdad. They desired to be repatriated to their ancestral home inside Turkey, but the new Turkish government refused to admit them and the British encouraged them to settle in Iraq. These non-Arab Christians wanted to retain their autonomy and distrusted the Iraqi authorities, who in turn regarded them with suspicion, in large part for their willingness to form a special military force under British command. When Iraq became independent in 1930, the government decommissioned the Assyrian "Levies," but strains persisted between the authorities and the Assyrians. In June 1933 a skirmish between Assyrians and the Iraqi army sparked an army massacre of several hundred Assyrians. Panic spread and 9,000 Assyrians fled into Syria, where they settled along the **Khabur River** in **Jazira** province. For eight years the League of Nations operated a special administration to assist their settlement and economic integration.

Today the largest concentration of Assyrians is found in **Qamishli**, settled in 1925. Smaller communities live in **Aleppo**, **al-Hasaka**, and **Homs**, the site of the patriarchate. They established private schools that give instruction in their language in the Aramaic alphabet, and they have maintained a vibrant cultural life through the church, clubs, and scouts. These associations perform plays and stage art exhibitions to keep their **minority** culture alive. Song and dance troupes perform at Syrian folklore festivals. For a number of years after Syrian independence, the Assyrians published their own periodicals. Their most famous cultural figure is John Aleksan, a writer and historian. **Arab nationalist** policies since 1963 aspire to dilute the concentration of Syria's various minorities and to assimilate them by placing schools under the Ministry of Education and encouraging Arabs to settle around Qamishli.

ATABEGS. In general, the term refers to dignitaries in the **Saljuk** regime. In the Syrian context, the atabegs were military slaves, or **mamluks**, who acted as the regents of the Saljuk princes of **Damascus** and **Aleppo**. In 1104, Duqaq, the last Saljuk prince of Damascus, died, and the atabeg Tughtagin ruled in his own right. Upon his death in 1128 power passed to his son Buri, and the Burid line lasted until 1154 and the **Zangid** conquest of Damascus by **Nur al-Din Mahmud**, himself from a line of northern Syrian atabegs. The Burid atabegs governed Damascus and its environs, a small territory squeezed between the **Fatimids** in **Egypt**, the Franks of the first **Crusade**, and their most dangerous enemies, the Zangid atabegs of northern Syria. The last Saljuk prince of Aleppo died in 1113, and there followed 15 years of struggle for control of Aleppo among Muslim and Crusader powers. This contest concluded in 1128 with the entry of the atabeg **Imad al-Din al-Zangi**, who had already established his rule over Mosul in northern **Iraq**. He and his successors, known as the Zangids, were often involved in warfare against the Crusaders.

ATASI, HASHIM AL- (1876-1960). Born in **Homs**, prime minister under Amir **Faysal** in 1920, a founding member and first chief of the **National Bloc**. He was one of the foremost nationalist politicians during the **French Mandate**. Atasi headed the Syrian delegation that negotiated the **Franco-Syrian Treaty of 1936**, and he then became president of Syria during the National Bloc government of 1936-1939. In the early independence period he was a founding member of the northern-oriented **People's Party** and served as prime minister under **Sami al-Hinnawi**'s short-lived regime. Atasi later became president under **Adib al-Shishakli**'s first regime, but he resigned after Shishakli's November 1951 military coup and dissolution of parliament. He then emerged as a central figure in the movement that overthrew Shishakli in February 1954. At the age of 78, Atasi became president following Shishakli's removal, but he resigned in September 1955.

ATASI, NUR AL-DIN AL- (c. 1929-1992). Medical doctor and member of the radical **neo-Ba`th**. In the first Ba`th Party regime, Atasi was a member of the **National Revolutionary Command Council**, minister of the interior, and then deputy prime minister. In the neo-Ba`thist regime, this **Sunni** from a respected **Homs** family was head of state, but he sided with **Salah al-Jadid** against **Hafiz al-Asad** in the party's internecine struggle. When Asad's faction prevailed in November 1970, Atasi was thrown into prison. He was released in August 1992 because of poor health, and he died a few months later in Paris.

ATRASH, SULTAN AL- (1887-1982). Druze leader of the **Great Revolt** of 1925-1927 against the **French Mandate** and member of the foremost clan in **Jabal Druze**. At the beginning of the mandate, the French tried to cooperate with the Atrash chiefs, but Sultan al-Atrash sought to minimize **France**'s authority in Jabal Druze. From 1922 to 1923, he led an uprising against the French, but was forced to flee to **Transjordan**. Two years later, however, he was back in Syria and planned a better organized, more widespread revolt. In July 1925, he launched an uprising that expelled the French from Jabal Druze and then spread to the rest of Syria. When the French crushed the revolt two years later, Sultan al-Atrash fled first to Transjordan and then Arabia. While in Transjordan, Atrash developed links with its **Hashemite** ruler Amir Abdallah and sustained them for many years after his return to Syria. Atrash returned from his exile at Kerak in May 1937. His ties with Abdallah were part of a more general connection between the Hashemites and the Druzes for the next two decades. During the early independence period, Atrash was prominent in the affairs of Jabal Druze, although his clan's power declined.

ATTAR, ISAM AL- (1925-   ). A **Damascus** high school teacher who became leader of the Syrian **Muslim Brothers** from 1957 until his exile in 1964. Attar was not known as a religious leader, but he was close to the organization's first leader, **Mustafa al-Siba`i**, and was married to the daughter of a prominent shaykh. Shortly after Attar became leader of the Brothers, the **United Arab Republic** banned them because of Egyptian President Gamal Abd al-Nasir's hostility to the movement, which had violently opposed him during the 1950s. The Muslim Brothers re-emerged following Syria's secession from the UAR and won 10 seats in the December 1961 elections to parliament. Attar was one of the Brothers' candidates to gain a seat. But when the **Ba`th Party** came to power in 1963, the Brothers again faced a hostile regime. Attar's public sermons against the Ba`th's secularism led the regime to briefly imprison him. In 1964, he went to Mecca for the pilgrimage and when he tried to return home, the authorities refused to allow him entry. For two years he resided in **Lebanon** and was then expelled. Meanwhile, the Ba`thists banned the Muslim Brothers. In 1968, Attar went to West Germany to direct an **Islamic** Center and publish an Islamic periodical.

Attar represented the Brothers' moderate wing, which opposed armed struggle against the government. In 1972, he had to relinquish his leadership to more militant elements determined to pursue a violent strategy in a bid to overthrow the government, but the Damascus faction remained loyal to him and his voice continued to matter in Syrian Islamist circles. In the middle of 1980, his journal came around to supporting the armed struggle against the Ba`thist regime. In retaliation, agents of the Syrian government murdered Attar's wife in Germany in March 1981. Given the depth of the regime's enmity toward him, it was peculiar that his sister Najah al-Attar served as minister of culture for many years.

AYN JALUT, BATTLE OF. On 3 September 1260, **Mamluk** and **Mongol** forces met in one of the major battles of Muslim history at this site, where according to legend David slew Goliath. The Mamluk Sultan Qutuz led his troops from **Egypt** to meet the advancing Mongols, who had swept south through Syria, brushing aside the feeble **Ayyubid** princes of central Syria. The Mamluk sultan and the chief commander of the vanguard, **Baybars**, gathered a much larger force than the Mongols had mustered and inflicted a decisive defeat on the Central Asian invaders, the first such military setback in more than four decades of Mongol assaults on Muslim armies. The outcome of the battle ended the immediate Mongol threat to Egypt and marked the beginning of the Mamluks' rise to power over Syria.

AYYUBID DYNASTY. The Kurdish clansmen of Najm al-Din Ayyub rose to prominence through service to the Zangid rulers of Mosul and **Aleppo**. One of Najm al-Din's kinsmen, **Saladin**, established dynastic rule over **Egypt** in 1171, and over most of Syria by 1183. His successors divided their empire into autonomous hereditary principalities centered in Aleppo, **Damascus**, **Hama**, and **Homs** while the main branch of the dynasty ruled Egypt. During their 90-year rule, the Ayyubids fought each other as often as they fought the **Crusader** states, with which they often negotiated truces. Their tolerance toward the Franks led them to allow the first Italian merchants to establish themselves in Damascus. The last Ayyubid ruler of Egypt, al-Salih Ayyub, relied on military slaves, or **mamluks**, to an unprecedented degree. The ethnic homogeneity of his mamluks and their isolation from Egyptian society contributed to their determination to seize power in 1250, an event that led to the establishment of the **Mamluk sultanate**. Ten years later, the **Mongol** invasion crushed the remaining Ayyubid domains in Syria.

AZM. The most prominent political family in Syria during the 18th century. Isma`il Pasha al-Azm (d. 1730) launched his clan's fortunes when the **Ottomans** appointed him governor of central Syrian districts, then of

Tripoli, and in 1725 of **Damascus**. During his tenure, **janissary** factions created troubles in the city. He promoted the careers of his brother Sulayman and son Ibrahim as governors of Tripoli and Sidon. Isma`il fell from favor in Istanbul in 1730 and was exiled to Crete. Sulayman Pasha (d. 1743) served as governor of Tripoli, then of Damascus from 1733 to 1738 and 1741 to 1743. He was no more effective than his brother Isma`il in quelling janissary unruliness. At his death, his nephew As`ad (d. 1758) became the next Azm governor of Damascus and served for an unusually long time (1743-1757). His long tenure can be attributed to his crushing of the local janissaries in 1746. This enabled him to establish his unchallenged authority over the city. He used some of his family's vast wealth to construct a splendid monument to 18th-century Ottoman Arab architecture and art, the Azm Palace. As`ad al-Azm was also known for relaxing restraints on **Christians**; for instance, he allowed them to drink alcohol in public. His rule represented the apex of Azm influence in Syria, as other members of the clan governed Sidon, Tripoli, **Aleppo**, and even Mosul. As`ad Pasha himself ultimately fell from grace with Ottoman officials, was forced to give up his post, and was executed in 1758.

For the next 13 years it appeared the era of Azm prominence had ended, but in 1771 the Ottomans appointed Isma`il's grandson, Muhammad al-Azm (d. 1783), governor of Damascus. During his first tenure, the governor of southern Syria, Zahir al-Umar, built up his power at the expense of the province of Damascus. The Ottomans dismissed Muhammad Pasha for failing to cope with Zahir and his Egyptian ally, the **mamluk** Ali Bey, but Azm returned to the post the following year. For the remainder of his second tenure (which ended when he died), Muhammad Pasha witnessed the fall of Zahir al-Umar and the rise of **Ahmad Pasha al-Jazzar**. He did, however, generously support urban construction and patronized religious and literary activities. The last member of the clan to govern Damascus was Abdallah Pasha. He held office three times between 1790 and 1808. He also served as governor of Tripoli and of Aleppo. During his time, Syria was threatened by **Wahhabi** raids from Arabia and a French invasion led by **Napoleon Bonaparte**. While the Ottomans did not appoint any more members of the Azm clan to govern Damascus, the clan remained one of the country's wealthiest and most influential families well into the 20th century.

AZM, HAQQI AL- (1864-1955). First prime minister of an elected Syrian government in 1932 until the French dismissed him in 1934. In the late **Ottoman** era he held posts in the civil service, but then became active in

Arab nationalist politics and joined the **Ottoman Party of Administrative Decentralization** that formed in 1912. At the start of the **French Mandate**, Azm decided to cooperate with the new rulers of Syria, and in November 1920, the French appointed him governor of the Damascus state, which they had created to administer southern Syria. He turned the office into a nest of nepotism and corruption, which scandalized Damascene public opinion. His inability to garner support from any quarter except for his extended family led the French to force him to resign in January 1923. Azm later formed the Reform Party to contest the elections of December 1931 to January 1932 and he gained a seat from **Damascus**. In June 1932, he became prime minister and signed France's first proposal for a **Franco-Syrian Treaty** in November 1933. Nationalist opposition to the treaty arose from its provision that the **Druze** and **Alawi** regions would remain separate from the rest of Syria. Azm's inability to deliver support for the treaty led the French High Commissioner to dismiss him in March 1934.

AZM, KHALID AL- (1895-1965). A leading independent politician from the late 1940s until the early 1960s, and known as the "Red Pasha" for his alliance with the **Syrian Communist Party** and support for better relations with the **Soviet Union**. Azm became prime minister to resolve a parliamentary crisis in December 1948, following Syria's defeat in the **Palestine War of 1948**. He was deposed by the March 1949 coup d'état of **Husni al-Za`im**, but after **Sami al-Hinnawi**'s military coup in August he became finance minister. In December 1949, after **Adib al-Shishakli** seized power, he named Azm prime minister, but his government fell after just five months because of feuding among cabinet members and disruption by **Akram al-Hawrani**. He returned as prime minister yet again in March 1951, this time with Hawrani's support as well as that of the **National Party** and the army. The common denominator was opposition to the **People's Party**, which held a plurality in the national assembly. Once again Azm's tenure was brief as his government was brought down when the People's Party inspired demonstrations at the end of July. Azm won renewed influence in the 1955 cabinet of **Sabri al-Asali** as its neutralist foreign minister. In this capacity Azm cultivated good relations with the Soviet Union to fend off Western pressures exercised through **Iraq** and **Turkey**. His good relations with the Soviets were mirrored in Syrian politics by his close ties to **Khalid Bakdash**, the leader of the SCP.

After Syria's secession from the **United Arab Republic**, Azm returned as prime minister again in September 1962 with a platform to restore democratic liberties that had been suspended under the UAR. In December he rescinded emergency laws and promised multiparty elections. This threat to curtail the army's role in politics generated a new round of plotting by several cliques of army officers, leading to the **March 8, 1963 coup** that overthrew the Azm government. He departed Syria and spent his remaining years in **Lebanon**.

AZMA, BASHIR AL- (1910-   ). During the **secessionist regime**, he served as prime minister of the cabinet that formed after the 28 March 1962 military coup against a conservative civilian government. Azma was an independent politician who had been head of the Syrian Doctors Association. His government moved to heal Syrian relations with **Egypt**, which had soured because of Syria's secession from the **United Arab Republic**. Nonetheless, Egypt continued to criticize the Syrian government, and at the end of July the Syrians announced the discovery of a Nasirist plot to seize power. On the domestic front, the Azma government reversed some conservative measures by restoring the 1958 **land reform** law and renationalizing a number of large **banks**. Under strong political pressure to restore democratic liberties, he allowed the National Assembly to reconvene on 14 September and vote for a new government under **Khalid al-Azm**. Azma then became deputy prime minister, a position he held until the **March 8, 1963 coup**. *See also* SOCIALIST DECREES.

-B-

BAB SAGHIR. The old, walled portion of **Damascus** had seven ancient gates. Al-Bab al-Saghir, "the Little Gate," is situated on the city's southern flank and gives its name to a cemetery just outside the walls that contains the graves of many notable figures from early **Islamic** history. The cemetery is a destination for **Shi`i** Muslim pilgrims who wish to visit the tombs of the Prophet's family. These include the sister of Husayn ibn **Ali**, Umm Kulthum, and Husayn's two daughters Sakina and Ruqayya. Two of the Prophet's wives, Umm Salma and Umm Habiba, are buried there. Bab Saghir's cemetery also contains the grave of the first muezzin (one who gives the public call to prayer), Bilal al-Habashi.

BAGHDAD PACT. Great Britain was the moving force behind this pro-Western military alliance formed by **Iraq** and **Turkey** on 24 February 1955. Much of the following year's regional politics focused on the struggle to include Syria in the pact or to keep it out. **Egypt** and **Saudi Arabia** supported Syrian parties and politicians who favored nonalignment. In Syrian politics this episode was eventful in generating a coalition among hitherto rival groups, especially the **Ba`th Party** and the **Syrian Communist Party**, and between the Ba`th and Egypt, which supported the former's determination to prevent Syria from joining the Baghdad Pact. In early March 1955, a Syrian-Egyptian-Saudi Arabian alliance was proposed as an alternative security arrangement (it remained a diplomatic, not a military fact), effectively scuttling the prospect of Syrian participation in the British plan. Britain nonetheless adhered to the Baghdad Pact in April. The episode marked Syria's refusal to take sides in the Cold War by following a neutralist line. In the next three years, Syria's neutralism strained its relations with Great Britain and the **United States**. Both powers increased pressures on the Syrian government. As a result, the Syrians improved relations with the **Soviet Union**, which offered economic, military, and political support.

BAKDASH, KHALID (1912-1995). Born in **Damascus**, he was the durable leader of the **Syrian Communist Party**. Bakdash joined the party in 1930 while a student at the Damascus School of Law, where he met some **Armenian** communists. His own Kurdish background attracted many young educated **Kurds** to the party. The French imprisoned Bakdash for his political activities in 1931 for several months and arrested him again in 1933, but he escaped and traveled to the **Soviet Union**. About this time he produced the first Arabic translation of *The Communist Manifesto*. In the USSR, he studied at the Communist University of the Toilers of the East until 1936, when he returned to Syria and became secretary-general of the SCP. The same year, Bakdash went to Paris to assist the Syrian delegation negotiating the **Franco-Syrian Treaty**. He was instrumental in obtaining the French Communist Party's support for the Syrians. He then directed the party to support the **National Bloc**'s demands for independence. During **World War II** Bakdash steered the SCP on a strictly nationalist line, delaying the class struggle until independence could be attained.

In the independence era, Bakdash defined the party's platform as opposition to imperialism, support for civil liberties, and helping the poor. He reached the peak of his influence between 1954 and 1958, when he forged a common front with the independent politician **Khalid al-Azm** and Ba`thist leader **Akram al-Hawrani**. In 1954, Bakdash won a seat in parliament, the first communist to be elected in an Arab country. He then benefited from Syria's turn to the Soviet Union for support against Western pressures to join an anticommunist alliance. But when Syria and **Egypt** formed the **United Arab Republic** in 1958, he concluded that the virulently anticommunist Egyptian President Gamal Abd al-Nasir would suppress the SCP, and he went into exile in eastern Europe. Bakdash spent most of the next eight years in Prague, then in 1966 the **neo-Ba`th** regime invited him to return. When **Hafiz al-Asad** came to power, he included the SCP in the National Progressive Front, a coalition of leftist parties headed by the **Ba`th Party**, but Bakdash's movements were closely circumscribed until his death in 1995.

BAKRI, NASIB AL- (1888-1966). Nationalist leader from **Damascus**, active in **al-Fatat** during the **Ottoman** era and a participant in the **Arab Revolt**, in which his chief task was to organize a **Druze** rising against the Ottomans. In the course of those activities he developed a close association with Druze leader **Sultan al-Atrash**. Under Amir **Faysal**'s 1918-1920 government, Bakri was rewarded for his efforts against the Ottomans with a high post. During the **French Mandate** era he played a crucial role in the **Great Revolt** of 1925-1927 as a link between Damascus-based nationalists of the **People's Party** and Druze leaders. When the French suppressed the revolt, he was forced into exile. He returned to Syria in 1928 and four years later resumed his nationalist activities by joining the **National Bloc** in return for its support for his election to parliament. In the factional politics of the Bloc, Bakri lined up with the moderate leader **Jamil Mardam**. When Mardam became prime minister in 1936, he appointed Bakri governor of **Jabal Druze** because of his extensive experience in the region. Yet the appointment of a non-Druze rankled the Druze, especially those who opposed the incorporation of their region with the rest of Syria (from 1922 to 1936 Jabal Druze had administrative autonomy). To appease Druze sentiment, Prime Minister Mardam agreed to limit Bakri's tenure to six months. In 1938 Bakri left the Bloc, even though he was its vice president at the time, and switched over to its rival **Abd al-Rahman Shahbandar**. In the independence era, Bakri belonged to the second People's Party and was elected to parliament in 1949.

BANIYAS. This modern port is at the site of an ancient Phoenician settlement lying between **Latakia** and **Tartus**. It is the terminal of an oil pipeline from **Iraq** and the site of an oil refinery that has operated since 1980. **Tourists** frequent the town because it is located near a **Crusader** era castle, al-Marqab, and it is not far from the medieval **Assassin** stronghold at **Masyaf**.

BANIYAS RIVER. This modest stream rises from springs on the **Golan Heights** and flows into the Jordan River. It contributes roughly one-fifth of the water to its upper reaches (the other tributaries of the upper Jordan rise in **Lebanon** and **Israel**). Even though the Baniyas River is a small stream, it has political importance because it replenishes the Jordan River, one of Israel's main water sources. Between 1964 and 1966, Syria developed plans to divert its waters to the **Yarmuk River** in order to inflict economic damage on Israel in retaliation for Israel's encroachment on supposedly neutral territory in the **demilitarized zones**. When Syrian machinery began work on the diversion, Israel launched military strikes on work sites to block the effort. Clashes over this water diversion project contributed to the political crisis that resulted in the **June 1967 War**, when Israel conquered the Golan Heights. Since that time, Israel has controlled the Baniyas River and some Israelis argue that it would be folly to return control over that water source to Syria as part of a peace settlement. Given the very small quantity of water that the Baniyas contributes, however, that is not one of the major issues obstructing a settlement.

BANKING. During the **French Mandate**, all of Syria's banks were owned by Europeans and the function of issuing **currency** resided in the privately held Bank of Syria and **Lebanon**. After independence it took the government about 10 years to form a Central Bank to issue currency and to supervise the private, mostly Arab, banking sector. During that period, the **Agricultural** Bank was the sole government bank from which Syrians could borrow. Private banks served short-term commercial needs at very modest levels. Traditional forms of credit extended by landowners and moneylenders persisted in towns and villages, usually at extremely high interest rates. The weak financial infrastructure inhibited private investment in large-scale development projects with the important exception of financing pumps and tractors for the extension of cultivation in **al-Jazira**.

The financial sector got a huge jolt in 1961, when the **United Arab Republic** passed the **Socialist Decrees** nationalizing foreign-owned banks and partially nationalizing local banks. The **secessionist regime** reversed these measures, but the **Ba'th Party** regime renationalized all banks in May 1963. Since that time, Syria has had no private banks.

The Central Bank handles money supply and an assortment of state-owned banks issue credit for specific sectors of the **economy**. Thus, the Commercial Bank, the only bank authorized to manage foreign currency exchange, offers credit to **public sector** companies. The Real Estate

Bank finances construction of hospitals, schools, and hotels. The People's Credit Bank arranges loans to the service sector. The Industrial Bank and the Agricultural Cooperative Bank support public sector companies in their respective spheres.

An acute foreign exchange crisis in 1986 and endemic economic malaise caused the regime to phase in more leeway for certain private financial transactions so that in the early 1990s foreign banks could operate in seven designated free trade zones. Private Syrian firms may obtain foreign credit only if they are based in one of those zones. Restricted liberalization of banking yielded only modest results, and in a few years it was apparent to most observers that the state-run banking system was still obstructing economic growth and development. In addition to regulatory problems, the financial system suffers from technical obsolescence such as the small number of computers.

In early 2001, **Bashar al-Asad**'s cabinet approved private banks on condition of majority ownership by Syrians but did not create an independent regulatory agency to oversee private banking. In the first three years of Asad's supposedly reformist regime, there has been minimal progress in modernizing the banking sector because entrenched political interests block substantial change. Consequently, public sector companies have preserved their privileged access to capital and the private sector has very few resources.

BARADA RIVER. Known in the Bible as the Abana, the Barada River rises from springs in the Anti-Lebanon Mountains and runs eastward until it descends to the plain of **Damascus**, which depends on its waters for urban and **agricultural** use. Quite simply, without this river there would be no Damascus. Since ancient times, the Nabataeans, Aramaeans, Romans, and **Umayyads** have dug channels to distribute the river's waters over a broad area. By Roman times, six branches of the Barada had been artificially created to bring water to Damascus for use in public baths, fountains, and houses. After passing through Damascus, the branches extend into the surrounding **Ghuta** oasis, which is irrigated by them. Beyond the Ghuta, the river terminates in a marshy area east of Damascus.

BA`TH PARTY.** *Ba`th* means "rebirth" or "renaissance." The party's full name from 1947 to 1953 was the Arab Renaissance Party; in 1953, it was renamed the Arab Socialist Renaissance Party. It was formally established by **Michel Aflaq and **Salah al-Din al-Bitar** in 1947, and went on to become the most influential political party in Arab politics during the

1950s and 1960s, and the ruling party in Syria since 1963. Its platform stresses Arab unity, freedom, and socialism.

Early history. The cofounders were teachers at a secondary school in **Damascus** in the 1930s, when Syria was still under the **French Mandate**. In the early 1940s, Aflaq and Bitar resigned their teaching posts to pursue their political aspirations. Even before formally constituting the movement as a party, it attracted a following among their pupils, many of whom went on to become teachers who would in turn recruit their own pupils to the movement. The founding congress of the Ba`th Party was held in Damascus on 4-6 April 1947. True to its pan-Arab ideology, the congress attracted members from **Iraq**, **Jordan**, and **Lebanon** as well as various parts of Syria. Michel Aflaq was elected secretary-general of the party, a title he would retain as its chief ideologue until 1965.

Ideology. The Ba`th Party's ideology is encapsulated in its slogan, "Unity, Freedom, and Socialism. One Arab nation with an eternal mission." For Aflaq and Bitar, **Arab nationalism** was the underlying idea for all three elements of the slogan. They wanted to overcome the division of the Arab world into many states and to achieve the unity of the Arab nation. Freedom for the various Arab countries under European rule and domination would be necessary to bring about unity. Then the united Arab nation would have to conquer its internal enemies, namely feudal and reactionary institutions, to clear the way for the establishment of a just social order. The socialist element in Ba`thist ideology would remain secondary until the 1960s and the rise of a new generation of party activists opposed to Aflaq and Bitar.

Structure. The Second National Congress held in June 1954 formally defined the party's organizational structure to consist of a hierarchy of six units. The basic unit is the circle comprising between three and seven members. Above the circle is the division, which is made of three to seven circles. Two or more divisions comprise a section, the leadership of which is a congress that elects a section command. Above the section is a branch composed of two or more sections and usually encompassing a city or province. The second highest unit is a region, which corresponds to an Arab country, so that Syria, Iraq, Lebanon, and Jordan would each have a regional congress and a regional command. The highest unit is the national command, which oversees party activity in the various countries in which it is active.

History. The party entered the national political stage in 1949 when it won a single seat in national parliamentary elections. Under **Husni al-Za`im**, the Ba`th was suppressed along with other political parties. During the brief dictatorship of **Sami al-Hinnawi**, Aflaq served as minister of **education**. When **Adib al-Shishakli** seized power at the end of 1949, the party hoped that Syria's new ruler would give it space to win new support, but by 1952 Shishakli was clearly unwilling to countenance organized political activity outside his control. The Ba'th's leaders then joined with the **National Party**, the **People's Party**, and the **Syrian Communist Party** in 1953 to find a way to bring down the regime. Around the same time, Aflaq and Bitar joined forces with **Akram al-Hawrani**'s **Arab Socialist Party** to form the Arab Socialist Renaissance Party. After Shishakli's overthrow, the Ba'th won 22 seats in the national parliamentary elections of September 1954, in large measure because of the popular base Hawrani added to the party with his following in **Jabal Druze**, **Hama**, and the army. Hawrani, Bitar, and **Wahib al-Ghanim** all won seats. The Ba'th continued to grow in influence and it established close ties with **Egypt** during the struggle against Syria's adherence to the **Baghdad Pact**. In 1955-1956, Hawrani's faction formed a tactical alliance with the SCP to oppose pro-Western political forces seeking union with Iraq or alignment with the US. Aflaq and Bitar, however, became alarmed at the SCP's increasing popularity, which it owed in part to the growth of military and economic support from communist countries. In June 1956, the Ba'th gained the foreign relations portfolio for Bitar. In late 1957 and early 1958 the party played a key role in the political developments that led to union with Egypt.

When the **United Arab Republic** formed in February 1958, the Ba'th leadership was optimistic regarding the opportunity the union would present them to dominate Syrian affairs even though Gamal Abd al-Nasir insisted on the party's dissolution as a condition for forming the union. But Nasir's handling of the July 1959 elections to a National Union, wherein he obstructed Ba'th members from getting elected, alienated party leaders from the union experiment. At the end of the year, the UAR's Ba'thist ministers resigned from the government. Because the party voluntarily dissolved itself at the outset of the union, the Syrian Ba'th entered a period of disarray that permanently weakened the party's original leadership. Moreover, younger party members blamed Aflaq, Bitar, and Hawrani for leading Syria into the union, which had been a disaster for the party. Some of these critics secretly continued party activities and kept its structures intact in a number of towns. When Syria seceded from the UAR in September 1961, the reconstituted Ba'th was dominated by younger men referred to as "regionalists" for their greater interest in pursuing socialism at home than unity with other Arab countries. Another development that weakened the old leadership was the emergence of the secret **Military Committee** as a powerful organization. In 1962, it was evident that Aflaq's star had dimmed in the Ba`thist firmament and that Bitar no longer enjoyed the respect of the rank and file. Hawrani, moreover, left the party and revived his own Arab Socialist Party.

Eighteen months after the failure of the UAR, a coalition of Ba`thist, Nasirist, and independent officers seized power in the **March 8, 1963 coup.** Strong sentiment for Nasir in the army and society at large, however, meant that the Ba`th's position was not yet secure. So in April, the Military Committee ordered a purge of Nasirists from the army. Then pro-Nasir riots broke out in Damascus and **Aleppo,** which the regime harshly suppressed and followed with further purges of Nasirists from the bureaucracy. The decisive moment in the Ba`thist-Nasirist struggle occurred on 18 July 1963, when a Nasirist uprising of officers and civilians in Damascus was bloodily repressed by Ba`thist forces. These events further poisoned relations between Egypt and Syria.

Meanwhile, the party's internal divisions became more severe. On the one hand, the original leadership of Michel Aflaq and Salah al-Din al-Bitar gave priority to Arab unity. They were opposed, however, by younger members who tended to come from the provinces and favored rapid implementation of the party's socialist platform. The younger Ba`thists, later dubbed the **neo-Ba`th,** eventually sided with the Military Committee against the Aflaq-Bitar wing of the party. The radical faction took control of the Regional Command in September 1963 when it excluded Aflaq from its membership.

In addition to strife within the party, the regime faced strong opposition from conservative social forces. Preachers in mosques began to condemn the Ba`th for its socialism and secularism. In early 1964 violent clashes erupted in Aleppo, Hama, and **Homs.** In Hama an antigovernment rising broke out in April under the slogan "**Islam** or the Ba`th," and the **Muslim Brothers** organized armed attacks on government and party officials. In retaliation, the regime sent tanks into the city and shelled it into submission. To quell the unrest, General **Amin al-Hafiz** issued a new **constitution** under which he became president and Bitar the prime minister. But in October, Hafiz dismissed Bitar, assumed the office of prime minister himself, and appointed members of the Ba`thist left to the cabinet. The regime then embarked on a more radical phase of economic reforms. In December 1964, it banned all oil concessions, effectively nationalizing the Syrian oil industry, and on 1 January 1965 it enacted sweeping nationalization measures targeting industry, including electricity, cotton ginning, and most foreign **trade.** The Regional Command, dominated by the Military Committee and the regionalists, then concentrated power in its hands in March 1965 when it assumed full powers and designated its secretary-general as head of state. Two months later, Aflaq was ousted as secretary-general of the National Command. Aflaq and Bitar tried to reassert their leadership in November, but could not dislodge their rivals from the Regional Command. In February 1966, the remaining representatives of the old guard in the National Command fired the members of the Regional Command and dismissed members of the Military Committee from the **National Revolutionary Command Council**. Then in the **February 23, 1966 coup** the regionalists and the Military Committee took the decisive steps to remove their rivals, thus permanently dividing the party between the old guard (whose supporters would come to power in Iraq two years later) and the neo-Ba`th. Ever since, relations between the two wings of the formerly single party have been marked by venomous propaganda and subversion. The party founders, Aflaq and Bitar, fled to Beirut.

During the period of neo-Ba`thist rule, 1966 to 1970, the party evolved distinct civilian and military wings loyal to **Salah al-Jadid** and **Hafiz al-Asad**, respectively. After the **June 1967 War**, tensions mounted between the two wings over domestic and **foreign policy**, and in November 1970 Asad overthrew the civilian branch in the **corrective movement**. Asad initially took steps to increase party membership and to broaden the base of his regime beyond the Ba`th Party, but during the Islamic insurgency of 1978 to 1982 he fell back on the party for support. Membership grew from around 65,000 in 1971 to over one million in the early 1990s. Such expansion entailed the dilution of the party's ideological character and reinforced its role as a mechanism for allocating patronage (jobs, licenses, and favors). An expanded membership also made the Ba`th an organ for spying on citizens by placing party members in government offices, **public sector** companies, schools, and universities. Another fundamental change under Asad was in the procedure for electing party leaders. These elections had formerly expressed the wishes of party members, but under Asad the Regional Command appointed leaders to lower level party organs. This helped turn the party into yet another mechanism for sustaining a personality cult surrounding President Asad.

The government's turn to gradual **economic reform** in the late 1980s threatened the Ba`th Party's socialist plank. Another symptom of the party's diminished power was Asad's decision to allot a larger proportion of seats (87 out of 250) in the People's Assembly to independent deputies since 1990. Finally, 15 years would pass after the general party congress of 1985, and the congress of June 2000 was scheduled as part of Asad's carefully executed transition of power to his son **Bashar al-Asad**. The president died just one week before the congress was to open. It elected Bashar to the Regional Command and nominated him as the only candidate for the presidency, a selection ratified in a national referendum. In other business, the congress passed bland resolutions affirming the policy of economic reform and administrative revamping. There were no major changes in the party leadership. The impression of stability and even stagnation, however, was challenged in spring 2003, 40 years after the Ba'th Party came to power in Syria. The American invasion of Iraq deposed that country's Ba'thist regime and several outspoken American pundits called for the overthrow of the party in Syria as well. How much longer the party that claims to represent Arab nationalism would rule in its original homeland suddenly became an open question, but the absence of a national opposition movement augured well for the Ba'th in the near to middle term.

BAYBARS, SULTAN (1223-1277). The second **Mamluk** ruler and the founder of the Mamluk sultanate's authority over Syria. He first appeared as a dependent of a late **Ayyubid** sultan, and he was probably behind the murder of the last Ayyubid ruler in 1250. A decade later, after playing an important part in the Mamluk defeat of the **Mongols** at the battle of **Ayn Jalut**, he plotted and partook in the assassination of the first Mamluk sultan, Qutuz, in order to seize power. He then made thorough preparations for warfare in Syria against the **Crusader** states and the Mongols. Between 1260 and 1265, Baybars eliminated and absorbed the remaining Ayyubid principalities scattered throughout Syria. He then launched a six-year war against the Crusaders' strongholds, beginning in **Palestine**, moving north to Antioch, and finally taking Safita and **Hisn al-Akrad**. When Sultan Baybars died in **Damascus** in 1277, he had set the Mamluk sultanate on a firm military foundation and reunified most of Syria under a single authority that would last until the Ottoman conquest in 1516. His mausoleum in al-Zahiriyya **madrasa** became the site of Syria's first national library in 1879.

BEDOUIN. Throughout the history of Syria, the countryside of the interior has been strongly influenced, and at times completely dominated, by bedouin—pastoral nomads belonging to various tribes. The bedouins' livelihood depended on pasturing their sheep and camel herds. The pursuit of grazing lands determined the pattern of annual migration between winter domains in the desert of the east and south and summer pastures closer to and sometimes in the western and northern regions of rain-fed **agriculture**. At times of drought or government weakness, the bedouin completely took over lands that were marginally suited to cultivation. Alternatively, the zone of cultivation pushed eastward during periods of strong sedentary authority. The bedouin occupied a special niche in Syrian **trade** for centuries. They exchanged the products of their livestock (wool, hides, meat, and dairy products) for grain and manufactures, and they provided the animals that transported goods in overland trade.

In modern times the **Ottoman Empire** took measures to contain the bedouin during the second half of the 19th century in the **Tanzimat** era. The Ottomans stationed larger and better-equipped military forces; built permanent garrisons and government offices at strategic points on the **Euphrates River** like **al-Raqqa** and **Dayr al-Zur**; induced cultivators to colonize deserted villages; and enticed bedouin shaykhs to cooperate by giving them property rights to tribal lands. By the early 20th century, the balance of power had shifted against the bedouin, and relations within tribes altered. The shaykhs were becoming landlords over immigrant sharecroppers from other parts of Syria and fellow tribesmen who had given up pastoral nomadism.

The bedouins' numbers have declined in the 20th century as they increasingly became sedentary. In 1930, the bedouin numbered 360,000, or nearly 13 percent of the total population. Thirty years later, their numbers had dwindled to just over 210,000, or five percent of the total population. Most tribesmen have left the pastoral **economy** for agriculture; some have migrated to towns and cities to work in construction and transport; a small portion still raise livestock but no longer follow the old migratory patterns, preferring to use trucks to transport their animals and to bring them food and water.

BIMARISTAN. A Persian word meaning "a place for the sick," it is the term for hospitals in early **Islamic** times. **Abbasid** rulers in Baghdad supported the earlier **Iranian** tradition of royal patronage for medical **education** and treatment at hospitals. Sultan **Nur al-Din** brought the bimaristan to Syria in the mid-12th century, ordering their construction in **Damascus**, **Aleppo**, and **al-Raqqa**. Descriptions of medieval hospitals indicate that their functions included treatment of both physical and mental illness, teaching, and shelter for ailing indigent townsmen.

BITAR, SALAH AL-DIN AL- (1912-1980). Cofounder of the **Ba'th Party** along with **Michel Aflaq**. Bitar was a **Sunni** Muslim from **Damascus**. He studied political science at the Sorbonne in Paris, then returned to

Damascus to teach high school. In cooperating with Aflaq, Bitar actively engaged in politics, while Aflaq played the role of party ideologue and writer. From 1947 to 1954, Bitar was on the Ba`th Party's executive committee, and when the party reorganized its structure, he became a member of its National Command. In 1954, he gained a seat in parliament after two earlier unsuccessful attempts. He became foreign minister in 1956 and used that office to campaign for the Ba`th Party's platform of Arab unity. In early 1958, Bitar headed a government committee to push forward efforts for union with Egypt. When the **United Arab Republic** was formed, he served on its cabinets until the end of 1959, when his disillusionment with the union experiment led him to resign from office. As a condition of joining the UAR regime, he had already withdrawn from the Ba`th Party's National Command. By 1960, Bitar was strongly opposed to the union with Egypt that he had so vigorously pursued, and when Syria seceded in September 1961, he publicly lauded the act.

At the beginning of the first Ba`thist regime in March 1963, Bitar served as prime minister a number of times, but he was pushed aside when more radical factions of the party rose to dominance. After the **February 23, 1966 coup**, the **neo-Ba`th** leaders imprisoned Bitar, but in August he escaped and fled across the border to **Lebanon**. When the **Lebanese Civil War** erupted in 1975, Bitar moved to **France**, where he remained active in publishing and commenting on Arab affairs. In particular, he expressed his regret at the failure of his and Aflaq's political enterprise. **Hafiz al-Asad**'s regime suspected Bitar of plotting against it, and on 21 July 1980, he was assassinated in Paris by Syrian agents.

BIZRI, AFIF AL- (1914-1994). First rose to prominence as head of the court-martial that tried officers implicated in the **conspiracy of 1956** orchestrated by **Iraq** and Great Britain. The following year he joined forces with **Abd al-Hamid al-Sarraj** to form the revolutionary command council, an extra-governmental body under leftist officers that would dominate Syria's **foreign policy**. In August 1957 Major-General Bizri, by then well-known for his sympathies with the **Syrian Communist Party**, became chief of staff as part of a leftist purge of pro-Western officers. He played a leading role in pushing for the union with **Egypt**, which created the **United Arab Republic** in February 1958, but Egyptian President Gamal Abd al-Nasir dismissed him just one month after the union for objecting to purges of the Syrian officer corps.

In June 1959 Bizri left Syria and settled in Beirut. He issued a public manifesto criticizing Egyptian domination of the UAR and calling for the restoration of political liberties. He favored retaining the union but modifying its form by moving to a federal system in which Syria and Egypt would each have separate parliaments while continuing to handle defense and foreign relations under a central government. Nasir interpreted Bizri's statement as a summons to agitation by communists in Syria, so he ordered a crackdown on the SCP. Unlike most army officers who took active roles in politics, Bizri was serious about ideological issues and in the mid-1960s contributed to debates among reformist communists who broke away from the SCP.

BLUDAN CONFERENCE. In September 1937, **Arab nationalists** from several countries met to express broad support for the **Palestinians**' revolt against Zionism and the British Mandate in general, and against Britain's recent proposal to partition **Palestine** into Jewish and Arab states. The Bludan Conference is historically noteworthy as an early demonstration of pan-Arab concern over Palestine.

BONAPARTE, NAPOLEON (1769-1821). Napoleon's relevance to Syrian history stems from the French invasion of **Egypt** that he led in July 1798. To secure his position there he led an expedition to Syria in February 1799. His 13,000-man army overcame **Ottoman** garrisons at al-Arish in the Sinai Peninsula and at Gaza in southern **Palestine**. In March, the French force proceeded toward Acre, the well-fortified stronghold of **Ahmad Pasha al-Jazzar**. Napoleon planned a land and marine blockade to besiege Acre, but a squadron of Ottoman and British ships intercepted French naval forces off the coast of Acre and drove them off. Meanwhile Ahmad al-Jazzar prepared Acre to withstand a siege, and England assisted him with military supplies. The siege began in the middle of March. Ottoman forces tenaciously defended the town, while the governor of **Damascus** dispatched forces to attack the French from the rear, but the French repulsed them near Nazareth. The siege dragged on for two months and Napoleon was losing troops to bubonic plague, so on 20 May he broke the siege and began a retreat to Egypt. Altogether, some 2,000 French soldiers perished during the siege, half of them from the plague.

BYZANTINE EMPIRE. In 324 the Roman emperor Constantine moved the imperial court from Rome to Byzantium, the site of present-day Istanbul in **Turkey**, known for centuries after the emperor as Constantinople. Also known as the Eastern Roman Empire, the Byzantine Empire represented a continuation of Roman rule over Syria and lasted until the Arab conquest in the 630s. Thereafter, the Byzantine Empire remained the nemesis of Muslim Syria until the 12th century and the era of the **Crusades**. In **Umayyad** and early **Abbasid** times, Muslim armies launched annual raids against the Byzantines along the Syrian-Asia Minor front. The Umayyads made a number of unsuccessful attempts to conquer the Byzantine capital, Constantinople. By the time the Abbasids rose to power in 750, the military frontier between the Arabs and the Byzantines had stabilized in southeast Asia Minor. A number of energetic rulers revived the empire's military power toward the end of the 10th century and led campaigns into northern Syria. They recovered Antioch and forced the **Hamdanid** and **Mirdasid** dynasties based in **Aleppo** to pay tribute. Further expansion southward was blocked by the ascendant **Fatimid** dynasty with its center in **Egypt** and domains in southern Syria. Byzantine power in eastern Asia Minor received a stunning blow in 1071 when the **Saljuks** defeated them at the Battle of Manzikert. Byzantine appeals to Christian Europe for military support against the Muslims contributed to the launching of the First Crusade. The Crusaders posed a grave military threat to Muslim Syria, but they did not strengthen the position of the Byzantines in Asia Minor. Instead, their power steadily dwindled as wave after wave of Turkish tribesmen made their way westward during the 12th and 13th centuries, fundamentally altering the demography of Asia Minor and ending its role as a launching pad for Christian offensives against Syria.

-C-

CALIPHATE. After the death of Muhammad, the Prophet of **Islam**, Muslims created this institution to represent the continuation of his political and spiritual authority. The first four caliphs, Abu Bakr (632-634), Umar (634-644), Uthman (644-656), and **Ali** (656-661), are known as the rightly guided caliphs and they governed the growing Arab empire from the Arabian town of Medina, located in present-day **Saudi Arabia**. Following the assassination of Ali, **Mu`awiya** established the **Umayyad** caliphate with **Damascus** as the capital. The Umayyad dynasty lasted until 750 when it was replaced by the Abbasid caliphate, which moved the imperial center to **Iraq** and built a new city, Baghdad, to serve as the capital. The Abbasid caliphate represented the pinnacle of Islamic political and cultural achievement during the eighth and ninth centuries. By the middle of the 10th century, though, the caliphate had ceased to wield effective authority beyond the confines of Iraq. Syria had already fallen under the control of local forces and dynasties based in **Egypt**, such as the **Fatimid** dynasty, which put forth a competing claim to the caliphate. With the fall of the Abbasid dynasty to **Mongol** invaders in 1258, the institution ceased to have any real political power, although the **Mamluk** sultanate and later the **Ottoman Empire** sustained a "shadow" caliphate until its final abolition by the Republic of **Turkey** in 1924.

CATHOLIC. A latecomer to Syrian Christianity, the Roman Catholic Church established a foothold during the 17th century when the Jesuits began a proselytizing mission, not to convert Muslims to Christianity, but to bring eastern **Christians** into the fold of Catholicism. Jesuit and Capuchin priests went to **Aleppo** in 1626, and members of the Carmelite order followed. These efforts bore fruit during the 17th and 18th centuries when the **Chaldaean** Church broke from the **Nestorian** Church, the **Greek Catholics** from the **Greek Orthodox**, **Syrian Catholics** from the **Syrian Orthodox** (or **Jacobite**), and the **Armenian** Catholics from the Armenian Orthodox. An important incentive for conversion had little to do with theology and everything to do with mundane matters, for **France** was the primary European sponsor of Catholic efforts and had extensive economic and diplomatic influence in the **Ottoman Empire**. Apart from missionaries, French merchants and consuls encouraged eastern Christians to become Catholic with promises of economic benefits and protection from Christian piracy. The strong European commercial presence in Aleppo during the 18th century provided a bridge for Catholic missions, whose activities increased the city's Catholic population from 4,000 in 1700 to nearly 15,000 by 1850. The eastern churches' hierarchies regarded the Catholics as interlopers and adopted a hostile attitude toward Rome and the various **Uniate** churches. In the late 1990s, the Catholics of various rites (Armenian, Chaldaean, Latin, Maronite, Syrian, and Greek) numbered just over 300,000, of whom nearly two-thirds are Greek Catholics.

CENSORSHIP. Since the introduction of **print media** during the late **Ottoman** era, government authorities have regularly limited freedom of expression. Sultan **Abdulhamid II** instituted strict guidelines for imperial censors to prevent the publication of words and phrases alluding to liberal ideas. The 1908 **constitutional** restoration inaugurated a spell of journalistic exuberance marked by a proliferation of periodicals and lifting of censorship. The imposition of martial law during **World War I** reintroduced strict censorship. In the **French Mandate** period, the propagation of nationalist political views frequently resulted in the closure of publications and arrest of writers.

After independence, government agencies to implement censorship developed during periods of military rule. The **United Arab Republic** created a special body committed to this function in the newly established Ministry of Culture and Information. Under the **Ba`th Party** regime, Article 4b of the Emergency Law gives the government the authority to censor all forms of expression—print, electronic, visual—on grounds of protecting national security. The Ba`thist regime does not apply censorship evenly to all forms of expression or even consistently to the closely regulated official press. The absence of clear, specific guidelines means that writers for the official newspapers may get in trouble by unintentionally violating taboos that apparently exist in the minds of the regime's most powerful figures but not on paper. A heavy hand also falls on books that deal with politics and **religion**. These must secure the approval of censors in a special bureau of the Ba`th Party. In **literary** fields of creative writing like fiction, drama, and poetry, authors submit manuscripts to censors from either the Ministry of Culture, the Ministry of Information, or the Arab Writers' Union (controlled by the Ba`th Party). As long as creative writers avoid direct criticism of the regime, they may, and frequently do, address urgent political, social, and cultural issues by treating them in historical settings or through symbolic messages.

As for broadcast media, the Ministry of Information operates all **radio and television** programs. This meant that before the spread of satellite dishes, Syrian television viewers in most of the country could watch official news reports, serial dramas, movies, sports events, and documentaries on the regime's economic and social achievements. Syrians living near **Jordan**, **Lebanon**, or **Turkey** could view television broadcasts from neighboring countries for a greater variety of programs. Another way to mitigate the effects of censorship is to tune in to foreign radio broadcasts, especially the British Broadcasting Corporation (BBC) Arabic service and Radio Monte Carlo. While Syria's censorship regime is not completely effective in preventing the spread of critical ideas, it does severely constrict their circulation and the fear of harsh punishment induces self-censorship.

CHALDAEAN. Uniate branch of the ancient **Nestorian** church established in 1672. Its patriarch resides in Baghdad. About 15,000 Chaldaeans live in **Jazira** and **Aleppo**, but most of them are in **Iraq**.

CHRISTIANS. They comprise about 10 percent of the population and live throughout the country. When the Muslim Arabs conquered Syria in the seventh century, most of the population was Christian and would remain so for several centuries. Although historians have not been able to determine with precision the pace of conversion to **Islam**, it appears that Christians became a **minority** no later than the 13th century. Their status under Muslim dominion was that of a protected minority, or *dhimmi*, that was liable to pay a special tax and was excluded from political office, but otherwise exercised religious and communal freedoms. Anti-Christian persecution did erupt periodically, the best-known examples occurring in the **Fatimid**

and **Mamluk** eras when **Byzantine** and **Crusader** military threats inflamed communal passions. But generally speaking, Christians in medieval and early modern Syria did not suffer harsh treatment or pressure to convert.

Their status began to change, however, in the 18th century with the growth of commerce with Europe, a **trade** from which Christians benefited as cultural brokers. Then, in the 19th century, the **Ottoman** reform program, or **Tanzimat**, further improved Christians' standing by declaring legal equality for all subjects regardless of religion. Many Muslims then resented Christians' economic prosperity and believed that the Ottomans were favoring the Christians in order to placate the Europeans. A violent Muslim backlash exploded in the **Aleppo massacre of 1850** and the **July 1860 Damascus massacre**. Although these events struck terror into Syrian Christians, their communities did not suffer any further attacks and they continued to prosper well into the 20th century because of their European contacts. Since the late **French Mandate** era, Syrian Christians, particularly the **Greek Orthodox**, have played a significant role in **Arab nationalist** movements. Moreover, the status of Christians has continued to improve with the gradual secularization of law and society.

There are eight historical denominations. The three Orthodox churches are the **Greek Orthodox**, whose liturgy is in Greek and Arabic; the **Syrian Orthodox**, or Jacobite, whose liturgy is in Syriac; and the **Armenian** Orthodox, or Gregorian, whose liturgy is in Armenian. The five **Uniate** churches are in communion with Rome but retain their own liturgies. The Uniate groups are the Maronites (entered into union with Rome in 1180), the **Syrian Catholics** (former Syrian Orthodox, established in 1783), the **Greek Catholics** (former Greek Orthodox, established in 1724), the **Chaldaean Catholics** (former **Nestorians** who became Uniates beginning in 1672), and the Armenian Catholics (former Armenian Orthodox, established in 1742). The Nestorians or East Syrian Christian Church have a Syriac liturgy and are separate from the Uniate and Orthodox churches. The distribution of different Christian denominations shows a preponderance of Greek Orthodox and a much smaller number of Greek Catholics along the coast, in the **Orontes River** valley, around **Damascus**, and in the **Hawran**. The Syrian interior, beginning with **Homs** and **Hama**, then extending north toward **Aleppo** and northeastward into **Jazira** is the domain of Jacobite, Armenian, and Nestorian Christians.

CINEMA. The first motion pictures played in **Aleppo** and **Damascus** in the early 20th century. During **World War I**, the **Ottoman** authorities showed German newsreels. American and French silent films gained a following during the **French Mandate** years. Syrian villagers became familiar with the medium when the French authorities toured with educational films and newsreels. The first attempts by Syrians to produce films suffered from insufficient capital, technical difficulties, and **censorship** by the French authorities for their own political reasons and because of pressure from Muslim and **Christian** religious leaders anxious about the cinema's possible effects on morality. Censors continued to monitor film content for political, religious, and sexual material after independence. Furthermore, filmmakers must obtain the government's permission to make a film and to exhibit it once they have shot it. The small number of cinemas in the country has limited the prospects for the growth of a private film industry; consequently, filmmakers have depended on government backing.

In the 1950s and 1960s, Egyptian, American, and European films saturated Syrian cinemas. The creation in 1958 of a Ministry of Culture and Guidance offered a firmer foundation for Syrians keen on making films. The ministry had a division for films that concentrated on such themes as folklore and **archaeology**. In 1963, the ministry established the General Film Organization to subsidize filmmakers and concentrate equipment in one agency. In the 1970s, directors from **Egypt, Lebanon**, and **Iraq** made most of the films in Syria. At that time, films addressed political themes, especially the **Palestinian** issue and social inequality. In the 1980s, Syrian directors emerged to put their stamp on the **art**, which they shifted to more subjective and unconventional themes. The most popular and successful figure is **Durayd al-Lahham**, who along with Nihad al-Qal`i made more than 20 comic films beginning in 1964.

CIRCASSIANS. Non-Arab **Sunni** Muslims who fled the Russian conquest of their homeland in the Caucasus Mountains in the late 1800s. In the 1860s the first Circassian refugees settled in small towns and villages north of **Aleppo** and in **Jazira** along the **Khabur River**, but high mortality rates from disease rapidly reduced their numbers. A second wave of refugees arrived in 1878 in the course of the Russo-**Ottoman** war of 1877-1878. This time the Ottomans directed them to settle in southern Syria, including the **Hawran, Golan**, and **Transjordan**, where the colonists founded Amman. A small number took up residence in villages east of **Homs** and **Hama**. In the **French Mandate** era, Circassians, like other minorities, were recruited into the **Troupes Spéciales du Levant**, which the French authorities used to repress nationalist strikes and demonstrations. During the **June 1967 War**, some 25,000 Circassians living in the Golan Heights were expelled. Most of the refugees resettled in **Damascus** and nearby villages; some emigrated to the **United States**.

CIVIL SOCIETY. Many observers of the rapid collapse of authoritarian communist regimes in Eastern Europe and the **Soviet Union** between 1989 and 1991 considered the proliferation of independent citizen associations a major contributor to these democratic political transitions. The concept of "civil society" gained popularity as an analytical category for social scientists and an aspiration for liberal reformers in authoritarian countries. Syrians hoping for a comparable political transformation at that time were disappointed at the **Ba`th Party** regime's resilience.

In the early months of **Bashar al-Asad**'s presidency, he gave indications that he might retreat from his father **Hafiz al-Asad**'s legacy of authoritarian rule. Many Syrians hoped that the country's new leader would initiate measures to liberalize the political system. In September 2000, the government announced it would allow discussion of political reform at individuals' homes and public venues. Widespread eagerness for open discussion and a freer political climate spurred groups of professionals, intellectuals, and independent members of the People's Assembly to hold meetings to discuss ways to introduce the rule of law, political pluralism, and security for individual rights. These groups, known as Civil Society Forums, appeared in **Damascus** and spread to other cities.

One of the most remarkable moments in that time was the 27 September 2000 publication by a London Arabic-language newspaper of a call for fundamental political reform. The statement was signed by 99 prominent intellectuals, artists, and professionals who had not previously expressed dissent. The list included the poet **Adonis**, novelists **Haydar Haydar** and Nabil Sulayman, political philosophers Sadiq al-Azm and Tayyib Tizini, filmmakers, actors, professors, lawyers, physicians, and others. The short manifesto urged the lifting of emergency and martial law, amnesty and release of political prisoners, establishment of basic political freedoms, and abolishing government surveillance of citizens.

In Damascus, a number of small meetings were held to set up Committees for the Revival of Civil Society, but their organizers wound up clashing with Bashar al-Asad when their political aspirations clearly exceeded the limits he would tolerate. An official backlash began in early 2001 when government officials condemned the committees and even criticized use of the term civil society. President Asad warned that criticizing the Ba`th Party, the policies of his late father, and the **armed forces** served the interests of Syria's enemies. In August and September, the government took a series of measures to suppress the civil society movement with arrests of its most outspoken and influential figures. They included two independent members of parliament, Ma'mun al-Humsi and **Riyad al-Sayf**, leader of the Communist Party-Political Bureau and former political prisoner **Riyad al-Turk** (released in November

2002), economist and one of the founders of the Committees for the Revival of Civil Society Arif Dalila, and several **human rights** activists. At the same time as this wave of arrests, the regime issued a decree that reinforced and extended government powers to punish expression deemed harmful to "state dignity, national unity, the morale of the army and the armed forces . . . . national **economy** and **currency**." The arrests marked the end of Syria's flirtation with a movement for substantial political reform.

COFFEEHOUSES. When coffee became part of Middle Eastern consumption and leisure in the early 16th century, coffeehouses (serving men only) followed close behind. The popularity of the beverage and public places devoted to it soon overwhelmed suspicions of its permissibility under Islamic law (**shari`a**) even though pious opinion continued to regard the coffeehouse as a threat to morality because of its association with drug use and illicit sexual liaisons. In the 17th century, centrally located, large coffeehouses and smaller neighborhood establishments became typical features of Syrian cities. Patrons also enjoyed going to the outskirts of town to tree-shaded coffeehouses situated along rivers. The coffeehouse attracted a diverse clientele and hosted such entertainment as recitation of poetry, music, storytelling, and performance of *karagoz*, or puppet shadow plays. Customers could also smoke tobacco in a water pipe while playing cards or backgammon. Their low overhead and popularity ensured their profitability, and hence they frequently formed part of philanthropic bequests (**waqfs**) as steady sources of revenue for mosques and religious schools. Since the late 19th century, coffeehouses have served as incubators for social and political change because they provided educated youth a public setting to discuss current issues.

COMMITTEE OF UNION AND PROGRESS. A secret society, also referred to as the Young Turks, founded by advocates of **constitutional** government for the **Ottoman Empire** in 1889. First established among students at Istanbul's military college, the movement's early membership included educated young men from various parts of the empire. During the 1890s, graduates stationed as bureaucrats and army officers in **Aleppo**, **Damascus**, **Dayr al-Zur**, **Hama**, and **Homs** set up cells that attracted the interest and support of educated youth, **ulama**, civil servants, and urban notables. Authorities in Syria first detected CUP activities in 1896 among Turkish officers disgruntled over arrears in salaries and shortages in provisions. An investigation led to charges against several officers, civil administrators, and Damascus notables. After the arrest and exile of several members, no further evidence of Young Turk activity appeared until 1906, when a new cell was set up by junior officers upset with the endemic problem of arrears in salaries.

In July 1908 military units stationed in Macedonia and loyal to the CUP mutinied against Sultan **Abdulhamid** and forced him to restore the 1876 constitution. The CUP initially stayed in the background of politics, but its leaders increasingly asserted themselves until they seized power in a coup d'état in 1913. The CUP advocated policies designed to strengthen central control over the empire's provinces, including the exclusive use of the Turkish **language** in official business and **education**. Some Syrian Arabs believed the CUP sought to "turkify" the empire, that is, forcibly impose Turkish language and culture on the polyglot population. This perception prompted a defensive cultural reaction that sowed the seeds of the first **Arab nationalist** groups.

In 1914, the CUP's leadership governed the empire and took the fateful decision to enter **World War I** on the side of Germany. At the end of the war, with the Ottoman Empire defeated and occupied by foreign armies, the CUP leaders fled to Germany and the **Soviet Union**. *See also* JAZA'IRI, TAHIR AL-; QASIMI, JAMAL AL-DIN AL-.

CONSPIRACY OF 1956. A far-reaching plot, code-named "Operation Straggle," hatched in Beirut to overthrow Syria's neutralist government and install a pro-Western regime. It was conceived by Syrian exiles in **Lebanon**, including members of the **Syrian Social National Party** and purged army officers, who had support from the government of **Iraq**. **Adib al-Shishakli**, who had seized power in a military coup in 1949 and ruled until 1954, was living in **France** at the time and initially showed some interest in the plot, but he ditched the enterprise when he calculated its low chances for success. Great Britain was to provide weapons and funds, and a number of civilian politicians were to help execute a coup. SSNP militiamen were to infiltrate Syria, assassinate leading leftist politicians, and trigger **Druze** and **Alawi** risings, which would be armed with weapons smuggled from Iraq. Military intelligence uncovered the plot and on 23 November 1956 announced the arrest of those participants living in Syria. The coup was timed to coincide with the attack on **Egypt** by Great Britain, France, and **Israel** at the end of October in a bid to eliminate the two neutralist Arab governments of Egypt and Syria and restore Western dominance in Arab politics. The arrests and trials of the conspirators damaged conservative political forces and boosted the standing of leftist parties.

CONSTITUTION. Syria first experienced a constitutional regime when it was still part of the **Ottoman Empire** from 1876 to 1877 and 1908 to 1918.

After **World War I**, Amir **Faysal** tried to set up an independent Arab kingdom in Syria, and he handed the **Syrian Congress** the task of drafting a constitution. A draft was produced, but the Congress's consideration of it was interrupted by **France**'s invasion in July 1920. The abortive constitution provided for a monarchy and bicameral legislature. During the **French Mandate** era, elections to a constituent assembly were held in April 1928. The assembly convened in June and issued a draft constitution by August. This first Syrian constitution provided for a parliamentary republic, equality for members of all **religions** and religious freedom, and a Muslim president. The French objected to articles declaring the unity of Syria, **Lebanon**, **Palestine**, and **Transjordan**; Syrian control over a national army; and presidential powers to conduct **foreign policy**. Consequently, French High Commissioner Henri Ponsot adjourned the assembly. Following two years of political stalemate, the French enacted a modified version of the 1928 draft. When Syria became independent in 1943, it was under the terms of the constitution of 1930.

Alterations in the Syrian constitution were first heralded during the brief regime of **Husni al-Za`im**, who called for the drafting of a new document and appointed a special committee that produced a new constitution in July 1949. But **Sami al-Hinnawi**'s coup in mid-August aborted that project and he authorized elections for a constituent assembly. These were held in November and the second **People's Party**, which generally supported Hinnawi, gained a plurality of seats. **Adib al-Shishakli**'s overthrow of Hinnawi in December interrupted the constituent assembly's work, but it convened in 1950 and drew up a new constitution. Its most controversial article was one declaring **Islam** to be the religion of the state. The **Syrian Social National Party**, the **Syrian Communist Party**, the **Ba`th Party**, and the country's various **Christian** communities all argued for a secular constitution, while the **Muslim Brothers** supported the condition concerning religion. Ultimately, the constituent assembly agreed on a solution by preserving the 1930 constitution's stipulation that the head of state be a Muslim, and in September 1950 the assembly ratified the new document. Its main departures from the 1930 constitution lay in the proclamation of detailed civil liberties and the greater powers it assigned to the legislative branch compared to the executive branch. Shishakli challenged the constitution when he assumed dictatorial powers in November 1951. In March 1953 he called for a new constituent assembly to draw up yet another constitution. The 1953 document tipped the balance of power back in favor of the executive branch, but when Shishakli was overthrown in February 1954, Syria's civilian government restored the 1950 constitution.

With the formation in 1958 of the **United Arab Republic**, Syria came under a new constitutional arrangement that submerged Syrian representation in an Egyptian-dominated assembly and assigned broad powers to President Gamal Abd al-Nasir. When Syria seceded from the UAR, the 1950 constitution was restored but a new provisional constitution was issued in November 1961 to govern elections for a constituent assembly. The military's continuous interference in politics, however, prevented implementation of that plan. The Ba`th Party regime introduced one more provisional constitution in April 1964. This document assigned executive powers to a new body called the Presidential Council and legislative powers to the **National Revolutionary Command Council**, stipulated state ownership of **industry** and minerals, and diluted the place of Islam by stating that **shari`a** comprises "a" source of legislation rather than "the" source.

The most recent constitutional changes began in May 1969 when the **neo-Ba`th** regime issued a new provisional constitution declaring Syria a democratic socialist republic. The regime of **Hafiz al-Asad** promulgated a permanent constitution in March 1973 that was similar to the 1969 document. It, too, stated that the head of state must be a Muslim, that Islamic law is the source of legislation, and that the Ba`th Party is the country's vanguard party. In keeping with Asad's supreme authority, the constitution also provides for strong presidential powers: He was commander-in-chief of the armed forces, appointed the prime minister and cabinet members, and had the power to dissolve the legislature and rule by decree. The legislative branch consists of a unicameral People's Assembly, whose members are elected every four years and vote on legislation drafted by the executive branch but may not initiate legislation. As for the judicial branch, the constitution provides for its independence.

When Hafiz al-Asad died in June 2000, he had been preparing his son **Bashar al-Asad** to succeed him, but the constitution stipulated a minimum age of 40 for the head of state. The People's Assembly then amended the constitution by lowering the minimum to 34 years, precisely Bashar's age at the time, to make his succession formally legal.

CORRECTIVE MOVEMENT. The 13 November 1970 coup d'état launched by **Hafiz al-Asad** against the radical **neo-Ba`th** regime headed by **Salah al-Jadid**. Tensions had been growing between the two former comrades, who had been founding members of the **Military Committee** a decade earlier in Cairo. Jadid's power base lay in the **Ba`th Party** while Asad controlled the **armed forces**. On 30 October, Jadid convened an emergency party congress, which dismissed Asad from the army and expelled him from the party. The congress ended on 12 November, and the very next day Asad arrested Jadid and other rivals. Asad publicly announced that his seizure of power was intended to rectify the excesses of the previous regime, and he moved to broaden his political base by building a coalition with other political parties, enlarging the private sector's role in the **economy**, and mending relations with other Arab states. The corrective movement was the last in a long line of military coups dating to March 1949.

CORRUPTION. In **Ottoman** times, the sultan was the ultimate owner of all wealth, and his appointed officials, essentially his servants, were generally expected to help themselves to whatever they could accumulate. There was not a well-defined line between compensation for fulfilling duties and illicit private gain. The most obvious case obtained for tax collectors. They were expected to acquire their own compensation from the same pool of revenue that fed the imperial treasury, so the opportunity to embezzle could prove irresistible. On the other hand, the ill-gotten assets of the sultan's servants could be suddenly confiscated upon dismissal or death, whereupon they reverted to their "legal" owner, the sultan.

Given the clandestine nature of corruption in both historical and contemporary eras, it is resistant to systematic analysis. Nonetheless, many observers of Syria's political and economic structures consider it a salient feature. There is both petty corruption on the scale of small bribes for favors from low-ranking party officials and government bureaucrats and much grander instances in which powerful military officers and government figures use their positions to accumulate fortunes through smuggling, kickbacks, and embezzlement.

The causes of corruption are several. Loyalty is more important than competence in climbing the ranks of military, civilian, and party hierarchies. There is little institutional control or oversight of **public sector** companies that might legally import equipment for manufacturing projects and then resell it to private businessmen for a substantial profit. In addition, the **armed forces** operate completely outside the purview of the rest of the government, so for years officers smuggled drugs cultivated in **Lebanon** with impunity until international political pressure brought about the curtailment of that illicit **trade**.

Another ubiquitous cultural factor that breeds corruption is patronage, which operates through connections or "*wasta*." An individual with many connections is said to have a lot of "vitamin w," for wasta. These personal connections express the expectation that an individual will assist a **family** member, fellow villager, or coreligionist if one can. To refuse such assistance would violate norms of honorable behavior and reciprocity.

Given the anecdotal nature of evidence about corruption, it is not possible to calculate how much it costs the Syrian **economy**, but the anecdotes are so numerous that corruption undoubtedly weighs it down. The political benefits, however, are such that the **Ba`th Party** regime is very unlikely to attack it in a comprehensive manner. In fact, occasional, high profile anticorruption campaigns are designed to "crack down" on the worst abusers and satisfy a public demand that "something finally be done" about the problem. It is noteworthy that **Bashar al-Asad** held the anticorruption "portfolio" for a few years before becoming president, as though it would mark him as a fresh, clean leader and set him apart from his father's tainted cronies. The first few years of his regime, however, have not been marked by the disappearance of corruption even though several high-ranking officials in public sector firms have been convicted for "economic crimes" and sentenced to prison terms.

CRUSADES. When this invasion of Syria commenced in 1097, the land was divided among **Saljuk** princes under the influence of their regents, or **atabegs**. The conquest of Antioch in 1098 marked the Crusaders' first success. Their primary aim was the recovery for Christendom of Jerusalem (conquered in 1099), so most campaigns focused on seizing and defending the holy city and on securing the Syrian coast for communications and transport to Europe. Consequently, the Crusaders threatened, but did not rule over the Syrian interior or its major towns. The four Frankish states were the County of Edessa (1098-1144), the Principality of Antioch (1098-1268), the Latin Kingdom of Jerusalem (1099-1187, moved to Acre when the Muslims regained Jerusalem, 1192-1291), and the County of Tripoli (1109-1289).

The first Muslim leader of counterattacks against the Crusaders was the atabeg **Imad al-Din al-Zangi** (r. 1127-1146), the ruler of **Aleppo** and Mosul. The Muslim offensive was pursued by **Nur al-Din Mahmud** and **Saladin** until 1192. Although the Europeans briefly recovered Jerusalem (1239-1244), the first half of the 13th century mostly saw minor skirmishes between Latin kingdoms and **Ayyubid** principalities. The Franks' military energies focused instead on **Egypt** because of the access it offered to the Red Sea and Indian Ocean **trade**. The final Muslim assault on the Latin kingdoms came under the command of Syria's new Turkish masters, the **Mamluk** sultans, beginning in the 1260s with the storming of coastal and inland holdings from Nazareth to Antioch. The last toehold of the Crusades, the Island of Arwad, fell in 1303.

CURRENCY. The first modern Syrian currency was issued during the **French Mandate** period. In 1924, the Banque de Syrie et du Grand Liban, a private bank with French-majority ownership, issued the Syrian-Lebanese pound, or *lira*. The lira was tied to the French franc until 1941, when British forces invaded Syria to overthrow the Vichy regime and pegged the lira to the British sterling.

The Syrian pound is the basic unit of currency and is comprised of 100 piasters. It is a nonconvertible currency. In 1963, the **Ba`th Party** regime imposed strict controls on foreign exchange transactions. Since that time, the government has maintained as many as five different exchange rates that vastly overvalue the Syrian pound. The most common rates are known as the official rate, the flexible rate, and a special "promotion" rate for travelers and **tourists**. The gap between the official rate and the black market rate widened in the 1970s. By 1981, one dollar fetched roughly 40 Syrian pounds but the official rate was only four pounds to the dollar. The artificial exchange rate and a decline in Arab aid contributed to an acute shortage of foreign exchange in the mid-1980s. That crisis prompted the government to devalue the currency from four Syrian pounds per dollar to 11.2 per dollar. At the same time, the government tried to curb the black market currency dealers with a decree that stiffened the penalty for possession of foreign currency by imposing prison sentences of 15 to 25 years. The decree only diverted the activity of Syrian currency traders to **Lebanese banks**. In the mid-1990s, the government closed the gap between the free market rate (about 50 Syrian pounds to the dollar) and the official rate (around 45 Syrian pounds to the dollar). The ban on foreign currency trading was repealed as part of the economic relaxation measures taken in the second half of 2000 under **Bashar al-Asad**. *See also* INFLATION.

-D-

DAMASCUS. The capital and largest city in modern Syria, Damascus is located on the eastern slopes of the Anti-Lebanon range on the edge of the desert. Situated in an arid region, Damascus has been the site of urban settlement for more than 4,000 years because of the waters borne by the **Barada River** and their exploitation to irrigate the **Ghuta** oasis around the city. The city is mentioned in pharaonic records of the 15th century B.C. and it served as the main city of the Aramaean kingdom of Aram beginning in the 11th century B.C. Like the rest of Syria, Damascus passed under a series of Mesopotamian powers between the eighth and sixth centuries B.C., then a period of Persian domination before Alexander the Great's conquest in 333 B.C. initiated nearly a millennium of Greco-Roman hegemony. The walls that surround much of the old city and its main thoroughfares date from Roman times.

In the course of the Muslim Arab conquest of Syria, the townspeople negotiated a peaceful Arab occupation in 635, but the next year, a powerful **Byzantine** army marched toward Damascus with the intention of recovering it. The Arabs withdrew south to the **Yarmuk River**, where the decisive Battle of **Yarmuk** took place in August 636. The Arabs then permanently retook the city at the end of the year. Damascus played its greatest role in Islamic history when the **Umayyad caliphs** (661-750) used it as their capital, but when the **Abbasid** dynasty (750-1258) came to power, the city was relegated to provincial status. For the next four centuries different powers ruled northern and southern Syria, and Damascus remained the most important city in the south. In 1154 it became the capital of a reunified Syria under the rule of **Nur al-Din Mahmud**, who fortified the city's defenses and revived its religious institutions. When **Saladin** incorporated Damascus into the **Ayyubid** (1176-1260) sultanate, the city was again reduced to a provincial capital, this time ruled from **Egypt**. Domination by rulers based in Egypt continued during the **Mamluk** sultanate (1260-1516) until the **Ottoman** conquest, which marked the beginning of 400-year rule from Istanbul.

During the 18th century, Damascus gained a greater degree of autonomy under the rule of various **Azm** governors and in the early 19th century it briefly came under the authority of **Muhammad Ali**, the ambitious ruler of Egypt. Following the Ottoman recovery of Syria in 1840, Damascus entered a period of transition characterized by the Ottoman reforms known as the **Tanzimat** and increasing economic interaction with Europe. The stresses these forces brought to the fore erupted in the **July 1860 massacre** of many of the city's **Christians** by **Sunni** townsmen and **Druzes** from the nearby countryside. The Ottomans responded with measures to tighten central control over the provincial capital, a process reinforced by improvements in **transportation** such as the railway linking Damascus to Beirut in 1894.

After Ottoman rule ended in 1918, Damascus became the capital of Amir **Faysal**'s short-lived state, then the seat of the **French Mandate**'s representative in Syria, and the capital of independent Syria in 1946. Since the late Ottoman period, the city has undergone physical expansion and population growth, from 230,000 in the 1940s to around four million today. In the early 20th century, a number of extramural suburbs sprouted up, and during the French Mandate, these new quarters overran garden areas that had ringed the walled city for centuries and replaced them with modern commercial and residential districts. The last 50 years have seen the capital engulf outlying villages and creep up the lower slopes of Mount **Qasiyun**.

The dramatic increases in size and population have resulted from a steady flow of rural migrants to the capital seeking jobs and amenities often lacking in villages. City residents maintain a keen awareness of the distinction between old Damascene families and newcomers, but the casual visitor will not notice tensions and will instead be drawn to the well-preserved historic quarters, mosques, and monuments. As for the appearance of contemporary Damascus, the modern **architecture** serves practical rather than ornamental purposes so the "streetscape" is unimpressive. The steady drift of dust from Mount Qasiyun ordinarily gives the city a drab appearance at the street level except during the brief spring when wildflowers dot the hills and planters along boulevards or after the occasional snowfall whitens the mountain slopes.

Everyday life does not revolve around the city's historic axis but the two main hubs of livelihood, private commerce and public agencies. The latter naturally include government ministries but also **public sector** companies and **Ba`th Party** offices. The social life of most Damascenes, like other Syrians, centers on the **family**, with members visiting each other's homes on a routine basis. Commercial thoroughfares and public parks attract evening strollers. Cultural venues like **cinemas** and the **theater** engage the interest of a fairly small segment of the population while the traditional setting of the all-male **coffeehouse** still has some appeal.

DAWALIBI, MA`RUF AL- (1907-). Professor of law at Damascus University, Dawalibi was elected to represent his native **Aleppo** in the 1947 parliament and the 1949 constituent assembly. He joined the **People's Party** in 1948, and by 1951 was one of the leading figures in the faction that favored a neutralist **foreign policy** and social reform at home. During the cabinet crisis of November 1951, he stepped forward to form a government that promised to establish civilian control over the gendarmerie and Ministry of Defense. If he had been able to follow through on this, **Adib al-Shishakli** would have lost his grip on power, so he disbanded Dawalibi's cabinet on 29 November, twelve hours after it had been formed.

A decade later Dawalibi gained a second chance to lead the country after Syria seceded from the **United Arab Republic** in September 1961. After the People's Party prevailed in national elections that December, he formed the **secessionist regime**'s first elected cabinet from the conservative People's and **National** parties. Prime Minister Dawalibi criticized the UAR's record on the **economy** for imposing stifling restrictions on the private sector and disrupting **agricultural** production. He tried to balance the demands of private capital and the popular measures instituted under the UAR, so he pledged to preserve legislation benefiting peasants and workers and to reverse the government's intrusion in **trade** and **industry** by rescinding the July 1961 nationalization of industry and trade. In contrast to a liberal economic policy, Dawalibi retained the UAR's emergency laws to use against the press, trade unions, and the **Syrian Communist Party**, whose leader,

Khalid Bakdash, was refused entry when he attempted to return to Syria. Dawalibi also left in place the network of state security courts and put the army in control of district administration.

As in 1951, Dawalibi refused to be hemmed in by the army's insistence on a role in politics; indeed on 24 March 1962 he publicly criticized officers for meddling. The army command then demanded that President **Nazim al-Qudsi** dissolve Dawalibi's cabinet, but he refused. Four days later **Abd al-Karim al-Nahlawi** carried out a coup that led to two weeks of political strife that ended in Dawalibi's resignation. During the decades of **Ba`th Party** rule, this veteran politician has spent most of his life in **Saudi Arabia**, where he advised the rulers for a number of years before retiring. As of spring 2003, he was still living in the Saudi kingdom. *See also* SOCIALIST DECREES.

DAYR AL-ZUR. This town of about 150,000 is a provincial seat situated on the **Euphrates River**. **Ottoman** authorities established Dayr al-Zur as a district center during the **Tanzimat** era as part of Istanbul's effort to establish its authority over **bedouin** tribes in the Middle Euphrates region. Nowadays it is a convenient base for **tourist** excursions to ancient and classical (Hellenistic, **Byzantine**) **archaeological** sites like Mari and Dura Europos. A suspension bridge constructed during the **French Mandate** period spans the Euphrates. The town is near the country's major **petroleum** fields and **mining** resources.

DEMILITARIZED ZONES. The **Armistice of 1949** created three demilitarized zones between Syria and **Israel**. Although Article Five of the armistice declared that sovereignty over the zones had yet to be determined, Israel pushed its claim to possess the land. Syria's refusal to concede this point led to a series of escalating clashes between 1951 and 1967. Israel initiated projects to develop **water** resources and cultivate lands in the zones. Arab villages that obstructed Israeli expansion were destroyed and their inhabitants expelled. In response, Syrian forces would fire on the Israelis, whereupon Israel would retaliate. Fishing rights on the Sea of Galilee provided another point of conflict. In December 1955, Syrian forces tried to prevent Israeli fishing boats from plying waters near the DMZ. In retaliation, Israeli forces launched a broad attack on the Syrians. When Syrian fishermen ventured into the Sea of Galilee, Israeli gunboats would fire on them. In February 1960, Israel pursued cultivation of lands in the southern DMZ, again triggering Syrian fire. This time, Israeli land and air forces attacked a Syrian village and military positions overlooking the DMZ. Fighting escalated further in 1964 when Syria threatened to divert tributaries of the Jordan River in order to thwart Israel's National Water Carrier project. Israel's use of armor, artillery, and airpower forced the Syrians to halt their diversion of the tributaries, but they then resorted to shelling Israeli settlements in the DMZ. Between August 1966 and June 1967, the neo-Ba`th regime began an aggressive policy of launching air strikes in addition to frequent shelling of Israeli settlements. On 6 April 1967, there occurred a major air battle in which Syria lost six fighter planes. At that point, Syria requested Egyptian support. President Gamal Abd al-Nasir's handling of the crisis led to the outbreak of the **June 1967 War** in which Israel drove the Syrians away from the 1949 armistice lines and occupied the **Golan Heights**.

DESERT PALACES. Some of the earliest specimens of Arab **architecture** are a string of palace complexes in the desert between the **Euphrates River** and eastern portions of **Jordan**. The best-preserved and most thoroughly excavated sites are Qasr al-Hayr al-Gharbi (Western) and Qasr al-Hayr al-Sharqi (Eastern) located near **Palmyra**. The earliest construction at the former site dates to the Roman era. The **Umayyad caliph** al-Hisham (r. 724-743) developed both locales with caravanserais, mosques, baths, and aristocratic residences. The palaces are notable for their exuberant **art** and decoration in stucco relief, tiles, and painting of hunting scenes and human figures, contrary to common notions of an Arab Muslim taboo against any representation of living creatures. Al-Hisham's purpose for developing these sites is unknown because the written records are mute, so we must depend on the interpretative speculation of archaeologists to tease their meaning from the material remains.

DRUZES. Members of this heterodox religious sect call themselves *muwahhidun*, "those who declare God's oneness." The Druzes comprise around three percent of the population. Three-quarters of the Druze reside in **Suwayda** province, or **Jabal Druze**, where they account for nearly 90 percent of the population. Other concentrations of Druze settlement include the **Golan Heights**, **Damascus** and its environs, and the mountains west of **Aleppo**.

Historically, the Druze **religion** is an offshoot of **Isma`ili Shi`ism**, which appeared in the time of the **Fatimid caliph** al-Hakim (996-1021), who claimed to be the incarnation of God. An early preacher in the cult of al-Hakim was a Persian Isma`ili, Hamza ibn Ahmad. He recruited a band of missionaries to spread the faith throughout the Fatimid domains in Arabia, **Egypt**, and Syria. The name "Druze" is derived from one of the new religion's propagandists, Muhammad ibn Isma`il al-Darazi. Other preachers won followers throughout Syria, especially in Aleppo and Damascus. When al-Hakim suddenly and mysteriously disappeared in 1021, official support for the new religion ended, and the next caliph ruthlessly suppressed it, so that Druzism survived only in isolated pockets of **Lebanon** and northern Syria. Active leadership of the movement passed to an associate of Hamza ibn Ahmad named Baha al-Din al-Muqtana, also called al-Samuqi. This latter figure played the central role in creating a formal structure for the incipient religion and in gaining new converts. By the time of Baha al-Din's death in 1043, a corpus of Druze teachings had been established in six books known as *The Noble Wisdom*, which contain 111 epistles by Hamza, Baha al-Din, and Isma`il al-Tamimi.

The beliefs and practices of the Druze religion are supposed to be kept secret from all outsiders, but in recent years scholars have published their religious texts. They teach belief in one God who was incarnate in the person of al-Hakim, and they hold that the believer must accept God's actions and submit to Him. Conversely, the Druzes must reject Satan. The epistles also emphasize truthfulness and the imperative of maintaining communal solidarity. Druzes believe their religion stands as a successor to ancient monotheistic cults reaching back to such Hellenistic figures as Pythagoras, Plato, and Plotinus, as well as the prophets of the Bible and the Qur'an. The Druzes do not observe the Muslim rituals of prayer, fasting, or pilgrimage. Another difference between the Druze religion and **Islam** is that, for the most part, the Druzes do not accept converts. They possess their own specialized religious leaders who manage civil matters like marriage (unlike Muslims, the Druzes do not allow polygamy) and inheritance. Full knowledge of their teachings is reserved for the religious hierarchy because one must demonstrate one's worthiness before initiation into esoteric knowledge.

Most Druzes lived in Lebanon until the 18th century, when some of them migrated to a plateau east of the **Hawran** in Jabal Druze. In **Ottoman** times they preserved their autonomy in the face of Istanbul's attempts to impose regular taxation in the late 19th century. When the **French Mandate** was imposed in 1920, the Druzes sought to keep apart from a centrally administered regime, and the French placated them by creating an autonomous regime similar to the one they developed for the **Alawis** in northwest Syria. Nonetheless, French meddling in Jabal Druze sparked a rebellion under the leadership of **Sultan al-Atrash** that spread to the rest of Syria in the **Great Revolt** of 1925 to 1927. After the suppression of the revolt, the French continued the separate administration of Jabal Druze until 1936, when it was annexed to the rest of Syria. Damascus appointed **Nasib al-Bakri** to govern the province, but Druze opposition to rule by a non-Druze led the government to appoint a Druze to the office in 1937. France reinstated a separate administration in 1939 that lasted until 1942.

In the independence era, the Druzes continued to affect Syrian politics. In the early years, they supported politicians who leaned toward unity with **Transjordan** because of the ties forged between its **Hashemite** ruler Abdallah and a number of Druze leaders. In 1947 President **Shukri al-Quwwatli** tried to break Druze autonomist tendencies by inciting a peasant uprising against the landlord families that traditionally opposed central authority. The powerful Atrash clan, however, rallied its loyal supporters to quell the peasant rising. In March 1949, **Husni al-Za`im** seized power with support from the Druzes in return for a pledge to follow policies to their liking, but when he did not fulfill his promise, they began to plot against him. Za`im then dispatched an armored battalion to Jabal Druze, a move that quickened efforts that led to his overthrow in August. The Druzes also played a significant part in the 1954 overthrow of **Adib al-Shishakli** by launching a revolt against him in January. The last manifestation of traditional Druze autonomy is the existence of a separate set of personal status laws for the community.

DUBA, ALI (1933-). From 1974 to 2000, he was the head of military intelligence, the most powerful and strategically sensitive of Syria's several **security forces**. This made him one of the most powerful figures in the regime of **Hafiz al-Asad**. Like most other members of that regime, Duba hailed from modest circumstances. He was born in a small **Alawi** village near **Latakia** and joined the **Ba`th Party** in high school. Given the nature of the position, he is known to have participated in some of the most critical episodes in the Asad regime's history, including the **Hama** uprising of 1982 and the confrontation between President Asad and his brother **Rif`at**. Duba's power exceeded the narrow definition of military intelligence. He sat on government committees that advised the prime minister on economic and administrative matters, and he handled sensitive political missions. In 1984, he contacted **Muslim Brother** leaders in European exile to arrange their amnesty in exchange for public renunciation of their previous involvement in armed insurrection.

Duba's abrupt removal from office in February 2000 caught Syria watchers by surprise. The move reportedly came at the behest of **Bashar al-Asad**. Observers speculated that Bashar took that step, with his father's approval, in order to remove a possible challenger to his place as successor. A second interpretation holds that Bashar was pursuing his anticorruption campaign because for years there had been rumors linking Duba to suspect deals. In retrospect, Duba's dismissal appears to have been the first step in a broader shake-up of powerful veteran members of the ruling elite that continued in March to pave the way for Bashar's succession in July 2000, weeks after his father's death.

-E-

ECONOMIC REFORM. During the early 1980s, sluggish economic performance, large budget expenditures for defense, and a drop in foreign financial assistance and remittances from Syrian workers in Arab Gulf countries contributed to an acute economic crisis in 1985-1986. The most dangerous aspect of this crisis was the near exhaustion of foreign exchange reserves. Since that time, the Syrian government has adopted measures to reform the state-dominated **economy**.

In contrast to **Egypt**'s more sweeping program of economic liberalization, Syria's economic reform has been cautious, controlled, and intermittent. Nearly 20 years after the first steps to expand private sector opportunities, the government and **public sector** companies remain dominant and the well-known inefficiencies of such economies continue to inhibit growth. The major reason for the regime's refusal to embrace a structural adjustment program along the lines of International Monetary Fund recommendations is apprehension that it would pave the way to political liberalization and perhaps even a loss of power.

In 1985-1986, the government issued decrees to promote private investment in **tourism** and to encourage joint **agricultural** ventures between private and public companies to cultivate crops for export to the Gulf countries. In order to broaden the field for private investment, a more ambitious 1991 law granted tax exemptions and relaxed restrictions on foreign exchange transactions to large capital projects that dovetailed with national economic goals. The results have been modest, but reform has led to the emergence of a newly prosperous business sector, improvements in productivity in certain areas of manufacturing and services, and most importantly for the regime, a respite from the foreign exchange crunch of the mid-1980s.

While there are economic and political pressures for further opening the economy, the government is mindful of the disruptive consequences that accompany structural readjustment. **Inflation** and unemployment would hit tens of thousands of public sector employees and civil servants, and they comprise an essential part of the regime's political base. Nonetheless, the high rate of population growth means the economy will need to create over 250,000 new jobs per year for young men and women entering the **labor force** during the first decade of the 21st century. Since 1990, the private sector has surpassed the public sector's contribution to capital investment;

there is no indication that the government will find natural resources inside Syria or financial resources outside the country to restore public sector dominance. It appears, then, that the government will eventually have to choose between social unrest arising from unemployment and underemployment or the risks of more sweeping economic reform. *See also* CURRENCY.

ECONOMY. To give a comparative sense of Syria's economy, the World Bank ranks it as a lower middle income country as measured by per capita gross domestic product. This puts it in the same category as **Jordan**, **Iran**, Tunisia, Romania, and Colombia, but a combination of high population growth rate—about 2.5 percent—and sluggish economic growth has driven Syria into the lower ranks of that class in the last decade.

Since independence, Syria's economy has gone through three main phases: capitalist (1946 to 1961), socialist (1961 to 1989), and selective **economic reform** (1989 to the present). During the capitalist phase, **agriculture** expanded through private investment in **water** pumps and farm machinery. Public spending assisted that expansion by extending the national **transportation** infrastructure from new Mediterranean ports to the **Jazira** region. In 1961, the **United Arab Republic** promulgated the **Socialist Decrees**, inaugurating nearly three decades of state domination of **industry**, **trade**, and **finance**. During the 1960s, **Ba`th Party** regimes extended those measures and deepened **land reform** to break up the old political elite's power. The socialist phase brought Soviet-style **five-year plans** and massive investment in a dam on the **Euphrates River** at **Tabqa** to boost electricity production and increase the amount of irrigated land. The creation of **public sector** companies to manage **banks**, industries, and foreign trade had greater political benefits for the Ba`th Party regime than long-term economic advantages. The only way Syria was able to sustain economic growth for much of the socialist period was by obtaining enormous sums of aid from oil-rich Arab Gulf states and developing its own **petroleum** reserves with the assistance of Western firms. By the mid-1980s, endemic problems in the public sector firms and **corruption** in government agencies created an economic dead end and the government shifted toward selective opening of the economy, particularly in **tourism**, real estate, and construction.

As for the rhythm of economic growth and stagnation, the overall trend was generally upward until the mid-1980s and seesawing between spurts of growth and stretches of stagnation since then. In the 1960s, the average rate of growth was 4.5 percent, while in the 1970s it exceeded 6 percent. The latter period had such high growth (5.5 percent from 1969 to 1974, 7.1 percent from 1974 to 1979) largely because President **Hafiz al-Asad** instituted policies to encourage foreign investment and Arab aid at the same time that Syria's own production and export of petroleum was increasing. Arab aid rose from $50 million per year before the **October 1973 War** to $600 million per year afterward to a peak of $1.6 billion in 1979. Other factors that contributed to economic growth included loans and grants from the World Bank, Europe, and the **United States**, and remittances from Syrians working in Arab Gulf countries. Moreover, during this period, petroleum surpassed cotton as Syria's main export because of the rise in oil prices in 1973 and 1974.

This robust era of economic expansion ended in the mid-1980s when the gross domestic product shrank nearly 3 percent per year from 1983 to 1987 and 9 percent in 1987, while population growth continued at 3.8 percent per year. Part of the reason for the slowdown was a cut in financial support from Arab Gulf regimes upset at Syria's support for **Iran** against **Iraq** in the first Gulf War. Furthermore, much of the capital received in the 1970s had been invested in public sector industries that operated with appalling inefficiency. When a severe crisis hit the country's foreign exchange, these industries lacked the capital to import parts and equipment necessary to continue in operation. Consequently, in the mid-1980s production at several factories came to a complete stop. The Asad regime responded to this distress by introducing measures to slowly liberalize the economy, including gradual moves that allowed the private sector to import goods that had previously been restricted to state companies and that made it easier for foreign companies to invest. The result was a recovery in economic growth at a rate of 6 percent in the early 1990s before slowing again in the last years of the decades, when there were three consecutive years of recession. The first years of the 21st century have seen a modest recovery stimulated by steady petroleum prices, favorable weather, and gradual opening to foreign investment and trade, especially with the **European Union**. *See also* BANKING; CURRENCY; ENERGY; GHAB; INFLATION; LABOR FORCE AND UNEMPLOYMENT; MINING.

EDUCATION. During the 18th century, European missions established schools in various parts of Syria, such as the Lazarist school that opened in **Damascus** in 1775. These tended to attract Syrian **Christians**. The spread of foreign mission schools received a boost during the **Egyptian** occupation in the 1830s. The Egyptians also opened the first public schools, but they shut down with the restoration of **Ottoman** rule in 1840. A thorough program to modernize education in Syria was first implemented under the terms of the Ottoman Empire's 1869 law, which provided for the establishment of a system of elementary, intermediate, secondary, and high schools. One purpose of the new educational system was to oppose the influence of mission schools, which tended to inculcate loyalty to the nation sponsoring the school, usually **France** or Great Britain. The era of higher public education dawned in Syria in 1903 when the Ottoman Medical School was founded in Damascus. The following year, a military preparatory school was opened in the city. During the brief rule of Amir **Faysal**, the Damascus Law Faculty was founded in 1919.

In the **French Mandate** era, there were government schools and private foreign schools operated by **Catholic** orders like the Jesuits and Dominicans. Government schools reached beyond their limited elite clientele of the late Ottoman era to embrace youths from urban middle-class families. In 1923, the Syrian University was founded in Damascus by combining the Law and Medicine faculties. For the most part, though, the French invested little in education; consequently, at independence, Syria had a high rate of illiteracy and a low proportion of youths in schools.

Since independence in 1946, Syrian governments of various stripes have devoted large portions of the budget to educational development: 13.4 percent from 1946 to 1949, 14.5 percent from 1956 to 1959, and 18.6 percent from 1975 to 1982. This expenditure has not only made primary and secondary education widely available, but also established adult literacy programs and vocational training. Primary education is free and mandatory through the sixth year; secondary education is also free, but not compulsory. Primary and secondary education are under the authority of the Ministry of Education; postsecondary education is the responsibility of the Ministry of Higher Education.

To qualify for entrance to a university, Syrians must pass a national examination at the completion of secondary school. One's admittance to a particular faculty depends on one's score on that exam. Those with the highest scores may attend the Faculty of Medicine. Other preferred faculties include pharmacy, dentistry, engineering, and commerce. Attendance at university is tuition free. In 1958 Syrian University was renamed the University of Damascus. In the early 1980s it had around 75,000 students. The second-oldest center of higher learning is the University of **Aleppo**, which grew out of the Faculty of Engineering established in 1946 and became an independent university in 1958 with the addition of the Faculty of **Agriculture**. By the early 1980s it had around 30,000 students. Two smaller universities have been established by the **Ba`th Party** regime of **Hafiz al-Asad**: Tishrin University at **Latakia** (founded in 1971) and Ba`th University at **Homs** (founded in 1979).

The general tendency in the independence period has been for the state to take over education. Private religious and foreign schools founded in the 19th century remained open, but their importance diminished with the rapid expansion of public schools. In 1967 the **neo-Ba`thist** regime extended state control over all schools when it gave the Ministry of Education supervision of private schools. This regime also placed greater emphasis on technical and scientific elements in the curriculum. Agricultural schools were established at the secondary-education level. New institutions include the Veterinary Institute in **Hama** and the Electrical and Petrochemical Engineering Institute in Homs.

The Ba`thist regimes directed a greater share of the budget to education, with the result that during the 1960s the number of students at secondary schools rose from 140,000 to 480,000; the number of teachers grew from 6,000 to 28,000; and the number of such schools increased from 400 to 1,150. As for primary education, by 1971, 63 percent of children were in schools (80 percent of boys, 47 percent of girls), but a shortage of qualified teachers has hampered the expansion of education. In spite of these gains, illiteracy has remained high. In 1960, 60 percent of the population was still illiterate, 43 percent of men and 77 percent of women, of whom 94 percent were illiterate in rural areas. Nonetheless, the proportion of girl pupils in primary schools rose from 29 percent in 1946 to 34 percent in 1969, while the percentage of girls in secondary schools stayed at 24 percent. By the early 1990s, the illiteracy rate had fallen to 36 percent, 22 percent among males and 49 percent among females. *See also* IBRAHIM PASHA.

EGYPT. When Syria became independent, Egypt's primary concern was to keep it out of any union plans proposed by the **Hashemite** rulers of **Jordan** and **Iraq**. In the inter-Arab contest for influence over Syria, Egypt tended to side with **Saudi Arabia**, which also sought to contain Hashemite ambitions. When the Cold War impinged on the Middle East in the mid-1950s, Egyptian president Gamal Abd al-Nasir supported Syrians inclined to adopt a neutral **foreign policy**. Therefore Egypt and Saudi Arabia proposed a military alliance with Syria in March 1955 to counterbalance the **Baghdad Pact**'s pro-Western alliance of Iraq and **Turkey**. This was the first official step in bringing Egypt and Syria closer together as the vanguard of Arab neutralism. The first steps toward Syrian-Egyptian unity were taken in July 1957 when Foreign Minister **Salah al-Din al-Bitar** traveled to Cairo for talks. During the August-October 1957 crisis in Syrian relations with the **United States**, Egypt dispatched 2,000 soldiers as a gesture of solidarity against Western pressures on the neutralist government. The upshot of the crisis was a sense of even greater urgency to unite with Egypt, if only to defend Syria against Western pressures coming from the US, Turkey, and Iraq. On 1 February 1958, Syria and Egypt merged in the **United Arab Republic**. Egyptian domination of the UAR, though, generated widespread discontent in Syria, and in September 1961 Syria seceded from the union.

Syria and Egypt then entered a period of hostile relations as the two governments blamed each other for the failure of the UAR. An improvement in relations appeared possible following the **March 8, 1963 coup**, but the **Ba`th Party**'s purge of Nasirists from the army and government ensured the continuation of poor relations. When the **neo-Ba`th** came to power in 1966 and backed a series of provocative raids on **Israel** by **Palestinian** guerrillas, Nasir tried to increase his influence over Syria's actions by arranging a defense pact, and the two countries exchanged ambassadors for the first time since the formation of the UAR in 1958. But Nasir's inept handling of a military crisis with Israel in May 1967 led to the **June 1967 War** in which both Egypt and Syria lost territory. For the next three years, Syrian-Egyptian relations again soured because of Egypt's acceptance of **United Nations Resolution 242** as a basis for resolving the conflict with Israel, while Syria rejected the resolution.

In the autumn of 1970 important changes in leadership occurred in both countries. Nasir died and Anwar Sadat succeeded him as president of Egypt; and **Hafiz al-Asad** seized power in the **corrective movement**. The two new leaders strove to improve relations, and they cooperated in devising plans for a surprise attack on Israel. This resulted in the **October 1973 War**, a unique instance of coordinated Arab military action against Israel. After the war, though, Sadat took Egypt on a separate course of disengagement from the conflict, and once again its relations with Syria were marked by serious strains. These tensions became complete rupture when Sadat made a separate peace with Israel in 1979. Syria then severed relations and embarked on a military buildup in order to confront Israel alone. Largely because of the war between **Iran** and Iraq, Egypt gradually restored its ties with Arab governments in the mid-1980s. When the war ended in Iraq's favor in July 1988, Syria was isolated in the Arab world for its support of Iran. To improve its regional position, Syria renewed relations with Egypt at the end of 1989. The extent of the Syrian-Egyptian rapprochement was evident in their agreement to send troops to Saudi Arabia in 1990 in response to Iraq's invasion of Kuwait and in Syria's assent to attend the **Madrid Conference** of December 1991.

During the 1990s, the two countries maintained correct but cool relations. The chief point of friction remained Egypt's peace treaty with Israel. Syria drew closer to Cairo after the election of Israel's Benjamin Netanyahu in May 1996 augured the suspension of peace talks. Efforts to knit together a coalition of Egypt, Syria, Saudi Arabia, and Iran to confront Israel faltered because of Egypt's close ties to the United States. As long as Syria's dispute with Israel remains unresolved, close ties with Egypt will lack a solid foundation.

EISENHOWER DOCTRINE. American policy announced on 5 January 1957 to commit **United States** military power to defend any Middle Eastern country against external or internal communist subversion. American fear of communist influence in the Arab world increased with the decline of British and **French** power in the aftermath of the 1956 Suez war. Furthermore, the **Soviet Union** had succeeded in deepening its relations with Egypt and Syria in the previous two years. Syria immediately rejected the doctrine's assumption that any Arab country was threatened by communist takeover. There followed several months of worsening relations with the United States, climaxed by the expulsion in August of three American diplomats for allegedly plotting a coup d'état. Syrian fears of an American plot persisted until October, when **Saudi Arabia** initiated a successful diplomatic campaign to reduce tensions.

ENERGY. One of the notable achievements of Syria's **Ba`thist** regimes is the extension of electrical power to most parts of the country. Presently, 97 percent of the population is connected to the national power grid. The problem for the government, which has controlled the generation and distribution of power since the early 1960s, is increasing the supply of energy to meet the demands of a young and growing population. In the early 1990s, observers estimated demand at 2,500 megawatts but capacity at only 1,900 megawatts. Consequently, Syrians cope with chronic electricity cuts. Part of the problem is that planners vastly overestimated the capacity of the country's major hydroelectric project at the **Tabqa Dam** on the **Euphrates River**. Instead of generating 800 megawatts per day, in the early 1990s its capacity was a mere 150 megawatts, and average daily output even less. While government officials dodge blame by accusing **Turkey** of diverting Euphrates River **water** to its own energy and agricultural needs, foreign observers consider inferior maintenance at Tabqa to be the main problem.

The centrality of energy to **industrial** production and even political stability prompted President **Hafiz al-Asad** in 1993 to intervene and break through the typical bureaucratic knot obstructing effective measures. Since that time, the private sector has been permitted to participate in efforts to increase production, and the government has solicited Arab and Japanese funds to finance the construction of new generators. Finally, Syria joined a regional effort to knit together the electricity grids of Turkey, **Iraq**, **Lebanon**, **Jordan**, and **Egypt** that should eventually make it possible to match demand and supply.

ENVIRONMENT. As in most parts of the developing world, shifts in the population and **economy** are degrading the environment. The imperative to feed a growing population has spurred efforts to intensify cultivation in semiarid regions, primarily by irrigating more land. Inadequate drainage of irrigated fields has resulted in raising the soil's salinity and has rendered large tracts uncultivable. The desert is spreading because of overgrazing, cutting of trees, and the utilization of off-road motor vehicles to shepherd livestock. The economic effect of this specific form of environmental damage is to reduce the amount of arable land. Recent efforts to restore rangeland have had no success because they do not address the basic imbalance between the number of animals and available pasture.

The Syrian coast has a special set of environmental problems. As the population and economic activities have grown in **Latakia**, **Baniyas**, and **Tartus**, a higher volume of industrial, **agricultural**, and human waste is spoiling the Mediterranean Sea's marine environment. In terms of economic production, such pollution is hurting the fisheries sector. In general, the urban environment is worsening as well. Migration from rural areas and natural growth have fostered overcrowding in major cities and put pressure on sanitation facilities. **Industry** and motor vehicles are sources of air pollution. Official recognition of the need to monitor and remedy environmental problems is evident in the 1979 appointment of a minister of state for environmental affairs. Perhaps the most important agency for mitigating environmental harm is ICARDA, based at **Aleppo**. It operates projects to reclaim semiarid zones and introduce sustainable grazing patterns. International bodies like the World Bank also play a role in fostering regulations and administrative commitment to introducing local procedures to stem environmental degradation.

EUPHRATES RIVER. This waterway runs through Syria for 670 kilometers between the borders of **Turkey** and **Iraq** and provides 80 percent of Syria's **water**. The Euphrates' total length is 2,333 kilometers. About 90 percent of its water comes from streams in Turkey, and its flow decreases near the border with Syria. The level of the Euphrates fluctuates sharply between high levels reached between November and May and low levels during the hot season. Before modern times, settlement along the river was sparse, the region being dominated by the **bedouin**. But beginning in the late **Ottoman** era, central government authority was extended by posting garrisons and developing towns around them. This process facilitated **agricultural** colonization and the settlement of most bedouin.

Al-Raqqa and **Dayr al-Zur** are the main towns along the river, each with populations around 150,000.

Since independence, Syrian planners have developed projects to more fully exploit the river for **energy** and agriculture. The Euphrates Dam at **Tabqa** was built between 1968 and 1973. It has increased the amount of land that can be irrigated and it generates most of Syria's electrical power. The **Jazira** region depends heavily on the river and its major tributary, the **Khabur**. Cities like al-Raqqa, Dayr al-Zur, **al-Hasaka**, and **Aleppo** draw from the Euphrates for municipal use, and the surrounding region's agricultural production is completely dependent on them.

The river's prominence in the national **economy** is the major reason for tensions with Turkey and Iraq. Because the river rises in Turkey, it controls the volume of flow downriver. If Turkey uses too much water, the level of **Lake Asad** behind the Tabqa Dam drops too low to operate the dam's eight turbines. By the same token, increases in Syrian use of Euphrates' waters lessens the flow into Iraq. In recent years, Turkey has been developing a massive hydraulic scheme, the Southeast Anatolia Development Project, or GAP, to construct a series of enormous dams to provide power and irrigation. The GAP irrigation projects could cut the river's flow into Syria by one-third. Furthermore, the smaller flow might contain higher levels of pollution because the river could carry Turkey's agricultural and industrial waste. It is possible that Turkey's and Syria's economic development plans will not result in either shortage or pollution but that anxieties about water security will remain. Water sharing is also a sore subject in Syria's relations with Iraq. In 1975, Baghdad accused Damascus of harming its economy when Syria filled Lake Asad and temporarily cut the river's flow from 15 to 9.5 billion cubic meters. Mediation by the **Soviet Union** and the **League of Arab States** lowered bilateral tensions. In 1990, the two countries agreed on an allocation of water whereby Syria promised Iraq about 60 percent of the Euphrates' flow entering Syria from Turkey.

EUROPEAN UNION. A large portion of Syria's **trade** is with European Union members. In 2000, more than half of Syria's exports went to EU markets and around 30 percent of its imports came from EU members. The EU provides technical and financial assistance in several fields, including irrigation and drainage on the **Euphrates River**, urban **water** supply in **Hama**, modernization of **banking**, and technical training. In 2001, the EU and Syria signed a new agreement covering management of electricity production, the establishment of a new business school,

tourism development, and telecommunications. Assistance takes the form of training, funds, and such equipment as new computers. The various projects are shaped to encourage **economic reform**, especially the development of a robust private sector.

In spite of the positive efforts on both sides, trade relations are not free of friction. For example, the EU accused Syria of dumping textile manufactures. On the other hand, Syria became eligible for loans from the European Investment Bank again at the end of 2000 by paying off debts it owed to Germany. It appears that **Bashar al-Asad**'s economic reform plan will rely on improved and increased cooperation with the EU.

-F-

FAMILY. Kinship ties play a central but variable role in the lives of Syrians. The common image of the extended multigenerational Arab family living in a single domicile, arranged marriage at a young age to a cousin, and many children represents at most a cultural ideal and almost certainly not historical reality for most Syrians through the ages. Nonetheless, an individual's kinship ties have weighed heavily in determining livelihood, place of residence, and personal interactions. Islamic civilization generally achieved a high degree of social and spatial mobility when compared to premodern societies in Europe, South Asia, and China. Yet it is still probably the case that most Syrians before modern times were born, grew up, and died in the same village or town or with the same **bedouin** clan; that the selection of a spouse occurred through networks of close relations; and that livelihood as cultivator, merchant, artisan, or scribe passed from one generation to the next within families.

It is not possible to describe in much detail the history of the family in Syria because historical research on the subject is a new field of inquiry and the results so far must be considered preliminary findings. The most developed field of inquiry is family life in **Ottoman** cities, where it is evident that kinship groups had important political, economic, and social functions. Certain families established multigenerational "dynasties" in specific fields of activity like religious prestige, political service to Istanbul, and participation in long-distance **trade**. Such families comprised a compact, conspicuous elite and usually possessed the material resources to attain the ideal of multigenerational families inhabiting a large common domicile or adjoining residences. These notable lineages used marriage to preserve their wealth and to sustain alliances. Research in law court records in Syrian towns have shown that monogamy was the norm since at least the 18th century.

In modern times, various forces have altered family dynamics in Syria. Urbanization has divided families between rural and urban branches and made it rare for extended families to live together. Economic change has created opportunities for livelihoods in professions and large-scale organizations like government offices, industrial enterprises, and commercial firms. The government's assumption of welfare functions in **education, health,** and employment has created new options for Syrians in need of such services. The effects of these changes are uneven. For example, it is clear that rural Syrians tend to marry at a younger age and have more children than city dwellers. Furthermore, the notion that modernization would marginalize the family is mistaken. Instead, the family has evolved and adapted to new circumstances. Thus, it is common for Syrians to tap family connections to gain access to jobs and public services. According to modern norms, such behavior constitutes nepotism (**corruption**), but for many, if not most Syrians, it represents loyalty to a higher value, the family.

FARZAT, ALI (c. 1945-). One of the foremost political cartoonists in the Arab world. Farzat rose to prominence in the late 1970s with his eloquent uncaptioned pictures. He established a repertoire of stock images to express his messages. Those images include medals for military leaders' phony claims to valor and heroism, and ornate desks for **corrupt,** incompetent bureaucrats. His popularity is such that when an official Syrian newspaper dropped his cartoons because they were deemed too critical, circulation plummeted, and the newspaper resumed carrying his work. Farzat made a bit of history in February 2001 when he received permission to publish Syria's first private periodical since the **Ba`th Party** first seized power in 1963. *The Lamplighter* (*al-Dumari*) is a weekly magazine dedicated to political satire. The first issue quickly sold out all 25,000 copies. It was reported that readers were interested less in reading the articles than viewing the cartoons that lampooned official corruption and military officers' abuses of power. The political opening under **Bashar al-Asad** proved ephemeral, and in June 2001 Farzat encountered pressures to stop publishing because of an article about Prime Minister **Muhammad Miru.** Nonetheless, Farzat has managed to keep the enterprise alive in the face of diminishing circulation and mixed signals from the regime.

AL-FATAT. The Young Arab Society (*al-Jam`iyya al-arabiyya al-fatat*) was a secret society organized by Arab students in Paris in 1911 to promote Arabs' rights in the **Ottoman Empire.** In 1913, al-Fatat members in Paris convened an Arab Congress to advance their demands with the support of other groups for greater Arab autonomy in the provinces. During **World War I**, al-Fatat abandoned its original program and began to strive for Arab independence from the Ottoman Empire and the establishment of a unitary state in Arab provinces of the empire. The group secretly met with Amir **Faysal** in 1915 and supported the **Hashemite**-led **Arab Revolt** that broke out the following year. When Faysal established his Arab government in 1918, members of al-Fatat played a leading role as government officials, military officers, and members of Faysal's staff. Many members of al-Fatat went on to become nationalist leaders during the **French Mandate** era.

FATIMID DYNASTY. This **Isma`ili Shi`i** dynasty first rose in North Africa (present-day Tunisia) in 909. After conquering **Egypt** in 969, they fought with fellow Isma`ili **Qarmatis** based in Bahrain for control over southern Syria. The Fatimids consolidated their authority in **Damascus** in 983, and then contended with the **Hamdanids** for supremacy in the north. For a century the Fatimids ruled southern Syria and wavered between direct rule and accommodation to other powers' influence in northern Syria. Thus, they coexisted with the Hamdanids and the **Mirdasids**. In Damascus the Fatimids began the practice of installing Turkish garrisons to maintain order in the city and its environs. When the Fatimids attempted to rule northern Syria, they came into conflict with the **Byzantines** on several occasions in the late 10th and early 11th centuries. Because of the Byzantines' greater military power, the Fatimids sometimes acquiesced to the emperor's claim on **Aleppo** and the rest of northern Syria as tributaries.

One of the curious episodes of Fatimid history involves the Caliph al-Hakim (r. 996-1021), certainly one of the most eccentric rulers in all Islamic history and the focal point for the development of the **Druze** religion. His reign was notable for other aspects. Early Fatimid policy toward **Jews** and **Christians** had been markedly tolerant to the extent that a number of high posts were assigned to them. By contrast, al-Hakim persecuted non-Muslims, seized their properties, and destroyed churches. In 1009 he outraged Christians in the Middle East and Europe by having the Church of the Holy Sepulchre in Jerusalem demolished. Four years later he relaxed restrictions on Christians and Jews, for he frequently reversed policies. Among his constructive acts was the establishment of a special institute for the study of Shi`i doctrines and to train Isma`ili propagandists. Al-Hakim also succeeded in extending direct Fatimid authority to Aleppo for the first time in 1017. The Mirdasids took the city six years later, but for the next five decades they usually acknowledged Fatimid suzerainty. Also in 1017 the first signs of a new religion appeared among Isma`ili propagandists suggesting that al-Hakim was not merely the **imam** but also the divine incarnation. This teaching angered not only **Sunnis** but also traditional Isma`ilis, and early Druze teachers came under attack in Egypt. After al-Hakim's disappearance in 1021, Druze missionaries left Egypt to spread the religion in Syria.

Soon after al-Hakim's reign, Fatimid power in Syria began to wane as local forces challenged the Isma`ili caliphate and bands of **Turkomen** migrated into Syria. To complicate matters for the Fatimids, their own garrisons in Syrian towns were riven with feuds between Turkish and Berber factions. In 1076, a Turcoman chief, who had served the Fatimids in campaigns against **bedouin** tribes, revolted and seized Damascus. Three years later, the Turcoman handed power over to the new great power of the region, the **Saljuk** Turks, thereby ending a century of Fatimid preeminence in Syria.

FAYSAL IBN HUSAYN AL-HASHIMI (1885-1933). A son of Sharif **Husayn ibn Ali**, leader of the **Arab Revolt** against the **Ottoman Empire** during **World War I**, and ruler of a short-lived independent Syrian state from October 1918 until July 1920. A year before the outbreak of the Arab Revolt, Faysal, a native of Mecca in western Arabia, visited **Damascus**, where he forged the basis for cooperation with members of the secret **Arab nationalist** society **al-Fatat**. When the revolt broke out a year later, Faysal led Arab forces on their march into Syria and entered Damascus in October 1918. He then established a provisional military government supported by his wartime Arab nationalist allies as well as subsidies and diplomatic backing from Great Britain. Faysal's nascent state was nonetheless vulnerable to French pressures. Moreover, he came to Syrian politics as an outsider and therefore lacked a solid political base. His efforts to secure Syrian independence by attending the Paris Peace Conference in 1918-1919 were ultimately futile because of **France**'s insistence on establishing direct control over the interior. Faysal's fate was sealed in November 1919 when British troops began to withdraw from Syria, leaving the way open to French occupation.

Faysal convened the **Syrian Congress** in March 1920. The Congress formally declared Syria's independence, proclaimed Faysal king of Syria, and formed a government under a prime minister appointed by Faysal. He then tried to negotiate with France and offered to recognize its primary standing among foreign powers in Syria, but his willingness to compromise Arab sovereignty undermined his position among nationalists at home. When French troops invaded, the outmatched Syrian forces resisted at the Battle of **Maysalun**, near Damascus, on 24 July 1920. The French commander drove Faysal out of Damascus, and on 1 August he left Syria, although he did later become king of **Iraq**. While Faysal's brief rule is primarily known for its tumultuous politics, a number of notable cultural institutions, such as a museum and a scientific academy, were established as an expression of Syria's increasingly Arab nationalist culture.

FEBRUARY 23, 1966 COUP. This coup by the **neo-Ba`th** against the first Ba`thist regime brought to power Syria's most radical government. It was precipitated by a heightening in the power struggle between the **Ba`th Party**'s old guard and younger factions. On 21 February, supporters of the old guard in the army ordered the transfer of their rivals. Two days later, the **Military Committee**, backing the younger factions, launched a coup that entailed bloody fighting in **Aleppo**, **Damascus**, **Dayr al-Zur**, and **Latakia**. As a result of the coup, the party's historical founders fled the country and spent the rest of their lives in exile. The coup also created a permanent schism between Syrian and **Iraqi** branches of the party.

FERTILE CRESCENT PLAN. An Iraqi **Hashemite** plan for the union of **Iraq** with Syria, **Lebanon**, **Palestine**, and **Transjordan**. Iraq's Prime Minister Nuri al-Sa`id broached the plan to British officials during **World War II**, when it appeared that **France** had become too weak to hold on to Syria. This Arab unity scheme faced opposition from those Syrians who did not wish to live under a monarchy or enter a pro-British alliance. During the independence period, the Iraqi government poured money into the pockets of Syrian politicians who favored unity. In addition, the second **People's Party**, representing northern Syrian commercial and landholding interests, favored the Fertile Crescent Plan and initiated diplomatic steps to implement it. On the other hand, the **National Party** and factions in the army were determined to block any plans for unity with Iraq as long as it had a military treaty with Great Britain. The closest the plan came to fruition was during the regime (August–December 1949) of Colonel **Sami al-Hinnawi**, who had installed a People's Party government that entered negotiations to achieve unity. The opportunity was aborted by Colonel **Adib al-Shishakli**'s coup d'état. Any remaining glimmer of hope for the Fertile Crescent Plan vanished with the over-throw of Iraq's monarchy in July 1958.

FIVE-YEAR PLANS. Syria introduced its first five-year plan for 1960 to 1965 during the **United Arab Republic** period. It aimed to develop **agriculture** and **mining** resources, as well as to launch construction of a railroad between **Latakia** and **Qamishli**, but the political turmoil of those years hampered implementation of the plan. The second plan (1966-1970) devoted the greatest share of investment to developing the **petroleum** industry and the **Euphrates** Dam at **Tabqa**, which was supposed to expand the area of irrigated agriculture and generate electricity. Large sums also went to **transportation**, communications, public works, and housing. The third five-year plan (1971-1975) sought to complete the Euphrates Dam and to further develop industrial production and **energy** resources. Endemic problems in achieving the plans' goals shaped the fourth plan (1976-1980) as did shortages in agricultural products. This plan tried to revive agriculture by giving it a quarter of public investment (compared with 10 percent in the third plan). The fifth plan (1981-1985) mainly invested in finishing projects left over from previous plans and reduced investment in agriculture. Since the mid-1980s, the regime of **Hafiz al-Asad** has had to rely more on the private sector as the engine of economic growth and to diminish the state's role in the **economy**. Consequently, while a sixth plan (1986-1990) was drawn up, the regime did not try to implement it, and a seventh plan for 1991 to 1995 was never completed, marking the end of centralized economic planning.

FOREIGN POLICY. Since gaining independence in 1946, Syria has passed through two main phases in its foreign relations. The first period lasted until around 1970. It was notable for the ability of outside powers to meddle in its affairs in order to draw Syria into one orbit or another. The second period has been characterized by Syria's ability to deflect such manipulation and to even project its influence into neighboring countries, most notably **Lebanon**. To understand the complex vicissitudes of the country's foreign relations, it helps to consider them as overlapping sets of issues in three contexts: the Arab-Israeli conflict, regional Arab politics, and superpower rivalry.

Syria's domestic instability in the 1940s and 1950s made it the object of Arab intrigue. The neighboring **Hashemite** kingdoms of **Jordan** and **Iraq** both sought to pull Syria into close alignment to oppose their **Egyptian** and **Saudi** rivals. By the same token, Cairo and Riyadh strove to ensure their position by swaying **Damascus** to support them. Consequently, Syrian foreign policy seesawed from one pole to another, but popular sentiment became increasingly pro-Egyptian, especially after President Gamal Abd al-Nasir's rise to heroic stature for defying Great

Britain and **France** over the Suez Canal. Throughout the period, the **United States** and the **Soviet Union** worked to swing Damascus into their respective camps. In early 1958, the neutralist and pro-Egyptian impulse prevailed with the creation of the **United Arab Republic**, and for the next three years Syria did not have an independent foreign policy but notably moved closer to the Soviet Union. As for **Israel**, Syria's military vulnerability in the **demilitarized zones** that had emerged from **armistice** talks after the **Palestine War of 1948** meant that its leaders might occasionally make bellicose pronouncements but they lacked the means to back them up and the armistice remained in place.

After the breakup of the UAR, Syria entered yet another prolonged stretch of volatility in its foreign relations in a more radical regional political climate. The most important change had occurred in Iraq, where the pro-Western monarchy fell in 1958 and a succession of military regimes followed. Damascus contributed to the radical mood when the **Ba`th Party** seized power in 1963 with a pan-Arab agenda at the head of a foreign policy driven by ideology. There ensued fruitless talks with Baghdad and Cairo to forge a basis for Arab unity. Even though the Ba`thist leaders declared their desire to attain Arab unity, their actions and rhetoric alienated most Arab regimes, which they viewed as either reactionary (pro-Western) or capitulationist (unwilling to go to war against Israel). By 1970, Damascus was more isolated in Arab politics than ever before.

The second key element in the Ba`th Party's foreign policy was an emphasis on the duty to liberate **Palestine** from Zionist occupation. As a result, the mid-1960s saw the development of ties between Damascus and **Palestinian** guerrilla organizations in Jordan and Lebanon. Syria's backing for guerrilla raids on Israel precipitated the May 1967 crisis which resulted in the **June 1967 War**. In that conflict Syria lost the **Golan Heights** to Israel and regaining that territory has been one of the foremost objectives of foreign policy ever since. The 1967 War was also a turning point for Syria's relations with superpowers. Damascus cut ties with Washington because of its support for Israel and drew even closer to Moscow for political and military support.

The **Corrective Movement** of 1970 marked a turn away from ideology to pragmatism, exemplified by President **Hafiz al-Asad**'s collaboration with Egyptian President Anwar al-Sadat in planning the **October 1973 War**. After the war, Asad again displayed pragmatism in restoring relations with Washington, but Egyptian President Anwar al-Sadat's pursuit of a separate arrangement with Israel forced Asad to resort to a foreign policy of "balancing" a coalition of regional forces against

Israel. Other Arab countries rallied to Syria as the main "confrontation" state facing Israel. On the one hand, this left Syria exposed to Israel's military might; on the other, it meant that Syria would receive billions of dollars in aid from Arab Gulf states. This spelled a moderation of Syria's foreign policy and its move to the center of Arab regional politics. That position, however, would be difficult to maintain after Syria's intervention in the **Lebanese Civil War** in 1976 and even more so when Syria supported **Iran** in its eight-year war with **Iraq** (1980-1988).

The next shift in foreign relations came in 1990 when Syrian President Hafiz al-Asad reacted to the dissolution of the Soviet Union by drawing closer to Washington and decided to support the United States effort to expel Iraqi forces from Kuwait. The aftermath of "Desert Storm" saw Asad agree to participate in an American endeavor to achieve a comprehensive settlement to the Arab-Israeli conflict by attending the **Madrid Conference**. Throughout the 1990s, Asad pursued his main foreign policy goal of recovering the Golan Heights in the **Syrian-Israeli peace talks** sponsored by the United States. In concrete terms, Syria gained from its cooperation with the Washington coalition by receiving a new injection of financial aid from the Gulf states and by obtaining America's implicit approval for imposing the *Pax Syriana* in Lebanon.

The new millennium brought more dangerous strategic conditions. Negotiations with the Israelis came closer than ever to clarifying the terms for a peace treaty, but the parties failed to close the deal in January 2000 in talks held at **Shepherdstown** in the United States. Then there was a dismal summit meeting at Geneva in March between Hafiz al-Asad and President Bill Clinton. Those developments turned out to be the last chapters in the prolonged peace process launched at Madrid in October 1991 because events in the next six months fundamentally altered the regional political climate. First, Israel unilaterally withdrew from Lebanon in May without negotiating a treaty with Beirut. By doing so, the Israelis removed an instrument for Damascus to apply pressure, namely guerrilla attacks on Israeli forces in Lebanon. Second, Hafiz al-Asad died in June, and his son Bashar succeeded him and needed time to consolidate his position rather than immediately renew diplomatic efforts. Third, in July, an attempt to resolve final status issues between Israel and the Palestinians through intensive American-mediated negotiations at Camp David collapsed in an angry atmosphere of mutual recriminations. At the end of September, a Palestinian uprising broke out against Israel's occupation in the West Bank and Gaza. Finally, in January 2001, Israeli elections resulted in a victory for veteran hawk Ariel Sharon, who became the new prime minister. A little over a year earlier, it had looked like a Syrian-

Israeli peace treaty was in reach, but in the first half of 2001, that prospect was as remote as ever.

Bashar al-Asad has continued his father's policy of finding partners to "balance" a stronger Israeli adversary. Damascus maintained close ties with Egypt and Saudi Arabia, boosted trade with Jordan and **Turkey**, countries that had had difficulties with Damascus in the 1990s, and deepened overtures to Baghdad begun in 1997. In response to the George W. Bush administration's call for allies in the war on terror in the wake of the September 11, 2001, attacks on the United States, Syria proclaimed its readiness to cooperate against Usama bin Laden's al-Qa`ida network. At the same time, Asad insisted that Palestinian attacks on Israelis were not instances of terrorism but acts of resistance against occupation, a position at odds with the official American view. For a while in 2002, it seemed possible that Syria might further drift into a chilly relationship with Washington over American belligerence toward Saddam Husayn's regime. The wish to avoid gratuitously antagonizing Washington resulted in Syria voting in favor of **United Nations** Security Council Resolution 1441 in November 2002 even though most Syrians strongly opposed an American invasion of Iraq. Syria's international position was dangerously exposed after the United States invaded and deposed the Ba`thist regime in Baghdad and threatened Damascus to refrain from any provocative behavior. In the war's immediate aftermath, Syria's leadership responded cautiously to the new regional situation of unprecedented American military domination, waiting to see what sort of regime would emerge in Iraq and whether the Americans would exert pressure on Syria to alter its policies on Lebanon, Israel, and the Palestinians.

FRANCE. In July 1920, French armed forces invaded Syria from **Lebanon** to impose France's rule under the terms of a mandate it had received from the League of Nations by the **San Remo Agreement** the previous April. French interests in Syria dated to the 18th century in the form of **Catholic** missions and a strong commercial presence in **Aleppo**. In the last decades of **Ottoman** rule, France became the European power with the largest economic stake in the Ottoman Empire. French companies had investments in various **transportation** projects, public utilities, financial institutions, and tobacco. During **World War I**, French and British diplomats concluded the **Sykes-Picot Agreement**, which divided the Ottoman Arab lands into spheres of influence. This plan assigned Syria (including Lebanon) to France. At the end of the war, however, British troops occupied Syria and assisted the establishment of an independent regime under Amir **Faysal**. The French suspected Britain of intentionally violating the terms of Sykes-Picot in order to undermine France's position in the region. There followed intense negotiations at Versailles that ended with Britain's agreement in September 1919 to withdraw its forces from Syria. Faysal tried to negotiate an arrangement with France whereby the latter would recognize Syria's independence in return for his promise to grant France exclusive control over **foreign policy** and the right to provide assistance in developing Syria's nascent military and administrative institutions. The French government, however, was determined to directly control Syria, so it expelled Faysal and dismantled his government in July 1920, thereby inaugurating the **French Mandate** that would persist for nearly 26 years. *See also* FRANCO-SYRIAN TREATY OF 1936.

FRANCO-SYRIAN TREATY OF 1936. During the **French Mandate**, Syrian nationalists came to realize that **France** would not grant Syria independence unconditionally, but that a treaty guaranteeing France's special status in the country's affairs after independence might bring about an early end to the mandate. Negotiations between an elected Syrian government under **Haqqi al-Azm** and French High Commissioner Damien de Martel reached agreement in November 1933, but the Syrian Chamber of Deputies gave the draft treaty a chilly reception because it left **Jabal Druze** and the **Alawi** state in **Jabal Ansariyya** under separate administrations. Martel reacted by suspending the Chamber for the next two years. In March 1936 the French High Commissioner allowed a Syrian delegation, headed by **Hashim al-Atasi**, to travel to Paris to negotiate a treaty directly with the French government. The atmosphere for talks improved that June with the election in France of the leftist Popular Front government, and the two sides reached agreement in September.

In the Franco-Syrian Treaty, Paris conceded the inclusion of Jabal Druze and the Alawi region in a unified Syrian state but under special administrations, while the Syrians consented to clauses granting France air bases and garrisons. For the treaty to come into force, it needed ratification by Syrian and French parliaments and then Syrian admission to the League of Nations. In the end, the treaty failed. The **National Bloc**, which triumphed in Syria's November 1936 elections, formed a government to guide Syria toward treaty ratification and independence. The Syrian parliament ratified the treaty and the French High Commissioner signed it in December, but the agreement's opponents in France rallied conservative sentiment to prevent its ratification by the French parliament. The French government then sought modifications to the treaty in order to mollify conservative critics, but when Syrian prime minister **Jamil Mardam** showed flexibility, he was undercut by his own nationalist hard-liners. By the end of 1938, it was clear that the 1936 treaty would never be implemented, and Syria would face eight more years of French rule.

FRANKLIN-BOUILLON AGREEMENT. By this October 1921 accord between **France** and **Turkey**, France relinquished its claims to a sphere of influence in southeastern Anatolia and disputed lands on the northern Turkey-Syria frontier. The Agreement stipulated a special regime for the Sanjak of **Alexandretta** by which it would be kept separate from the rest of Syria under French control and Turkish would be recognized as an official **language**. In return, the Turkish government agreed to stop supporting the rebel movements of **Ibrahim Hananu** and **Shaykh Salih al-Ali**.

FRENCH MANDATE. Between July 1920 and April 1946, **France** ruled Syria under the terms of the mandate system, which was created after **World War I** by the League of Nations to provide a legal basis and mechanisms for European rule over areas of the Middle East occupied during the war. In theory, certain countries were not prepared to rule themselves; therefore, European countries assumed the duty to guide and prepare such countries for independence. France received a provisional mandate over Syria and **Lebanon** in April 1920 under the **San Remo Agreement**. According to the League of Nations terms for the mandate, France was supposed to draft a **constitution** and guide the development of governing institutions. The mandate also made France responsible for Syria's defense, internal security, and **foreign policy**. Three months after San Remo, a French expeditionary force put teeth into the mandate by invading Syria and at the Battle of **Maysalun** defeated **Arab nationalists** defending Amir **Faysal**'s fragile state. France then detached several regions from Syria and attached them to Lebanon in August 1920, thereby creating the modern boundaries of an enlarged Lebanon. The mandatory power divided Syria into four separate districts: **Aleppo**, **Damascus**, **Jabal Druze**, and **Latakia** (for the **Alawis**). In 1925, France created a Syrian state by combining Damascus and Aleppo, but it left the Druze and Alawi regions under separate administrations, and **Alexandretta** became a special district as a concession to **Turkey**'s concerns over the future of Turks living there.

During the mandate's first five years, Syrian resistance took various forms: revolts in the north led by **Ibrahim Hananu** and **Shaykh Salih al-**

Ali and organized political movements such as **Abd al-Rahman Shahbandar**'s **People's Party**. The first serious threat to French authority came from a 1925 uprising that spread from Jabal Druze to the rest of the country in the **Great Revolt**, which lasted for two years before French reinforcements suppressed it. In order to meet Syrian demands for political evolution and to satisfy European pressures for a policy besides repression, France organized elections for a constituent assembly in April 1928. The leading nationalist organization, the **National Bloc**, was able to dominate the assembly's proceedings even though its members were a minority, and by the end of July the assembly issued a draft constitution. But because the constitution contained articles that effectively eliminated France's legal authority in Syria, the High Commissioner rejected the draft and adjourned the assembly. There followed two years of political stalemate that ended in May 1930 when France promulgated a modified version of the 1928 draft as the basis for national elections to parliament. When these were held in December 1931-January 1932, the National Bloc won just 17 out of 69 seats.

The next major political matter was negotiating a **Franco-Syrian Treaty** to govern relations between the two countries in the event of Syria gaining its independence. Because the National Bloc's parliamentary members prevented the passage of formulations preferred by France, the High Commissioner suspended parliament in November 1933. Stalemate on the treaty continued until the **General Strike** of January-March 1936 induced the French to invite Bloc leaders to Paris to negotiate the terms of a treaty. This time, efforts to reach agreement bore fruit, and the draft treaty provided mechanisms for Syria's eventual independence and admittance to the League of Nations. Fresh from this diplomatic triumph, the National Bloc swept national elections to parliament, and before the end of the year, Syria had its first elected nationalist government. At the same time, Jabal Druze and the Alawi Territory, previously under separate administrations, were incorporated into Syria. Against these achievements, however, Syrians had to reckon with France's bowing to Turkey's ambitions to annex Alexandretta in order to gain Turkish neutrality in the event of a war with Italy. This debacle and the failure to secure French ratification of the 1936 treaty led the government to resign in February 1939. On the eve of **World War II** the High Commissioner suspended the constitution, dissolved parliament, and resumed separate administrations for Jabal Druze and Latakia.

When France fell to Axis forces in 1940, a pro-Vichy regime was established in Syria, but a combined British-Free French force invaded Syria and Lebanon in 1941 to remove Vichy officials. The preponderance of British troops in the invasion force made Britain the dominant military power and drastically diminished France's ability to determine its own policy toward Syria. Meanwhile, the Free French authorities had declared Syria's independence on the eve of the invasion and after consolidating their authority, but they moved very slowly in actually transferring power to the Syrians. The French ended separate administrations for Jabal Druze and Latakia, then in 1943 allowed national elections, which were swept by **Shukri al-Quwwatli**'s **National Party**, the successor to the National Bloc. In early 1945, the French sought to prolong their rule. That triggered a new round of nationalist demonstrations in May. The French suppressed the protests with a bombardment of Damascus that killed 400 Syrians, whereupon British forces seized control from the French. The last French troops withdrew on 17 April 1946.

-G-

GENERAL STRIKE OF 1936. This protest gave fresh momentum to the nationalist movement, which had been stalled since the 1933 suspension of parliament. When **French Mandate** authorities arrested prominent members of the **National Bloc** and closed its offices in **Damascus**, demonstrations in that city, **Aleppo**, **Hama**, and **Homs** shattered a lull in anti-French activities on 20 January. Merchants then went on a strike that spread to all major towns, and demonstrations spread throughout the country. Confrontations between protestors and troops resulted in dozens of deaths. The **League of National Action**, a radical pan-Arab movement, organized protest marches in Damascus, while the National Bloc demanded the restoration of the 1930 **constitution** before the strike would be called off. For five weeks commercial activity was frozen and students boycotted schools. Finally, on 2 March the French agreed to the formation of a Syrian delegation to travel to Paris to negotiate a **Franco-Syrian Treaty**. When French authorities released the nationalist leaders they had arrested, the Bloc ended the strike.

GHAB. A low-lying rift northwest of **Hama** between the eastern edge of the **Jabal Ansariyya** and the Zawiya Mountains. It measures 80 kilometers from north to south and about 15 kilometers from east to west. The **Orontes River** passes through it from south to north. Until the 20th century, the Ghab was a vast swamp, but two barrages on the Orontes and drainage of the marshes have reclaimed the land for **agriculture**. Work on reclamation began in 1954 with the deepening of the riverbed, the diversion of the river, and the construction of a dam to channel water to irrigation canals. When the project was completed in 1968, the new irrigation system made possible the cultivation of wheat and barley in the winter, and cotton, rice, and sugar beets in the summer.

GHANIM, WAHIB AL- (1919-2003). Early member of the **Ba`th Party** and an associate of **Zaki al-Arsuzi** when they both lived in **Alexandretta** and then **Damascus**. Ghanim got his training in medicine and then opened a practice in **Latakia**, where he recruited educated youths, including future president **Hafiz al-Asad**, into the party. In 1947, party cofounders **Michel Aflaq** and **Salah al-Din al-Bitar** met with Ghanim and persuaded him to bring some of Arsuzi's followers into their movement. Consequently, he attended the Ba`th's founding congress in April 1947, and was elected to its four-man executive committee. In 1954 Ghanim was one of 22 party members to win a seat in parliament, and he became Minister of Health in **Sabri al-Asali**'s February to September 1955 government. The party's Syrian branch dissolved itself on the eve of the **United Arab Republic**'s formation, causing deep disarray and internal strife. When the Ba`th reemerged after Syria's secession from the UAR, Ghanim was no longer a member, but he ran for parliament and won in the December 1961 election, this time as an independent from Latakia. Following the **March 8, 1963 coup**, though, he dropped out of politics.

GHAZZI, SA`ID AL- (1897-1967). Nonpartisan prime minister from 19 June to 14 October 1954, and again from 13 September 1955 to 2 June 1956. This lawyer from an old **Damascus** family belonged to the **National Bloc** from 1928 to 1936, and served in cabinets during the early independence period. The first time Ghazzi was prime minister his task was to form a nonpartisan government that would preside over parliamentary elections in September 1954, Syria's first free elections after four years of military dictatorship under **Adib al-Shishakli**. Ghazzi pledged to keep the government from interfering in the election. The result was a large gain for leftist parties, particularly the **Ba`th Party**, which won 22 seats. The **Syrian Communist Party**'s **Khalid Bakdash** and the neutralist **Khalid al-Azm** were also elected. After the elections a new cabinet formed and Ghazzi stepped down.

In September 1955, President **Shukri al-Quwwatli** invited Ghazzi to head another government that pursued a neutralist foreign policy, meaning that Syria would not join the **Baghdad Pact**. To stiffen Syria's resistance to Western pressures for adherence to the Pact, Ghazzi's government negotiated the Egyptian-Syrian Defense Pact in October and developed closer ties to the **Soviet Union**, concluding military and commercial agreements with the Soviet bloc. In June 1956, the shaky conservative coalition that kept his cabinet together came unraveled and Ghazzi resigned.

GHUTA. This is a general term for a cultivated area in the midst of arid land that is dependent on springwater diverted to irrigation channels. More specifically, the Ghuta is the broad cultivated area of 10 by 12 miles around **Damascus** watered by the **Barada River** and its six man-made branches. There are several large villages and many smaller ones in this densely populated oasis. A great variety of crops are cultivated: cucumbers, grapes, onions, melons, and eggplants; the orchards include apricot, almond, cherry, fig, walnut, peach, pear, and plum trees.

GOLAN HEIGHTS. The high plateau in southwestern Syria that **Israel** occupied in the **June 1967 War**. The Heights average 1,000 meters in altitude and comprise an area of approximately 1,750 square kilometers. From north to south the Heights run for 65 kilometers and have a width of 12 to 25 kilometers. The region is of key strategic significance because it dominates the topography where the borders of Israel, **Lebanon**, and Syria converge. Moreover, the sources of the Jordan and **Yarmuk Rivers** spring from the Golan Heights.

During the 1967 war about 35,000 Syrians fled their homes, and by early 1968 the Israeli occupation had displaced another 100,000 Syrians; the Israelis allowed only about 10,000 Syrians, mostly **Druzes**, to remain. In 1968 Israel established its first settlement on the Golan Heights. In the next four years, Israel introduced only about 600 settlers, but after the **October 1973 War**, that number grew to 1,800 in one year and to 7,000 by 1980. By 1990, Israel had constructed 35 more settlements with a total Jewish population of 13,000; the Syrian population in the six remaining Arab villages numbered 16,000. Moreover, in December 1981, Israel declared the extension of its law to the Heights, effectively annexing them.

Israel's 1967 occupation of the Golan Heights changed the nature of its conflict with Syria. It was no longer a matter of Arab solidarity; now the confrontation involved the recovery of occupied territory. Syrian determination to recover the Heights lay behind President **Hafiz al-Asad**'s collaboration with Egyptian President Anwar Sadat to launch the October 1973 War. After the war, Syria recovered a small portion of the Heights, including the district center **Qunaytra**, which had been demolished by the Israelis. Syria's primary goal in the **Syrian-Israeli peace talks** since 1991 has been the recovery of the entire region, whereas Israel has declared its willingness to undertake a partial withdrawal in exchange for normal relations.

GREAT REVOLT. This Syrian revolt of 1925 to 1927 against the **French Mandate** began in **Jabal Druze** and spread to the rest of the country. In the first few years of the mandate, **Druze** notables objected to the erosion of their traditional authority. When French officials arrested a number of Druze chiefs in **Damascus, Sultan al-Atrash** launched a revolt to drive the French out of their region beginning on 18 July 1925. A month later, nationalist leaders of the first **People's Party** met in Damascus with representatives of Atrash to agree on a plan to widen the revolt. In October and November, Damascus, **Hama**, and other towns also rose in revolt, but for the most part rebel activities were confined to the Syrian countryside south of Damascus and between Damascus and **Homs**. On 18 October, several hundred armed nationalists entered the old city of Damascus and took it over. The French responded with artillery and air attacks on the old city for the next two days, killing several hundred civilians.

In March 1926, the French initiated a major campaign to regain control over rebel-held territory in central and southern Syria. The next month, French forces seized **Suwayda**, the main city in Jabal Druze. Then on 7 May, French warplanes bombarded the Maydan quarter of Damascus to destroy rebel strongholds there and to expel the rebels from the city. As the French poured in thousands of troops in 1926, they made headway in suppressing the revolt, and by the end of the year had regained control over most of the country. In July 1927, the Great Revolt came to an end as the French pacified the last pockets of resistance around Hama and in Jabal Druze. Syrians consider the Great Revolt the first nationalist uprising in their history.

GREATER SYRIA. This term refers to the territory of historical Syria and includes the contemporary nations of **Israel, Jordan, Lebanon**, Syria, and the Turkish province of Hatay (**Alexandretta**). Since **France** and Great Britain partitioned historical Syria after **World War I** into four separate territories, there have been various political movements and forces seeking to establish a unified Greater Syrian state. Amir Abdallah, the **Hashemite** ruler of **Transjordan**, hoped to annex Syria, Lebanon, and **Palestine** to his domain. During **World War II**, when it was apparent that the **French Mandate** would soon expire, Abdallah campaigned for the unification of Syria and Transjordan under his throne. The first elected president of Syria, **Shukri al-Quwwatli**, a longtime supporter of

Saudi Arabia's interests, made it clear that Syria would not join on Abdallah's terms, but that Transjordan could become part of the Syrian Republic. The Hashemite ruler's attention was also drawn to Palestine, and his forces occupied portions of that land in the **Palestine War of 1948**. After Abdallah's death in 1951, leadership in the Hashemite family passed to his nephew Abdul-Ilah, the regent of **Iraq** and advocate of the rival **Fertile Crescent Plan** for Iraqi hegemony. The **Syrian Social National Party** founded by **Antun al-Sa`ada** also sought to restore what he considered to be Syria's natural unity.

GREEK CATHOLIC. Former **Greek Orthodox Christians** who since 1724 have converted to the **Catholic** rite. They are also known as Roman Catholics and as Melkites. In the 18th century, Greek Catholics tended to come from the wealthier and better-educated ranks of urban Christians, particularly in **Aleppo** and **Damascus**. In the second half of that century, a number of Greek Catholics, under pressure from the Orthodox, emigrated to coastal towns of **Lebanon** and **Palestine** as well as to **Egypt**, where they became crucial players in that country's growing trade with Europe. Their patriarch of Antioch is currently resident in Damascus. Today Greek Catholics live mostly in Damascus and Aleppo, and they number around 190,000.

GREEK ORTHODOX. The largest **Christian** community in Syria and until 1453 also known as Melkites. The Greek Orthodox church consists of four patriarchates: Constantinople, Alexandria, Jerusalem, and Antioch. Syrian followers are under the see of Antioch, which is mostly Arab. These Christians adhered to the official imperial dogma of the **Byzantine Empire**, and because of their affiliation with the Byzantine church, for centuries a formidable military foe of Muslim dynasties, the Greek Orthodox suffered greater intolerance and suspicion than did other eastern Christians. They did not get along well with the **Crusaders**, who represented Latin Christianity, yet Muslims suspected the Melkites of sympathy with the Frankish invaders.

During the **Ottoman** era, the patriarch of Constantinople reasserted his authority over his Syrian flock, but by the 17th century, the Greek Orthodox of Syria had abandoned the Greek liturgy and adopted Arabic in its stead, setting the stage for friction with the patriarchate between speakers of Greek and Arabic. In the 19th century, they sought the support and protection of the Russian Empire. In the 20th century, Orthodox Arabs have shown a strong propensity for **Arab nationalism**. Antioch was the seat of the patriarch, but in modern Syria his residence is in **Damascus**, and the patriarch has been an Arab since 1899. Greek Orthodox Christians presently number around 800,000 and are concentrated in Damascus, **Latakia**, **Homs**, **Hama**, and villages along the Homs Gap in a region called the Valley of the Christians (*Wadi al-Nasara*).

GYPSIES. In Syria, the most common term for this numerically small, widely dispersed people is "*nawar*." They seem to have migrated to Syria from the east in **Byzantine** times. As in other lands, they keep apart from the rest of the population, which regards them as dishonorable yet clever folk. The gypsies have traditionally provided **musical** entertainment at weddings and celebrations. The participation of gypsy **women** in such activities is lucrative, yet at the same time it reinforces the group's low status. Gypsies also appear at festivals to ply their trade as fortune-tellers, sorcerers, and animal trainers. In contemporary Syria, one may still encounter gypsy encampments in rural areas.

-H-

HAFFAR, LUTFI AL- (1885-1968). A wealthy merchant and prominent nationalist politician who served as minister in several cabinets during the **French Mandate** and early independence periods. His first political association was with **Abd al-Rahman Shahbandar** and the **People's Party** established in 1925. After the suppression of this party, Haffar became a founding member of the **National Bloc** and acquired a reputation for advocating economic nationalism. He was the guiding force behind the construction of the first public **water** system for **Damascus**, completed in 1932, under the auspices of one of Syria's first publicly held companies, the Ayn al-Fija Company. During the brief period of National Bloc rule, 1936 to 1939, Haffar became prime minister in February 1939. His cabinet was buffeted by criticism from radical nationalists for a willingness to compromise with France and by the incipient revolt of **Sulayman al-Murshid** in the northwest. Haffar stepped down after a month in office.

In the independence era, Haffar was elected to parliament and served as minister of the interior from 1943 to 1946. He also participated in founding the **National Party** and briefly served as its chief.

HAFIZ, AMIN AL- (1920-). Strongman of the first Ba'thist regime, from 1963 to 1966. Hafiz was a **Sunni** officer from **Aleppo** who had participated in the February 1954 coup against **Adib al-Shishakli**. During the **United Arab Republic** era, he was posted to Cairo, where members of the **Military Committee** met him and grew to trust him even though he was not a member of the **Ba`th Party**. In December 1961, he was sent to Argentina as military attaché, but following the **March 8, 1963 coup**, he was invited to return to Syria and become minister of the interior, essentially to serve as the front man for the Military Committee. In June Hafiz added the Ministry of Defense to his portfolio, and the following month he became chief of staff and chairman of the **National Revolutionary Command Council**. In November he replaced **Salah al-Din al-Bitar** as prime minister. Following the April 1964 riots in **Hama**, he stepped down as prime minister, but returned to office again in September.

In terms of the Ba`th Party's internal power struggles, Hafiz at first leaned toward neither the original leadership nor the Military Committee, the two main factions that struggled for control. But as power within the party shifted from the old guard to younger, more radical officers, Hafiz sided with the former group. When the Military Committee launched its **February 23, 1966 coup**, it sent a large and well-armed force to his villa in **Damascus** and a pitched battle ensued that ended in 50 deaths and Hafiz's surrender. At first, the **neo-Ba`th** regime imprisoned him, but it later allowed him to leave the country. He initially went to Beirut and then to Baghdad when **Iraqi** Ba`thists seized power in July 1968. Since that time, he has been active in various groups seeking to overthrow the regime in Syria.

HAKIM, HASAN AL- (1886-1988). Nationalist politician during the **French Mandate**, member of the **Iron Hand Society** and the first **People's Party**, and a close associate of **Abd al-Rahman Shahbandar**. The French chose him to be prime minister from September 1941 until April 1942. Hakim was a leading independent pro-**Hashemite** politician in the early years of independence and favored unity with **Iraq**, **Jordan**, and **Lebanon**. He also called for Syria to align itself with the West in the context of the Cold War. In the unstable political climate of **Adib al-Shishakli**'s first two years, governments rose and fell rapidly. With relations between the army and the People's Party deteriorating, Hakim was called upon in August 1951 to form the fifth government in less than two years. The major issue during his brief tenure was whether Syria should participate in a pro-Western Middle Eastern defense organization put forward by Great Britain, **France**, and the **United States** in October. When his foreign minister bluntly attacked the proposal, the pro-Western Hakim could not hold his cabinet together, and he resigned in November.

HAMA. Biblical name is Hamath. This city straddles the banks of the **Orontes River** 54 kilometers north of **Homs** and 150 kilometers south of **Aleppo**. It is in a region of orchards and cereal cultivation, and its proximity to the Syrian desert has made it a market town for **bedouin** throughout history. In medieval times Arab rulers of various dynasties struggled to control the town. It is widely known for its many **norias**, or waterwheels, the greatest of which rises 22 meters above the Orontes to lift water to the city's aqueducts which conduct the **water** to city homes and outlying fields. Hama's population has greatly increased in the 20th century, rising from 60,000 in 1930 to about 315,000 today.

Since the **Ba`th Party** came to power in 1963, Hama has been the center of strong religious opposition because of its special historical relationship with the **Alawi** countryside to its west. A handful of **Sunni** families owned most of the lands of nearby villages and wielded complete economic and political domination over their Alawi inhabitants. The Ba`thist regime promoted secularism and implemented **land reform** that undermined the basis of landlord domination over the countryside, policies that the city's Sunnis perceived as purposefully inflicting sectarian-class vengeance and attacking Islam's preeminence in Syria. There were demonstrations and violent attacks on the regime in April 1964, and in February 1982 the **Muslim Brothers** launched a full-scale revolt against the government of **Hafiz al-Asad**. Government forces killed between 5,000 and 20,000 people and leveled much of the city in two weeks of bitter fighting. The government then rapidly reconstructed the city's devastated portions, but memories of the episode may take many years to fade.

HAMDANID DYNASTY. From its capital in **Aleppo** this dynasty ruled over northern and parts of central Syria between 944 and 1016. The Hamdanids came from **Jazira**, where their ancestral tribe had dwelled since pre-Islamic times. In the early 10th century, the weakness of the **Abbasid caliphate** in Baghdad facilitated the emergence of several regional dynasties, including the Hamdanids in the northern Iraqi city of Mosul. Like other such powers, the Hamdanids began their rise by keeping order on behalf of the Abbasids, fighting **Kharijis**, defending against **Qarmati** raids, and participating in the restoration of Abbasid authority in southern Syria by helping to oust the Tulunids.

The founder of Hamdanid power in northern Syria was Sayf al-Dawla (r. 944-967), younger brother of the Hamdanid ruler in Mosul. In 944, he seized Aleppo and **Homs** from the Ikhshidids. From Aleppo he led Muslim forces against **Byzantine** armies encroaching on northern Syria after a hiatus in conflict on that frontier since early Abbasid times more than a century before. In the course of these campaigns, the Byzantines took the offensive a number of times and occupied portions of northern Syria, including Aleppo in 962 and 969. The Christian power raided as far south as Homs and along much of the Syrian littoral (Antioch fell in 969) as far as Tripoli. The Hamdanids thus became de facto tributaries to the Byzantine Empire. In 1016, the last Hamdanid ruler of Aleppo, little more than a dependent of the Byzantines, fled from **Mirdasid** forces seeking to avenge the murder of their clansmen. In Islamic history, this short-lived dynasty is famed for its rulers' generous patronage, which attracted a brilliant circle of poets, including **al-Mutannabi**, philosophers such as al-Farabi, and scientists.

HANANU, IBRAHIM (1869-1935). Leader of resistance to the establishment of the **French Mandate** in northern Syria. He came from a **Kurdish** landowning family in a rural area near **Aleppo**. In the **Ottoman** era he worked in the provincial administration, yet he participated in the **Arab Revolt** against the Ottomans. When the threat of a French invasion loomed, Hananu organized a militia called the League of National Defense, and in the fall of 1919 he launched a revolt in nearby rural districts. His movement depended on support from Turkish nationalist forces fighting the French for control over southeastern **Turkey**. The revolt crested in late 1920 when large portions of northwest Syria were controlled by Hananu's forces. The tide turned against him, however, in 1921 with the arrival of French reinforcements and the conclusion of the **Franklin-Bouillon Agreement** between Turkey and **France**. Turkish support then vanished, French forces went on the offensive, Hananu fled to **Transjordan**, and the revolt was suppressed.

When he returned to Syria, he became a leader of the **National Bloc**'s radical Aleppan faction. In 1928 Hananu was elected to the constituent assembly and was named chairman of the committee to draft the **constitution**. When France promulgated a constitution that excluded articles strengthening Syrian self-rule, Hananu strenuously opposed all moves to cooperate on the basis of what he considered an illegal document. In particular, he rejected Bloc chief **Jamil Mardam**'s tactic of "honorable cooperation" and engineered Mardam's resignation as prime minister rather than sign a treaty that compromised Syrian unity. Hananu directed the Bloc's Aleppan faction until his death in 1935.

HARIRI, ZIYAD AL- (1930-). General Hariri was a key figure in the **March 8, 1963 coup** that toppled the 18-month **secessionist regime** that followed the **United Arab Republic**. A brother-in-law of **Akram al-Hawrani**, Hariri did not belong to any political party, but he cooperated with **Ba`thist** and Nasirist officers in the coup. His purpose in seizing power was to reestablish the UAR, but the Ba`thist officers were completely against such a move. The Ba`thist **Military Committee** maneuvered to consolidate its power, but the existence of units loyal to Hariri demanded caution in getting rid of the general. An opportunity arose when he traveled to Algeria in June. The Military Committee and Minister of Interior **Amin al-Hafiz** forced about 30 of Hariri's officer allies to retire, so that when he returned, the **National Revolutionary Command Council** was able to remove Hariri as Chief of Staff of the armed forces. On 8 July 1963 Hariri left Syria for exile in **France**.

HASAKA, AL-. Located 500 kilometers east of **Aleppo**, in the heart of **Jazira**. This northeastern town is the seat of the country's largest governorate (population one million) of the same name. Its economic importance lies in livestock, grain cultivation—watered by irrigation from the **Khabur River**—and in **petroleum** production. The city's population is mostly **Kurdish** and **Christian**. The 1994 census counted roughly 120,000 residents.

HASANI, TAJ AL-DIN AL- (1890-1943). A prominent politician of the **French Mandate** era who cooperated with the French and opposed the nationalists. The French rewarded him by appointing him prime minister in 1928 in preparation for elections to a constituent assembly, and he lasted in office until 1932. The French again designated Hasani prime minister in 1934, following the failure of negotiations with the **National Bloc** on terms of a **Franco-Syrian Treaty**. Less than two years later, though, Hasani had to resign during the 1936 **General Strike**, which compelled the French to return nationalists to government. His last moment in the limelight came after the Free French-British invasion during **World War II**. On this occasion, the French appointed him president in October 1941, but he had so little credibility by then that it was difficult for nationalist cabinets to work with him. His fall from office in January 1943 preceded the nationalists' vindication in elections by six months.

HASHEMITES. A family of religious dignitaries originally from Mecca. They rose to prominence in modern Arab history during **World War I** when the Hashemite sharif of Mecca, **Husayn ibn Ali**, launched the **Arab Revolt** against **Ottoman** rule in 1916. His ambition was to establish

Hashemite rule over Arabia, Syria, and **Iraq**. Husayn's son **Faysal** established a short-lived kingdom in Syria between 1918 and 1920, and then set up a monarchy in Iraq that lasted from 1921 until 1958. Abdallah, another of Husayn's sons, established a second Hashemite regime in **Transjordan** that has lasted from 1921 to the present. Abdallah aspired to add Syria to his kingdom throughout the **French Mandate** era. He supported **Sultan al-Atrash**'s 1925 to 1927 revolt, in the course of which he developed strong ties with the **Druzes**, who thereafter tended to favor his ambitions. Among mandate-era **Arab nationalists**, **Abd al-Rahman Shahbandar** led pro-Hashemite forces in Syria. When Syria gained independence, the Hashemite rulers of **Jordan** and Iraq sought to establish their authority over Syria through a variety of unity schemes. **Saudi Arabia** and **Egypt** consistently and successfully opposed these plans. The fall of the Hashemite monarchy in Iraq in July 1958 sharply reduced the family's power as it left Jordan the sole remaining possession. Even though the Hashemites rule a lesser Arab power, their historical rivals in Saudi Arabia regard them warily as possible contenders for influence in Iraq and even the Muslim holy cities of Mecca and Medina.

HAWRAN. The region in southern Syria located between **Jabal Druze** and the **Golan Heights**. Its economy is based on the cultivation of cereals because the area receives a fair amount of annual rainfall and cultivators can exploit abundant springs. The Hawran is a chief source of grain for **Damascus**. Its main town is Dar`a, with a population of about 50,000.

HAWRANI, AKRAM AL- (1914-1996). Populist politician from a prominent **Sunni** family in **Hama**, he initiated Syria's first major peasant movement and played an important role in giving the **Ba`th Party** a popular base. During the **French Mandate**, Hawrani led a local youth movement and tried to coordinate its activities with the **Syrian Social National Party**. In the early 1930s he belonged to the pan-Arab **League of National Action**. In addition to these activities, Hawrani showed a bent for dramatic action, as when he rushed to **Iraq** to back a 1941 anti-British revolt. Two years later he was elected to the Syrian parliament where he opposed the **National Bloc** for its indifference to social and economic issues. At the same time, he began to mobilize peasants around Hama in a movement against big landowners. Hawrani's penchant for direct action gained him further notoriety in 1945 when he and two officers, including future dictator **Adib al-Shishakli**, seized the citadel in Hama from French forces.

In the early independence period, he founded the **Arab Socialist Party**, drifted from the SSNP, and developed ties with young army officers. When the **Palestine War of 1948** erupted, he enlisted with irregular forces that attacked Jewish settlements. In 1949, Hawrani initially helped establish **Husni al-Za`im**'s regime, but moved into opposition when the colonel designated a member of a large landowning family his prime minister. During the **Sami al-Hinnawi** regime, Hawrani served as minister of **agriculture**, but he conspired with Adib al-Shishakli against Hinnawi when it appeared that the elected government might vote for union with **Iraq**, a move he opposed because of his strong republican sentiments. After Shishakli's December 1949 coup, he became minister of defense. He and Shishakli came from Hama and had similar early political tendencies, so for a time Shishakli permitted Hawrani to organize attacks on landowner families in central Syria and to hold an "antifeudal" rally of peasants in **Aleppo**. The two men had a falling out following the colonel's November 1951 abolition of civilian government and Hawrani fled to **Lebanon**. He met with **Michel Aflaq** and **Salah al-Din al-Bitar** in Beirut and they agreed to merge his party with the Ba`th Party, thereby bringing his following among army officers and peasants into the ranks of the Ba`th's supporters. It was in large measure thanks to Hawrani's popular base that the Ba`th Party won 22 seats in the 1954 elections held after Shishakli's overthrow.

As Syrian politics veered left in the next three years, Hawrani's influence increased, partly because of his informal alliance with the independent **Khalid al-Azm** and **Syrian Communist Party** leader **Khalid Bakdash**. By early 1958 Hawrani favored the establishment of the **United Arab Republic** and indeed he joined its cabinet as one of four vice presidents, and in November 1958 became minister of justice. But as Egyptian President Gamal Abd al-Nasir limited the scope of his and other Ba`thists' roles in government, Hawrani became disenchanted with the union experiment, resigned from the government at the end of 1959, and retired to Hama, nursing deep resentment at Egyptian domination of the UAR. He signed a public manifesto in support of the September 1961 **secessionist** coup that ended the UAR. He then successfully ran for a seat in parliament, where he defended the **land reform** legislation passed under the UAR against proposals to soften their impact on large landholders. His bitter public criticism of Nasir and the UAR indicated his growing differences with the Ba`th's leadership, and on 20 June 1962, he formally left the party and revived the Arab Socialist Party. He had no links with the Ba`thist regimes that have ruled Syria since 1963, spending the rest of his life outside the country. He died in Jordan in 1996.

HAWWA, SA`ID AL- (1935-1989). The foremost ideologue in the moderate wing of the **Muslim Brothers** during the 1960s and 1970s. He grew up in a petty merchant family of **Hama** in modest circumstances and inherited a disposition to political activism from his father, who had supported **Akram al-Hawrani's Arab Socialist Party** in the 1950s. At secondary school, a charismatic teacher attracted Hawwa to his religious circle at the city's primary mosque and persuaded him to join the Muslim Brothers at age 18. Hawwa enrolled at the Islamic Law Faculty at Damascus University, where he met Muslim Brother leader **Mustafa al-Siba`i**. During the 1964 protests in Hama, Hawwa supported the commercial strike but broke with the Brothers' militant wing, which was bent on a violent course of action that led to the government's crushing of the protest. In 1966, government pressure compelled him to move to **Saudi Arabia**, where he wrote the books that made him a leading Islamist ideologue. When he returned to Syria in 1971, his efforts to reconcile the militant and moderate factions of the Muslim Brothers did not bear fruit. He went to prison in 1973 for his role in organizing protests against the 1973 **constitution** over the inclusion of an article stipulating that the head of state be Muslim. Hawwa spent his five years' incarceration writing on **sufism** and the Qur'an. He left the country for **Jordan** shortly after his release in January 1978 and played no role in the bloody confrontation between Islamists and the regime that lasted from 1979 to 1982. From his exile, he continued to write and speak on behalf of the Syrian Muslim Brothers until his death.

Hawwa's writings express a strong desire to unify the diverse strands of religious sentiment that ranged from the political quiescence and piety of sufi orders to militant Islamists espousing the radical views of the Egyptian ideologue Sayyid Qutb, whose views on Muslim history and society he considered wrongheaded. In the period of intense polarization between the secularizing **Ba`thist** regime and its religious foes, Hawwa's call for a patient, protracted campaign to construct a broad Islamic coalition had little impact.

HAYDAR HAYDAR (1936-). One of the country's leading authors of novels and short stories, from a small town near **Tartus**. He spent a number of years working as a teacher in Algeria and **Lebanon** before returning to Syria in the 1980s. His prolific output addresses social and political frustrations confronting not only Syrians but Arabs more generally. Thus, the settings in Haydar's works include Syrian villages but also the marshes of **Iraq** and the streets of Algiers. In spring 2000, one of his novels, *Banquet for Seaweed*, first published in 1983, appeared in a new edition in **Egypt**. Even though this long, complex novel's central theme is the failure of communist and nationalist movements in the Arab world, an Islamist pundit in Cairo created a sharp controversy by twisting the meaning of one sentence in the novel to accuse government officials of promoting blasphemy. In Egypt the affair triggered student demonstrations and a series of legal and political confrontations but it barely registered in Syria, where the secular regime had ruthlessly tamed Islamist activism since the early 1980s. *See also* LITERATURE.

HEALTH. The earliest public endeavors to support medical care in Syria occurred in medieval times under the **Zangid** rulers, who constructed hospitals, or **bimaristans**, in **Damascus** and **Aleppo**. Literary and **archaeological** records are insufficient for reconstructing more than a sketchy history of health care before the 20th century.

One of the measures of national economic development in modern times is the improvement of sanitary conditions, medical care, and public health. Local health departments were formed under the auspices of **French Mandate** authorities in the 1920s. Their initial efforts sought to reduce the incidence of malaria, introduce better hygiene to public eating places, and deliver safe drinking **water**. The period of French rule saw an increase in the number of hospitals, clinics, and medical doctors.

At independence in 1946, medical facilities were fairly limited. The country had 35 hospitals and around 1,700 beds for a population of 3.5 million. Residents of major towns had access to hospital care, but the northeastern region had only two hospitals serving a vast area. Improving medical services would require construction of hospitals in underserved regions and training of physicians and nurses. Government policy has supported these objectives under different regimes by devoting resources to **education** and sometimes requiring recent graduates of medical school to begin their practices in villages and small towns. With respect to general health conditions, endemic diseases included malaria and tuberculosis among the adult population and diarrhea among small children. Government programs to improve health during the early years of independence included spraying against mosquitoes, public education, and developing sanitary drinking water supplies.

One of the hallmarks of the **Ba'th Party** regimes since the early 1960s has been a concerted effort to address endemic diseases and improve public health and sanitation. The result as measured in gross statistics has been a substantial improvement in health conditions for Syrian citizens. By the early 1970s, malaria and tuberculosis were largely contained, and nearly two-thirds of urban Syrians and one-half of rural Syrians had access to clean drinking water. Unlike wealthier, oil-producing Arab countries, Syria has not created a national health insurance system, but workers in the public sector and government offices do benefit from coverage.

Overall, health care has shown marked improvement in recent decades. The mortality rate for children fell from 201 per thousand in 1960 to 25 per thousand in 2003: the mortality rate for infants per thousand also declined, from 136 in 1960 to 27 in 1997. Average life expectancy in 2001 approached 71 years, 69 for men and 73 for **women**, up from just 56 years in 1970. These improvements are related not only to government health programs, such as an effective campaign to immunize against childhood diseases, but also to better nutrition made possible by subsidies for basic needs. In 2000, 80 percent of the population was connected to treated water, but the difference between urban and rural rates is substantial: 95 percent in cities and just 65 percent in rural areas. A series of measures reduced the incidence of malaria and tuberculosis and eliminated smallpox altogether. As for HIV/AIDS, the World Health Organization reports a fairly low level of incidence and a growing program of testing for the virus. Access to medical care remains unevenly distributed. The national rate of 144 doctors per 100,000 does not reflect disparities between the ready availability of general practitioners, specialists, and hospital beds in cities and their persistent scarcity in the countryside. Even though a succession of governments since 1951 has discouraged newly licensed physicians from setting up practice in major cities, rural Syrians have much less access to health care compared to their urban brethren.

HINDAWI AFFAIR. Nizar Hindawi was a young **Jordanian** recruited by one of the Syrian **security forces** to plant a bomb on an **Israeli** civilian aircraft at London's Heathrow Airport on 17 April 1986. An Israeli security guard discovered the explosive in a false bottom of a piece of luggage carried by Hindawi's girlfriend (who was by all accounts unaware of the bag's contents). In his confession to British authorities, Hindawi directly implicated the head of Syrian air force intelligence and employees of Syria's national airline. Hindawi recanted at his trial in October, but a jury found him guilty and sentenced him to a 45-year jail term. At the announcement of the verdict, Britain formally cut relations with Syria. The **United States** and Canada withdrew their ambassadors, while the European Community imposed political and economic sanctions. For several months Syria endured its worst diplomatic isolation since the **neo-**

Ba`th regime of the 1960s. President **Hafiz al-Asad** managed to crack the diplomatic quarantine when he closed down the offices of the notorious Abu Nidal **terrorist** group in June 1987. The following month, the European Community withdrew its sanctions. Relations with the United States also improved, but Britain did not restore ties until November 1990, after Syria joined the anti-**Iraq** coalition in Desert Shield.

HINNAWI, SAMI AL- (1898-1950). Leader of Syria's second military coup of 1949. Born in **Aleppo**, Hinnawi joined the **Troupes Spéciales** in 1927. He overthrew and executed **Husni al-Za`im** on 14 August. Unlike his predecessor, Hinnawi immediately designated a civilian government headed by **Hashim al-Atasi** and crowded with members of the Aleppo-based, pro-**Hashemite People's Party** such as **Nazim al-Qudsi**. He also appointed to the cabinet such leftist politicians as **Akram al-Hawrani** and **Ba`th Party** leader **Michel Aflaq**. Colonel Hinnawi handed the civilian government the task of conducting national elections to a constituent assembly. Elections for 114 seats were held on 15 November 1949, and the People's Party won 45 seats, while 40 seats went to independents; the Ba`th Party won just one seat in **Dayr al-Zur**. Supporters of union with **Iraq**, backed by Hinnawi, hoped that the constituent assembly would fashion a document to facilitate such a union. Opponents of union feared just that prospect. Hinnawi was deposed on 19 December by anti-Hashemite officers led by Colonel **Adib al-Shishakli**, imprisoned until September 1950, and assassinated in Beirut on 31 October by a cousin of former prime minister Muhsin al-Barazi, who had been executed on Hinnawi's orders a year earlier.

HISN AL-AKRAD. Also known by its French name Crac des Chevaliers, this is the best-preserved castle from the era of the **Crusades**. It is situated at the southern end of **Jabal Ansariyya** and dominates the Homs Gap between Tripoli and **Tartus** on the Mediterranean and **Homs**. The castle covers an area of 2.5 hectares and stands 300 meters above the surrounding Buqay`a plain. It had been the site of a fortress since ancient times, and in the 11th century the **Mirdasid** dynasty of **Aleppo** settled **Kurdish** troops there, hence the Arabic name "Fortress of the Kurds."

In 1099, Raymond of St.-Gilles briefly occupied Hisn al-Akrad, and it was taken over by Tancred of Antioch in 1110. The Crusaders incorporated it into a network of fortresses designed to defend against Muslim attack that might strike at the County of Tripoli from the northeast. The knights used flares and signals to communicate with nearby castles. In

1142, the Order of the Hospitallers took control of Hisn al-Akrad. **Saladin**'s attempt to seize it in 1188 was repulsed. A series of earthquakes at the turn of the 13th century damaged the castle, and the present structure dates from repairs and enlargements constructed after those tremors. The Crusader knights resisted several Muslim attempts to expel them in the early 13th century. The **Mamluk** Sultan **Baybars** laid siege in late 1270 and overwhelmed the defenders in April 1271.

HIZBALLAH. In the early days of the **Lebanese War of 1982**, Syria facilitated the establishment of this Lebanese **Shi`i** organization, whose name means "Party of God." Funds, arms, and ideological inspiration for Hizballah have come primarily from **Iran**'s Islamic Republic, but the Syrian government has played an essential role in facilitating contacts between the group and Iran by keeping open the route from **Lebanon** to **Damascus**. In the 1980s, Hizballah played a central role in Syria's struggle against the efforts of **Israel** and the **United States** to create a pro-Western regime in Lebanon. The organization carried out suicide bomb attacks, guerrilla strikes against Israeli forces, and kidnappings of Westerners. Hizballah never admitted to holding Western hostages, but hostages themselves testified upon their release that their captors were cells of the organization.

With the termination of the **Lebanese Civil War** in 1991, Hizballah entered the political scene by contesting elections to the Chamber of Deputies, and in the 2003 Chamber it had 11 deputies (out of 128 total). The turn to legal political activities did not, however, spell the end of the group's violent facet. It continued to spearhead armed resistance to Israeli occupation in southern Lebanon until Israel withdrew in May 2000. Many Lebanese who generally have little sympathy for Hizballah's religious zeal and populist message credited the organization with causing Israel to abandon Lebanon by steadily inflicting casualties on its troops.

Syria has benefited from Hizballah's activities even though its **Islamic fundamentalist** ideology is at odds with the **Ba`th Party** regime's secular policies. The alliance of mutual convenience has outlasted the struggle to oust Israel from Lebanon. Presently, both Hizballah and the Syrian government maintain that Israel continues to occupy a small slice of Lebanese territory called Shab`a Farm, and Hizballah has attacked Israeli forces there from time to time. For its part, Israel claims that this piece of land is Syrian territory it conquered in the **June 1967 War**, and the **United Nations** has supported the Israeli position with old maps of the Lebanese-Syrian boundary clearly demonstrating the location of Shab`a Farm in Syria. Hizballah, however, has a stake in low-level conflict to boost its credentials as a patriotic movement against an external enemy. Moreover, leaders and members possess a zealous commitment to continuing their fight against Israel as an Islamic cause. Syria supports Hizballah because it wishes to make Israel uncomfortable with the status quo and exert pressure on Israel to withdraw from the **Golan Heights**. Support for Hizballah, however, causes problems for Syrian relations with the United States, which considers it a **terrorist** organization responsible for killing civilians in Lebanon and South America. It is likely that as long as the Syrian-Israeli stalemate over the Golan Heights continues, Hizballah will remain a factor in Lebanon.

HOLIDAYS. Syria officially observes patriotic and traditional religious—Muslim and **Christian**—holidays. The patriotic holidays are Evacuation Day on 17 April to celebrate the end of **French** rule in 1946, Revolution Day on 8 March to observe the occasion of the ruling **Ba`th Party**'s rise to power, and October Liberation War Day on 6 October to observe the **October 1973 War**. There are two extended, three-day official Muslim holidays for the Ramadan Feast (*Id al-Fitr*) and the Feast of the Sacrifice (*Id al-Adha*) at the end of the Meccan pilgrimage rites. In addition, Syrians observe the Prophet's birthday (*mawlid al-nabi*) and the Muslim New Year. Christians publicly celebrate **Catholic** and Orthodox Christmas and Easter. The country also closes government offices on New Year's Day.

HOMS. *Hims* in Arabic, *Emesa* in Latin; a central Syrian city on the eastern bank of the **Orontes River**. Several factors make Homs the major city on the route between **Damascus** and **Aleppo**. It is at the eastern end of the Homs Gap, a pass between **Jabal Ansariyya** and the Lebanon Mountains that leads from Tripoli to the Syrian interior. Because of the Gap, the area around Homs receives much more rainfall than interior regions to its north and south. Thus, the city lies at the center of a cultivated region (crops include wheat, barley, lentils, cotton, sugar beets, vines), as well as serving as a point of exchange between the sedentary zone and the desert. Moreover, because of easy access to the Mediterranean Sea, Homs has attracted overland **trade** from the Persian Gulf, just as in recent history an oil pipeline from northern **Iraq** passed through Homs on its way to Tripoli and **Baniyas**. Syria's major oil refinery is in Homs. Furthermore, Homs is roughly halfway between Aleppo and Damascus, so it participates in trade with and between these centers.

Homs may have been founded by the Seleucids. During Roman times, the city contributed two emperors, Marcus Aurelius Antoninus and his successor Alexander Severus. **Umayyad** rulers based in Damascus used Homs to launch military campaigns against the **Byzantines**, but with the rise of the **Abbasids** and the shift of imperial power to Baghdad, Homs declined in status. The city suffered several Byzantine occupations and much destruction in the late 10th century. During the era of the **Crusades**, the **atabegs** and **Ayyubids** turned Homs into a major staging point for campaigns against the Franks. In modern times, the city's population has grown from 50,000 in 1912 to about 640,000 today. It is one of several important provincial centers of **industrial** production.

HOMS, BATTLE OF. In 1281, the **Mongols** launched their largest and best-planned invasion of **Mamluk**-ruled Syria. A Mongol force of 80,000 engaged a Mamluk army of unknown size just outside of **Homs**. From Muslim chronicles it appears that the Mamluks were on the verge of defeat when their field commander cleverly devised a ruse to allow his forces to outmaneuver the Mongols and attack their main force from the rear, thereby turning the battle into a rout. While this was not the last Mongol incursion into Syria, it was in certain respects the most decisive one in that the Mamluks demonstrated their ability to defeat a large, well-organized Mongol offensive. Thus, the Battle of Homs contributed to the legitimacy of Mamluk rule in Syria at the beginning of its third decade.

HUMAN RIGHTS. Except for a few brief periods of civilian democratic rule, independent Syria has a terrible record of human rights abuses. Since 1963, the **Ba`th Party** regime has forged a formidable framework of emergency laws, decrees, and regulations that deny freedoms of expression and association and citizens' rights to fair trials and humane conditions of incarceration. The regime has also developed an elaborate set of **security forces** to intimidate and harass citizens who dare to question its policies. Observers of Syrian politics consider the human rights nightmare a barometer of the regime's lack of legitimacy and fragility. Whatever the cause, the high degree of surveillance and the suppression of dissent suggest a fear that without ceaseless vigilance, the regime's enemies would topple it.

The human rights situation hit its nadir during the political disturbances of the late 1970s and early 1980s. The two most infamous events from that period were the June 1980 massacre of approximately 500 political prisoners at the Tadmor (**Palmyra**) military prison after an unsuccessful attempt to assassinate President **Hafiz al-Asad**, and the February 1982 killing of thousands of civilians in **Hama** when government forces recaptured the city from Islamist insurgents. The early 1980s probably represented the high point in sweeping arbitrary arrests, detention without trial, and summary proceedings against suspected political activists. Documented accounts of torture of political prisoners are numerous and include many instances of permanent disability and death from torture. The largest number of prisoners are members of different Islamist groups and communist parties.

During the 1990s, the government declared amnesties for hundreds of political prisoners. For example, in March 1995, between 500 and 600 political prisoners were released. Many Syrians hoped that when **Bashar al-Asad** became president in July 2000 he would improve the human rights situation, and in the first months of his presidency, several reform associations mobilized to press for the lifting of the emergency law and respect for human rights. These groups include the Committees for the Defense of Democratic Freedoms and Human Rights in Syria and several associations to promote **civil society**. In November 2000, Bashar al-Asad granted amnesty to around 600 political prisoners to mark the 30th anniversary of the 1970 **Corrective Movement**. Any hopes that the new president would steer the country to a more liberal path were dashed in August-September 2001, when he promulgated a new draconian decree that reinforced and extended government powers to punish the expression of views deemed harmful to the state, the **armed forces**, and national unity. At the same time, the government unleashed a campaign to muzzle calls for reform by arresting leaders, including members of the People's Assembly. International criticism from the **United Nations** Human Rights Committee, Amnesty International, and Human Rights Watch apparently had no effect on the regime, which insisted that it was protecting its citizens from misguided individuals and malicious plots.

HUSAYN IBN ALI, SHARIF (c. 1853-1931). Chief religious dignitary of Mecca who organized the 1916 **Arab Revolt** against the **Ottoman Empire** and head of the **Hashemite** clan in the early 20th century. "Sharif" was the title of the local *amirs*, or princes, who claimed descent from the Prophet Muhammad and shared power with the Ottoman governor. Their primary responsibility was to act as custodians of the Meccan shrine and ensure the proper conduct of the pilgrimage. Husayn became the sharif of Mecca in November 1908, at the same time that Istanbul was seeking to establish firmer control over the empire's provinces. For his part, Sharif Husayn strove to balance Mecca's traditional autonomy with support for the Ottomans against rebellions in western Arabia. His ambition to secure his status in the holy city eventually blossomed into a plan for an Arab kingdom independent of the Ottoman Empire.

In February 1914, he had his son Abdallah contact British officials in Cairo to seek their support in case the Ottomans should try to remove him. Later that year, the Ottomans entered **World War I** against Great Britain, and Husayn explored further the possibility of British support for his position as an independent Arab ruler. There ensued a series of exchanges known as the **Husayn-McMahon Correspondence** that laid the foundation for the Arab Revolt. The sharif hoped to establish an Arab kingdom over Arabia, Syria, and **Iraq**. By the end of the war he realized his ambition of becoming king of Hijaz, western Arabia including the holy cities of Mecca and Medina, and his son **Faysal** established a short-lived government in Syria. But the French drove Faysal out of Syria in 1920, and four years later the rising Saudi state of central Arabia drove Husayn out of his kingdom. He died in Amman, **Transjordan**, in 1931.

HUSAYN-MCMAHON CORRESPONDENCE. A series of letters exchanged between Sharif **Husayn ibn Ali** and Sir Henry McMahon, British High Commissioner in **Egypt**, between July 1915 and March 1916. In this exchange, Husayn sought a British commitment to support the creation of an independent Arab kingdom that would encompass the **Ottoman** Arab provinces east of Egypt. The British wanted Husayn to launch an **Arab Revolt** that would sap Ottoman power (Britain and the Ottoman Empire were **World War I** adversaries) and dilute Muslim sympathy for the empire's war efforts.

The correspondents failed to agree on the extent of the proposed Arab kingdom because Britain had to consider its ally **France**'s ambition to establish a sphere of influence over Syria. As a result, McMahon explicitly excluded coastal Syria, the districts west of **Aleppo**, **Hama**, **Homs**, and **Damascus**, roughly from **Alexandretta** to Beirut. Nonetheless, Sharif Husayn proceeded to launch the Arab Revolt in June 1916. After the war, the British acquiesced to France's demand to control all of Syria, an act that Arabs have always considered to be a violation of Britain's pledges in the Husayn-McMahon correspondence to support an independent Arab kingdom. *See also* HASHEMITES; SYKES-PICOT AGREEMENT.

-I-

IBN ABI USAYBI`A (after 1194-1270). During the height of medical scholarship in medieval Syria, the Nuri **bimaristan** (hospital) in **Damas-**

cus boasted a number of outstanding physician-scholars. Muwaffaq al-Din ibn Abi Usaybi`a wrote medical works on subjects like bonesetting, but his significance for historians rests in a work on the lives of nearly 400 physicians and scholars. After studies under his father and other scholars, he worked at hospitals in Damascus and Cairo before joining the court of an **Ayyubid** prince at Salkhad in **Jabal Druze.**

IBN TAYMIYYA, TAQI AL-DIN AHMAD (1263-1328). A renowned religious scholar whose intellectual influence resonates in the 20th-century Muslim world. He was born in Harran (in present-day **Turkey**), but his family had to flee in 1269 because of the **Mongol** threat, and they settled in **Mamluk Damascus,** where Ibn Taymiyya spent most of his life. He entered into many religious controversies and gained a popular following for his exhortations to participate in jihad against the Mongols and the Twelver **Shi`is** in **Lebanon.** On a number of occasions, rival **ulama** incited the Mamluk authorities against him, and he endured several periods of imprisonment in Cairo and Damascus. In fact, he died a prisoner in the citadel of Damascus.

Ibn Taymiyya wrote prolifically in several fields of Islamic scholarship, particularly theology, law, doctrine, and heresiography. The modern revival of his teachings stems at least in part from the **Wahhabi** movement's adoption of his views in the 18th century, then the **salafiyya** movement's propagation of them. Today his works are widely popular throughout the Arab world among **Islamic fundamentalist** groups.

IBRAHIM PASHA (1789-1848). Leader of Egyptian forces that invaded and occupied Syria from 1831 to 1832. His previous military achievements included the subjugation of rebels in Upper **Egypt** to the rule of his father, **Muhammad Ali,** and the quelling of anti-**Ottoman** revolts in Arabia and Greece. He commanded Egyptian forces invading **Palestine** in November 1831 and took **Damascus** on 2 June 1832. The following month his troops routed Ottoman forces at a battle near **Homs.** Soon after that, all of Syria was under Egyptian rule and the Ottomans formally recognized Muhammad Ali's authority in May 1833 in return for annual tribute.

The powerful Egyptian army, modeled on early 19th-century European armies, brought a higher degree of security and order to the Syrian countryside, particularly in curbing the **bedouin.** The Egyptian occupation also improved the status of Syrian **Christians,** included their representatives in local consultative councils, and even designated Christians to head the councils in Damascus and **Aleppo.** Such measures fostered a climate more favorable to **trade** with Europe, and in 1833 Ibrahim allowed the establishment of a British consulate in Damascus. The Egyptian regime also encouraged economic growth by introducing new crops, extending the margins of cultivation, and providing assistance to peasants. Furthermore, Ibrahim promoted **education** by creating primary and secondary schools, setting up military colleges in Damascus, Aleppo, and Antioch, and allowing more mission schools.

In general, Ibrahim Pasha tried to reproduce in Syria the strong central authority his father had imposed on Egypt. This entailed the reorganization and centralization of administration, regular taxation, conscription, and disarming the population. The imposition of a head tax galled Muslims, who considered such a tax equivalent to the traditional levy on Christians and **Jews**. Uprisings against these measures erupted among **Druze** in the south and **Alawis** in the northwest. Discontent among **Sunni** townsmen swirled around the Egyptians' favorable treatment of Christians. Finally, all Syrians resented heavy new taxes to pay for a large army of occupation. Encouraged by local revolts, the Ottomans resumed war against Ibrahim Pasha in June 1839, but he defeated them yet again. This time, however, an alliance of European powers intervened to compel Ibrahim to evacuate Syria. In return, the Ottomans offered to designate Muhammad Ali the hereditary governor of Egypt. Ibrahim Pasha personally led the Egyptian withdrawal in the closing days of 1840, and Ottoman rule was restored to Syria.

IMAM. An Arabic term for the leader of Muslim congregational prayer, it also has special connotations for **Shi`i** Muslims. In their usage, the imam is the legitimate spiritual and political head of the Muslim community. They regard **Ali ibn Abi Talib** as the first imam and his male descendants as successors to that status. In the first three Islamic centuries, Shi`is disagreed on the identity of the imam, particularly following the death of the sixth imam, Ja`far al-Sadiq. From these differences arose a variety of Shi`i sects, including the Twelvers, **Isma`ilis**, **Nizaris**, and **Qarmatis**, as well as offshoots of Shi`ism such as the **Druzes** and the **Alawis**.

INDUSTRY. In medieval times, Syrian manufactures acquired broad fame for their high quality craftsmanship and technical ingenuity. **Damascus** steel was prized for swords and armor, and weavers spun fine blends of cotton and silk for the urban elite. For centuries, the major industry consisted of cotton, wool, and silk textiles manufactured in **Aleppo**, **Damascus**, **Homs**, and **Hama**. Artisans manufactured both luxury cloths and ordinary textiles for use as clothing and household furnishings. Metal, glass, and leather products were also important in traditional industry. Modern industry appeared in the late 1920s in the fields of cement, textiles, and food processing. Forty years later, Syrian industry was still concentrated in textiles, processed foods, soap, matches, glass, and cement.

The heyday of private industry abruptly ended under the **United Arab Republic** in July 1961, when Gamal Abd al-Nasir issued the sweeping **Socialist Decrees** nationalizing **banks**, insurance companies, and large industrial firms. Altogether, nearly 80 firms were affected. The **secessionist** cabinet of **Ma`ruf al-Dawalibi** rescinded the measures the following year, but the **Ba`th Party** regime settled the fate of private industry for at least a generation with a series of measures in 1965 that nationalized wholly and in part more than 100 businesses.

Private investment in industry gained new breathing space in the 1970s under **Hafiz al-Asad**'s regime, which allowed foreign participation in large ventures and increased public investment in industrial development. Consequently, during the 1970s, industry grew fairly rapidly at around 13 percent per year. New industrial enterprises in the 1980s included oil refineries, and factories producing fertilizer, cement, and paper. In the field of food processing, new investment in sugar refineries led to higher output. To the older cement factories in Aleppo and Hama, Syria added two new ones in **Tartus** and Adra around 1980, allowing a doubling of production. Phosphate deposits are present in the desert near **Palmyra**, and a phosphate fertilizer plant was built near Homs to exploit this resource. Phosphate plants in the Homs region produce fertilizer for domestic consumption and export. An indication of the growing importance of industry is the increase in its share of the **labor force** from 20 percent in 1965 to 30 percent in 1990.

State control of large industry was supposed to rationalize the allocation of scarce capital and resources in order to maximize productivity and achieve optimal distribution of benefits among producers and consumers. Instead, **public sector** companies operated according to political rather than economic criteria and have failed to contribute much to the country's economic development. One positive result has been the dispersal of manufacturing centers among several regions rather than their concentration in one or two cities. Thus, the medium-sized town of Hama is the center of iron, cement, and textile production. Homs is the site of fertilizer manufacturers that exploit phosphates mined near Palmyra. The newest and largest oil refinery is at the coastal town of **Baniyas**.

INFLATION. In the last 40 years, the Syrian **economy** has been buffeted by periods of high inflation. While analysts question the accuracy of official statistics, it is possible to describe in broad strokes the main patterns of price fluctuations. During the 1960s, **Ba`th Party** regimes established government control over large portions of the economy and that had the effect of triggering a massive flight of private capital out of the country. In spite of these disruptions, it is estimated that inflation averaged around 3 percent per year. The mid-1970s were a time of sharp inflation with annual rates in the range of 20 percent per year. This spike was caused by several factors, including global inflation pursuant to the rise in **energy** costs and local events like the arrival of 400,000 refugees fleeing the **Lebanese Civil War**. The government attempted to mitigate the effects of inflation on poor Syrians by controlling prices on select items.

The 1980s were a decade of stubbornly high inflation, usually between 15 and 20 percent per year. Price increases were especially burdensome on **public sector** employees and civil servants, whose wage increases trailed the inflation rate. A combination of austerity measures and very slow economic growth in the late 1990s finally brought inflation down from 16 percent in 1993 to about 1 percent in 2000. *See also* CURRENCY.

INTERNET. Until 1997, the Internet was banned because of the **Ba`th Party** regime's desire to control the flow of information in and out of Syria. Initially, the government permitted **public sector** companies and ministries and then a few private businesses to use the Internet through a single portal operated by the public sector Syrian Telecommunications Establishment.

Not long after becoming president in July 2000, **Bashar al-Asad** pushed the door open a bit wider by allowing some Internet cafes to operate, but Syrians could still not access it from their homes. Before succeeding his father, Bashar had headed the Syria Computer Society, a sign of his interest in technological advancement. He wanted to move quickly to increase Internet connections from just 7,000 at universities and hotels to 200,000 in one year, but by the end of 2001, there were probably only around 30,000 connections and still a single provider. The authorities fear the Internet's potential for political subversion, so it is not surprising that the regime routinely blocks sites and tries to keep tabs on e-mail. Personal computers are still fairly rare, only about 15 per 1,000 people in 2000.

IRAN. Relations with Iran were of secondary importance to both countries during Syria's first few decades of independence. Mohammed Reza Shah (r. 1941-1979) adopted a decidedly pro-Western **foreign policy** that included warm ties with the **United States** and official relations with **Israel**, to which he sold **petroleum**. Bilateral relations assumed greater importance after the 1978-1979 Iranian revolution brought to power an Islamic regime opposed to American influence in the Middle East and avowedly hostile to Israel.

When **Iraq** invaded Iran in September 1980, Syria took the side of non-Arab Iran against the rival **Ba`th Party** regime of Baghdad. President **Hafiz al-Asad**'s policy isolated Syria in the Arab world, but it brought tangible benefits, primarily preferential deals for Iranian oil imports. Observers pointed out the ostensible anomaly of a close relationship between the Islamic Republic of Iran, avowedly dedicated to spreading Islamic revolution, and Ba`thist Syria, a secular regime combating an **Islamic fundamentalist** led by the **Muslim Brothers**. In fact, a delegation of Syrian Muslim Brothers visited Tehran and met with Ayatollah Ruhollah Khomeini, requesting that he support their struggle to overthrow Asad's regime. But despite the Islamic Republic's greater ideological affinity with the Muslim Brothers than with the **Ba`th Party**, Khomeini maintained a pragmatic foreign policy toward Syria, and the Muslim Brothers were left to draw the conclusion that they were victims of a **Shi`i** plot.

The **Lebanese War of 1982** further strengthened Syrian-Iranian relations. During the war, Syria permitted Iranian Revolutionary Guards to establish bases in the Bekaa Valley and to organize Lebanese Shi`is into the **Hizballah** organization, which became a potent force in **Lebanon**'s politics and its military struggle against the Israeli occupation of southern Lebanon. There was a certain irony in Syria's facilitating the establishment of an Islamic party in Lebanon at the same time the regime was battling Islamic fundamentalists at home, but Asad calculated that he could keep the two spheres separate. Hizballah's anti-Western actions suited Asad's strategy in Lebanon during the 1980s when he confronted an Israeli-American bid to exclude Syria from Lebanon's political recovery. Since Israel and the United States abandoned their ambitions, friction between Syria and Hizballah has intermittently strained Syria's relations with Iran. Hizballah is financially dependent on Iran, and Iran's access to Lebanon is dependent on Syria, so ultimately Syria holds the keys to Hizballah's fortunes.

The cooperative relationship between Iran and Syria persisted during the 1990s in spite of strains over Syria's pursuit of a diplomatic settlement with Israel while Iran hewed to a militant line. A related sore point was the Asad regime's occasional attempts to press Hizballah to limit attacks on Israeli forces in southern Lebanon when those threatened to disrupt the

Syrian-Israeli peace talks. A second area of some difficulty for Tehran and Damascus was Iran's dispute with the United Arab Emirates over three small islands in the Persian Gulf that Iran had occupied in the 1970s. Syria signed joint Arab statements demanding the return of the islands to UAE sovereignty. The Syrians and Iranians, however, did not allow these secondary policy disagreements to shake their warm relations based on more crucial interests. Thus, Hafiz al-Asad was the first foreign leader to visit Muhammad Khatami when he was elected president of Iran in 1997, and Khatami in turn traveled to **Damascus** in 1999 to shore up bilateral relations and cooperation on Hizballah's military resistance against Israel in Lebanon.

IRAQ. During the first decade of Syria's independence, Iraq's **Hashemite** rulers sought to establish dominance in the Arab East by drawing Syria into their orbit through the **Fertile Crescent Plan**. Iraqi leaders courted Syrian politicians, in particular the pro-Iraqi **People's Party**, and provided them with funds to boost their status in the Syrian political arena. Iraqi intrigue contributed to the downfalls of **Husni al-Za`im** and **Adib al-Shishakli**, but pro-Iraqi politicians were never able to bring about unity between the two countries. **France, Egypt**, and **Saudi Arabia** all opposed such a union, while Great Britain was cool to the notion.

In the fall of 1963, the **Ba`th Party** regimes in Iraq and Syria proposed a union of the two countries, but this initiative proved abortive because on 18 November a military coup removed the Ba`th from power in Iraq. Five years later, the Ba`th Party again seized power in Iraq, but the Iraqi Ba`th represented the faction that was loyal to **Michel Aflaq**, which had been violently driven from power in Syria by the **February 23, 1966 coup**. Thus two hostile factions of the same party inherited the pattern of troubled relations between Damascus and Baghdad. Notwithstanding ideological and personal animosities between the two regimes, during the **October 1973 War** Iraq sent two armored divisions and infantry units to support Syrian troops fighting **Israel** in the **Golan Heights**. But when Syria agreed to a cease-fire, the Iraqis withdrew their forces to indicate their disapproval. Relations deteriorated again in 1975 in a dispute over **Euphrates River water**, then briefly improved when Egypt made peace with Israel three years later. There were even new moves toward unity in late 1978 and early 1979, but they halted following the rise to power of Saddam Husayn in Baghdad in July 1979 and his accusation that Syria was plotting to subvert the government.

In September 1980, Iraq invaded **Iran** in a bid to overthrow the newly established Islamic Republic that Baghdad's leaders accused of subversion. Syria immediately criticized Iraq for diverting Arab resources from the confrontation with Israel, and in retaliation Iraq severed relations. April 1982 saw the final steps on the road to a break between Damascus and Baghdad: Syria closed the border, then shut down the **Iraqi-Syrian pipeline**, and finally severed diplomatic relations on 18 April. When Iraq emerged victorious at war's end in July 1988, Saddam Husayn sought to punish **Hafiz al-Asad** for supporting Iran by sending arms to General Michel Aoun, who at the time was seeking to expel Syria from **Lebanon**.

After Iraq invaded Kuwait in August 1990, Asad struck back at Saddam by siding with the **United States** and its Arab coalition partners, who invited Western intervention to expel the Iraqis. In September, Syria sent 20,000 troops to Saudi Arabia, ostensibly to defend the kingdom against Iraqi attack. These troops did not participate in the assault on Iraq, but for a time it appeared that the Iraqi threat would lead to a permanent joint force of Syrian and Egyptian troops to defend the Gulf Arab states. The Saudis and Kuwaitis, however, decided against a permanent Arab military presence and sent the Syrian soldiers home.

One of the more notable shifts in Syrian **foreign policy** in the late 1990s was the rapprochement with Iraq. The first crack in the wall of hostility came in early 1996 when low-level government officials met to discuss their common frustration with **Turkey**'s reduction of the Euphrates River's flow into their countries. In 1997, the **United Nations** modified sanctions on Saddam Husayn's regime by instituting an "oil for food" program, and Syria renewed trade ties. Moreover, Asad felt that he needed added leverage against the new Israel-Turkey axis sealed by a formal military pact. Iraq wished to break out of the isolation it endured for failing to implement United Nations resolutions passed at the end of the Gulf War. Therefore, the rival Ba'thist regimes exchanged diplomatic missions and permitted the resumption of **trade** across their borders. Syrian vendors gained access to Iraqi markets for food and medical supplies, Iraqi exports arrived at **Tartus** and **Latakia**, and the pipeline from Kirkuk to **Baniyas**, closed since 1982, was reopened. The thaw in relations went further than signing formal commercial agreements. Syria made important political gestures like shutting down radio broadcasts by Iraqi dissidents and airing frequent criticism of American air attacks on Iraqi military targets.

When **Bashar al-Asad** became president in 2000, he continued the policy of eroding United Nations sanctions on Iraq. He cooperated with the Egyptian government to increase trade and improve political ties to Baghdad. In summer 2000, the railway between Iraq and **Aleppo** reopened. In early 2001, direct flights between **Damascus** and Baghdad resumed for the first time since 1980. Of greatest concern to the United States was Syria's flouting of United Nations rules on oil for food. In fall 2000, it was estimated that Syria was purchasing between 100,000 and 150,000 barrels per day of **petroleum** at a discounted price, thus allowing Damascus to increase its foreign exchange earnings by exporting a larger quantity of its own petroleum production. American efforts in 2001 to persuade Syria to comply with UN rules on oil for food elicited a disingenuous denial of breaking those rules.

A handful of strategic factors spawned this new chapter in Syrian-Iraqi relations. The initial phase coincided with a lull in **Syrian-Israeli peace talks** when Benjamin Netanyahu was elected prime minister. After Bashar al-Asad became president in 2000, foreign policy remained under the direction of veterans like **Faruq al-Shara`** and **Abd al-Halim al-Khaddam**, and in all likelihood they have resorted to the senior Asad's typical balancing tactic against increasingly belligerent American and Israeli postures by reaching out to Baghdad. Syria's relations with the United States entered a difficult passage in fall 2002 when Washington was campaigning for a new UN resolution to bring Iraq into compliance on inspections for weapons of mass destruction. At the time, Syria was a rotating member of the Security Council and voted in favor of Resolution 1441 even though popular opinion at home was opposed to what many viewed as American bullying and hypocrisy. But when the United States invaded Iraq in March 2003, the Syrian government condemned it and called for Arab solidarity with the Iraqi people. The future of Syria's relations with its Arab neighbor is impossible to predict in the immediate aftermath of the United States victory over Saddam Husayn, but developments in Iraq are likely to have significant effects on Syria's own political and economic trajectory.

IRAQI-SYRIAN PIPELINE. In 1952, the pipeline began delivery of **petroleum** from Kirkuk in northern **Iraq** to the central Syrian town of **Homs**, and from there to the Mediterranean ports of **Baniyas** in Syria and Tripoli in **Lebanon**. From 1968 to 1973, Iraq and Syria bickered over the latter's demand for a large increase in the transit fee. This led the Iraqis to develop alternative pipelines to **Turkey** and the Gulf. In April 1976 Iraq stopped sending oil through the pipeline and left it shut for nearly three years. After Syria sided with **Iran** against Iraq in the Gulf War, it closed the pipeline on 10 April 1982. A rapprochement between Baghdad and **Damascus** led to its reopening after Syrian and Iraqi oil ministers exchanged visits in summer 1998. The **United States** viewed this step as a violation of the **United Nations** resolution governing the oil for food program.

IRON HAND SOCIETY. The first nationalist group to emerge in **Damascus** under the **French Mandate**. It was led by **Abd al-Rahman Shahbandar**, who organized its spread to **Homs** and **Hama**. In **Aleppo** a similar organization called the Red Hand Society also agitated against French rule. The French arrested Shahbandar and other members in 1922 and suppressed the society.

ISLAM. Since the Arab conquest in the seventh century, Islam has been the **religion** of the ruling authorities except for the country's coastal regions during the **Crusades**. The majority of the population converted to the new monotheistic religion by the early 10th century but its doctrine of toleration for other Abrahamic faiths ensured their survival. The basic teaching of Islam is that one God, in Arabic called *Allah*, is the creator and that he sent a series of messengers to humanity to reveal his will and the otherwise unknowable destiny of humans in the afterlife. These messengers include Abraham, Noah, Moses, Jesus, and others familiar to **Jews** and **Christians**. Muslims believe the last messenger was Muhammad, a resident of Mecca in the early seventh century whose recitation of divine revelations comprise the Qur'an and whose exemplary behavior, or *Sunna*, sets a model for believers in his message. The Muslim Prophet endured persecution in Mecca for propagating a new faith and emigrated with his followers to Medina, where he consolidated the Muslims as an autonomous, dynamic community that vanquished his adversaries and established the first Muslim polity.

Not long after Muhammad's death in 632, his community divided over the question of leadership into tendencies that evolved into **Sunni** and **Shi`i** sects. The power of these sects has fluctuated. In the 10th and 11th centuries, different Shi`i dynasties held sway in much of the country, but the **Saljuk** Turks began a Sunni revival that eventually pushed Shi`is to the geographical periphery—remote mountain regions—where they have remained ever since.

In addition to Islam's political centrality, its ritual and doctrinal facets have left a huge imprint on Syria's history. Rulers and townsmen constructed grand and modest mosques where believers may perform the obligatory prayers. **Damascus** assumed a key role as staging point for the annual pilgrimage to Mecca, an event that brought marked economic benefits to the city and surrounding areas. **Educational** institutions evolved to meet religious expectations and needs. Qur'an schools taught young children to memorize the holy book and **madrasas** trained advanced pupils in a range of Islamic sciences that qualified the brightest to interpret **shari`a**, Islamic law. In the major cities, wealthy patrons created endowments (**waqfs**) for the madrasas, which often assumed splendid **architectural** form as emblems of the community's commitment to preserving sacred learning.

Overlapping with the scholastic tradition, Syria has had a vibrant tradition of mystical orders known as **sufi** brotherhoods since their emergence in the 13th century. The brotherhoods vary in character; some are urban, others are rural; some cater to educated townsmen, others to illiterate believers. Damascus contains the tomb of one of Islamic mysticism's most celebrated figures, Muhyi al-Din Ibn Arabi, the author of sophisticated meditations on the relationship between the human and the divine. In more recent times, another sufi immigrant to Damascus, Khalid al-Naqshbandi (d. 1826), established a revivalist tradition in Syria that continues to influence both contemporary sufis and **Islamic fundamentalists** in the **Muslim Brothers**.

In numerous aspects of daily life Muslims conformed to the requirements of shari`a, including marriage, divorce, burial, inheritance, commerce, charity, and **art**. But to assert that Islam regulated all aspects of life is an exaggeration and even an idealization of the past by contemporary Islamic fundamentalist ideologues. Nonetheless, premodern Syrian society, particular in the towns, bore a strong religious imprint.

The modern era, however, has redefined religion throughout the world, and Syria is no exception. The first moves to narrow Islam's sway occurred in the era of **Ottoman** reform known as **Tanzimat**. Initiatives in law and education created a bifurcation between religious and secular subcultures that has not gone away. The **French Mandate** and a sequence of regimes since independence widened the secular sphere, but a religious reaction challenged this historical tendency, starting in the late Ottoman period and culminating with an armed uprising against the secular nationalist **Ba`th Party** regime in the late 1970s and early 1980s. Since the fierce suppression of that uprising's last eruption at **Hama** in 1982, the place of Islam in public life has not been openly debated inside the country but it is probably still regarded as an unsettled question by Syrians uncomfortable with a secular regime. *See also* ALAWI; DRUZES; ISMA`ILI; NIZARI.

ISLAMIC FUNDAMENTALISM. In the 20th century, much of the Muslim world saw a new form of **religious** activism that is commonly referred to as Islamic fundamentalism. The hallmarks of this trend are the call for observing what its proponents consider correct forms of worship and morality along with opposition to secular tendencies in law and govern- ment. To the extent that it claims to seek a return to correct religious belief and practice, it is similar to revivalist movements in earlier periods of Islamic civilization. The stamp of modernity, however, is evident in Islamic fundamentalism's organizational forms, ideological formulations, and political aspirations. In short, it is not a traditional form of **Islam** but an expression of traditionalism, the idea that Muslims must preserve certain traditions and discard others. Moreover, it is important to distinguish between fundamentalism with its activist character and the much more common phenomenon of piety without a political or public agenda.

In Syria, a cluster of fundamentalist themes appeared in the late **Ottoman** period. **Sultan Abdulhamid II** attracted support for policies that emphasized the Ottoman Empire's Islamic character and diminished the secular cast of the **Tanzimat** period. The first call for a return to proper religious practice and belief issued from Syrian **ulama** in the **salafiyya** movement. Also in the Ottoman period, conservative ulama published the first periodical to address fundamentalist issues like criticism of knee-jerk imitation of European culture.

During the **French Mandate** period, the impulse to shelter indige- nous culture against the occupying foreigner found expression in avowedly Islamic societies in the main cities in the 1920s and 1930s. They combated vices like alcohol and gambling, the influence of **Christian** missionary schools, and public mixing of men and **women** at dances and **cinemas**. Members of these groups gravitated to the Society of **Muslim Brothers**, a movement that originated in **Egypt** in 1928 and established a Syrian branch in 1946.

In the early years of independence, the fundamentalist movement, largely represented by the Muslim Brothers, combated efforts to spread Western forms of consumption and entertainment. In the 1950s, the Brothers adopted a more explicit political posture when they opposed the growing influence of socialist and communist trends. The real high point for fundamentalist activism occurred when the avowedly secular **Ba`th Party** seized power in 1963. For nearly 20 years, Ba`thist regimes confronted persistent criticism and at times violent opposition from the Muslim Brothers and smaller fundamentalist groups like the Vanguard of Muhammad and the Islamic Liberation Party. During the countrywide disturbances between 1978 and 1982, the fundamentalist movement split. On one side were those who believed it was necessary to resort to violence to overthrow the Ba`thist regime, which they considered a tool of the **minority Alawi** sect to which President **Hafiz al-Asad** belonged. On the other side were those, like **Sa`id al-Hawwa**, who argued that the regime was too powerful to dislodge and that armed struggle would be self-destructive. The latter view proved correct. One of the more discouraging facets of that period for Islamic fundamentalists was the prospect of an avowedly Islamic regime in **Iran** forming a strategic alliance with the secular Ba`thists at the very moment when the latter were ruthlessly suppressing Syrians seeking to create an Islamic regime in **Damascus**.

During the late 1970s and early 1980s, Asad's repressive forces arrested hundreds of members and suspected members of fundamentalist groups. Other members and sympathizers fled the country. After the February 1982 uprising at **Hama**, the climax of fundamentalist assertion in Syria, the movement underwent further schisms and then efforts to heal them. The headquarters of fundamentalist organizations relocated to Europe. The Asad regime offered amnesty to key figures in exchange for a pledge to refrain from political activity. Syria's secularist order had suppressed and tamed the Islamic fundamentalists. Nonetheless, the late 1980s and the 1990s did not see Syrian Muslims completely embrace Western culture and manners either. Rather, public culture demonstrates an eclectic mix of personal piety in dress and habit by Muslims who might or might not also quietly harbor fundamentalist aspirations of overturning the present secular trend should political conditions ever offer the opportunity.

ISMA`ILI.** A **Shi`i Muslim sect whose members have long lived in parts of central Syria in the vicinity of **Hama** and in **Latakia** province. Its members account for about 1.5 percent of the population. This Shi`i sect gave rise to several important movements and dynasties in the 10th and 11th centuries, including the **Fatimids**, **Nizaris**, and **Qarmatis**. The Isma`ilis differed with other Shi`is over succession to the sixth **imam**, Ja`far al-Sadiq, who died in 765. Some of Ja`far's followers believed that he had designated his son Isma`il to succeed him, but Isma`il predeceased his father, and Isma`il's party then split into two groups. The first held that the line of imams had ended with Isma`il, that he was still alive, and that he would return as the *mahdi*, the messianic figure in popular Islam who would inaugurate a millennial reign of justice. The second party believed that Isma`il's son Muhammad was the true imam. When he died, his followers divided into two more sects. Some paid allegiance to Muhammad as the last imam, who would return as the mahdi. This group became the Qarmatis. Others supported the claim of a certain Ubayd

Allah that he was a direct descendant of Muhammad ibn Isma`il and the rightful imam. This figure established the Fatimid movement, which founded a dynasty in North Africa in 909, and later conquered **Egypt** and Syria. In the late 11th century a schism arose in Fatimid Isma`ilism when the Nizaris broke away and founded their own state based in **Iran** and with loyal bases scattered in parts of central Syria.

In early modern times a few thousand Isma`ilis were concentrated in villages in **Jabal Ansariyya**, particularly near the ancient fortresses of Qadmus and **Masyaf**. Endemic feuding with the more numerous **Alawis** of the region constituted a permanent threat to their prospects in that part of Syria. In 1849, the **Ottoman** authorities encouraged the Isma`ilis to emigrate to the district of **Salamiyya**, 30 kilometers southeast of **Hama**. In medieval times the town had served as one of the sect's strongholds, and in the 19th century it became the center of a new Isma`ili region as immigrants from Jabal Ansariyya settled and revived villages east and west of Salamiyya. By 1940, Isma`ilis in the vicinity of Salamiyya numbered 16,000 compared with only 4,000 remaining in the mountains. There are presently 40,000 Isma`ilis in Salamiyya district and 15,000 in the mountains.

ISRAEL. Much of Syria's history since 1948 has been deeply affected by the formation of a Jewish state in **Palestine**. Syria's **armed forces** fought in the **Palestine War of 1948**, but the small and poorly equipped army could do no more than occupy a sliver of territory that **France** and Great Britain had attached to Palestine in 1920, but that Syria considered its own. With the conclusion of the **Armistice of 1949**, Syria and Israel agreed to designate the disputed territories **demilitarized zones** whose ultimate possession would be determined in later negotiations. Israel, however, pursued its claim to the DMZs by gradually taking them over by force. Syria resisted such moves, and armed clashes became commonplace. While Syrian leaders often called for reversing the verdict of the 1948 war, Israel's military superiority induced a cautious policy of containing conflict to small-scale fighting in the DMZs.

Such prudent policy, however, was abandoned under the **Ba`th Party** regimes of the 1960s. Indeed, the **neo-Ba`th** regime adopted a provocative stance because some of its members favored a "people's war" modeled on the Algerian war for independence against France and the Vietnamese war against the **United States**. The **June 1967 War** erupted in the wake of a crisis generated by Syria's confrontations with Israel over the DMZ. Syria lost the **Golan Heights** to Israeli forces in the fighting, so the issue at stake grew from disputes over the bits of land in the DMZ to the much larger and far more strategically valuable Golan. **United Nations Resolution 242** provided for Syria's recovery of its territory in exchange for peace with Israel, but the neo-Ba'th regime flatly rejected the resolution.

The **corrective movement** brought **Hafiz al-Asad** to power in November 1970. He had been minister of defense during the 1967 war, so he had additional personal motivation to retrieve Syria's lost territory. To pursue this aim, Asad allied with Egyptian President Anwar Sadat and launched the **October 1973 War**, in which Syrian forces briefly regained much of the Golan Heights, but then lost them and more territory to an Israeli counteroffensive. After the war, Syria and Israel accepted American mediation that led to a 1974 separation of forces and the stationing of the **United Nations Disengagement Observer Force** in a buffer zone. Since then, no fighting between Syria and Israel has taken place on that front. Moreover, in 1975 Asad indicated his willingness to negotiate a peace treaty, but Israelis mistrusted Syrian intentions and therefore showed little interest in exchanging land for peace. Israelis, for their part, regarded the continued occupation of at least part of the Heights as a necessary strategic buffer against any possible future Syrian attack.

Syria's position vis-à-vis Israel notably weakened when **Egypt** signed a separate peace treaty in 1979, making it possible for Israel to concentrate its formidable military might on its northern front. Syria then embarked on a massive arms buildup that lasted well into the 1980s and put a drag on the **economy**. The next major development was the **Lebanese War of 1982**. In June 1982, Israeli forces invaded **Lebanon** in an attempt to eliminate the **Palestine Liberation Organization** and bring Lebanon into Israel's sphere of influence. Israeli forces attacked Syrian units stationed in eastern Lebanon but failed to dislodge them, and the two sides agreed to a cease-fire after a few days. For the next three years, Syria and Israel struggled to gain supremacy in Lebanon in the war's aftermath, and Syria prevailed, but the stalemate over the Golan Heights continued.

The first real breakthrough in diplomacy took place following Syria's participation in the coalition to evict **Iraq** from Kuwait and the rapid decline of the **Soviet Union**. A few months after the conclusion of Desert Storm, President Asad dropped his insistence that the United Nations oversee negotiations and accepted the United States' invitation to attend an international peace conference to be held in **Madrid** in October 1991, and then to enter direct negotiations with Israel in Washington. Nine years of intermittent **Syrian-Israeli peace talks** brought substantial progress to resolving their differences but failed to reach a final settlement. Syria insists on recovering all of the Golan Heights up to the 4 June 1967 line in return for a peace treaty. On the Israeli side, Labor Party governments have come closest to meeting that condition while Likud Party governments tend to view retention of the Golan Heights as essential to Israel's security. The situation of no war, no peace that has prevailed since the October 1973 War appears likely to continue for the foreseeable future.

ISTIQLAL PARTY. An **Arab nationalist** party, whose name means independence, established by members of **al-Fatat** and al-Ahd during Amir **Faysal**'s short-lived regime of 1918-1920. The party was intended to serve as a public organization while al-Fatat remained a secret group. Istiqlal called for the independence and unity of the Arab lands under a constitutional monarchy that would reign over a federation of autonomous regions. Its members included men who rose to preeminence during the **French Mandate** era, including **Jamil Mardam** and **Shukri al-Quwwatli**. In the early years of the mandate era, the Istiqlal Party was a rival of **Abd al-Rahman Shahbandar**'s **People's Party**.

-J-

JABAL ANSARIYYA. Also known as Jabal al-Nusayriya and Jabal al-Alawi, this range in northwestern Syria has an average height of 1,200 meters with the highest peak (Nabi Yunus) of 1,600 meters. The western slopes facing the Mediterranean Sea receive enough rainfall to support **agriculture** and have a slight enough incline to allow for intensive cultivation and dense settlement. The steeper and drier eastern slopes are more sparsely inhabited. Much of the population of the Ansariyya range has long been primarily **Alawi**, but there are a fair number of **Christian** and a few **Isma`ili** villages as well. Until recent decades, the Alawi peasants of the mountain were dominated by wealthy **Sunni** townsmen of **Hama** and **Latakia**.

Throughout history, the rugged terrain of Jabal Ansariyya has made it difficult for outsiders to rule it directly. The **Ottoman Empire** began to assert central authority more effectively in the last decades of the 19th century. When Ottoman rule ended in 1918, autonomist tendencies appeared in **Shaykh Salih al-Ali**'s revolt, and **French Mandate** policies reinforced them by creating an administration separate from the rest of Syria. From 1936 to 1939, Jabal Ansariyya was ruled by a national government in **Damascus**, then **France** granted it separate status from 1939 to 1942. When Syria became independent in 1946, **Sulayman al-**

Murshid led an autonomist movement that the government quickly suppressed. Since that time, the region has been an integral part of Syria.

JABAL DRUZE. A rugged volcanic plateau east of the **Hawran** in southern Syria. The main town and provincial center is **Suwayda**. Its eastern portion consists of a maze of lava flows, hills, and caves that have made it an ideal refuge for political dissenters, as indicated by its Arabic name **al-Laja'**, which means refuge. In the 17th century, **Druzes** came from **Lebanon** to settle. For most of the three centuries of Druze settlement there, they guarded their autonomy against outside domination. In a process similar to the case of **Jabal Ansariyya**, the **Ottoman Empire** increased its authority in the late 19th century. The **French Mandate** accorded Jabal Druze separate status, but meddling by the French authorities turned the region into the center of the **Great Revolt** of 1925-1927. More recently Jabal Druze was the site of Syria's first **petroleum** discovery. The district's present population is 90 percent Druze and 10 percent **Christian**, mostly **Greek Orthodox**.

JABIRI, SA`DALLAH AL- (1893-1947). From one of **Aleppo**'s leading families, he was active in **Arab nationalist** politics in the late **Ottoman** era, a participant in **Ibrahim Hananu**'s revolt, and a prominent nationalist leader during the **French Mandate**. In 1922 Jabiri organized the Red Hand, a short-lived nationalist movement modeled on the **Iron Hand Society** based in **Damascus**. The French arrested and exiled Jabiri for his role in the **Great Revolt** of 1925-1927, but granted him amnesty in 1928. When the **National Bloc** formed its executive leadership in 1932, Jabiri became its vice president and a leader of one of Aleppo's factions in the Bloc. He served in the 1936-1938 cabinet of **Jamil Mardam** and became prime minister of independent Syria's first elected government in August 1943.

Jabiri proved incapable of governing the country in a manner that would have strengthened its fledgling parliamentary system. Graft and nepotism were rampant; the government harassed its critics with arrests, suspensions of newspapers, and bans on their organizations. He resigned in October 1944, but became prime minister again the following October. During his second tenure, in May 1946, Jabiri obtained extra-constitutional powers to issue decrees, such as one to eliminate independent oversight of the accounts of government departments, and his parliamentary bloc rammed through measures without regard for legal procedure. Moreover, the government used the gendarmerie to keep officials and parliamentary deputies under surveillance. Finally, feuding among cabinet members and his own declining health prompted President **Shukri al-Quwwatli** and Interior Minister **Sabri al-Asali** to induce Jabiri to resign in December 1946, six months before his death.

JABIYA, AL-. An ancient settlement in the **Golan Heights** and an important military outpost in **Byzantine** and very early Islamic times. Al-Jabiya served as a center for the Ghassanids, pre-Islamic Arab vassals of Byzantium. The Muslim Arabs used it as a military headquarters for campaigns against the Byzantines, including the decisive Battle of **Yarmuk**. After that Arab victory, the **caliph** Umar convened a meeting of Muslim leaders to organize Syria's affairs. Once the Muslims consolidated power in **Palestine** and southern Syria, the center of military activity against the Byzantines shifted north, and al-Jabiya fell into neglect and became uninhabited.

JACOBITE. *See* **SYRIAN ORTHODOX.**

JADID, SALAH AL- **(1926-1993).** Dominant figure in the **neo-Ba`thist** regime of 1966 to 1970. An **Alawi** from Jabla, a small town south of **Latakia**, Jadid's first political involvement was with the **Syrian Social National Party** and then the **Ba`th Party**. He was a founding member of the **Military Committee** that formed in **Egypt** in 1959. In the first Ba`thist regime of 1963 to 1966, Jadid became chief of the Officers' Bureau and the Personnel Branch, positions that gave him the authority to dismiss, transfer, and appoint officers. He used these positions to entrench members of the Military Committee in key commands, including **Hafiz al-Asad** as commander of the Air Force and Muhammad Umran as commander of a key armored brigade stationed near **Damascus**. Jadid also engineered a purge of **Sunni** officers, whom he replaced with Alawi, **Druze**, and **Isma`ili** men. In December 1964, Jadid was promoted to chief of staff and became the leading figure in the Military Committee's struggle against the party old guard in 1965 to 1966. It was Jadid who plotted the **February 23, 1966 coup** that brought the neo-Ba`th to power.

In the neo-Ba`thist regime, Jadid was the most powerful figure, but he satisfied himself with a modest official position as assistant secretary-general of the Ba`th Party's Regional Command. He supported the regime's radical economic measures and its sponsoring of **Palestinian** raids against **Israel**. After Syria's defeat in the **June 1967 War**, Jadid and Asad became rivals for power as Asad took effective control of the **armed forces** while Jadid remained the master of the party. When a climactic clash occurred in November 1970, Asad easily prevailed, arresting Jadid and throwing him into prison, where he remained until his death in August 1993.

JAMAL PASHA, AHMAD (1872-1922). A member of the **Committee of Union and Progress** ruling triumvirate that dominated **Ottoman** politics from 1912 until 1918. He arrived in Syria in 1914 as governor and commander of the Ottoman Fourth Army to defend Syria against British forces stationed in **Egypt** that threatened to invade during **World War I**. Jamal ordered a massive conscription of Syrian manpower for military service and to build military roads and railways. In February 1915, he launched a surprise attack on British forces defending the Suez Canal, but the campaign stalled. He tried again a year later, but British defenses again held their lines.

One of Jamal Pasha's main concerns was to stamp out any sign of disloyalty among Syrians active in the nascent **Arab nationalist** movement. Most prominent Syrians were disposed to support the empire during the war; others were easily coopted; those he suspected of disloyalty, he exiled to Asia Minor. In April and May 1916, Jamal Pasha ordered the execution of 21 Arab nationalists in Beirut and **Damascus**. As a result, he is known in Arab nationalist historiography as a ruthless tyrant. He remained responsible for Syria's defense until the middle of 1917 when a German general took command; in early 1918, Istanbul recalled Jamal Pasha from Syria. At the end of the war, he fled to Germany and then traveled to Afghanistan, where he assisted the government's drive to modernize its army. In the meantime, the Ottoman government court-martialed and passed a death sentence on him in absentia. In July 1922, he was assassinated in Tbilisi by two **Armenian** gunmen seeking vengeance for Ottoman atrocities against their countrymen during the recent war.

JANISSARIES. **Ottoman** infantry corps that was at the forefront in the empire's conquests in Europe and Asia. In Syrian history, their significance lay in the garrisons established in the major cities of **Aleppo** and **Damascus**, where they constituted virtually autonomous power blocs that took over sections of the local economies and could challenge the authority of Ottoman governors. In 17th-century Damascus, a distinction arose between "local" janissaries (*yarliyya*), who were artisans, other townsmen, and troops who struck roots in the local **economy**, and imperial janissaries (*kapi kullari*), troops dispatched to counter the rebelliousness of the local janissaries. Twice during the 18th century, in 1726 and 1740, the two factions fought for supremacy in Damascus. In 1741, the imperial janissaries were expelled, leaving the local janissaries in a dominant position until their defeat at the hands of the Ottoman governor As'ad Pasha al-**Azm**, who then reestablished a corps of imperial janissaries under his firm control. But the two factions resumed their feuds following As'ad Pasha's dismissal in 1757.

In the 18th and early 19th centuries, the janissaries of Aleppo contended for dominance with the **ashraf**, religious leaders claiming descent from the Prophet Muhammad. In the early 1800s, the janissaries completely dominated the city against the will of governors appointed by Istanbul. This situation abruptly ended in 1813, when the Ottoman governor carried out a massacre of leading janissaries that effectively reduced the group's collective power. The janissaries remained elements in local urban politics until Sultan Mahmud II eliminated the corps by means of a well-planned massacre in March 1826 in Istanbul.

JAZA'IRI, TAHIR AL- (1852-1920). A prominent figure in the early stages of the **salafiyya** movement. Tahir al-Jaza'iri's most lasting achievement was the foundation of the Zahiriyya Library, Syria's first public library. From 1898 to 1907, he served as curator of libraries in the province of **Damascus** and set up libraries in **Homs**, **Hama**, Jerusalem, and Tripoli. Jaza'iri was also a pioneer in the development of modern **education** and he enjoyed **Midhat Pasha**'s backing in his efforts to lay the foundations of a system of state schools in the province. As superintendent of schools in the early 1880s, he developed curricula and composed textbooks. Furthermore, Jaza'iri took a keen interest in the works of the 13th-century religious reformer **Taqi al-Din Ahmad ibn Taymiyya**, and he participated in the salafi revival of his works by seeking and circulating his manuscripts.

Jaza'iri was at the center of reformist trends in Damascus, and his private salons attracted Turkish officials, Arab **ulama**, and younger Arab students. This group, known as the senior circle, favored the restoration of the 1876 Ottoman **constitution** as well as educational reform. Ottoman authorities learned of his political leanings and began to harass him in the early 1900s. Jaza'iri got fed up with searches of his personal library and confiscation of his papers, so in 1907 he left Syria to settle in **Egypt**. Even though he had enjoyed good relations with Turkish partisans of constitutional government, he distrusted the **Committee of Union and Progress** and remained in Egypt after it came to power. During **World War I**, Jaza'iri supported the **Arab Revolt**. He did not return to Syria until 1919 when he was seriously ill, and he died shortly thereafter.

JAZIRA. In Arabic, *jazira* means an island or peninsula, and by extension refers to land lying between two rivers, in this case the **Euphrates** and Tigris Rivers. The Jazira region in Syria consists mostly of a low plateau broken by several mountain ranges that give rise to tributaries of the Euphrates such as the **Khabur** and Balikh Rivers. Throughout history, Jazira has been of strategic importance as a channel for communications between **Iraq** and Syria. The Arabs conquered it from the **Byzantines** in a series of campaigns between 639 and 641. In the early Islamic period it was a haven for religious dissidents and the site of frequent strife between Arab tribes competing for scarce grazing lands. The most famous sons of Jazira are the founders of the 10th-century **Hamdanid** dynasty that established splendid courts in **Aleppo** and Mosul.

Until modern times Jazira was a sparsely settled region, mostly inhabited by **bedouin**, but after **World War I**, **France** encouraged the settlement of refugees from **Turkey**, mostly **Armenians** and other **Christians**. During the **French Mandate** other refugees from Turkey and Iraq included **Kurds** and **Assyrians**. These 20th-century migrations have made Jazira the country's most heterogeneous province. New towns sprang up, most notably **al-Hasaka**, which has a Christian majority, and **Qamishli**, at the same time that bedouin were induced to settle down. Qamishli in particular, located near the Turkish border along a railway running to Aleppo, became the center of a regional economic boom based on the export of **agricultural** and pastoral products. Among Kurds, Armenians, and Assyrians sentiment for autonomy was quite strong, but France did not create a separate regime as it had for **Jabal Druze** and the **Alawi** districts. When the 1936 **National Bloc** government assumed responsibility for administering the Jazira, however, a strong movement for autonomy developed. The government appointed a **Sunni** from **Damascus** to govern the restive province. He failed to reconcile autonomist elements to the new order, and soon a revolt of Kurds and Christians erupted, forcing the governor to flee Qamishli. Continued troubles led the French to establish a separate regime for Jazira in July 1939, but Syrian control was restored the following year.

During the 1940s and 1950s, population and agricultural production grew rapidly. Aleppan merchants invested in machinery to cultivate this vast region and induced peasants from western Syria to migrate to Jazira to work the land. In a decade, the amount of land under cultivation doubled. The province has witnessed ongoing economic development and population growth, but it appears that further agricultural expansion will be costly and slow because of difficulties with irrigation, drainage, and sedimentation in projects along the Euphrates and Khabur Rivers. The region's major cities are Qamishli (150,000), **Dayr al-Zur** (140,000), **al-Raqqa** (165,000), and al-Hasaka (120,000).

JEWS. Syria's Jewish community has its origins in antiquity with their migration to the area in the 13th century B.C. After the seventh-century Arab conquest, they continued to live in **Aleppo** and **Damascus**. Like the **Christians** under Muslim rule, the Jews did not experience pressure to convert or persecution; rather, they were permitted to practice their **religion** and govern their communal relations with minimal interference by the Muslim authorities.

One of the hallmarks of Jewish history in Syria is immigration and settlement in several phases. As a result, close study of Syrian Jews reveals a variety of communities rather than a monolithic group. At different times, there were special institutions for **Iraqi** Jews, who arrived from Baghdad in the ninth and 10th centuries, for Spanish Jews who came in the 16th century, and for southern European Jews who came in the 18th century. A second feature is the fluctuation in their fortunes. Communities flourished during the centuries of **Fatimid** and **Ayyubid** rule when Jews held influential positions as administrators and physicians, and religious scholarship flourished. Their position deteriorated under **Mamluk** rule.

In the 16th century, the expulsion of Jews from Spain and efforts by the **Ottoman Empire** to attract Jewish traders and craftsmen led to a substantial immigration of Jews to Aleppo, where they formed separate institutions with their own synagogues and cemeteries. The Ottoman era marked a high point in the fortunes of Syrian Jews, many of whom prospered in long-distance **trade**, finance, and official service. During the 18th century, Aleppo's flourishing commerce with **Iran** and India enticed Jews from Italy and **France** to settle there, where they formed a distinct group known as Francos who occasionally clashed with native Jews over tax exemption and communal autonomy. In Damascus, the intellectual vitality of Jewish life was evident in a Hebrew press that produced a printed text in 1605. During the middle 18th and early 19th centuries, the Farhi family in Damascus attained wealth and influence as treasurers for Ottoman governors and through private financial transactions.

Neither the end of the Ottoman Empire nor the imposition of the **French Mandate** affected the Jews' status, but the Zionist movement and the threat it posed to the Arabs of **Palestine** fundamentally altered the conditions of life for Syrian Jews. Anti-Jewish sentiment emerged in the mid-1930s because of Syrian opposition to Zionism and the suspicion that Syrian Jews sympathized with the movement to turn Palestine into a Jewish state. A few attacks on Jews in Damascus occurred in 1936 and

1945. After the **United Nations** passed a resolution calling for the partition of Palestine into Jewish and Arab states in November 1947, anti-Jewish violence erupted in Aleppo, where a number of synagogues was set afire and destroyed. During the **Palestine War of 1948**, there were further attacks on Jewish property in Damascus.

As recently as 1943 there were nearly 30,000 Jews in Syria, but that number dropped sharply to around 6,000 because of emigration in the years surrounding the 1948 creation of **Israel**. Ongoing hostility between Syria and Israel meant that the remaining Syrian Jews were viewed with suspicion by the government and people. By 1990, the Jewish population was divided among 4,500 in Damascus, 1,000 in Aleppo, and about 100 in the northeastern city of **Qamishli**. In 1994, the Syrian government made a gesture of goodwill toward Israel when it announced a free emigration policy for Syrian Jews. Around 3,000 Jews left, leaving just several hundred in the country and probably spelling the sad end of their distinguished historical tradition there.

JORDAN. Known as **Transjordan** before 1949. Amir Abdallah, the son of Sharif **Husayn ibn Ali**, ruled Transjordan from the time of its establishment in 1921. He always harbored the ambition of adding Syria to his kingdom. Ultimately, Abdallah did add to his kingdom portions of eastern Palestine in the course of the **Palestine War of 1948**. From the time of Syrian independence in 1946 until Abdallah's assassination in July 1951, he pursued his ambition to rule Syria by meddling in its internal affairs. After his death, though, Syria became more aggressive toward Jordan and its new ruler King Husayn. In the Arab cold war of the 1950s and 1960s, Syria and Jordan consistently found themselves on opposing sides because of Syria's republican nature and opposition to Western influence on one hand and Jordan's monarchical government and support for Western interests on the other. Relations deteriorated when the **neo-Ba`th** regime came to power in 1966. It accused Jordan of supporting an abortive plot that year and struck back with a car bomb at a border crossing the next year. That led to a brief cut in relations. Further occasions for disagreement included Syrian support for an independent **Palestinian** guerrilla organization, Fatah, and support for the 1970 rising of Palestinian guerrillas against the Jordanian monarchy. Once again relations were cut in July 1971.

Hafiz al-Asad's policy of moderation in **foreign policy** led to the improvement of ties with Jordan on the eve of the **October 1973 War**, but in the late 1970s relations again worsened when the Syrians accused Jordan of harboring **Muslim Brothers** seeking to overthrow the Asad regime. Jordan then developed strong ties to **Iraq** as a counter against Syria and staunchly supported Iraq in its war against **Iran** throughout the 1980s. Furthermore, for most of the 1980s Syria suspected King Husayn of willingness to enter a peace process sponsored by the **United States** that would exclude Syria. After the 1990-1991 crisis and war over Kuwait, Syria and Jordan found themselves in similar circumstances as both countries agreed to participate in peace talks with **Israel**, and for a time there were signs that the need to coordinate policies would dictate better relations, but Jordan's signing of a peace treaty with Israel in October 1994 again demonstrated the divergence in the two countries' interests and policies.

For the next five years, relations remained cool between Amman and **Damascus** because of Jordan's peace treaty with Israel. When King Husayn died in February 1999, President Asad attended his funeral along with his veteran foreign policy advisers **Abd al-Halim al-Khaddam** and **Faruq al-Shara`**. Asad met with King Husayn's son and successor, King Abdallah II. Later that month, Asad's son **Bashar** met with the new ruler. Shortly afterward, a two-day visit to Damascus by King Abdallah II resulted in improved relations on **trade** and cooperation on sharing **water** resources in the **Yarmuk River** watershed. In that year and the next, Syria provided water to alleviate Jordan's severe drought. In June 2000, King Abdallah visited Damascus for Hafiz al-Asad's funeral. Bilateral relations have recently improved, especially in the area of economic cooperation. Thus, in 2001, Syria joined an electricity network shared by **Egypt** and Jordan. A persistent sore point in their relations is Jordan's allegation that Syria holds an estimated 700 Jordanians under detention.

JULY 1860 DAMASCUS MASSACRE. One of the major events in 19th-century Syrian history. On 9 July 1860, Muslims began several days of attacks against **Christian** townsmen of the Bab Tuma quarter, looting and burning churches, homes, and shops, and massacring Christians. Anti-Christian sentiment was stoked during the **Egyptian** occupation (1831-1840) by **Ibrahim Pasha**'s favorable treatment of Christians. The 1860 outbreak came in the context of rising anti-Christian sentiment in the **Ottoman Empire** due to the **Tanzimat** reforms, particularly the 1856 edict declaring equality between Muslims and non-Muslims, and the improving commercial prospects of Christians more generally. More immediately, the violence came on the heels of fighting between **Druzes** and Maronites in **Lebanon**.

Communal tensions rose in the first week of July as townsmen digested reports of Druze military victories over Christians. Damascene

Muslims taunted and threatened the town's Christians. At that point the Algerian hero Abd al-Qadir al-Jaza'iri, resident in **Damascus** since 1855, urged the city's Muslim leaders to prevent a violent outbreak that could lead to European intervention in Syria, but his warnings failed to prevent the riots. The incident that ignited the violence involved a number of Muslim youths who drew crosses on streets so that Christians would have to step on them. The Ottoman governor punished the boys by making them remove the markings. Muslims in the marketplace then forced the guards to let the youths go, and a furious Muslim crowd formed that initiated eight days of attacks in Bab Tuma. By no means did all Damascene Muslims condone the violence. Indeed, prominent notables offered refuge, and Jaza'iri took a contingent of armed men into the Christian quarter to rescue terrified Christians. In all, some 5,000 of the city's 20,000 Christians were killed; of the 15,000 survivors, Jaza'iri and his men saved 10,000, and the rest resided in other parts of the city where their Muslim neighbors provided protection.

News of the atrocities caused outrage in Europe and triggered military intervention by several powers, chiefly **France**. In order to demonstrate Ottoman resolve and to fend off European demands for closer supervision of Ottoman governance, the authorities declared martial law and inflicted harsh punishment on the town's Muslims for committing the outrages and on their own officials for failing to prevent or halt the violence. The Ottoman governor was executed, a collective fine imposed on the city's Muslims, around 250 Muslims were executed for their crimes, and nearly 150 were exiled, including some of the city's leading dignitaries. To drive home the point that Ottoman authority was not to be challenged, Damascenes were disarmed and conscripted, something that had been tried three times before in the 1840s and 1850s but had encountered violent resistance. By October 1860, 3,000 men had been drafted and sent to Anatolia, and conscription became an annual event thereafter. An indemnity was levied on the entire province equal to two years' annual revenues, and it was used to reimburse Christians for destroyed property and for the reconstruction of Bab Tuma, which was completed by 1864. In spite of these punitive and restorative measures and indications of Ottoman concern for Christians' welfare, hundreds left Damascus for safer confines in Lebanon. In the broader historical scheme, the events of 1860 marked a turning point in relations between Istanbul and Syria: thereafter, the Ottomans subjected the province to much closer and more effective control.

JUNE 1967 WAR. Also known as the Six Day War, this conflict fundamentally altered the contours of the Arab-Israeli conflict. In a sense, Syria's **neo-Ba`thist** regime planted the seeds of war with its provocations of **Israel** in the **demilitarized zones.** As military clashes escalated, it appeared possible that Israel might strike at **Damascus** to punish the Syrians. On 13 May 1967, reports reached **Egypt** that Israel was preparing to invade Syria. Egyptian President Gamal Abd al-Nasir responded by ordering the withdrawal of **United Nations** forces stationed in Gaza and in Sinai at the entrance of the Gulf of Aqaba. Nasir then sent troops into Sinai and announced the closure of the Gulf of Aqaba to Israeli shipping. Diplomatic efforts to defuse the crisis were still being pursued when Israel's leaders decided to launch surprise attacks on Syria, Egypt, and **Jordan**.

On the war's first day, 5 June, Israeli warplanes destroyed the air forces of all three Arab countries. In the first four days of fighting, Israel conquered the Sinai Peninsula and Gaza Strip from Egypt and the West Bank from Jordan while Syria launched token artillery attacks from the **Golan Heights.** By the evening of 8 June, Egypt had accepted a cease-fire and Syria followed the next morning. But Israeli Minister of Defense Moshe Dayan, without consulting the Israeli cabinet, ordered a full attack on the Syrian front. When a cease-fire took effect the following evening, Israeli forces had occupied the entire Golan Heights. The war was a devastating blow to what little legitimacy the neo-Ba`th regime could claim and damaged the reputation of Defense Minister **Hafiz al-Asad.** An enduring legacy of the war is the Israeli occupation of the Golan Heights. Syria claims that **United Nations Resolution 242** passed in November 1967 requires Israel to completely withdraw from land it conquered in June, but so far Israeli governments have not agreed to Syria's terms. The absence of any progress toward a diplomatic remedy for Syria's territorial loss led to the **October 1973 War.**

-K-

KAFTARU, AHMAD (1915-). The **Sunni** chief jurisprudent, or mufti, of Syria since 1964. Kaftaru received a traditional **Islamic** religious **education** and became a teacher of **religion** in **Qunaytra** in 1948. He then became mufti of **Damascus** in 1951 and was active in several religious associations. Kaftaru is particularly interested in interfaith dialogue and has traveled widely to participate in conferences devoted to dialogue among adherents of different religions.

KAN`AN, GHAZI AL- (c. 1943- ).** From 1982 until 2002, Lieutenant-General Kan`an presided over Syrian military intelligence in **Lebanon. He assumed that politically and strategically sensitive position after **Israel**'s 1982 invasion of Lebanon, and for two decades he acted as de facto viceroy for Syrian interests. Lebanese political leaders frequently visited the headquarters he established at the border town of Anjar. He left the post when **Bashar al-Asad** appointed him to head the domestic political security agency back in **Damascus**.

KASM, ABD AL-RA'UF AL- (1932-). Prime minister under **Hafiz al-Asad** from January 1980 until October 1987. Kasm was the son of a well-known religious scholar of **Damascus**. He had become acquainted with Asad in the early 1950s when both were active as student members of the **Ba`th Party**. Kasm went on to become a professor of urban planning at Damascus University. In the midst of the largely **Islamic fundamentalist** insurrection, Asad appointed Kasm prime minister in an attempt to sway the **Sunni** Muslims of Damascus. Kasm took several steps to placate Sunni public opinion, but they had practically no effect in quelling the unrest. As prime minister, Kasm presided over a vast civilian bureaucracy that was frequently bent to the needs of the more powerful military branch of government. On several occasions he tried to curtail different generals' smuggling and siphoning resources from the **public sector**, but these efforts were ultimately futile. Kasm's dismissal came at a time of economic hardship, but at the time, his tenure had been the longest of any prime minister since independence.

KAWAKIBI, ABD AL-RAHMAN AL- (1849-1903). An influential writer and advocate of **Islamic** reform, Kawakibi was born to an influential family of **Aleppo**. He was active in the earliest stages of Arabic journalism, working first for the official **Ottoman** paper and later issuing a short-lived private newspaper as well. In his journalistic writings Kawakibi criticized Ottoman governors and other officials. As a result, his publications were banned and he got embroiled in disputes with the Ottoman governor of Aleppo. His troubles led him to emigrate to **Egypt** in 1898.

Kawakibi is best known for two essays that criticized the Ottoman political order at the time of Sultan **Abdulhamid**. The title of the first work refers to the Arabic nickname for Mecca, Mother of Cities, and calls for the restoration of the **caliphate** to the Arab clan of Quraysh. According to Kawakibi, this renewed caliphate would spark an Islamic spiritual revival but not provide a focus for Muslim political unity. His second work details the evils of unrestrained despotism and was intended as a sharp criticism of Ottoman misrule.

KHABUR RIVER. A major tributary of the **Euphrates River** that rises in **Turkey** and flows for 486 kilometers in Syria's **Jazira** region before joining the Euphrates south of **Dayr al-Zur.** Government projects to construct barrages and drain off salt have enabled the development of **agriculture** along the Khabur. In the 1990s, however, upstream projects in Turkey reportedly reduced the river's volume by half. **Al-Hasaka** (population 120,000) is the major town along this river.

KHADDAM, ABD AL-HALIM AL- (1932-). This **Sunni** Muslim from the coastal town of **Baniyas** became one of President **Hafiz al-Asad**'s closest advisers and a central figure in formulating the country's **foreign policy.** Khaddam joined the **Ba`th Party** when still in high school. He became acquainted with Asad when the two were party activists in **Latakia** in the early 1950s. Khaddam went on to study law at **Damascus** University. After completing his studies, he had a practice in Damascus until the **March 8, 1963 coup** brought the Ba`th to power.

In the first Ba`thist regime, Khaddam was governor of **Hama** when antigovernment protests erupted in April 1964. Three years later, he had the misfortune to be governor of **Qunaytra** when it was lost to **Israel** in the **June 1967 War.** In the **neo-Ba`th** regime, Khaddam entered the cabinet as minister of economy and foreign trade. When Asad seized power in 1970, he made Khaddam his foreign minister, a post he held until 1984 when he was promoted to first vice president. In the late 1970s and 1980s, he helped shape Syria's close relations with the **Soviet Union.** After Syria's decisive intervention in the **Lebanese Civil War** in 1976, Khaddam represented Syrian interests there along with the head of Syrian military intelligence in Lebanon **Ghazi al-Kan`an.** In 1999, however, President Asad reportedly put his son **Bashar al-Asad** in charge of "the Lebanon portfolio" as part of his preparation to succeed him as president.

When Hafiz al-Asad died in June 2000, Vice President Khaddam served as head of the transitional government prior to Bashar al-Asad's official succession. After a brief flirtation with a political opening, the younger Asad cracked down on dissent, and Khaddam acted as one of the leading spokesmen for the regime's reactionary faction. He accused political reformers of complicity in foreign plots and of sabotaging the nation's struggle against Israel. In the realm of foreign affairs, Khaddam has remained deeply involved in Lebanon and regional relations.

KHARIJI. A small Muslim sect that had its greatest importance in early **Islamic** history in the disputes over the **caliphate**. They emerged during the contest between **Ali ibn Abi Talib** and **Mu`awiya** when the former agreed to an arbitration to settle their dispute. Some of Ali's followers opposed his compromise and they seceded (*kharaja*) from his camp, then becoming his deadly enemies for what they considered to be his betrayal of fundamental religious principles. In 661, a Khariji assassinated Ali, but an attempt on Mu`awiya's life failed. In later years, Khariji revolts would plague the **Umayyad** dynasty and its successor, the **Abbasid** dynasty. The movement was strong in parts of **Iraq, Iran,** Arabia, and North Africa, while in Syria it established a strong presence among Arab tribes in **Jazira** until the 10th century.

KHURI, FARIS AL- (1877-1962). This prominent nationalist in the **French Mandate** era was unusually influential for a **Christian.** In the early mandate period Khuri was a political ally of **Abd al-Rahman Shahbandar** and served as vice president of the **People's Party.** For his role in supporting the **Great Revolt** of 1925-1927, the French briefly exiled him. In 1932 Khuri helped form the **National Bloc,** in whose leadership he would figure throughout the mandate era. He was part of the delegation that went to Paris in 1936 to negotiate the **Franco-Syrian Treaty,** and he served as speaker of parliament from 1936 to 1939, and again in 1943. He headed three short-lived ministries in 1944-1945 before returning to his position as speaker of parliament.

In the independence period, Khuri became prime minister in October 1954 following the first free national elections since 1947 and five years of military domination. His cabinet drew heavily from the conservative **National Party** and People's Party, both known for pro-Western stances in **foreign policy.** The increasingly popular neutralist impulse, though, was well represented in parliament, and Khuri had to declare his intention to keep Syria out of any pro-Western alliances. In January 1955, he attended an Arab ministers' conference in Cairo meant to coordinate opposition to **Iraq**'s participation in a security pact with **Turkey.** Khuri's refusal to condemn Iraq led to the fall of his cabinet on 7 February 1955.

KING-CRANE COMMISSION. At the Paris Peace Conference of 1918-1919, American President Woodrow Wilson proposed that the allies send a commission to the Arab lands to determine the wishes of the people regarding their political future. **France** and Great Britain refused to participate, but Wilson still sent an American team headed by Dr. Henry Churchill King and Mr. Charles R. Crane to conduct the inquiry. The commission visited **Damascus** from 25 June to 19 July 1919. During their visit, they met with the **Syrian Congress**, religious leaders, and various delegations. They reported overwhelming sentiment for the unity and independence of Syria, including **Palestine**, under a constitutional monarchy with Amir **Faysal** as king. Members of the commission learned that a limited mandate would be acceptable and that the **United States** was the preferred mandatory power. While a mandate held by Great Britain was also deemed acceptable, there was nearly complete opposition to France's aspirations in Syria. In October 1919, President Wilson suffered a stroke, and the United States withdrew from the diplomatic process. The commission's support for Syrian self-determination collided with French and British ambitions to carve out spheres of influence and its findings were completely ignored as the European powers established their rule over Arab lands against the will of the people.

KURD ALI, MUHAMMAD (1876-1953). Pioneer of journalism and author of popular works on Arab and Syrian history. He studied under the religious and educational reformer **Tahir al-Jaza'iri** and frequented circles calling for administrative and social reform in the **Ottoman Empire.** Kurd Ali gained early notoriety for publishing *al-Muqtabas*, one of the most influential newspapers in the years before **World War I**. In it he voiced support for the movement for Arab rights, but during World War I **Jamal Pasha** coopted him to back the Ottoman cause. After the war, Kurd Ali became prominent as a founder of the Arab Academy in 1919, and in 1922 he became its president. In the **French Mandate** era he was **education** minister in 1928. He established his place in Syrian intellectual life by publishing works on the history of **Damascus**.

KURDS. Most Kurds live in **Iran, Iraq**, and **Turkey**, but the predominantly Kurdish region of the Middle East, known as Kurdistan, also spills over into northern Syria. They are the country's largest non-Arab **minority** in Syria, as they comprise around 10 percent of the population. Syrian

Kurds speak the Bahdinani, or North Kurmanji, dialect of the Kurdish language that is spoken by the Kurds of Turkey and northern Iraq. Most Kurds live in the northern parts of the country near the Taurus Mountains, in **Jazira** province, and in the vicinity of **Aleppo**. They are mostly **Sunni** Muslim; a small number are Alevi, **Yazidi**, and **Christian**.

Kurds first became prominent in Syrian history during the 12th century when the **atabegs** included Kurdish soldiers in their armies. One Kurdish clan, the **Ayyubid**, whose most famous member was **Saladin**, established its rule over Syria and **Egypt** for 90 years. In recent history, most Kurds have been pastoral nomads living in sparsely populated regions of the north. The Kurdish population grew considerably between 1923 and 1938 when the Turkish government suppressed revolts against its strict nationalist and secular policies, and thousands of Kurds fled south. In Iran, Iraq, and Turkey, Kurdish autonomy movements have struggled against nationalist governments in the last 50 years. In Syria, on the other hand, there has been just one brief attempt to form a Kurdish political movement. In 1957, a Syrian branch of the Kurdish Democratic Party of Iraq was formed with the purpose of promoting cultural autonomy, but two years later it was banned under the **United Arab Republic**.

Throughout the 1960s, the UAR and the two **Ba'th Party** regimes strictly forbade any signs of Kurdish separateness. One enduring vestige of that period's discriminatory policy is the problem of stateless Kurds. In October 1962, the authorities conducted an exceptional census of **al-Hasaka** governorate as part of an effort to dilute the region's large Kurdish majority. The census reportedly stripped Syrian nationality from approximately 120,000 Kurds on the grounds that they could not prove residence as of 1945. They and their descendants fall into two categories. Some are classified as foreigners but possess a special identity card. Others are unregistered residents and have no official documents. Neither category may own property or businesses, obtain government or **public sector** jobs, acquire passports, or marry Syrian citizens. The government has acknowledged errors in the census and notes that individuals may petition to claim citizenship, something that a substantial minority has successfully attained. Because the children of stateless Kurds are not Syrian citizens, their numbers have grown to between 150,000 and 200,000.

The **Arab nationalist** ideology of Syrian government has discriminated against Kurds in other ways as well. In the early 1970s, the authorities encouraged Arab migrants to settle in villages near the border with Turkey to dilute the concentration of Kurds there. The government does not allow Kurdish language schools (unlike **Armenians** and **Circassians**), and Kurdish publications are sold but may not be published. In rural areas, they generally celebrate the customary Kurdish holiday Nawruz—or New Year's—without interference from the authorities. It is notable that a large number of Kurds living in the cities, especially **Damascus**, supported the **Syrian Communist Party**, in part because its leader, **Khalid Bakdash**, is Kurdish, and in part because it is one of the few Syrian political parties that is not Arab nationalist.

The Kurds play a role in the country's **foreign policy**. **Hafiz al-Asad** supported Kurdish movements in Iraq and Turkey. The Patriotic Union of Kurdistan, an Iraqi Kurdish party led by Jalal Talabani, was founded in Damascus in 1976. The Syrian government allowed the Kurdistan Workers' Party, a movement of Kurds in Turkey better known by its Kurdish acronym of PKK, to operate guerrilla bases in **Lebanon** and keep offices in Damascus from the early 1980s to 1997.

On the eve of the **United States** attack on **Iraq** in March 2003, Syria expressed concerns about the prospect of an independent Kurdish nation emerging in its aftermath. In December 2002, Kurds demonstrated outside the People's Assembly in Damascus protesting ethnic discrimination. In response to the unrest, President **Bashar al-Asad** visited Kurdish regions and met with leaders to hear their grievances and tell them that he considers them an integral part of the Syrian nation. That development may augur a welcome turn away from the record of Syrian governments' Arab ethnocentrism in dealings with the Kurds.

KUZBARI, MA'MUN AL- (c. 1914-1998). For a brief spell, he was the prime minister of the first **secessionist** government that formed after the breakup of the **United Arab Republic**. Kuzbari was an attorney and businessman from an old **Damascene** family that had a proud history of outstanding religious scholars (**ulama**) in the 18th and 19th centuries. He put together a cabinet of men from the two veteran conservative political parties, the **People's Party** and the **National Party**. He resigned after less than two months (29 September to 20 November 1961). The brevity of his tenure foreshadowed the rhythm of political life for the next 18 months, when the average tenure was three months until the **March 8, 1963 Ba`th Party coup** put an end to democratic politics.

-L-

LABOR FORCE AND UNEMPLOYMENT. Developing countries try to devise economic policies that generate gainful employment for their citizens and equip workers with technical skills needed to increase productivity in all sectors of the **economy**. Beyond these two common challenges, Syria faces the additional task of creating a large number of new jobs for its rapidly growing population. Efforts to develop the national economy and develop the potential of the work force have been complicated by significant changes in the population. Since independence, the population has quintupled, the ratio of urban to rural residence has shifted because of village to city migration, and the economy has changed from a primarily agrarian orientation to one with balance among **agriculture**, **industry**, and services.

Establishing exact figures about the labor force is difficult because observers doubt the accuracy of official statistical abstracts. Consequently, one finds wide variations in estimates on the changing shape of the labor force since independence. Nonetheless, the general tendency has been for the decline of agriculture's share of the labor force from more than one-half to around one-third (estimates range from 30 to 40 percent). Employment in the service sector, including government bodies and the **armed forces**, has increased from around 10 percent to as much as 40 percent. Industrial enterprises have raised their share of the labor force from perhaps 10 percent to about 20 percent. The figures on male-female participation in the labor force are considered more reliable. Female participation inched up from 13 percent to around 20 percent between 1980 and 2000. The largest field of work for **women** is agriculture, where the majority of the labor force is female.

Figures on unemployment are elusive. Many Syrians in the agriculture sector have only seasonal work. Overstaffing at **public sector** firms and government bodies masks a shortage of employment situations. Three-year compulsory military service for all men reduces the unemployment rate as well. One last factor that alleviates pressure on jobs is migration to the Gulf and **Lebanon**. Since 1970, government statistics usually show the unemployment rate in the vicinity of 8 percent but outside observers estimate the real rate to hover in the range of 20 percent.

While it is difficult to get a precise sense of unemployment statistics and the distribution of the labor force by sector, the primary perennial problem in Syrian manpower is crystal clear: a lack of technical capacity in the workforce. Part of the problem is that **Ba'th Party** regimes nationalized large enterprises and assumed responsibility for major infrastructure projects. Low salaries and mismanagement have caused many Syrians with professional and technical qualifications to seek work in the Gulf countries, where salaries are much higher and working conditions are better.

Another part of the problem is the failure to introduce adequate technical **education** in schools and universities. National education policy has raised literacy rates but there is an endemic shortage of skilled labor. Government authorities have grappled with this problem for decades but it persists into the new millennium and may well get worse as the costs of introducing and frequently replacing computer and scientific equipment remain beyond Syria's reach. Moreover, the government continues to adhere to an independent economic course that preserves economic sovereignty but sacrifices access to World Bank assistance let alone **United States** economic aid. The country's high birthrate means that job creation—about 200,000 to 250,000 per year to absorb young adults—will pose economic challenges that could have political ramifications in the next decade.

LABOR MOVEMENT. Syria's modern labor movement began in 1926 when Subhi Khatib founded the country's first trade union. Printers and textile workers established a number of unions in following years. The first national conference of trade unions convened in **Damascus** in 1936. Its members demanded restrictions on child labor, higher wages, a shorter work day, and legal guarantees for trade union activities. Two years later trade unions founded the General Trade Union Federation of Syria. In 1946, the Federation held a second conference at which it drafted a labor law for submission to parliament, which passed the measure. The Labor Law of 1946 marked a qualified gain for workers. On the one hand, it legalized trade unions and granted them a limited right to strike. On the other, it subordinated them to a government body, the Ministry of Labor and Social Welfare. Therefore, workers did not have a presumptive right to form trade unions but had to obtain government approval. Moreover, the Ministry of Labor vetted candidates for election to union leadership. Furthermore, the law prohibited trade unions from participating in political activity and peasants were not included among the workers who had the right to form unions. The law did promote **health** insurance and pensions for workers.

In the 1950s, the number of workers in unions grew from 28,000 in 1951 to 46,000 in 1958. Two-thirds of unionized workers were in the two main cities, **Damascus** and **Aleppo**. The Federation participated in the 1956 formation of the International Confederation of Arab Trade Unions, whose first president was Subhi Khatib.

While the first 12 years of independence had brought a number of gains to workers, the rise of nominally socialist regimes under the **United Arab Republic** and the **Ba`th Party** ironically resulted in curtailment of organized labor activity. During the UAR, the Ba`thist Ministry of Labor and Social Affairs brazenly meddled with trade union elections to stuff the leadership with Ba`th Party members and banished trade union groups under the influence of the **Syrian Communist Party**. UAR President Gamal Abd al-Nasir revoked the 1946 Labor Law that had granted the right to strike. The new UAR code provided for closer government control over trade unions. When union leaders protested the new measures, Nasir had them arrested. The UAR did, however, pass an **agricultural** relations law that extended certain safeguards to peasants, including minimum wages, regulations on child and **women**'s labor, and the right to form syndicates and to engage in collective bargaining. But like other unions, peasants did not gain a legal right to strike and were barred from political activity.

The labor code changed again under the Ba`th Party regime, which passed a new law in 1964 that affirmed the right of union members to hold elections for their leadership, but the party undermined the independence of unions and turned them into instruments for controlling workers. First, the regime packed the Ministry of Labor and Social Affairs with loyalists and then the ministry rigged union elections to defeat the more popular Nasirists. Likewise, the party took over the General Federation of Trade Unions and established a General Peasants Union along similar lines. The long-term effect of these measures has been to rein in the historically restive and fractious trade unions. On the other hand, the regime depends on labor for political support and must devote substantial, and often scarce, financial resources to pay for **public sector** workers' benefits. The persistent political significance of labor is evident from the regime's appointment of the General Federation of Trade Unions head to the highest government bodies deliberating economic policy, ensuring that workers' concerns are given a hearing if not often a decisive voice.

LAHHAM, DURAYD AL- (1934-   ). Syria's most famous popular performer has a long string of accomplishments in **theater, television,** and **cinema**. Before discovering his acting talent, Lahham taught chemistry at **Damascus** University, but an opportunity to appear in a television series in 1960 led him to switch from **education** to entertainment.

His comic character, Ghawar al-Tawsha, combines elements of Damascene popular culture with Chaplinesque touches of social satire. His critical success and popular acclaim stem in some measure from his collaboration with another talented performer, Nihad al-Qal`i, and with a leading literary figure, **Muhammad al-Maghut**. Lahham's grip on Syrians' hearts reportedly reached the extent that even President **Hafiz al-Asad** granted him special dispensation in stretching the limits on political expression in his theatrical satires targeting **corruption** and hypocrisy.

His most celebrated work is the play *Here's to You, O Homeland* (1979), a bitter commentary on the manifold failures of political leaders that resonated with audiences across the Arab world. The play uses farce to address grim matters like torture, as in the scene where a political prisoner laughs at his torturer preparing to subject him to electrical shocks because he knows that the country's endemic power cuts mean there will be no electric current.

In the 1990s, Lahham turned to producing movies and television shows for children, an initiative that gained him recognition from the **United Nations** Children Fund (UNICEF) and designation in 1991 as the Fund's ambassador for children in the Middle East and North Africa. This international honor was preceded by a series of awards from Arab leaders and institutions.

LAJA', AL-. This is a 900-square-kilometer region in southwestern Syria that consists in large measure of lava flows. Because of its rugged topography, the area became a refuge for dissident groups and even outlaws at different times, hence the name "*al-laja'*," which means "the refuge." Its southern portion abuts the **Jabal Druze**, the **Golan Heights**, and the **Hawran** regions. During the first millennium B.C., small towns and villages developed as the area combined **agriculture** and regional **trade** in the Roman and **Byzantine** eras. During the 19th and 20th centuries, **Druzes** and **bedouin** in southern Syria would retreat to al-Laja' when they rebelled against the **Ottomans** and the **French Mandate** authorities.

LAKE ASAD. An artificial body of water created by the **Tabqa Dam** to store water for irrigation. The lake also supplies nearly all of **Aleppo**'s drinking water.

LAND REFORM. During the last 60 years of **Ottoman** rule (c. 1860-1920), the bulk of cultivable land in central Syria from **Aleppo** to **Damascus** came under the control of urban absentee landlords. During the **French Mandate**, authorities continued the Ottoman effort at registering and surveying **agricultural** lands as well as favoring the expansion of large estates. The first proposals to limit landholdings came from **Husni al-Za`im** in 1949. A legal basis for land reform was laid in the **constitution** of 1950 under **Adib al-Shishakli**, and political pressure for measures to reform tenure and land distribution came from **Akram al-Hawrani**'s **Arab Socialist Party**. He convened a peasant conference at Aleppo in August 1951 to demonstrate mass support for land reform. The event succeeded in pushing parliament to pass a land reform bill in January 1952, but landlords then lobbied for it to be rescinded.

The first lasting measures were the **United Arab Republic**'s agrarian reforms of 1958. At the time less than one percent of the rural population controlled about half of the cultivated lands. The UAR's reform established ceilings on private holdings of 80 hectares for irrigated land and 300 hectares for unirrigated land. By 1961, the government had taken about one-third of the land that could be expropriated, but only a tiny portion had been distributed to landless peasants. Another provision of the UAR land reform was the establishment of agricultural cooperatives.

Following Syria's **secession** from the UAR, a short-lived conservative government raised the ceilings on landholdings, but then a more radical cabinet restored the UAR ceilings and strengthened the land reform law to accelerate the distribution of land to peasants. Then, in 1963, the first regime of the **Ba`th Party** enacted amendments that lowered the ceiling on allowable holdings, thereby increasing the amount of land liable to expropriation and distribution. From 1965 to 1971, Ba`thist regimes implemented the expropriation and distribution of land. These measures created a large class of peasants with medium-size holdings and reduced the share of large landowners to about 10 percent of cultivated lands. While the various phases of land reform certainly created more equitable conditions in the countryside, they also had a disruptive effect on production in the first decade before it recovered in the 1970s.

The results of land reform have fallen far short of achieving equitable distribution. Because poor peasants received small, unirrigated parcels and had only limited access to machinery and credit, they frequently fell into debt and relinquished their plots or rented them to others. For the most part, land reform did not improve the welfare of the rural poor, who have become landless laborers and sharecroppers or migrated to cities. On the other hand, peasants with medium-sized estates fared better and did benefit from new institutions like the Peasants Union and cooperatives. As for the old class of large landowners, many of them held on to large estates at the same time that high-ranking military officers and government officials formed a new class of wealthy landowners by investing in choice rural properties.

Forty years after land reform, the main changes have been the growth in number and wealth of medium-sized estates, the emergence of new large landowners, and the prominent role of government agencies in setting procurement prices for key crops and providing technical and credit facilities.

LANGUAGES. About 90 percent of Syrians speak Arabic as their mother tongue. Differences between regional dialects are noticeable, but they are not so great as to hamper easy interaction among citizens. They are, however, a source of light humor in popular culture, with **Aleppans** making fun of **Damascenes** for their lilt and Damascenes returning the favor for the heavier Aleppan accent. Arabic is the official language and is taught at all schools. As in other Arab countries, the gap between spoken Arabic and formal written Arabic, known as diglossia, is quite significant and a formidable obstacle to the acquisition of a high degree of literacy.

Even though a large majority of the citizens are Arab, there are several other languages still spoken and used in **Christian** religious services. Such linguistic pluralism is a vestige of premodern society before the rise of political and economic pressures for cultural homogeneity. **Kurdish** is spoken by about 10 percent of the population. Since the **United Arab Republic**, Kurdish-language **education** has been prohibited in schools, and except for a few spells of political leniency, it has been illegal to publish Kurdish-language books or periodicals. Because Syrian Kurds form part of a much larger Kurdish community that straddles **Iraq**, **Turkey**, and **Iran**, they are likely to preserve their language for the foreseeable future.

A small number of Syrian citizens speak languages other than Arabic or Kurdish, but the long-term tendency is for the young generation to Arabize because of national education and economic integration. The close-knit **Armenian** community keeps its language alive in the home and in the liturgy of its churches. Aramaic is spoken in a handful of villages in the vicinity of Damascus and is probably a dying language except for liturgical purposes. A related language, Syriac, is spoken by the **Assyrians** who live in the northeast along the **Khabur River**. **Circassian** is the language of Muslim refugees from Russian expansion in the Caucasus during the late 1800s. Circassian villages on and near the **Golan Heights** preserved their ancestral tongue. Finally, there is a small, scattered population of **Turkomen** who speak a Turkic language. They are descendants of Turkish nomads who settled in the region during **Ottoman** times and for centuries preserved a distinct identity, but like other small language groups are tending to Arabize.

LATAKIA. The major port of northern Syria and an ancient Phoenician settlement, it is named for the mother (Laodice) of the Seleucid ruler who laid out the Hellenistic city. Latakia is in the middle of a fertile coastal region at the western edge of **Jabal Ansariyya**. Although it was a major city in Greek and Roman times, its significance diminished in the **Islamic** era. When **France** ruled Syria, though, it made Latakia the capital of a separate **Alawi** state. The city's importance to Syria's future was determined by the 1938 cession of **Alexandretta**, which traditionally served as northern Syria's port, to **Turkey**. After independence, the Syrian government funded a project to enlarge and improve Latakia's port (1950-1957). The growth of **trade** required a second project (1958-1968). The city's population has grown from 7,000 at the turn of the century to about 350,000 today, making it the country's fourth largest city.

LEAGUE OF ARAB STATES. Also known as the Arab League. In 1943, Egyptian Prime Minister Mustafa al-Nahhas conducted talks with delegations from Syria, **Iraq, Lebanon, Saudi Arabia**, and **Transjordan** with a view to establishing a framework for Arab cooperation. Nahhas then persuaded the governments of those countries to send representatives to Alexandria to constitute a preparatory committee that would pave the way for founding a pan-Arab organization. The preparatory committee, including the prime ministers of Syria, Iraq, Lebanon, and Transjordan, duly convened in September 1944. On 7 October, they approved the

Alexandria Protocol, which called for the creation of the League of Arab States to promote political, economic, social, and cultural cooperation. Negotiations over the text of the League's pact were completed in March 1945, and the League was formally established 10 May 1945. It has provided a framework for inter-Arab relations and the resolution of conflict, although its effectiveness has been hamstrung by bitter disputes among member states.

LEAGUE OF NATIONAL ACTION. A pan-Arab nationalist movement founded in 1933 as a public successor to the secret Arab Liberation Society, which had been created in 1929 and modeled on the **Ottoman**-era Arab societies **al-Fatat** and al-Ahd. The League's pan-Arab ideology clearly distinguished it from the **National Bloc**, which focused on independence for Syria. In accord with its ideology, the League established branches in **Iraq** and **Palestine**. Although dissatisfied with the Bloc's moderation toward **French Mandate** authorities, the League lacked a mass base and therefore tended to cooperate with the Bloc. The French banned the League in March 1939. The ephemeral body's chief importance was as the political incubator of important personalities like **Akram al-Hawrani, Zaki al-Arsuzi**, and Jallal al-Sayyid, all of whom became involved in other political movements in the 1940s.

LEBANESE CIVIL WAR. This tragic conflict lasted from 1975 to 1990 and was the occasion for Syrian military intervention and occupation of much of the country. The civil war had its roots in long-simmering political tensions over a variety of issues, the central one in domestic affairs being the distribution of power in **Lebanon**'s political system. These tensions erupted into full-blown civil war in April 1975. On one side, leftist Lebanese and **Palestinian** militias fought for fundamental changes in Lebanon's political system, economic policy, and the government's stance toward the large Palestinian refugee population; on the other side, largely Maronite **Christian** militias supported the political status quo. In June 1976, Syrian forces entered Lebanon to prevent a victory by leftist-Palestinian forces. A stable cease-fire was negotiated among the various parties in October 1976.

The failure of Lebanon's various factions and militias to agree on a political resolution for the civil war prolonged Syria's occupation of much of the country. From 1977 to 1978, Syria's brief alliance with the Maronites broke down as the latter turned to **Israel** for support against the Palestinians and Lebanese left. A new element arose in 1981 when the

Lebanese Forces under Bashir Gemayel consolidated hegemony over the hitherto divided Maronite community and developed an alliance with Israel. Gemayel wanted Israel to invade Lebanon in order to force the Syrians out. In pursuit of this aim, he launched an attempt to take over the Bekaa Valley town of Zahle in April 1981. The Syrians counterattacked, and it took intensive diplomatic mediation by the **United States** to prevent the outbreak of hostilities between Israel and Syria. Gemayel's hopes for Israeli intervention, however, were merely delayed until Israel's June 1982 invasion began the **Lebanese War of 1982**. Despite Israel's military victory, Syria was able to regain its dominant position in Lebanon by the end of 1985 but could not bring about a resolution of the civil conflict.

The last chapter of the civil war began with the expiration of President Amin Gemayel's term in September 1988 and the failure of parliament to elect a successor. Gemayel designated General Michel Aoun head of a caretaker government, but the cabinet refused to recognize Aoun and insisted on its sole legitimacy to represent the government. Syria attempted to devise a formula for political reform to end the crisis, but Aoun declared that a Syrian withdrawal must precede any discussion of reform and he proclaimed a war of liberation to expel Syrian troops from the country. Arab mediation led to the **Ta'if Accord** of October 1989, providing for changes in the political system, but Aoun rejected the accord and the governments of first Rene Muawad and then Ilyas Hrawi elected according to its terms. Lebanon witnessed some of the war's worst fighting from 1989 to 1990 as Lebanese became divided between Aoun's enthusiastic followers and his enemies backed by Syria. The stalemate was broken in October 1990 after Syria agreed to participate in the coalition against **Iraq**'s annexation of Kuwait. In a gesture of gratitude, the **United States** gave Syria the green light to carry out an air attack on Aoun at the presidential palace, forcing him to flee to the French embassy and ending his challenge to Syrian domination. Since that time, Lebanon has gradually reconstituted itself along the lines laid down by the Ta'if Accord but Syria has not withdrawn its military force from its neighbor, so one of the casualties of the civil war has been Lebanon's sovereignty.

LEBANESE WAR OF 1982. In June 1982, **Israel** invaded **Lebanon** in order to destroy the **Palestine Liberation Organization**, which had established its headquarters in Beirut in the early 1970s. Initially, Syria stayed out of the conflict, but Israeli forces attacked Syrian troops in the Bekaa Valley, destroyed Syria's surface-to-air missile installations in Lebanon, and inflicted a huge defeat on the Syrian air force. Nonetheless, the bulk of Syrian ground forces merely staged a limited retreat to more defensible positions within Lebanon while a smaller number participated in defending Beirut against Israel. Meanwhile, the **Soviet Union**, chagrined at the dismal performance of its missile defense systems, resupplied the Syrian army and air force. On the other hand, Israel's eight-week siege of Beirut succeeded in forcing the PLO to withdraw from Lebanon by the end of August. Israel also engineered the election of its Lebanese ally Bashir Gemayel to the presidency with the expectation that he would negotiate a peace treaty and pressure Syrian forces to withdraw. Gemayel, however, was assassinated in early September and succeeded by his brother Amin Gemayel, who was less beholden to Israeli interests. After Bashir's assassination, Christian militiamen carried out a massacre of **Palestinian** civilians in two Beirut refugee camps. An Israeli government inquiry found several officials indirectly responsible for the atrocity at Sabra and Shatila camps. Furthermore, the massacres led to the deployment of a multinational force of American, French, and Italian troops, and the **United States** decided to keep its troops in Lebanon to support the Amin Gemayel government.

There followed an American initiative to arrange a treaty between Israel and Lebanon. Amin Gemayel's government negotiated with Israel an agreement that was signed on 17 May 1983. The agreement granted Israel the right to establish permanent surveillance posts in the south as well as to conduct land and air patrols. It also made an Israeli withdrawal contingent on one by Syria. In response, Syria rallied Lebanese forces that opposed the agreement and Gemayel's bid to restore Lebanon's pre-civil war political structure. By the beginning of 1984, Syria had forced Gemayel to abandon the May 1983 agreement with Israel. Moreover, Syrian support for Lebanese guerrilla attacks against Israeli soldiers induced its leaders to withdraw their troops to a strip of territory in southern Lebanon that Israel declared its security zone. In February 1984, President Gemayel formally revoked the accord with Israel. The aftermath of the war lasted another 16 years until May 2000 when Israel withdrew its troops following a protracted guerrilla war against **Hizballah** and other Syrian-backed Lebanese groups.

LEBANON. In the late **Ottoman** era, a special regime was established in Mount Lebanon, the central mountainous region of the present-day country. When **France** took over Syria and Lebanon after **World War I**, it formally divided the two and enlarged the province of Mount Lebanon by attaching to it predominantly Muslim regions to its north, east, and south, including the port cities of Beirut, Tripoli, Sidon, and Tyre. Reattachment of these districts and cities to Syria was a popular nationalist issue among Lebanese Muslims and Syrian nationalists during the early **French Mandate** period. By the outbreak of **World War II**, however, the permanence of Lebanon's boundaries had won grudging acceptance among Syrian and Lebanese Muslim leaders, although popular political movements in both countries would continue to oppose the new map.

In the independence era, a dispute arose between Lebanon and Syria over their unified customs regime, which dated to the mandate era. France had treated them as a unified administration until 1937, when the Lebanese and Syrian governments agreed to separate them, but could not reach accord on the division of revenues. In March 1950, the **Khalid al-Azm** government terminated the customs union, a move that caused severe disruption to the Syrian **economy**. The dispute ended two years later. Relations between the neighbors remained tense for much of the 1950s because of Syria's foreign policy of neutrality and Lebanon's pro-Western orientation. This difference became most evident in 1958 shortly after the formation of the **United Arab Republic** when Lebanese **Arab nationalists** agitated for adherence to the union. Lebanon's President Camille Chamoun invoked the **Eisenhower Doctrine**, which promised American support against communist subversion, and American marines landed in Lebanon to shore up the government. In the 1960s, Syria's **Ba`th Party** regimes castigated Lebanon for maintaining a pro-Western stance.

In the 1970s, Syria viewed Lebanon through the prism of its own strategic security vis-à-vis **Israel**. The loss of the **Golan Heights** in the **June 1967 War** and instability in Lebanon caused Syrian leaders to fear an Israeli attack through Lebanese territory. Consequently, since its 1976 intervention in the **Lebanese Civil War**, Syria has insisted that any resolution of that conflict take into consideration its strategic interests. To maintain a dominant position, **Damascus** has cultivated tactical alliances with Lebanese **Druze**, **Shi`i**, and **Sunni** groups to block the rise of radical political forces or the triumph of conservative elements backed by Israel. The most severe threat to Syria's position in Lebanon came during the **Lebanese War of 1982** when Israel invaded and occupied much of the country. Syria was able to dig in and assist Lebanese militias that waged a guerrilla struggle against Israeli forces that compelled their withdrawal to a narrow band of territory in the far south.

In 1989-1990, Syria played an important part in resolving the Lebanese Civil War and implementing the **Ta'if Accord** by disarming most of the militias. But even with the end of civil war, Syria did not withdraw its 35,000 troops, ensuring control over Beirut's foreign policy, influence on its domestic affairs, and enhancing its own military position vis-à-vis Israel. For the Lebanese, Syrian hegemony is part of the heavy price they paid to end the civil war.

During the 1980s and 1990s, Israel's occupation of a strip of Lebanese territory along the border, its "security zone," was the cause of persistent fighting. On one side, Israeli forces and their proxy allies, the South Lebanese Army, patrolled the zone to prevent infiltration into Israel. On the other side, **Hizballah** and other groups fought a guerrilla war to force Israeli troops out. In April 1996, Israeli Prime Minister Shimon Peres decided that Hizballah had gone too far in its attacks on Israeli troops, so he ordered a massive military strike called "Grapes of Wrath." Peres hoped to deter further attacks and to bolster his domestic position on the eve of national elections. The two-week operation utterly failed to change the situation to Israel's advantage and brought a torrent of international criticism when an Israeli shell killed more than 100 civilians. In 1998, the Israeli government proposed withdrawing on condition that the Lebanese government guarantee its security, but Syria's primacy ensured that Beirut would not agree to such a deal. Moreover, as long as Israel did not budge from the Golan Heights, Damascus saw Israel's presence in southern Lebanon as an opportunity to inflict casualties through Hizballah without risking direct military confrontation or escalation. In May 2000, however, Israeli Prime Minister Ehud Barak withdrew all forces in a rapid and somewhat disorganized fashion. That maneuver ostensibly removed a point where Syria could exert pressure on Israel, but both Beirut and Damascus subsequently insisted that Israel had not completely evacuated and claimed that Israel's occupation of a small enclave known as Shab`a Farms meant that Hizballah would continue to attack its troops there. Israel's insistence that it had indeed evacuated was upheld by a **United Nations** survey that declared Shab`a Farms is part of Syrian territory that Israel seized in the June 1967 War. Nevertheless, Hizballah strikes at Israeli troops from time to time.

Syria's military forces and an extensive network of security agents make Damascus the power broker in Lebanon's domestic politics. Disputes between parties, leaders, and factions often get resolved in Damascus rather than among the Lebanese themselves. In the 1996 parliamentary elections, for example, candidate lists reflected the interference of Syrian envoys and the majority of seats went to pro-Syrian candidates. At the time of the 1998 presidential election, **Hafiz al-Asad** essentially gave the nod to Emile Lahud for the office and that was that. The Syrians seem to have interfered less in the August-September 2000 national elections that gave a landslide victory to Rafiq al-Hariri for the prime minister's office.

Coordination between the two countries deepened with an October 1999 pact to reduce tariffs on certain goods and work on joint projects in communications and electricity. The ubiquitous Syrian **security forces** operate outside the bounds of Lebanese law and are known to have abducted Lebanese and Palestinian activists and transported them to prisons in Syria. Official denials were unpersuasive, and in March 1998, the Syrians released more than 100 Lebanese men it had abducted since 1978, primarily members of the Iraqi wing of the Ba`th Party and **Islamic fundamentalists**. Then again, in December 2000, Damascus set free another 54 Lebanese it had detained at various times since 1985.

Yet another facet of Syria's domination is the influx of up to one million workers filling low-wage jobs in construction and services. Many Lebanese deeply resent their neighbor's meddling in political and economic spheres. Opposition to the Syrians takes the form of public criticism and occasional violence. While the boldest voices for a Syrian pullout usually come from Maronite Christian institutions and political organizations, Lebanese of other religious communities generally share the sentiment. Militant Lebanese underground groups have carried out sporadic attacks on Syrian workers, and some bombings inside Syria have been attributed to them. Notwithstanding public criticism and occasional attacks, President **Bashar al-Asad** openly declared in February 2001 that Syria would keep its forces in Lebanon as long as Israel occupied the Golan Heights. Still, since June 2001, Syrian forces have undertaken three partial redeployments to diminish their presence in largely Christian areas. Maronite Christian political leaders had agitated for such a move for a decade. In addition to these shifts, the number of troops has shrunk to about 20,000.

LEGAL SYSTEM. Syria's modern legal framework began to take shape during the **Tanzimat** era, when **Ottoman** statesmen drew up new codes for commercial, penal, and civil law. The last major legal initiative under Ottoman auspices was a Family Relations Law passed in 1917. This measure slightly modified marriage and divorce law in favor of **women** but essentially preserved **Islamic** law (**shari`a**) as the foundation for

family relations. The **French Mandate** era saw little alteration in the legal system because of failure to advance toward a constitutional form of self-government under Mandatory authority. In the first few years after independence, the Syrian government enacted legal codes for commercial, civil, criminal, and penal matters. The last area to be codified was personal status law, which passed in 1953, as the Syrian Code of Personal Status. It combines elements from the Ottoman and Egyptian law.

Syria has six different kinds of court. The highest court in the land is the Supreme Constitutional Court composed of a chief justice and four other justices. Each member is appointed by the president of the republic to serve a four-year term. This court's jurisdiction encompasses the constitutionality of laws, election irregularities, conflicts between lower courts, and charges of misconduct by the president of the republic. The next highest level, the court of appeal, is represented in each of Syria's 54 districts. The courts of appeal are divided into three separate branches to deal with criminal, penal, and civil matters. A third category, the tribunal of first instance, is where most legal criminal and civil cases begin. Then, there are 227 tribunals of the peace to adjudicate civil and penal matters. The influence of the government is weakest in the realm of so-called personal status issues like marriage, divorce, and inheritance. Special courts handle such matters according to separate customary rules for Muslims, **Druzes**, Orthodox **Christians**, Roman **Catholics,** and Protestants. Finally, there are courts for minors.

The judiciary's independence is compromised by the existence of a parallel network of military and state security courts. These courts first appeared under the **United Arab Republic** and had jurisdiction over "economic crimes" involving currency transactions and foreign trade. They operate without civilian oversight or regard for due process. *See also* HUMAN RIGHTS; SECURITY FORCES.

LITERATURE. Throughout history, Syrian literature has encompassed the genres of Arabic literature found from **Iraq** to North Africa. Arabs have since pre-**Islamic** times considered poetry the highest literary form, and two of Arabic poetry's great geniuses, **al-Mutanabbi** and **al-Ma`arri**, were from Syria. Other traditional literary genres included popular storytelling, rhymed prose, and religious, often mystical (**sufi**), verse. The modern history of Arabic literature began in the 19th century with a movement called *al-nahda*, the Arab renaissance. The most influential figures in the Arab renaissance came from **Egypt** and **Lebanon**, but Francis Marrash (1836-1873) of **Aleppo** contributed to neoclassical poetry and the development of didactic fiction in the direction of the novel.

In the 20th century, Syria produced a larger number of significant poets, novelists, and short story writers who not only participated in Arabic literary creativity, but also pioneered new experiments in expression. The short story is the most fully developed genre in modern Syrian fiction. Authors have written in a wide variety of styles, including socialist realism, symbolism, and surrealism. Commonly addressed themes range from political commentary to social criticism of customs that value conformity rather than individual expression and fulfillment by pursuing higher **education** and a professional career rather than finding satisfaction in customary domestic life. Some writers focus on the depiction of particular settings like the Syrian village or traditional urban quarter.

The first modern short story writer was Fuad al-Shayib (1910-1970). He published an important anthology on the eve of independence that marked a shift from old-fashioned morality tales to more realistic and harsher themes. Since the 1960s, two **women** authors, Colette al-Khuri (b. 1937 in **Damascus**) and Ghada al-Samman (b. 1942 in Damascus), have attained prominence in the growing field of Arab women's literature. Their short stories and novels criticize the general cultural preference for boys, arranged marriage, and double standards for sexual fulfillment that wink at men's indiscretions while tolerating honor killings.

The first novels came out during the **French Mandate** era and celebrated the heroes of Islamic history and resistance to colonial domination. Abd al-Salam al-Ujayli (b. 1918 in **al-Raqqa**) is the first major Syrian novelist and one of the most prolific writers whose oeuvre includes stories, novels, plays, and poetry. He is noted for incorporating political themes dealing with socialism, communism, Arab unity, and the plight of economic backwardness. Hanna Mina (b. 1924 in **Latakia**) may be the country's most popular novelist. Since his first work came out in 1954, he has gained renown for recording daily life in rural settings rapidly disappearing before electricity and paved roads. A different slice of traditional life is found in the novels and short stories of Ulfat Idilbi, who gives a woman's perspective on the settings and relationships in Muslim **family** life in the old quarters of Damascus.

Since the 1960s, experimental approaches to fiction have become more common and they are well represented in the works of an Egyptian immigrant, Walid Ikhlasi. Many of his works create a mood rather than develop a plot and they frequently express alienation. Another experimental writer, **Haydar Haydar**, unintentionally sparked a political storm in Egypt with *Banquet for Seaweed*, his novel exploring the bankruptcy of Arab politics.

In the sphere of modern Arabic poetry, Syria's contributions have fit into broader regional trends alongside those from Egyptian, **Iraqi**, and Lebanese poets. Syria's poets of the 1920s and 1930s reflected the nationalist mood by recalling the heroes of Arab history. After 1948, the combative spirit of **Palestinian** poetry influenced Syrians like Sulayman al-Isa, himself displaced from Antioch after **Turkey** annexed **Alexandretta**.

Since the mid-1960s, three Syrians above all others have made their mark on the Arab literary scene. They are **Nizar Qabbani**, for his daring erotic poetry; **Adonis**, for his bold, erudite experiments in form and diction as well as for his penetrating critical essays; and **Muhammad al-Maghut**, for his highly personal form of expression in non-metrical prose poems. A number of Syrian women have also left their mark on contemporary poetry. The most prominent include al-Maghut's late wife Saniya Salih (1935-1984) and Samar al-`Attar (b. 1945), who is also a novelist.

-M-

MA`ARRI, ABU AL-ALA AL-** (973-1058). One of the great masters of classical Arabic poetry and prose, he spent most of his life in his native town, Ma`arrat al-Nu`man, a northern Syrian town between **Homs** and **Aleppo**. As a small child, Ma`arri was stricken by smallpox and became blind. He is known as the "twofold prisoner" because of his blindness and his decision to seclude himself in his room at the family home after his mother's death in 1010. The poet was also renowned for his asceticism, which included an austere vegetarian diet and a vow to never marry or have children. In fact, he requested that the inscription on his grave read, "This wrong was by my father done to me, but never by me to anyone." He lived during the era of **Hamdanid decline and **Mirdasid** ascendancy, a period of disarray and strife in northern Syria as the **Fatimids** and **Byzantines** contended for domination over the region. Around 1008, Ma`arri traveled to Baghdad, which had once been the peerless center of Arabic literary culture, but he found only a shadow of its former greatness. When he returned to Syria, he learned that his mother had just died. During nearly 50 years of seclusion, he corresponded with poets and officials in Syria, **Iraq**, and **Egypt**; for instance, he entered a debate with a Fatimid scholar who challenged the virtue of his vegetarianism.

His pensive, brooding poetry reflects a deep contemplation of religious and philosophical themes. Ma`arri expressed a strong faith in God, but he doubted the reality of resurrection, a fundamental tenet of **Islam**, and he emphasized the power of human reason. Such views caused some Muslims to call into question his religious orthodoxy. His contributions to Arabic prose include a commentary on contemporary political events and personalities delivered by animals, but his better-known work is "The Epistle of Forgiveness." In this work, prompted by an epistle from an Aleppan scholar, Ma`arri presents a drama set in Paradise and Hell that has led some modern critics to posit it, rather doubtfully, as an influence on Dante's *Divine Comedy*.

MADRASA. A madrasa is a Muslim religious school. For centuries, it was the most widespread form of organized learning in the Muslim world. A madrasa customarily consisted of a mosque, a school, and rooms for student lodgers. The institution first appeared in eastern **Iran** during the 11th century and spread westward. The first madrasa in Syria was erected in 1098 under a **Saljuk** prince of **Damascus**. **Nur al-Din Mahmud** (r. 1146-1174) and **Saladin** (r. 1174-1193) were the first avid builders of madrasas in Syria, and later **Ayyubid** and **Mamluk** rulers emulated them. By 1500, Damascus alone had more than 120 madrasas. The typical madrasa took a rectangular shape. One entered the main courtyard through an elaborately sculpted portal. The courtyard had one or more arcades along the perimeter and an interior prayer hall. The legal instrument for establishing a madrasa was a **waqf**, a deed of property and its income for charitable purposes in perpetuity. The donor usually specified how it was to be administered and what subjects were to be taught. In most instances, the major focus of instruction was **Islamic** jurisprudence, *fiqh*, according to one of the four traditional **Sunni** schools of law (sing. *madhhab*). Donors often created endowments for teachers' stipends and students' lodging and a food allowance.

From the 11th century until the late 19th century, the madrasa represented the pinnacle of learning. In the era of **Ottoman** reform, however, Western forms and curricula began to displace the madrasa. In modern times, higher learning in Islamic sciences has been incorporated into Damascus University's College of Islamic Law.

MADRID CONFERENCE. An international conference on the Arab-Israeli conflict held on 30 October to 3 November 1991. After the **United States** and coalition forces, including Syria, expelled **Iraq** from Kuwait, the first

George Bush administration took a bold diplomatic initiative to bring all parties to the Arab-Israeli conflict into a comprehensive process to reach a peace settlement. In July 1991, Syria announced its agreement to attend such an international conference sponsored by the United States and the **Soviet Union**. The Madrid Conference marked the first time since the **Armistice of 1949** talks that Syrian and Israeli representatives met in an official diplomatic forum. The conference itself was more ceremonial than substantial, but it marked a major breakthrough in attempts to end the conflict. It was followed by bilateral talks held in Washington and multilateral talks held at various sites in Europe and the Middle East. Syria refused to attend the multilateral talks on arms control, **water**, economic development, and the **environment**. Bilateral **Syrian-Israeli peace talks** continued intermittently throughout the 1990s, but they failed to reach a settlement.

MAGHUT, MUHAMMAD AL- (1934-). This versatile man of letters is best known for his contributions to modernist poetry but has also made a mark with short stories and plays. In the more popular medium of **television** screenwriting, he collaborated with the noted comic **Durayd al-Lahham** to create scripts for the actor's widely acclaimed character Ghawwar. Al-Maghut was born in **Salamiyya**, a medium-sized provincial town. Even though he did not have an advanced formal education in Arabic **literature** and was not familiar with modern European literature, he received critical acclaim for his first poetry anthology published in 1959. For many years he lived in Beirut and participated in its lively literary scene. He then lived for a time in **Damascus**, but like many creative writers and intellectuals, he found the repressive political climate intolerable and he moved to the Gulf.

Al-Maghut's poetry is notable for its concrete similes and the absence of the sort of pedantic allusions to classical Arabic phrases and modern European trends that are commonly found in modern Arabic verse. He eschews classical poetic forms and meter, preferring a more direct mode of composition. His oeuvre encompasses an impressive range of themes. They frequently convey the feeling of a villager adrift and lonely in the indifferent city. Al-Maghut, himself from a small provincial town, often uses rural imagery like the desert, **bedouins**, blossoms, and birds. Omens of death, pain, and hunger litter his poems. He is capable of causing even the distant reader to shudder at his images of the bleak political and social landscapes of Arab countries and the sheer terror of living in the shadow of omnipotent **security forces (*mukhabarat*)**. In a more personal vein, al-Maghut dedicated poems to his wife and fellow poet, Saniyya Salih.

MALKI, ADNAN AL- (1918-1955). Deputy chief of staff of the army, Colonel Malki's assassination on 22 April 1955, while he attended a soccer match, created a political firestorm. In December 1952, Malki had led an abortive coup against **Adib al-Shishakli** that resulted in his arrest. After Shishakli's downfall in February 1954, he was restored to his rank and he rallied army support for neutralist politicians and opposition to Syria's adherence to the **Baghdad Pact**. By the time of his murder, Malki was one of the most powerful figures in the **armed forces** and thus in national politics. The assassin, who committed suicide right after shooting Malki, was a sergeant who belonged to the pro-Western **Syrian Social National Party**, which was seeking influence in the army. But the event was the occasion for a campaign of repression against the party, which was banned and whose members were purged from the army and bureaucracy. The leftist parties—**Syrian Communist Party** and the **Ba'th Party**—exploited Malki's martyrdom to boost their own popularity as upholders of Syrian independence from foreign domination. There followed trials of SSNP members and several men accused of plotting the assassination. In June, 140 SSNP members were indicted for complicity in the crime and conspiring with the **United States** to install a pro-Western government. The trial lasted from August to December and resulted in harsh sentences for 26 SSNP members. In the larger political context, the Malki affair weakened conservatives and boosted the standing of leftists.

MA'LULA. The largest of three villages in modern Syria where a dialect of Aramaic is still spoken. Ma'lula is 60 kilometers southeast of **Damascus** at an elevation of 1,500 meters on a plateau at the southern end of the Anti-Lebanon range. It is famous for its ancient **Christian** holy places, including the monastery of St. Sergius, which dates from **Byzantine** times. Its current population of 2,000 is mostly **Greek Orthodox**. The younger generation is tending to use Arabic more in speech, although young people can understand their elders and speak Aramaic. The other two Aramaic-speaking villages are Bakh'a and Jabba'din.

MAMLUK. The Arabic term for a military slave. The **Abbasids** were the first Muslim dynasty to use mamluks. They would purchase non-Muslim slaves (**Islamic** law [**shari'a**] prohibits the enslavement of Muslims) and train them for service to the ruler. In the second half of the ninth century, the Abbasid **caliphate** came to depend on mamluks to serve as palace guards. Later Muslim dynasties perpetuated the practice. Mamluks constituted a crucial part of later **Ayyubid** armies, and eventually they seized power in **Egypt** and Syria in the middle of the 13th century. These slave soldiers established the **Mamluk sultanate**, which ruled Egypt, Syria, and much of Arabia until the **Ottoman** conquest of 1516-1517. The Ottomans eliminated the mamluks in Syria, but mamluk commanders and their cohorts remained an important element in Egypt throughout the first three centuries of Ottoman rule.

MAMLUK SULTANATE. A line of Turkish and **Circassian** sultans who ruled Syria from 1260 until 1516. The practice of relying on slave soldiers in Muslim societies went back to **Abbasid** times. The **Ayyubid** dynasty that ruled **Egypt** and Syria in the late 12th and early 13th centuries was just one of several Muslim powers to import, train, and depend on regiments of military slaves. In 1250, a band of these slaves seized power in Egypt and brought down the local Ayyubid line. The new regime would be based on the importation, training, and promotion to high office of military slaves from Central Asia and the Caucasus region.

The Mamluks initially entered Syria in 1260 in response to a **Mongol** invasion, and they were the first Muslim power to defeat the Mongols on the field of battle at **Ayn Jalut**. There followed five decades of intermittent Mongol-Mamluk warfare marked by Mamluk success in turning back Mongol invasions in 1281, 1299-1303, and finally 1313. They also effected the complete and final eviction of the Latin **Crusader** kingdoms. In 1268, Mamluk troops captured Antioch; in 1291, Acre fell, followed by Tyre, Sidon, and Beirut. Meanwhile, the remaining Ayyubid potentates scattered in Syria were absorbed by the Mamluk sultanate.

The Mamluks were not Arab, but their victories over Mongol and **Christian** invaders earned them a degree of political legitimacy that they augmented with generous support for monumental urban construction and patronage of religious institutions like **madrasas**. While Cairo remained the seat of the Mamluk sultanate, **Damascus** became a second capital from which Mamluk amirs ruled **Palestine** and coastal Syria. In fact, Damascus enjoyed a prolonged period of economic expansion and urban improvement during the 14th century. **Aleppo** was made the capital of northern Syria and also witnessed a long revival under Mamluk rule following its disastrous experiences under three Mongol occupations between 1260 and 1300. In these and other Syrian cities, the first century of Mamluk rule saw the construction and repair of dozens of mosques, schools, hospitals (**bimaristans**), and convents, as well as waterworks.

The prosperity and stability of Mamluk rule eroded during the last decade of the 14th century under the impact of civil wars among Mamluk factions contending for supremacy. These struggles left the Mamluks vulnerable to the Central Asian conqueror **Timur Leng**, who smashed Mamluk power in 1400 and wreaked havoc on Syrian cities. Sultan Barsbay (r. 1422-1438) restored order, but the last five decades of Mamluk rule, 1468-1516, were marked by wars against **Turkomen** powers to the north, Christian piracy in the Mediterranean, growing **bedouin** incursions on settled lands, and abuses of power by Mamluk amirs. Mamluk rule ended in October 1516, when the **Ottoman** Sultan **Selim I** conquered Syria.

MARCH 8, 1963 COUP. In this turning point of modern Syrian history, a coalition of three groups of officers overthrew the civilian government of **Khalid al-Azm**. The conspirators included **Ba`th Party** officers in the **Military Committee**, Nasirist officers, and an independent group led by Major-General **Ziyad al-Hariri**, whose brigade stationed in **Jabal Druze** marched on **Damascus** while other units seized the air force base outside Damascus. The new rulers then established a **National Revolutionary Command Council** of 20 members, including 12 Ba`thists and eight Nasirists and independents. The council declared a state of emergency that abolished the democratic liberties that the Azm government had reinstated only 10 weeks before. In the aftermath of the coup, a power struggle among the three groups of officers resulted in the triumph of the Military Committee by the beginning of August, thus inaugurating Ba`thist rule in Syria.

MARDAM, JAMIL (1894-1960). One of Syria's foremost political leaders during the **French Mandate** era. As a young man he was active in the **Arab nationalist** secret society **al-Fatat**. During the early years of the French Mandate, Mardam joined the **People's Party** and later was a founding member of the **National Bloc**, in which he led the moderate faction seeking to cooperate with the French. In 1933, his leadership of the Bloc was challenged by the more pan-Arab **Shukri al-Quwwatli**, who encouraged the growth of the **League of National Action** to strengthen his position in the Bloc. But Mardam held on to the leadership and served as prime minister of the National Bloc government of 1936 to 1939. That government's several failures, particularly its inability to secure ratification of the **Franco-Syrian Treaty** by French parliament or to prevent **Turkey**'s annexation of **Alexandretta**, severely damaged Mardam's standing in the Bloc. Moreover, his government encountered strong resistance in regions that the French had administered separately between 1922 and 1936: **Jabal Druze, Jabal Ansariyya**, and **Jazira**. Mardam suffered further blows when several prominent figures, including **Faris al-Khuri** and **Lutfi al-Haffar**, resigned from the Bloc's executive committee in 1938. He also faced opposition from **Abd al-Rahman Shahbandar**, who rallied those upset with the prime minister's handling of the Alexandretta issue and negotiations over the treaty. Mardam responded by censoring newspapers expressing Shahbandar's views and placed him under house arrest. The final blow to Mardam's government came in November 1938 when the French parliament voted against ratification of the treaty, but he did not resign until February 1939. Two months later, his longtime rival for leadership of the National Bloc, Shukrı al-Quwwatli, ascended to the position of party chief. When Shahbandar was assassinated in June 1940, the investigation charged Mardam with plotting the crime and he fled to **Iraq**, where he spent the next two years.

When he returned to Syria, the country was preparing for national elections scheduled for July 1943. Mardam and Quwwatli patched up their differences to strengthen the National Bloc's electoral prospects. After the Bloc swept the polls, **Sa`dallah al-Jabiri** formed a cabinet with Mardam as foreign minister. When the Jabiri government fell in December 1946, President Quwwatli invited Mardam to head a cabinet. After the elections of 1947 returned the **National Party** to power, Mardam formed a new cabinet, which plunged the country into the **Palestine War of 1948**. Syrian public opinion held the government responsible for the army's poor showing against **Israel** and rumors spread that Mardam embezzled funds collected for the war. He tried to restore public confidence by forming a new cabinet in August 1948, but few were convinced that it represented real change, and the country slipped into three months of turmoil and political violence. The crisis subsided when Mardam submitted his resignation on 1 December, spelling the end of his long run as one of Syria's leading politicians.

MARJ DABIQ. This small town on northern Syria's **Quwayq River** was the site of the decisive battle fought in August 1516, when **Ottoman** Sultan **Selim I** defeated **Mamluk** forces. That victory opened the way for Syria's incorporation into the Ottoman Empire.

MASHARQA, ZUHAYR AL- (1938-). A prominent member of the **Hafiz al-Asad** regime during the 1980s. He is from **Aleppo** and has a professional background in law. Unlike most other high-ranking officials in Asad's circle, Masharqa had a brief spell in the private **industrial** sector as manager of a manufacturing concern. In the 1970s, he was governor of **Hama**, then minister of **education** and deputy secretary-general of the **Ba`th Party**. He became one of three vice presidents in 1984 after the political crisis in the wake of Hafiz al-Asad's serious illness in fall 1983. Masharqa was vice president for education and cultural affairs alongside the other two vice presidents, **Abd al-Halim al-Khaddam** and **Rif`at al-Asad**.

MASYAF. Presently a small town in the **Jabal Ansariyya** between **Hama** and **Baniyas**. It emerged as a strategic stronghold during the First **Crusade** in the conflict among Franks, **Sunni** Muslim strongmen, and **Isma`ilis**. For a time, Masyaf (also called Masyad) was the seat of the **Nizari** leaders, including the renowned Rashid al-Din Sinan. The citadel, which is still standing, withstood a siege by **Saladin** in 1176. Masyaf remained a Nizari bastion until its subjugation by the **Mamluk** Sultan **Baybars** in 1270. Today this village attracts **tourists** to wander through its Crusader-era ruins, especially the fortress, referred to as "the Castle of the Assassins."

MAYSALUN, BATTLE OF. On 24 July 1920, French troops defeated Arab forces defending Amir **Faysal**'s kingdom and snuffed out hopes for Syrian independence. The battle marked the end of diplomatic maneuvering between Faysal and **France** that had begun soon after the end of **World War I**. While France sought to impose its authority over Syria, Faysal strove to preserve some independence for the government he had constructed since October 1918. In June 1920, the French government decided to eliminate Faysal's regime and gave orders to General Henri Gouraud, who commanded French troops in **Lebanon**, to occupy **Damascus** as soon as possible. On 14 July, Gouraud issued an ultimatum to Faysal demanding that he accept the **French Mandate**, halt conscription, limit the size of the Syrian army, use **currency** issued by France, and allow French forces to occupy stations along the railroad line that ran from northern Lebanon through **Homs** and **Hama** to **Aleppo**. Faysal had four days to accept these terms or Gouraud would invade. The amir sought clarifications and an extension of the deadline, which Gouraud granted. He gave Faysal until 20 July to accept the terms and begin implementing them.

Meanwhile nationalists in the **Syrian Congress** rejected the ultimatum and called for popular mobilization to resist a French occupation. Faysal in turn dissolved the Congress and wired his acceptance of Gouraud's latest demands on 19 July, but his surrender did not reach Gouraud because the telegraph wires had been cut. Consequently, a French force of 12,000 crossed the Lebanese-Syrian frontier and Syrian forces withdrew to Khan Maysalun, just 25 kilometers west of Damascus. On the morning of 24 July, Syrian troops and volunteers clashed with French forces. The Syrians had enough ammunition to fight for only a few hours while the French had air power and a handful of tanks in addition to plenty of ammunition. The battle commenced at dawn and was over by 10 A.M. France's decisive victory at Maysalun paved the way for its occupation of Syria and Faysal's flight from the country.

MELKITE. See **GREEK ORTHODOX** and **GREEK CATHOLIC.**

MIDHAT PASHA (1822-1884). Famous **Ottoman** reformer who served as governor of **Damascus** from 1878 to 1879. Midhat first came to Syria in 1840 when he was posted as a low-level clerk in Damascus for two years, and he returned in 1851 as inspector of the province's finances. He later served as provincial governor in Baghdad and Bulgaria. In both posts he created gendarmeries to bring greater security, ordered the construction of roads and bridges, and opened schools. He played a key role in the tumultuous events of late 1876 when Istanbul saw the deposition of two sultans and the accession of Sultan **Abdulhamid** in September in exchange for his promise to grant a **constitution** for the Ottoman Empire. The new sultan made Midhat the grand vizier, the head of the empire's vast bureaucracy, but two months later Abdulhamid dismissed him and removed him and other high officials associated with the constitutional movement from Istanbul by assigning them to provincial posts.

Midhat arrived in Damascus for the third time at the end of 1878, now as governor of the province. He concentrated on developing a better communications and **transportation** network, extending new telegraph lines, building post offices, and encouraging the construction of carriage roads to link the major towns. For instance, a road running from Damascus to **Homs**, Tripoli, and **Latakia** enabled the Ottomans to gain firmer control over **Jabal Ansariyya** and its historically autonomous **Alawi** inhabitants. Midhat also gave a boost to **education**, as 30 schools opened during his brief tenure. In Damascus he urged **Tahir al-Jaza'iri** to form a benevolent society to pursue educational reforms, and he appointed Jaza'iri superintendent of schools in the province. He also encouraged Jaza'iri's project to found Syria's first public library. The reformist governor's other achievements included improving the provincial gendarmerie and reforming tax collection. In spite of these efforts, the sultan suspected that Midhat was plotting to carve out an autonomous realm, and in August 1880, Abdulhamid ordered his transfer to a Turkish province, where the sultan's spies could keep a closer eye on him. The sultan later trumped up charges that Midhat had conspired to murder Sultan Abdulaziz in 1876. Midhat was tried, convicted, and imprisoned in the Arabian town of Ta'if, where the sultan's agents murdered him in prison in 1884.

MILITARY COMMITTEE. This secret faction of the **Ba`th Party** was founded in Cairo by five Syrian officers during the **United Arab Republic** era. The original members included three **Alawi** officers—**Salah al-Jadid, Hafiz al-Asad**, Muhammad al-Umran—and two **Isma`ili** officers—Abd al-Karim al-Jundi and Ahmad al-Mir. These men despised party founders **Michel Aflaq** and **Salah al-Din al-Bitar** for their "betrayal" of the party when they dissolved it at Gamal Abd al-Nasir's insistence as a condition of forming the UAR in 1958. The Military Committee members wanted to rebuild the party and preserve the union with **Egypt**. When they returned to Syria after its **secession** from the UAR, they contacted other officers, mostly Alawis, **Druzes**, and provincial **Sunnis**, with whom they conspired to overthrow the government.

Because the members of the Military Committee were dismissed from the **armed forces** on their return to Syria, they developed ties with Nasirist officers and the few remaining Ba`thist officers in order to plot a coup d'état. The first attempt was a mutiny by Nasirist and Ba`thist officers at **Aleppo** on 2 April 1962, but this adventure failed. The Military Committee then contacted Major-General **Ziyad al-Hariri**, who was not aligned with any of the factions but was apprehensive about Prime Minister **Khalid al-Azm**'s desire to restore full civilian authority over the army. The combination of Hariri, Nasirists, and Ba`thists brought off the **March 8, 1963 coup**. The Military Committee then augmented its membership so that it grew to include 10 officers, including men placed on the **National Revolutionary Command Council**.

The Military Committee maintained its cohesion in the first Ba`thist regime as it contended with Nasirists and the party's old guard for power, but tensions emerged when Umran called for more moderate economic and political measures to conciliate opposition to the regime. At the end of 1964, he was ousted from power and sent to Spain as the ambassador. The Military Committee won a trial of strength with the party old guard and seized power in the **February 23, 1966 coup**. Following the **June 1967 War**, tensions within the committee resurfaced between those who supported Jadid's aggressive policy toward **Israel** and economic radicalism at home and the supporters of Asad's call for restraint toward Israel and moderation in attacks on the Syrian bourgeoisie. By 1970, of the five original members, Asad and Jadid were on the verge of a decisive showdown, Umran was still in Spain, Mir was in exile in Beirut, and Jundi was dead. When Jadid forced the issue in the fall, Asad seized power in what he called the **corrective movement** and arrested Jadid, bringing about the final end of the Military Committee.

MINING. After **petroleum**, Syria's main mineral resource is phosphate rock. Mining of deposits near **Palmyra** began in 1971. During the 1980s, annual production ranged from 1.2 to 2 million tons, and then increased in the next decade to an average of 2.5 million tons. Syria usually exports 60 percent of production and processes the remainder to make ammonia urea and fertilizers. Other mineral resources, like salt near **Dayr al-Zur** and asphalt near **Latakia**, are of minor economic significance. Local minerals useful for construction include cement, marble, and gypsum.

MINORITIES. Analysts commonly break down Syria's population using two categories, **religion** and **language**. In religious terms, the majority of the population is **Sunni** Muslim and the country contains non-Sunni Muslims, **Christians**, and until recent years, **Jews**. In linguistic terms, Arabic speakers comprise the majority, and there are Syrians for whom **Kurdish**, **Armenian**, **Circassian**, Turkish, and **Assyrian** are the mother tongue. Until modern times, the different groups coexisted with little difficulty but that changed with the emergence of nationalism because of its tendency to impose ethnic and cultural homogeneity.

The first glimmers of modern communal tensions appeared in 19th-century attacks on Christians by Muslim crowds at **Aleppo** and **Damascus**. **Ottoman** measures held such tensions in check after 1860, but the **French Mandate** authorities deliberately exploited minorities as military and political assets to weaken and divide the country's primarily Sunni **Arab nationalist** movement. For instance, the French created military units comprised of Armenians, Kurds, and Circassians. They also devised administrative boundaries that accentuated minority aspirations for political autonomy in heavily **Druze** and **Alawi** regions. Collaboration by members of minorities with the French colored the outlook of Syria's mostly Sunni Arab leadership after independence, hence the common view that minorities are a danger to national integrity. Consequently, a succession of regimes has striven to emphasize the country's Arab character at the expense of linguistic minorities by making Arabic the only language of instruction in public schools and restricting other languages to private schools. The harshest measures against a language group have targeted the concentration of Kurds living along the border with **Turkey**. In the early 1960s, the government implemented a plan to break up that concentration by denying Kurdish villagers the sort of assistance for **agriculture** that it provided to Arab citizens and by colonizing the area with Arabs. On the other hand, apprehensions about religious tensions have led to efforts to foster a secular public culture and to guarantee the religious rights of non-Sunni citizens. Official policies, then, obstruct Kurds and Armenians from sustaining a lively culture in their languages; at the same time, religious minorities enjoy an atmosphere of toleration that is preferable to the situation in neighboring countries. The clear exception to this pattern is the Jewish community, which because of the animosity toward **Israel** faced severe restrictions until the mid-1990s when most Jews left the country.

MIRDASID DYNASTY. Tribal rulers of **Aleppo** and northern Syria from 1023 to 1079. They came from the Banu Kilab tribe that had supported the **Hamdanid** dynasty during the late 10th century. After the fall of the Hamdanids in 1016, Salih ibn Mirdas led the Banu Kilab in their contest for power against the **Byzantines** and the **Fatimids**. The Mirdasids survived as rulers of a buffer region between Byzantine and Fatimid forces and by balancing the interests of Aleppan townsmen with those of the Banu Kilab tribesmen. Throughout their five decades of ascendance, the Mirdasids fended off several attempts by the Fatimids to absorb Aleppo into their empire. This ephemeral dynasty fell in 1079 to an Arab vassal of the **Saljuk** Turkish sultans.

MIRU, MUHAMMAD MUSTAFA (1941-). Designated prime minister in a March 2000 cabinet reshuffle just a few months before **Hafiz al-Asad**'s death. A native of a small village north of **Damascus**, Miru's first public role, in 1971, was in the teachers union. He then held administrative positions in provincial governorates before making his mark as a capable technocrat as governor of **Aleppo** between 1993 and 2000. It is reported that he owed his elevation to the prime minister's post to **Bashar al-Asad**'s familiarity with his abilities and reputation for honesty in contrast to the air of **corruption** surrounding Miro's predecessor, **Mahmud al-Zu`bi**.

MONGOLS. Central Asian conquerors of the eastern half of the Muslim world. The Mongols first raided Muslim lands in 1218 when they conquered a Central Asian sultanate. Forty years later they sacked Baghdad and destroyed the **Abbasid caliphate**. They were then poised for further conquests in Syria and **Egypt**. Mongol forces overran **Aleppo** and **Hama** before a **Mamluk** army defeated them on 3 September 1260 at the Battle of **Ayn Jalut** (the Spring of Goliath) in **Palestine** and then drove the Mongols from Syria. There followed several decades of frontier warfare between the Mamluks and the Mongol Ilkhanid dynasty based in northwestern **Iran**. In 1280 and 1299, the Mongols invaded Syria. On the first occasion, the Mamluks defeated the Mongols near **Homs**. The second invasion, though, led to the occupation of **Damascus**, the destruction of much of the city, and a slaughter of its inhabitants. The Mongols then reached Gaza in southern Palestine before a Mamluk counteroffensive in 1303 drove the invaders out of Syria for the last time.

MOUNT HERMON. In Arabic *Jabal al-Shaykh*. This massive peak on the Syrian-**Lebanese** border is the highest point on the **Golan Heights** at 2,814 meters. It has been under **Israeli** control since the **June 1967 War**. Its location and elevation make its possession a strategic asset for whoever controls it. Consequently, it was the scene of fierce combat during the **October 1973 War**, when the Syrians seized it and then Israeli forces recaptured it. During the **Syrian-Israeli peace talks** of the 1990s, Israel expressed the desire to maintain an early warning listening post there in the event of its return to Syria, but **Damascus** rejected that condition. In addition to its commanding prospect over surrounding areas, the **water** runoff from Mt. Hermon's snowmelt feeds tributaries to the Jordan River and thereby contributes to Israel's water supply.

MU`ALLIM, WALID AL- (1941-). The Syrian ambassador to the **United States** in the 1990s. He headed the Syrian delegation that held diplomatic negotiations with **Israel** after the **Madrid Conference**.

MU`AWIYA (c. 600-680).** The first **Umayyad caliph** (r. 661-680) and founder of that dynasty, renowned in Arab history for his deft political touch that enabled him to provide two decades of political calm following the stormy contest to succeed the third Muslim caliph, Uthman. Mu`a-wiya's political tact is embodied in the aphorism attributed to him: "I apply not my lash where my tongue suffices, nor my sword where my whip is enough. And if there be one hair binding me to my fellow men, I let it not break. If they pull I loosen, and if they loosen I pull." The so-called "hair of Mu`awiya" became a proverbial expression for tact and diplomacy. Yet **Shi`i Muslims revile Mu`awiya for what they consider his usurpation of **Ali ibn Abi Talib**'s rightful claim to the caliphate.

In 639, the second rightly guided caliph, Umar, appointed Mu`awiya governor of Syria. He secured the loyalty of both immigrant Arabian tribes and Arab tribes that had long resided in Syria. Furthermore, he continued the early Muslim practice of relying on administrators, mostly **Christian** Arabs, who had served the **Byzantines**. Mu`awiya's favorite wife was a Christian, as were his court poet and physician. His lenience toward Syrian Arab Christians gained him broad political support in a land where the vast majority of the population adhered to the same religion as the Muslims' chief enemy, the Byzantines, who had only recently been displaced as rulers of Syria. Mu`awiya was governor of a frontier province, and like later Muslim rulers he used northern Syria as the springboard for military campaigns against Byzantine forces in Asia Minor. He also ordered the construction of the first Arab Muslim naval fleet, which he sent against Cyprus, Rhodes, and Sicily. In 655, Mu`awiya ordered his navy to conduct the first of many Muslim assaults on Constantinople.

When his kinsman the caliph Uthman was murdered in 656, Mu`a-wiya refused to recognize Ali's claim to the caliphate. They marshalled their forces for a battle at Siffin on the **Euphrates River** in 657, but after some fighting the two sides agreed to submit their dispute to arbitration. Mu`awiya had still refused to acknowledge Ali as the caliph when the latter was assassinated in 661, whereupon Mu`awiya became the uncontested claimant to the caliphate, the seat of which he moved from Medina in Arabia to **Damascus**.

The heartlands of the Arab Empire in Syria, Iraq, Arabia, and **Egypt** were stable and prosperous under Mu`awiya, and he devoted much of his energy to military campaigns of conquest. In 668, he dispatched an Arab army under the command of his son Yazid to seize Constantinople, but the Byzantines withstood a siege of several months. Mu`awiya tried again with a longer siege that lasted from 674 to 680, but in the end the Byzantines forced a retreat. On a different front, in 663, he sent an army from Egypt into Byzantine-ruled North Africa, thereby reviving the enterprise of Arab conquest that had been suspended during the turmoil following Uthman's assassination. By the time of Mu`awiya's death in 680, Arab armies had reached the borders of Algeria. On the eastern front, the caliph appointed Ziyad, a former supporter of Ali, to govern Iraq and **Iran**. Ziyad consolidated Arab rule over eastern Iran and extended the empire into Afghanistan. In 674, Ziyad's son struck out north of Afghanistan to conquer the Buddhist towns of Bukhara and Samarkand. Shortly before his death, Mu`awiya designated his son Yazid as his successor, thereby breaking with 50 years of Muslim practice that had not set a precedent for dynastic succession.

MUHAMMAD ALI (c. 1768-1849). Powerful ruler of **Egypt** (r. 1805-1848) who successfully challenged **Ottoman** authority by carving out a virtually autonomous realm over the Nile Valley. Muhammad Ali took advantage of Ottoman weakness when he had his son **Ibrahim Pasha** lead an army into Syria in 1831. As governor of Syria, Ibrahim instituted the same measures of state monopoly over valuable resources, efficient taxation, conscription, and disarmament of informal militias that had solidified Muhammad Ali's position in Egypt. These centralizing measures foreshadowed the **Tanzimat** reforms to come in the following decade and encountered stiff resistance in various parts of Syria. In 1840, European opposition to Muhammad Ali's growing power forced him to abandon Syria in return for recognition of his descendants' hereditary rights to govern Egypt under Ottoman suzerainty.

MUKHABARAT. The Arabic term for a variety of domestic and foreign intelligence agencies responsible for the regime's basic political security. *See also* SECURITY FORCES.

MURSHID, SULAYMAN AL- (1905-1946). Charismatic leader of an **Alawi** revivalist movement in the early years of the **French Mandate**. He was born Sulayman Yunus in a small village in **Jabal Ansariyya**. In 1922, he claimed to receive religious inspiration and attracted a following among the region's peasants. He then incited them to withhold taxes and defy the authorities, so the French arrested him in 1923. Upon his release, Murshid claimed the power to work miracles and his following grew. At that point, the French decided to develop friendly relations with him and turned him into an ally. Murshid became a prominent leader in Jabal Ansariyya, accumulating large amounts of land and marrying into influential Alawi families. In 1936, he was elected to the Syrian parliament, where he sought to preserve Alawi interests within a unified Syria. After independence in 1946, Murshid led a revolt. The government sent troops to **Latakia** province, captured him, and publicly executed him in **Damascus**.

MUSIC. If music may be likened to language, then Syria's musical tradition is comprised of dialects linked to the country's various religious groups and social milieus. **Christian** liturgical chants, **Jewish** songs, **sufi** music, and Arab musical traditions associated with **bedouin**, village, and city life give the country a rich and complex heritage. The tradition of Arab music in Syria goes back to the **Umayyad** dynasty when rulers held musical performances by singers, who performed a variety of Arabian, **Byzantine**, and Persian styles. In later centuries, music became an important part in the rituals of sufi orders, frequently to the accompaniment of a reed flute. The **Ottomans** influenced music in provinces like Syria with the formation of military bands, and the authorities regulated musicians and singers through specialized guilds. In the desert, bedouins enjoyed their own musical tradition in which the musician played a one-string fiddle to accompany a singer. Villages commonly played music to celebrate weddings and to express grief in funeral laments.

During the late 19th century, increased interaction with Europe brought familiarity with Western instrumentation and musical forms that fostered the development of Arab orchestral backing for singers, first in Cairo and then in other Arab cities. Since the 1960s, popular Western music has had a following among the young, and artists have created original syntheses of Arab melodies and rhythms with such Western genres as disco and rap.

MUSLIM BROTHERS. The most important **Islamic fundamentalist** movement of the 20th century. The Society of Muslim Brothers was founded in **Egypt** in 1928 by a schoolteacher named Hasan al-Banna. A Syrian branch of this organization devoted to reviving **Islam** formed in 1946 when several Islamic reform societies merged under the leadership of **Mustafa al-Siba`i**. In the 1920s and 1930s, there appeared Muslim benevolent societies aiming to revive Islam and to oppose Western cultural influences (**cinemas**, immodest **women**'s dress, mixing of genders in public). The direct ancestor of the Brothers was an Aleppan society called Dar al-Arqam, founded in 1935. From independence until

1958, the Brothers participated in elections and acquired a substantial following in **Damascus** but failed to attract much support in other parts of the country. In January 1952, the military ruler **Adib al-Shishakli** dissolved the organization, but it reemerged after his overthrow in 1954 in a diminished capacity. The government again banned the society during the **United Arab Republic** (1958-1961), and it has opposed each of the three regimes to rule in the name of the **Ba`th Party**. The society's leadership remained in the hands of Siba`i until poor health forced him to step down in 1957. **Isam al-Attar** then led the Muslim Brothers for the next 12 years.

In April 1964, the Muslim Brothers instigated antigovernment demonstrations in **Hama** over the Ba`th's secularism and socialist economic policies. The regime's violent suppression of this and later protests created a dilemma for the Brothers. Should they adopt armed struggle to overthrow the regime or pursue a nonviolent course in seeking to influence it? Attar favored the latter course, but in 1969 militant sections of the society ousted him. There emerged a new collective leadership, chief among whom was a teacher from Hama, Adnan Sa`d al-Din. This event marked the Brothers' turn to violent tactics, first in opposing the Ba`thist government, and then in trying to overthrow it. Moreover, the Brothers' propaganda began to emphasize the regime's **Alawi** complexion and accused it of seeking to destroy **Sunni** Islam.

In the late 1970s the Brothers carried out assassinations against members and supporters of the regime. Perhaps inspired by the Iranian Revolution, in 1980 the Muslim Brothers formed a coalition of Islamic groups called the Islamic Front in Syria. The Front's manifesto called upon all Syrians who opposed Asad's regime to join forces in a struggle for the restoration of civil and political freedoms, the independence of the judiciary, and private property rights. Meanwhile, an assortment of secular leftist groups and professional syndicates were organizing protests and demonstrations against the regime, an indication that it was not only religious circles that opposed government policies and practices. The country's urban centers, particularly in the northern towns of **Homs**, Hama, and **Aleppo**, witnessed a vicious struggle between the government and the Islamist rebels. In June 1979, for instance, the Brothers massacred more than 50 Alawi cadets at an Aleppan artillery school. After an assassination attempt against President **Hafiz al-Asad** in June 1980, the government made association with the Muslim Brothers a capital crime. The culmination of this virtual civil war took place in February 1982, when Islamist forces briefly took over Hama. In the course of two weeks of fighting, government forces retook the city, leveled huge stretches of urban landscape, and killed several thousand insurgents and civilians.

The Hama uprising marked the definitive victory of government forces. The Islamic Front then split. Some members had lost all confidence in armed struggle, while others sought to broaden their political base by allying with secular parties opposed to the Ba`thist government. In 1986, Asad offered amnesty to Muslim Brothers in exile if they pledged to refrain from political activities. The acceptance of this deal by a number of former leaders dealt another blow to the organization. By the early 1990s, the Muslim Brothers and the Islamic movement more generally in Syria were quiescent if not moribund. Since **Bashar al-Asad** became president in 2000, he has pardoned and released scores of political prisoners, including about 400 Muslim Brothers in November 2000. Such moves indicate the regime is confident that the Brothers no longer pose a threat, but some uncompromising elements in exile have refused offers to return in exchange for pledges to refrain from political activity.

MUTANABBI, ABU AL-TAYYIB AL- (915-965). One of the great classical Arab poets, especially as a master panegyrist, he was born in the **Iraqi** city of Kufa and spent much of his adult life in Syria. Some accounts of his life hold that in his early years he claimed prophetic powers, hence the sobriquet "al-Mutannabi," he who claims to be a prophet; that he led a political-religious revolt in central Syria, for which he was imprisoned in **Homs** for two years; or that he was a partisan of the **Qarmati Shi`i** movement. It is more certain that like other poets of his age, Mutanabbi drifted from one court to another, celebrating his patrons' achievements in panegyric verse. He gained renown in **Aleppo** as court poet of the **Hamdanid** ruler Sayf al-Dawla from 948 until 957. During that time, Mutannabi wrote long odes and panegyrics praising his master's military campaigns against the **Byzantines** and Arab tribes. The poet, however, fell out of Sayf al-Dawla's favor, probably because of his rivals' plotting against him, and for the next several years he moved from court to court between Cairo and **Iran**, until he was finally killed in a **bedouin** attack on a caravan.

Critics have observed that Mutanabbi's poetry is distinctive for its Arab chauvinism, religious skepticism, and pessimism. His style shifted from a neoclassical manner to spontaneous and personal moods until his mature poems showed a synthesis of the neoclassical with a freer style.

-N-

NAHLAWI, ABD AL-KARIM AL- (1926-). Lieutenant-Colonel Nahlawi
led the September 1961 coup to bring about Syria's **secession** from the
United Arab Republic. He and his army colleagues designated a civilian
government to be headed by the conservative **Ma'mun al-Kuzbari**, and
then stepped out of the political limelight while seeking to maintain
supervision over the government, in particular blocking any moves to
relax the strict controls over political life imposed by the UAR. On 28
March 1962, Nahlawi organized a coup against a conservative government that was repealing the **socialist decrees** and criticizing officers for
meddling in politics. He ordered the arrest of President **Nazim al-Qudsi**
and Prime Minister **Ma`ruf al-Dawalibi** as well as other cabinet members
and several parliamentary deputies. Then officers opposed to Nahlawi
rose up in **Homs** and **Aleppo**. The affair ended with the decision taken at
a meeting of officers held at Homs to exile Nahlawi and six others to
Switzerland. In January 1963, Nahlawi and other exiled officers crossed
the Turkish border back into Syria and incited junior officers to demand
the restoration of union with **Egypt**. Again he failed to gain support from
many other officers and he went back into exile.

NATIONAL BLOC. The major nationalist party of the **French Mandate** era,
it was first conceived at a conference of political leaders in Beirut in
October 1927. The National Bloc was formally established at the **Homs**
Congress of November 1932. While its leadership was officially committed to the unity and independence of Syria, its short-term goal was to
obtain a share in governing the country, a constitutional parliamentary
form of government, and a treaty with **France**. The Bloc was the most
broadly representative nationalist movement of the interwar period, with
leaders from each of the major cities: **Damascus, Aleppo, Homs**, and
Hama. The Bloc represented a more moderate approach to achieving
national aspirations than had the **Iron Hand Society** or the **People's
Party**, an approach dictated by France's success in totally suppressing the
Great Revolt in 1927.

Although it won just 22 of 70 seats to the constituent assembly in
1928 elections, the Bloc's confident, articulate representatives managed
to dominate the assembly's proceedings and its committee to draft a
constitution. Because this document contained articles the French found
unacceptable, High Commissioner Henri Ponsot adjourned the assembly.
In 1930 France promulgated a constitution, and even though it fell short

of the Bloc's demands, its leaders decided to participate in national parliamentary elections in 1931-1932. This willingness to compromise reflected the attitude of **Jamil Mardam**, who headed the National Bloc government that came to power in 1936 seeking to secure French ratification of the **Franco-Syrian Treaty**. This was the first nationalist government since Amir **Faysal's** fall 16 years earlier. During its three-year tenure, the nationalist government suffered a number of severe political failures: the loss of **Alexandretta** to **Turkey**; the refusal of the French parliament to ratify the treaty; and resistance to nationalist rule by areas heavily populated by non-**Sunnis**—**Jabal Druze**, **Jabal Ansariyya**, and **Jazira**. The government's failure led to Mardam's fall from party leadership and the ascent of his rival **Shukri al-Quwwatli**. In 1943, Quwwatli dissolved the Bloc and formed its successor, the **National Party**, to contest national elections.

NATIONAL PARTY. Created on the eve of independent Syria's first national elections in July 1943 as the successor to the **National Bloc**, the National Party headed by **Shukri al-Quwwatli** led the final push for complete, unfettered independence. The party swept the July 1943 elections and brought to power a cabinet headed by **Sa`dallah al-Jabiri** as prime minister; parliament then elected Quwwatli president. Lacking an ideological program or an organizational framework, the National Party resembled the Bloc in representing the personal influence of prominent men. Nonetheless, it stayed in power during Syria's difficult transition to liberation from French domination, enduring **France**'s May 1945 bombardment of **Damascus** and overseeing the final evacuation of French troops in April 1946. The National Party won national elections for a second time in July 1947, but the party's days as a powerful force were numbered. It had the misfortune to hold office during the **Palestine War of 1948**, in which the armies of several Arab countries proved unable to prevent the establishment of a Jewish state, **Israel**, in what had recently been an Arab land. **Husni al-Za`im**'s coup in March 1949 ended nearly six years of National Party domination, and the colonel forced its leaders to leave the country.

During the next five years of military domination, the party moved into the opposition, while its rival, the **People's Party**, occasionally gained the confidence of military strongmen. The National Party orchestrated strikes and demonstrations in September 1950 to protest an attempt by the Constituent Assembly, dominated by the People's Party, to convert itself into a four-year parliament. When democracy returned after the

Adib al-Shishakli dictatorship, the National Party was far weaker, yet in 1954 its new leader, **Sabri al-Asali**, formed a coalition government with the People's Party. But both parties, representing the political elite inherited from **Ottoman** times, spent the next four years feuding with each other and fending off the rising leftist current represented by the **Ba`th Party** and the **Syrian Communist Party**. The National Party practically self-destructed when it divided into factions for and against union with **Iraq**. By the time Syria entered the **United Arab Republic** with **Egypt** in 1958, the National Party was a shadow of the organization that had guided the country to independence.

NATIONAL REVOLUTIONARY COMMAND COUNCIL (NRCC). Following the **March 8, 1963 coup**, Syria's new military masters created this ruling body as the executive authority. At first, the members were all officers, including **Ziyad al-Hariri** and **Salah al-Jadid**. The NRCC was to formulate policy and delegate its implementation to a cabinet of ministers responsible to the NRCC. The provisional **constitution** of April 1964 passed the NRCC's executive functions to a Presidential Council.

NAYYUF, NIZAR (1962-). Perhaps the Syrian prisoner of conscience best known outside the country during the 1990s. Nayyuf is a journalist who in the early 1990s helped create a **human rights** organization, the Committee for the Defense of Democratic Freedom and Human Rights. In January 1992, the regime arrested him and four other members of the Committee. Nayyuf was tried for illegal political activities as editor of a human rights newsletter, *Voice of Democracy*, and sentenced to prison for 10 years. International human rights organizations protested the trial procedure but to no effect.

During his years in prison, Nayyuf endured torture so severe that it left him permanently disabled. He received several awards for his dedication to press freedom from the **United Nations** and from European and American organizations that publicized his case to persuade Syrian authorities to release him. The government finally let him out of prison in May 2001 during the visit of Pope John Paul II to Syria, but several weeks later, he was kidnapped in **Damascus** by one of the **security forces** and released the following day on **President Bashar al-Asad**'s orders. He then went to **France** to obtain medical treatment. While there he appeared on the Arab satellite television channel al-Jazira and publicly aired allegations of **corruption** by Syrian officials. After he returned to Syria, he reportedly endured more incidents of harassment.

NEO-BA`TH.** Radical faction of the Syrian **Ba`th Party that emerged during the first Ba`thist regime of 1963 to 1966. It included the **Military Committee** and the "regionalists," younger, more radical civilians and military officers, largely members of religious minorities and **Sunnis** from the provinces. In 1965, these radicals came to dominate the Syrian Regional Command of the party. In response, the moderate National Command under **Michel Aflaq** announced the Regional Command's dissolution on 19 December 1965 and dismissed the neo-Ba`thists from government. In the **February 23, 1966 coup,** neo-Ba`thist officers led by **Salah al-Jadid** seized power and purged the army and government of more than 400 men.

While Jadid was the regime's strongman, as a member of the **Alawi** minority, he preferred to manage affairs from behind the scenes, and he appointed two **Sunni** medical doctors of the party's regionalist faction to assume the high offices of state. Accordingly, **Nur al-Din al-Atasi** became head of state (the office of president was abolished) and **Yusuf al-Zu`ayyin** became prime minister. In general, though, the regime effected a thorough purge of Sunnis identified with the families that had dominated Syrian politics for several generations. The neo-Ba`th pursued a radical agenda in reforming the Syrian **economy**, ranging from state control over **industry** and **trade** to attempts to restructure agrarian relations and production through **land reform**. Its positive achievements include beginning construction of the **Tabqa Dam** on the **Euphrates River** to increase the amount of land under cultivation and electrical power. In part because of the regime's radicalism, in part because of its lack of a popular base, the neo-Ba`thists relied on support from the **Syrian Communist Party**. When the regime brought a communist onto the cabinet, it received a boost in aid from the **Soviet Union**.

In regional **foreign policy**, the regime advocated the overthrow of nearly every Arab regime, particularly the monarchies in **Jordan** and **Saudi Arabia**, so those two countries gave comfort and aid to the regime's many Syrian enemies living in exile. On the other hand, the neo-Ba`th made overtures to **Egypt**'s Gamal Abd al-Nasir, and the two countries restored official relations. Support for **Palestinian** guerrilla groups emerged as another hallmark of the regime, but Palestinian raids triggered retaliation by **Israel**. Violence along the border created a dangerous situation in the **demilitarized zones**, where limited conflict could easily escalate. This was Nasir's fear when he arranged a defense pact with Syria in the expectation that it would give him some leverage and prevent Israel from attacking Syria, in which event he would have to go to war. But a military clash between Syria and Israel in May 1967 and the ensuing steps taken by Nasir to demonstrate support for his ally led to the **June 1967 War**, which was a disaster for the regime.

After the war, a split in the leadership appeared between Minister of Defense **Hafiz al-Asad** and Salah al-Jadid. The former wanted to concentrate Syria's resources and energies on a military buildup in order to effectively confront Israel in the quest to regain the **Golan Heights** that were lost in the war. Jadid preferred a continuation of the regime's policies, including revolution at home and in the Arab world. Matters came to a head in February 1969 when units loyal to Asad seized control of the national media and all sensitive commands. Jadid retained control of the Ba`th Party, and on 30 October 1970, he convened an emergency national party congress that announced Asad's dismissal from the party and the government. But Asad ignored the decree and two weeks later launched his **corrective movement** in which he completed his takeover of the country and ended the neo-Ba`th's rule.

NESTORIAN. Also known as the East Syrian church. It dates to the second century. **Christian** opponents coined the term "Nestorian" after a fifth-century patriarch of Constantinople, Nestorius, whose theological views stressed Jesus Christ's humanity. In 431, the Council of Ephesus declared his views heretical and stripped him of office. Nestorius's teachings nevertheless gained a wide following in Syria and Mesopotamia, and in subsequent centuries, Nestorian Christians were important in proselytizing deep into Asia as far as China. In the history of ideas, Nestorian scholars were important for their many Syriac translations of Greek philosophy from which Arabic translations were made. Modern followers of this church are known as **Assyrians**, and they still use their own Syriac liturgy.

NIZARI. A branch of **Isma`ili Shi`is** more commonly but improperly known as the Assassins, a name derived from the Arabic word for users of hashish, *hashashiyyun*. It seems that their **Sunni** enemies accused Nizari leaders of manipulating followers by having them consume hashish. The Nizaris frequently resorted to political murder against Sunni rulers and religious officials. European **Crusaders** then circulated tales of fanatical Nizari agents under the influence of a magical potion carrying out their masters' orders to murder their enemies, so the name "hashashiyyun" passed into Western usage as Assassins.

The Nizaris emerged in the late 11th century in the course of a succession dispute within the Isma`ili **Fatimid** dynasty of **Egypt**. In 1094 the Fatimid **caliph** al-Mustansir died, leaving two sons, Nizar and al-Musta`li, to contend for succession. The military chief, who was the power behind the throne, selected the younger, more compliant Musta`li, and Nizar revolted, but his bid for power failed and he was put to death. Nizar's followers, however, gained the support of the powerful and persuasive Hasan-i Sabbah, who ruled over a network of Isma`ili mountain strongholds in **Iran** and formed a distinct branch of the sect called the New Preaching.

In Iran the Isma`ilis' chief adversary was the **Saljuk** sultanate, and several high ministers met their ends at the hands of Nizari agents. In the early 1100s, Hasan-i Sabbah sent agents to Syria to organize the New Preaching among Isma`ilis there. At that time, Saljuk rule was fragmenting among princes of the ruling house, and the Crusaders had just established their principalities along the coast. For about 30 years, the Saljuk princes of **Aleppo** and **Damascus** countenanced Nizari activities and tried to use them to further their own ambitions. Iranian Nizari missionaries worked to spread the New Preaching under Saljuk protection but made little headway. When the Saljuk prince of Aleppo died in 1113, his successor suppressed the Nizaris in that city, but in the 1120s, they managed to establish good relations with the ruler of Damascus, the **atabeg** Tughtigin. As in Aleppo, however, the Nizaris' dependence on relations with a single individual made their standing tenuous, and following Tughtigin's death in 1128, his successor, Buri, incited a mob to massacre several thousand Nizaris. In 1131, Nizari agents from Iran avenged their martyrs by murdering Buri.

With the failure to secure themselves in Syria's main cities, the Nizaris repeated the formula that had worked in Iran—that is, establishing fortresses in remote mountain areas, in this case the rugged **Jabal Ansariyya** in northwest Syria. Between 1132 and 1141 they obtained by conquest and negotiation several strongholds, including **Masyaf** and Qadmus, that became the nuclei for Nizari power for the next century. The Syrian Nizaris, then, comprised part of a larger Nizari polity based in northern Iran at the impregnable mountain fortress of Alamut near the Caspian Sea. The noncontiguous Nizari state included holdings in northwest Syria and western, northern, and eastern Iran. The Nizari ruler at Alamut was recognized as the supreme authority throughout this vast realm, and Nizari chiefs in Syria were always Persians sent by Alamut.

In the 12th century, the Nizaris became bitter enemies of the atabegs **Zangi** and **Nur al-Din Mahmud** as well as of **Saladin**, founder of the **Ayyubid** dynasty. The Nizaris reached the pinnacle of their influence in Syria under Rashid al-Din Sinan, who was their chief from 1162 until 1193. He twice tried to assassinate Saladin, in 1175 and 1176. Following the second attempt, the Ayyubid ruler invaded Jabal Ansariyya and besieged Masyaf, the chief Nizari stronghold, but failed to take it. By the early 13th century, relations between the Nizaris and Ayyubids had improved and they cooperated in warfare against Frankish enemies. The overthrow of the Ayyubids by the much more powerful **Mamluks**, however, drastically altered the Nizaris' prospects. In the 1260s, Sultan **Baybars** demanded and received tribute from them and then seized control of their mountain fortresses between 1271 and 1273, thereby extinguishing the independent Nizari state.

NONCONVENTIONAL WEAPONS. The earliest estimate for Syrian government efforts to develop chemical weapons is the 1970s when **Egypt** and **Soviet** bloc governments may have provided assistance. A special agency, the Scientific Studies and Research Center, is said to oversee projects related to nonconventional weapons. Since the 1980s, Syria has purchased equipment and materials from European pharmaceutical companies to develop the capacity to produce medicine. The same equipment and materials may be converted into chemical weapons. During the 1990s, Syria reportedly refined its expertise in this field with Russian assistance. Intelligence agencies in the **United States** and **Israel** estimate that Syria has the capacity to produce tons of chemicals annually. It is believed that Syria has the capacity to deliver chemical warheads, including VX and sarin nerve gas with surface-to-surface missiles, aircraft, and artillery. In the 1980s, Syria obtained ballistic missiles from the USSR, and in recent years has turned for assistance to North Korea and **Iran**. Observers think that Syria has not vigorously pursued the development of a nuclear capacity because of the costs it would involve, but in 1998, Russia agreed to help construct a small center for nuclear research. As for biological weapons, Syria is reportedly at an early phase of research. With regard to international treaties on nonconventional weapons, Syria is a signatory to the Treaty on the Non-Proliferation of Nuclear Weapons, but it has not ratified the biological weapons treaty or even signed the chemical weapons treaty. In view of Israel's possession of nuclear weapons, Syria's efforts in this field may be construed as an element of strategic deterrence or a possible threat, depending on one's perspective.

NORIA. Perhaps the most famous landmarks in **Hama** are the towering waterwheels, or norias, on the **Orontes River**. They are specimens of a hydraulic technology that dates to late antique times in the Fertile Crescent, and that in **Islamic** times spread all the way from **Iran** to Spain. Hama's 17 norias convey the river's **water** to an aqueduct which supplies the town and surrounding fields. The largest one measures 30 meters in diameter. Their graceful motion and constant low-pitched groaning make them a familiar city emblem and **tourist** attraction. The recent construction of dams upriver for irrigation has diminished the flow of the Orontes, so in the autumn months it is not unusual for the level to fall too low to drive the norias.

NUR AL-DIN MAHMUD (r. 1146-1174). Son of **Imad al-Din al-Zangi**, the **atabeg** of northern Syria and northern **Iraq**, Nur al-Din became the ruler of northern Syria upon Zangi's murder in 1146. He is renowned as an energetic leader of military campaigns against the **Crusader** states of Antioch and Jerusalem as well as against rival Muslim rulers. In 1154 he joined his northern Syrian domain to the south by conquering **Damascus**, thereby bringing the country under local unified control for the first time since the fall of the **Umayyad** dynasty 400 years before. Nur al-Din also made Damascus an important political capital for the first time since the Umayyads. He fortified the city's defenses and patronized **Sunni** religious institutions, including the Adiliyya **madrasa**, which in the early 20th century housed the Arab Academy, a historical and literary research institute.

Having secured his position in Damascus, Nur al-Din spent the following years struggling to impose his authority on rulers of petty states in central and southern Syria in addition to frequent campaigns against the Latin kingdom of Jerusalem. A new field of ambition opened up in 1163 when a palace revolt forced out the vizier, or chief minister, of the **Fatimid** dynasty in **Egypt**. This man, Shawar, went to Damascus to ask Nur al-Din to restore him to power in exchange for annual tribute and control over one of Egypt's rich **agricultural** districts. The following year, Nur al-Din's Kurdish vassal, Shirkuh, invaded and briefly occupied Egypt. Shirkuh brought along a nephew, **Saladin**, who became governor of Alexandria. The threat of attack by the Latin kingdom of Jerusalem on Egypt led Nur al-Din to again dispatch Shirkuh in 1168; this time he stayed, only to die several months later. Leadership of the expedition then passed to Saladin, who laid the foundations of **Ayyubid** rule in Egypt and brought about the end of the Fatimid dynasty in 1171. Nur al-Din then became alarmed at the potential threat represented by Saladin should the vassal decide to extend his rule to Damascus. Nur al-Din was preparing to attack Saladin in Egypt when his death in 1174 prevented conflict. Some writers emphasize Nur al-Din's contributions to the political revival of Sunni **Islam** in Egypt and Syria. For instance, he ordered his vassal Saladin to suppress the **Isma`ili** Fatimid **caliphate**; and he ordered the construction of 11 madrasas in Damascus and seven in **Aleppo**.

NUSAYRI. *See* **ALAWI.**

-O-

OCTOBER 1973 WAR. Also known as the Ramadan War to Arabs and the Yom Kippur War to Israelis. On 6 October, Syria and **Egypt** launched a surprise attack on **Israel** in order to recover the **Golan Heights** and the Sinai Peninsula, both of which Israel had conquered in the **June 1967 War**. At the outset, Syrian forces broke through Israeli defenses on the Golan Heights and advanced to within a few kilometers of Israel's border. On 9 October, however, the Syrian offensive ran out of steam in the face of stiff Israeli resistance, which inflicted high casualties on the attacking forces. In order to hamper the delivery of military supplies from the **Soviet Union**, Israel's air force attacked airport runways in **Damascus** and **Aleppo** in addition to Syria's main ports.

Egyptian forces had also scored early victories against Israel, most notably the unexpected feat of crossing to the east bank of the Suez Canal in the face of Israel's imposing network of defensive installations. When Egypt slowed its offensive in the Sinai Peninsula, however, Israel was able to mobilize its forces for a massive counterattack against the Syrians on 11-13 October. The Israeli offensive advanced several kilometers beyond the 1967 cease-fire line, but failed to capture a village on the road to Damascus that would have brought the Syrian capital within artillery range. Israel's military leaders then felt they had a secure situation in the north, so they turned their attention to the Egyptian front. Between 14 and 23 October, Israeli forces turned back an Egyptian attempt to advance farther and then launched a counterattack across the Suez Canal. On 22 October, the parties agreed to abide by a cease-fire resolution passed by the **United Nations** Security Council, but Israeli troops on the west bank of the Suez Canal pressed their advantage for the next two days as they tried to completely encircle portions of the Egyptian army on the canal's east bank. The Soviet Union then threatened to intervene directly, and this led the **United States** to exert pressure on Israel to abide by the cease-fire. At war's end, Syria had lost about 3,500 soldiers, Israel some 2,800, and Egypt 5,000 in fighting that included some of the largest tank battles in history. After the conclusion of hostilities, **United Nations Resolution 338** was passed in the hope that Israel and Syria might accept its terms for a negotiated resolution of their dispute. *See also* UNITED NATIONS DISENGAGEMENT OBSERVER FORCE.

ORONTES RIVER. *Al-Asi* in Arabic. Syria's second major river after the **Euphrates.** The Orontes rises in **Lebanon**'s Bekaa valley near Baalbak and then meanders northward into Syria through a number of lakes and marshes. About 470 of its 570-kilometer course runs through Syrian territory. The Orontes is the main waterway in central Syria and the region's main cities, **Homs** and **Hama**, are situated along its banks. The government built two dams in the 1950s, a fairly large one at Rastan and a small one at Mhardah to store **water** for irrigation. Because towns along the banks dump their waste into it, the Orontes' water is not fit for drinking. North of Hama it turns northwest into **Turkey** before heading west toward the Mediterranean Sea where it empties south of Antioch. Whereas the Euphrates is the subject of international dispute, the riparian states sharing the Orontes's waters have not clashed. In 1994, Syria and Lebanon agreed on a division of its water that allocates a modest portion to Lebanon which meets both present and anticipated future needs.

OTTOMAN EMPIRE. Ruled Syria from 1516 until 1918. The dynasty first rose in northwestern Asia Minor in the 1320s. Border fighting with the **Mamluks** began in the 1480s along the Syrian/Asia Minor frontier. In August 1516, **Sultan Selim I** led Ottoman forces, armed with artillery and other gunpowder weapons, to victory over the Mamluks near **Aleppo**. In the context of the enormous Ottoman Empire, Syria was reduced to the status of a minor province, but it held importance for the Ottoman dynasty's religious legitimacy because it was the staging point for the annual pilgrimage to Mecca. For the next 60 years, Ottoman authority was firmly established, but in the last three decades of the 16th century, Istanbul's hold weakened, and local forces centered on the **janissaries** asserted themselves against Ottoman governors in Aleppo and **Damascus**. This contest continued throughout the 17th century and into the 18th century until the Ottomans found reliable allies in the powerful **Azm** clan to serve as governors. For several decades, members of the Azm clan brought stability to much of Syria. The tendency to rely on local figures to govern Syria continued in the late 1700s and early 1800s under **Ahmad al-Jazzar**.

By the early 1800s, the Ottoman Empire faced threats from European powers and disarray within as conservative forces fended off attempts to reform the empire's administrative and military institutions. In Syria the Ottomans were shocked by the invasion launched in 1831 by **Muhammad Ali** of **Egypt**. The Ottomans did not recover the province until 1840, and then only with the assistance of the European powers. The rest of the 19th century saw a sustained effort to strengthen the empire's ability to defend itself and to control its lands and population. This drive for administrative and military modernization took place under both secular direction in the **Tanzimat** period and under religious leadership during the reign of Sultan **Abdulhamid II**.

In 1908, military officers belonging to the **Committee of Union and Progress** launched a mutiny to force the sultan to institute constitutional government, thereby shifting power at the center of the empire from the sultan to a group of officers and bureaucrats. The new rulers promoted cultural policies that many Syrians construed as anti-Arab, and in reaction the cultural prelude to **Arab nationalism** developed. The Ottoman Empire's leaders entered **World War I** on the side of Germany against Great Britain and **France**. The empire's disastrous defeat in the war terminated four centuries of Ottoman rule in Syria.

OTTOMAN LAND CODE OF 1858. During the **Tanzimat** era the **Ottoman Empire** embarked on an ambitious program to thoroughly reform its legal framework. The 1858 land code was a milestone not only in the empire's legal reform, but also in the history of land tenure in much of the Middle East. It established a land registry office to issue deeds, thereby formalizing long-standing property claims. The most profound effect of the code in Syria was to foster the rise of a class of absentee landowners among urban notables who exploited their control over credit and knowledge of land registration procedures to accumulate vast holdings. Their efforts were facilitated by peasants' apprehension that registration of their property could make it easier for the authorities to tax and conscript them. Consequently, many peasants registered the lands they cultivated in the names of urban notables; others became ensnared in debt to urban creditors and gave up their lands to lighten their debt. By the early 1900s, **Sunni** landowners in **Damascus, Aleppo, Homs, Hama,** and **Latakia** thoroughly dominated the Syrian countryside and used their agrarian wealth to become the leading economic stratum in the country. Furthermore, their wealth enabled them to play the leading part in politics for nearly a century until the **land reforms** of the **United Arab Republic** and **Ba`th Party** regimes wiped out the effects of the 1858 code and undermined the agrarian base of their power.

OTTOMAN PARTY OF ADMINISTRATIVE DECENTRALIZATION. Established in Cairo in January 1913 to promote the cause of provincial autonomy in the **Ottoman Empire**'s Arab regions. This short-lived party, largely composed of Syrian émigrés living in Cairo, opposed the **Committee of Union and Progress** regime's centralist policies that tightened Istanbul's hold on the provinces. The party joined with other groups in convening an Arab Congress in Paris in June 1913. Members of the congress issued the only formal public declarations of the Ottoman period claiming to represent the interests of the Arabs to the Ottoman rulers. Its resolutions specifically favored administrative decentralization and the use of Arabic in provincial administration. The government responded with indications of willingness to grant some demands, but eventually adopted a strong policy against the Arab autonomists.

-P-

PALESTINE. During the **Ottoman** era, Palestine was part of the province of **Damascus** and had strong economic, cultural, and social ties with Syria. When the European powers separated Palestine from Syria at the end of **World War I**, nationalists in both countries fought for the reintegration of southern Syria, that is, Palestine. Throughout the **French Mandate** era, the Syrian and Palestinian nationalist movements supported each other, but effective cooperation proved difficult because they faced two different colonial powers, **France** in Syria, Great Britain in Palestine. Moreover, the Palestinians confronted a unique challenge in the Zionist project to establish a Jewish state.

The first major demonstration of Syrian popular sympathy for the Palestine Arab cause was sparked by the latter's 1936 revolt against Zionist immigration and the British Mandate. Syrians launched strikes and demonstrations, donated funds, smuggled weapons, and recruited fighters in support of the revolt. The British, however, suppressed the Palestinian revolt and dispersed the Palestinian Arab leadership by spring 1939. At the same time as the Palestinian revolt, Syria's **National Bloc** was struggling to wrest from France a measure of self-government, an effort that failed in 1939. During **World War II**, British forces used Palestine to stage their 1941 invasion of Syria to remove a Vichy administration.

After the war, Syria gained its independence in April 1946. While the Arabs of Palestine waged a desperate political battle to keep their homeland intact in 1946-1948, the newly independent Syrian government was just taking shape and struggling to manage the basic tasks of administration. The strong sympathy of Syrians for their Arab brethren compelled the government to oppose the **United Nations** resolution to partition Palestine into Jewish and Arab states, and even to attempt military intervention, but the government lacked the capacity to prevent an **Israeli** victory in the **Palestine War of 1948**.

For the next 20 years, Syrian governments faced two political issues that emerged in the war's aftermath. Most immediately, Palestinian refugees in Syria and other countries sought repatriation as required by United Nations Resolution 194. Second, most Syrians and other Arabs wished to eliminate Israel and regain Palestine for the Palestinians. The **June 1967 War**, however, changed the territorial situation. Israel conquered the **Golan Heights** from Syria, the West Bank from **Jordan**, and **Gaza** and the Sinai Peninsula from **Egypt**. Gradually, Arab states drifted to the idea of trading land for peace on the basis of **United Nations Resolution 242**. Thus, if Syria were to regain the Golan Heights and the Palestinians were to establish an independent state in the West Bank and Gaza, peaceful relations with Israel could result. Syria formally embraced that formula at the **Madrid Conference** in 1991. For nine years after Madrid, it appeared that the parties might inch their way toward a comprehensive settlement, but Israel's talks with Syria collapsed in early 2000 and with the Palestinians later the same year. *See also* FOREIGN POLICY.

PALESTINE LIBERATION ORGANIZATION (PLO). From its foundation in 1964 until 1968, when guerrilla groups took control, the Palestine Liberation Organization was essentially an instrument of Egyptian foreign policy. During that period, Syria was at odds with **Egypt**; consequently, Syria supported Yasir Arafat's Fatah organization, then independent of the PLO, and helped Fatah launch raids against **Israel** beginning in 1965. There was a brief breakdown in relations between Fatah and the **neo-Ba'th** regime in 1966, but for the most part Syria supported Fatah before and well after the **June 1967 War**. In the September 1970 conflict between **Palestinians** and the government of **Jordan**, Syria sided with the PLO and   supported its establishment of new headquarters in **Lebanon** following its expulsion from Jordan.

In Lebanon's weak polity, the PLO developed a firm base of power that allowed it greater independence of action. When PLO actions did not coincide with Syrian interests, clashes ensued. During the **Lebanese Civil War**, the PLO decided to support Lebanese groups seeking to radically alter Lebanon's political system. Syria, on the other hand, opposed those groups and consequently collided with the PLO in the summer of 1976. The following year the two sides mended fences under the impetus of Maronite efforts to obtain support from Israel and Egyptian President Anwar Sadat's visit to Jerusalem. Israel's March 1978 invasion of south Lebanon further consolidated Syrian-PLO relations.

The aftermath of Israel's invasion that launched the **Lebanese War of 1982**, however, led to a rupture between Syria and the PLO when the latter party attempted to reconsolidate its position in northern Lebanon in order to regain some freedom to maneuver. Syria then supported a mutiny within Fatah against Yasir Arafat. At the end of 1983, Arafat and forces loyal to him were expelled from Tripoli by Syrian-backed Palestinians. Tensions between the PLO and Syria persisted as the former strove to find a way to participate in diplomatic efforts sponsored by the **United States** to resolve the Arab-Israeli conflict that omitted Syria. For the latter, the fundamental concern was to prevent progress on Arab-Israeli negotiations that did not address Israel's occupation of the **Golan Heights**.

Iraq's August 1990 invasion of Kuwait reshuffled regional relations as the PLO backed Saddam Husayn and Syria supported the American-led intervention. After the victory of the coalition forces, both Syria and the PLO agreed to attend the 1991 **Madrid Conference**, which led to negotiations between Israel and both parties. Relations again took a turn for the worse when the PLO struck a separate deal with Israel in the August 1993 Oslo Accords, thereby undermining Syria's strategy of presenting Israel with a unified Arab negotiating position. To weaken Arafat, Syrian President **Hafiz al-Asad** backed factions that rejected Arafat's diplomatic efforts. These factions included the Democratic Front for the Liberation of Palestine, the Popular Front for the Liberation of Palestine, and the Popular Front for the Liberation of Palestine-General Command. While they do not carry much weight in the West Bank and Gaza, they have effectively contended with Arafat's Fatah for influence among refugees in Lebanon and Syria. During the 1990s, Asad also provided support to organizations outside the PLO like the **Islamic fundamentalist** groups Hamas and Islamic Jihad.

When Ehud Barak became Israeli prime minister in May 1999 and indicated a stronger interest in talks with Damascus than with the Palestinians, Arafat sought to meet with Asad, who by then had decided that he could never rely on Arafat and must therefore pursue Syria's interests separately. These efforts failed, the Oslo talks hit a dead end in summer 2000, and the second Palestinian uprising broke out shortly afterward. The general failure of peace talks along with Hafiz al-Asad's death in June created the conditions for a rapprochement between the PLO and the Syrian government, but the history of tensions is likely to resume when either party ever gets an opportunity for a favorable deal from Israel.

PALESTINE WAR OF 1948. On 29 November 1947, the United Nations General Assembly voted in favor of a resolution to partition **Palestine** into Jewish and Arab states. Public opinion in Syria vehemently opposed partition. A mass strike was held in **Damascus**, and huge crowds stormed the buildings housing the legation of the **United States** and the cultural office of the **Soviet Union** because of their votes in favor of the UN resolution. Anti-Jewish riots in **Aleppo** destroyed hundreds of homes and 11 synagogues and killed more than 70 **Jews**. In the early months of 1948, Syrian volunteers began to enter Palestine in order to support Arab forces that were already fighting the Zionists and attacking Jewish settlements. As the 14 May deadline for British withdrawal from Palestine drew closer and Zionist military forces gained the upper hand, Arab public opinion pushed leaders to plan armed intervention. Syria's political leadership, including Prime Minister **Jamil Mardam**, boasted that Arab armies would easily triumph. Syria contributed between 3,000 and 4,000 troops to the joint Arab cause, but they were poorly trained and ill equipped for the conflict.

When the British completed their withdrawal, the Zionists proclaimed the independent state of **Israel**, whereupon **Egypt**, **Lebanon**, and Syria intervened to block partition. For its part, **Transjordan** outwardly participated in the Arab front but actually favored partition between the new Jewish state and itself. On 16 May, Syrian units entered northeastern Palestine, but most of the war's fighting centered on the Egyptian and Transjordanian fronts. During the phase of fighting before the first truce on 11 June, Syrian forces gained a foothold around Lake Huleh. Israel used the truce to obtain huge stores of arms and to mobilize more men, so that when fighting resumed on 8 July, its forces made large gains in central Palestine, but not against the Syrians, who managed to expand their hold in the northeast. As the war wound down in December, Syrian forces occupied small portions of Palestine that became **demilitarized zones**.

Syrian popular opinion had been led to expect a quick and easy victory, and Israel's military successes prompted widespread anger at the government for its incompetence. The ensuing political turmoil was a key factor in Colonel **Husni al-Za`im**'s 30 March 1949 military coup. The new regime agreed to a permanent cease-fire on 13 April 1949, and the two parties signed the **Armistice of 1949** on 20 July.

PALESTINIAN. During the **Palestine War of 1948**, more than 700,000 Palestinians became refugees in neighboring Arab countries. This mass exodus was caused by a combination of expulsions by **Israeli** forces and flight from wartime dangers. While the bulk of refugees settled in the West Bank, Gaza, and **Transjordan**, about 90,000 Palestinians went to Syria. A second, smaller wave of refugees came after the **June 1967 War**, and the **Lebanese War of 1982** triggered yet another exodus of several thousand Palestinian refugees into Syria, fleeing the fighting caused by the Israeli invasion.

The **United Nations** Relief and Works Agency (UNRWA) was created in 1950 to provide basic services to refugee camp residents. Its chief functions are in the areas of **education**, public sanitation, and vocational training. Three of the four largest camps—Sabayna, Qabr al-Sitt, and Khan Ashiya—are located outside **Damascus**. The other large camp, Nayrab, is near **Aleppo**. Smaller camps are located outside of **Homs, Hama**, and Dar`a. Besides the UN camps, there are three unofficial camps. The largest is Yarmuk, now a suburb of Damascus with over 100,000 residents. In addition to UN services, the Syrian government created a special administration for settling and providing aid to refugees.

The status of Palestinians has been governed by piecemeal legislation, mostly passed between 1949 and 1956, that granted them employment rights not held by other non-Syrian residents. For instance, Palestinians can work in the civil service and the modern professions. Moreover, the government has allowed them open access to public education through the university level. These legal provisions and the Palestinians' proportionately small numbers in the overall population have enabled them to integrate in the Syrian **economy** and society. Consequently, around 70 percent of the Palestinians no longer reside in refugee camps but have moved into nearby cities. The Palestinians have not been free to pursue independent political activities; rather, successive Syrian regimes, particularly since the 1960s, have strictly controlled Palestinian politics on Syrian soil.

As of 2002, the UNRWA counted over 400,000 registered refugees, of whom roughly 115,000 lived in the 10 official camps. The UN body was operating 111 schools with over 63,000 pupils. *See also* PALESTINE.

PALMYRA. This desert city is one of Syria's most renowned ancient sites. Inscriptions from the second millennium B.C. mention it as an oasis settlement and entrepôt for **trade** between the Mediterranean and Mesopotamia (**Iraq**). The ruins that **tourists** visit today date from the Roman era. A stroller down the main avenue may view facades of wealthy merchants' palaces as well as temples, **theaters**, and statues. The city is famous for the revolt waged by Queen Zenobia against Roman rule (267-272). The modern city of Tadmur has grown near Palmyra. It is a base for tourists and for Syria's phosphate **mining** and natural gas sectors. *See also* PETROLEUM.

PEOPLE'S PARTY. Two distinct parties have existed under this name. The first was established by **Abd al-Rahman Shahbandar** in June 1925 to promote the establishment of a constitutional regime in a unified Syria that would include **Palestine, Transjordan**, and portions of **Lebanon**. It was the first legal nationalist party under the **French Mandate**. The People's Party was active for only a brief period, during which it abetted the spread of the **Great Revolt** of 1925-1927. The French suppressed the party during that revolt. In its short history, the People's Party attracted members of the urban elite: wealthy landowner politicians, merchants, and educated professionals. It also enjoyed the financial support of the **Syrian-Palestine Congress** in Cairo.

The second People's Party formed in 1948 in opposition to the **National Party**. Both parties had roots in the **National Bloc**, but regional and personal rivalries tore the Bloc apart, and former members from Syria's northern cities—**Aleppo, Homs**, and **Hama**—established the new People's Party. Former National Bloc members included **Hashim al-Atasi** and **Nazim al-Qudsi**. In general, the party represented northern and central Syrian business and landowning interests in favor of economic union with **Iraq**, whose northern regions were historically important to the trade of northern Syria.

The party reached the peak of its influence between 1949 and 1951 under the military regimes of **Sami al-Hinnawi** and **Adib al-Shishakli**. It received a strong plurality of votes in November 1949 elections, and engaged in a duel with Shishakli over control of the gendarmerie and the army. Shishakli decisively won this struggle with his 28 November 1951 coup against the elected government and arrest of leading members of the party. People's Party leaders were among those who plotted Shishakli's overthrow two years later, and they regained some of their influence by taking over prominent cabinet posts and gaining a plurality of seats in the parliament elected in September 1954. But the next few years saw Syrian politics drift to the left, and the People's Party was unable to effectively combine with other conservative forces to stop that tendency.

PETROLEUM. While Syria is not a major oil producer for the global market, its modest output has been its most important export and source of foreign exchange since the early 1980s. The first commercially significant discovery of oil took place in 1959 in **Jabal Druze** near **Suwayda**. The German company which made the find did not receive a concession to develop the field. The **Ba`th Party** government nationalized petroleum in 1964 and created the General Petroleum Authority, but oil exports had to await construction of a pipeline to **Tartus** from the northeast oil fields in 1968.

Production did not take off until **Hafiz al-Asad**'s regime encouraged exploration by offering better concessionary terms to foreign firms. The result was the discovery of new fields in the desert near **Dayr al-Zur** and a doubling of production from 1974 to 1980. In 1987, Western firms opened production in more fields discovered in northeastern Syria. Output increased from 162,000 barrels per day in 1985 to 560,000 barrels per day in 1993. By the end of 1994, production had reached 600,000 barrels per day, enough to bring in 70 percent of the country's export earnings. The government invited foreign companies to explore for new oil fields near the borders of **Turkey** and **Iraq**. In the late 1990s, production stabilized in the range of 560,000 to 600,000 barrels per day thanks to additional exploration efforts by European, American, Japanese, and Malaysian firms. Based on a revised estimate of proven reserves in 1999 at 2.5 billion barrels, Syria could produce at that rate until around 2010. The output suffices for domestic consumption and a surplus is exported.

Petroleum exports, though modest in scale compared to those of Gulf countries, have been critical to keep Syria's **economy** afloat. In the 1980s, petroleum exports accounted for between 40 and 75 percent of total exports; during the 1990s, the figure hovered in the 55 to 65 percent range. Consequently, the national economy's future welfare heavily depends on further discoveries, particularly in light of the unimpressive results of **economic reform** in recent years.

The infrastructure for transporting and refining petroleum includes the **Iraqi-Syrian pipeline** (constructed in 1934) that goes from the Kirkuk field to two destinations, one in Tripoli, **Lebanon**, and another in **Baniyas** that opened in 1952. The major oil refinery is at **Homs**, with a second smaller one at Baniyas.

The petrochemical sector includes large reserves of natural gas in the desert near **Palmyra** and in **Jazira**. In the early 1990s, the Syrians developed a natural gas field producing between 4.5 and 7 million cubic meters per day. By the late 1990s, the quantity had risen to 14 million cubic meters per day, and the Syrian Petroleum Company plans to construct new pipelines to transport gas from the Palmyra fields to **Aleppo** and Lebanon.

PRINT MEDIA. The first newspapers and magazines appeared in Syria during the late **Ottoman** era when the provincial government in **Damascus** established a printing press to publish an official gazette. A handful of ephemeral private publications appeared in the 1890s, but **censorship** under Sultan **Abdulhamid II** hampered the spread of journalism. After the constitutional restoration in 1908, newspapers and magazines proliferated in several Syrian towns. For the next few years, print media played a crucial role in expressing diverse views on sensitive political, cultural, and religious controversies, especially those touching on the place of **religion** in Ottoman affairs and on the relations between Syrian Arabs and the largely Turkish political elite in Istanbul. During **World War I**, the Ottoman authorities again clamped down on free expression and used the press to rally popular support for the empire's desperate military struggle. The brief interval of Amir **Faysal**'s rule brought a relaxation of control over the press.

In the **French Mandate** period, newspapers and magazines again proliferated to new parts of the country and expanded in coverage. **Women**'s journals promoted emancipation from traditional customs and instructed readers in hygiene and child rearing. Cultural magazines published short stories, humorous columns, and sports news. During the independence era, there have been just a few brief episodes of press freedom between long stretches of strict censorship under military rule.

When the **Ba`th Party** seized power, it expanded state control over the mass media to propagate official positions and ideas as well as to censor dissenting views. The Ba`th Party regime controls newspapers and magazines through the Ministry of Information in accord with the emergency law of 1963 granting the government control over all media. Since that time, Syria has had three major national newspapers. As its name suggests, *Al-Ba`th*, published since 1946, expresses the outlook of the party. When the party seized power in 1963, the new regime created another newspaper, *al-Thawra* (Revolution). In the early years of **Hafiz al-Asad**'s regime, the last major official newspaper, *Tishrin* (October), was established. The reader finds little difference among them, not only because they must voice the official line, but also because many columns come from the same government agency, the Syrian Arab News Agency (SANA). The political news in these organs is typically one-sided and wooden, but they also carry features on sports and cultural affairs that ordinary Syrians like to follow.

In early 2001, President **Bashar al-Asad** permitted the publication of the first private periodical since 1963, a satirical weekly created by political cartoonist **Ali Farzat**. Political parties in the Ba`th-led Progressive National Front also gained approval to publish their own periodicals. *See also* RADIO AND TELEVISION.

PRIVATIZATION. *See* **ECONOMIC REFORM.**

PUBLIC SECTOR. Since the wave of nationalizations initiated by the **Ba`th Party** regime in the early 1960s, Syria's **economy** has been dominated by the public sector. The first steps to extend government control over economic activity were actually taken in the early years of independence by pro-business cabinets seeking to curtail foreign economic influence that had dominated Syria's economy during the **French Mandate**. They nationalized foreign companies operating **railways** and **water** and power utilities. During the 1950s, a fairly even balance of political power in the domestic arena prevented measures to expand the range of government economic activity until the **United Arab Republic**'s **Socialist Decrees** paved the way for public sector organizations to manage **banks**, insurance companies, **mining**, and **petroleum** production.

A deeper and more radical phase of instituting socialism occurred in the mid-1960s under the Ba`th Party regimes, largely as part of a political strategy to overwhelm rivals whose power stemmed from their connections to Syria's business community. The Ba`thist regimes created new bodies, usually called "General Organizations," to manage much of the economy. Examples would include the General Organizations for Insurance, Food Industries, Textile Industries, and Phosphates and Mining. The management of these firms has been handled by a mix of Ba`th Party officials, trade union representatives, and political appointees. The performance of public sector firms in economic terms is, not surprisingly, unimpressive. They tend to hire many more employees than needed to run an enterprise, but such overemployment is politically useful for co-opting men and **women** who would otherwise be jobless. Government ministries usually set prices at low levels as an indirect subsidy to the Syrian consumer. Low morale and pay tend to induce more talented and motivated workers to seek work for better remuneration in the private sector, leaving less productive employees behind.

Given the poor performance of public sector firms, they have received criticism from proponents of **economic reform**, but their political utility and clout has made the regime cautious about allowing private firms to compete with public sector companies. Observers of Syria's current economic prospects acknowledge the political constraints on a thorough reform of the public sector, but even the country's limited reform measures have swung the balance of economic dynamism in favor of the private sector. Many analysts believe it is a matter of how and when, not whether, the public sector will shrink.

-Q-

QABBANI, AHMAD ABU KHALIL AL- (c. 1833-1902). The founder of modern **theater** in Syria. He came from a **Damascus** family of traders. As a young man, he would entertain evening gatherings with his singing of poems. Inspired by the **Lebanese** productions of Marun al-Naqqash (1817-1855), he decided to stage a play for relatives around 1865. Soon afterward he gave the first public performance at a **coffeehouse**. Qabbani was a playwright, actor, singer, and composer of songs. Performances usually included songs, and his plays freely borrowed from Arabian Nights, popular legendary characters, and European plays. The reformist Ottoman governor **Midhat Pasha** encouraged his efforts and sponsored the construction of a playhouse for regular public performances. Not long after the governor's departure, however, conservative opinion pushed the **Ottomans** to close the theater and pressured Qabbani to leave **Damascus**. He briefly resided in **Homs** and then permanently moved to **Egypt**.

QABBANI, NIZAR (1923-1998). A leading contemporary poet best known for his early erotic compositions in the 1940s and 1950s. His frank treatment of young men's sexual desire and descriptions of **women** as objects of that desire made Qabbani a frequent center of controversy. In 1954, his poem "Bread, Hashish, and Moon" expressed a searing critique of Arab culture for its ignorance and backwardness, and conservative critics poured scorn on him for betraying cherished cultural values. At the same time that he was publishing his first collections of poetry, he worked in the Syrian foreign ministry and held diplomatic posts in the Middle East, Europe, and Asia, but in 1966 he quit the foreign service and moved to **Lebanon**.

Qabbani was as much a celebrity as a literary figure, and the Arab public eagerly followed his dramatic private life. He left his first wife when he fell in love with an Iraqi woman who became the subject of his love poetry in the 1970s. Tragedy struck his life when his oldest son was killed in an accident and his wife perished in a terrorist attack on the Iraqi embassy in Beirut. Controversy followed him even after he died in London, where conservative Muslims objected to a memorial service on the grounds that he was an atheist.

The social implications of Qabbani's oeuvre are complex. On the one hand, he expressed yearnings to emancipate the individual from stifling social conformity (he even made homosexual love a subject) and he sometimes poured scorn on **corrupt**, oppressive Arab regimes. On the other hand, his political poetry occasionally exalted an authoritarian cult of the strong leader, be that **Egypt**'s Gamal Abd al-Nasir in the 1960s or Iraq's Saddam Husayn in the 1990s, and he glorified clichés about revolution and armed struggle against **Israel** at a time when the public mood was moving in the direction of compromise. In sum, Qabbani's poetry fits the model of the 19th century European romantic movement that celebrated the individual and responded to broader social and political currents through emotion and sentimentalism. In the general sweep of modern Syrian **literature**, critics and ordinary folks highly esteem both his love poetry and his social criticism.

QAHTAN SOCIETY. In 1909, a few Syrians living in Istanbul formed this small secret society, named after an eponymous ancestor of the Arabs, to defend Arab rights against what its members perceived as the **Committee of Union and Progress**'s campaign to "turkify" the **Ottoman Empire**'s administration. The society sought the transformation of the empire into a dual monarchy similar to the Austro-Hungarian empire. In certain respects, the Qahtan Society anticipated the platform of the **Ottoman Party of Administrative Decentralization**, which appeared in 1913.

QAMISHLI. This city of about 170,000 in the country's northeastern corner developed after **World War I**, when **French Mandate** authorities settled **Assyrian, Armenian,** and **Kurdish** refugees from **Turkey** along the banks of the Juqjug River, a tributary of the **Khabur River**. Its largely non-Arab population reflects the historical character of upper Mesopotamia. Modern Syrian governments have encouraged Arab settlement in and around Qamishli, perhaps from the belief that ethnic arabization is essential to maintaining national unity. Given the heterogeneous population, there has been intermittent tension, particularly between Assyrians and Kurds, as recently as 1970. Qamishli also attracted a colony of Syrian **Jews**, but they departed in the early 1990s like many of their coreligionists.

On the Turkish side of the border is the ancient town of Nusaybin. Because of unfriendly bilateral relations, the border crossing has ordinarily been closed, cutting off residents of the two towns, many of whom are related to one another. Qamishli's location near the juncture of Syria's border with **Iraq** and Turkey has made it an important **transportation** hub with railway lines linking the three countries.

QARMATI. Isma`ili Shi`i sect named for Hamdan Qarmat, who preached among the peasants of southern **Iraq** in the 870s and directed other preachers to spread Isma`ili teachings among **bedouin** tribes in the Syrian and north Arabian deserts. In 899 the Qarmatis split from those Isma`ilis who followed the leadership of Ubayd Allah when he claimed to be the **imam**. The Qarmatis held that the line of imams had already ended and that the seventh imam would soon return as the *mahdi*, the rightly guided messianic figure anticipated in Shi`i **Islam**. Ten years later, Ubayd Allah's movement established an Isma`ili **caliphate** in North Africa and founded the **Fatimid** dynasty. In the meantime, bedouin tribes under Qarmati leadership attacked and briefly occupied **Damascus, Homs,** and **Hama** between 902 and 906. Counterattacks by forces loyal to the **Abbasid** caliph in Baghdad drove the Qarmatis from the Syrian desert, but they created a separate state in the region of Bahrain in eastern Arabia. Hamdan Qarmat disappeared in Iraq shortly thereafter.

While the Qarmati state consolidated itself in Bahrain, the Fatimids built up their power in North Africa and prepared for the conquest of **Egypt**, which they achieved in 969. Qarmati armies became active in

Syria again in the 960s with attacks on Damascus, towns in **Palestine**, and even Egypt. One year before the Fatimid invasion of Syria, Qarmati forces from Bahrain occupied Damascus, thus setting the stage for a violent confrontation between two wings of the same Shi'i sect. For 10 years, Qarmati and Fatimid armies struggled for domination over southern Syria. First, a Fatimid force seized Damascus in 970, but the following year the Qarmatis formed an alliance with the **Hamdanids** of **Aleppo** and the Buyid princes of Baghdad and regained the city. The Qarmatis' dependence on tribal forces unwilling to permanently settle in a city, however, meant they could not hold on to Damascus. In 971 and 974 the Qarmatis carried the offensive into Egypt, laying siege to Cairo, the new capital of Egypt founded by the Fatimids. Finally the Fatimids dealt the Qarmatis a decisive defeat in 978, and drove them out of Syria permanently. The Qarmati state in Bahrain, however, survived for yet another century.

QASIMI, JAMAL AL-DIN (1866-1914). The leading figure in the **salafiyya** movement of the early 20th century. Qasimi was the prayer leader at the Sinaniyya Mosque in **Damascus**, the second most prestigious mosque in the city. He was a prolific writer in various fields of religious knowledge, history, and contemporary affairs. The central themes in his works were the essential rationality of **Islam** and the need for Muslims to overcome divisions between followers of different legal schools. Qasimi believed that Muslims would remain backward in relation to Europe until they rediscovered Islam's true nature as a **religion** that is based on reason so that it encourages a positive attitude toward science and technical progress. With respect to divisions among Muslims, he argued that it was necessary to return to Islam's sources (the Qur'an and the tradition of the Prophet) to provide a common ground and to abandon beliefs and practices that had developed over the long course of Muslim history but were not part of Islam's essence.

More conservative **ulama** attacked Qasimi's ideas because they represented a strong criticism of their own view of Islam. Consequently, on several occasions they stirred the **Ottoman** authorities to harass him and they incited mobs against him. Although Qasimi did not win a wide following in his lifetime, contemporary salafis hold him in high regard and his works continue to circulate among reformist Muslims in the Arab world.

QASIYUN. Damascus lies at the foot of the massive, towering Mount Qasiyun, a spur of the Anti-Lebanon mountain range. In local lore, the

1,200-meter peak has religious significance as the site of several grottoes, including the one where Cain is supposed to have slain Abel. Another one is associated with the Qur'anic tale of the People of the Cave (Sura 18) and another is where 40 prophets are supposed to have died of starvation. During the medieval and early modern eras, a handful of suburbs spread up the lower slopes as extensions of Damascus. In recent years, its higher slopes have become dotted with restaurants and **coffeehouses** that Damascenes frequent on summer evenings to escape the heat and to enjoy the sweeping vista of city lights spread out on the plain below.

QAWUQJI, FAWZI AL- (1887-1976). He was a captain in the Syrian Legion, created by **France** as the core of a national army, when the **Great Revolt** against the **French Mandate** broke out in July 1925. In early October, Qawuqji led **bedouin** and mutinous soldiers in an uprising against the French presence in **Hama**. A few days later, a French aerial bombardment spearheaded a counterattack to secure the town and drive the rebels into the countryside, where Qawuqji continued to lead rebel efforts until the end of the revolt nearly two years later. He then fled to **Iraq**. He entered the spotlight again during the **Palestine** Arab Revolt of 1936 to 1939, when he led Syrian volunteers who went to Palestine to fight British and Zionist forces. In the months preceding the 1948 partition of Palestine and the **Palestine War of 1948**, Qawuqji also led a militia of Arab volunteers called the Arab Liberation Army.

QINNASRIN. This small village on the banks of the **Quwayq River** south of **Aleppo** was once the primary military stronghold in northwest Syria for the **Byzantines** and then the **Umayyads**. Qinnasrin continued to serve its strategic function for later Muslim dynasties until a series of Byzantine raids in the late 10th and early 11th centuries reduced it to a minor settlement serving caravans between the **Euphrates River** and the coast.

QUDSI, NAZIM AL- (1906-1998). Nationalist lawyer from **Aleppo** who was active in the **National Bloc**'s radical Aleppan faction during the **French Mandate**. In the independence period, Qudsi grew estranged from the **National Party** leadership, and on the eve of 1947 elections, he and other Aleppan dignitaries formed the Liberal Party. A few months later, he participated in the creation of a broader opposition party, the second **People's Party**. During **Sami al-Hinnawi**'s brief rule in 1949, Prime Minister **Hashim al-Atasi** formed a government dominated by the People's Party and he appointed Qudsi minister of foreign affairs. The

Atasi government wanted to create a new constitutional order for Syria, so it decided to hold elections for a constituent assembly. In the September 1949 elections, the People's Party gained a plurality, and the assembly named Qudsi to head a committee to draft a new **constitution**. The draft document underwent some modification when the assembly debated its articles, and it was ratified in September 1950. Meanwhile, **Adib al-Shishakli** had seized power the previous December, and in June 1950 he .chose Qudsi to form a government. As prime minister, he faced strong opposition from the National Party and was frustrated by the army's encroachment on civilian control over the gendarmerie, yet he did achieve the first nationalizations of French and British utility companies before he resigned in March 1951.

After Syria's **secession** from the **United Arab Republic** in September 1961, the People's Party gained the largest bloc of seats in national elections, and its leader, Qudsi, became president of the **Syrian Arab Republic**. At the time of the abortive coups d'état of March-April 1962, Qudsi was placed under arrest for two weeks but was then restored to office. The **March 8, 1963 coup**, however, swept him from power. The **National Revolutionary Command Council** then formally stripped him of his civil rights and imprisoned him until the end of the year. The veteran political leader left Syria and spent the rest of his life in exile, first in **Lebanon**, then in **Jordan** from 1986 until his death in 1998.

QUNAYTRA. In 1873, Russia's conquests in the Caucasus Mountains triggered the flight of **Circassian** refugees to the **Ottoman Empire**. The Turkish authorities resettled them on the **Golan Heights**, where they established Qunaytra and other villages nearby. In 1967, it was a town of 17,000. **Israel** occupied Qunaytra during the **June 1967 War** and forced the population to flee, leaving it a ghost town for several years. After the **October 1973 War**, the 1974 disengagement agreement stipulated that Israel return Qunaytra to Syria. Before withdrawing, Israeli troops systematically dynamited houses, both those damaged in the two wars and those that had escaped harm. The destruction of Qunaytra further poisoned Syrian attitudes toward Israel.

QUWAYQ RIVER. This rather small river flows from the foothills of the Taurus Mountains into northwest Syria. Along its banks **Aleppo** developed in remote antiquity. For centuries the Quwayq River supplied the city and watered its renowned pistachio orchards, but in recent decades population growth has led to excessive exploitation to the point it is barely a trickle anymore. Aleppo now obtains **water** for municipal use from the **Euphrates River**'s **Lake Asad**.

QUWWATLI, SHUKRI AL- (1891-1967). A leading nationalist during the **French Mandate** and president for nine of Syria's first 15 years of independence. Quwwatli joined **al-Fatat** during **World War I** and supported the **Arab Revolt**; for his nationalist activities, the **Ottomans** imprisoned him. During Amir **Faysal**'s brief reign, Quwwatli was active in the nationalist **Istiqlal Party**. When **France** occupied Syria in 1920, he fled to **Egypt**, where he joined the **Syrian-Palestine Congress**. He spent the next 10 years in exile, like many other nationalists the French considered too dangerous to allow back into Syria. In 1930, however, France issued a general amnesty and Quwwatli returned. He reentered the political arena in 1932 when he joined the **National Bloc**, and he soon became the head of the more radical faction that challenged party chief **Jamil Mardam**'s leadership. In 1936, Quwwatli was elected to parliament and Mardam named him minister of defense and finance. Mardam's leadership of the National Bloc government failed to advance Syrian nationalist goals, and in 1939 Quwwatli defeated him in a contest for leadership of the Bloc.

When elections were held for Syria's first independent government in July 1943, Quwwatli was elected president. His tenure saw the final evacuation of French forces and the eruption of the **Palestine War of 1948**. Syria's poor performance in the conflict contributed to **Husni al-Za`im**'s military coup of March 1949 that ended Quwwatli's presidency. He then moved to Egypt as he had nearly 30 years before.

After Shishakli's overthrow, he returned to Syria in August 1954 to boost the **National Party**'s election campaign. In September 1955, Quwwatli again became president, but with far less authority than before. He led Syria through crises over the **Baghdad Pact**, the Suez War, the **conspiracy of 1956**, military threats by **Turkey**, and finally unity talks with Egypt. Quwwatli's last political act was to resign as president of Syria in order to allow Gamal Abd al-Nasir to assume the presidency of the **United Arab Republic**.

-R-

RADIO AND TELEVISION. Electronic media have been under complete state control since the early 1960s. Typical radio broadcasts include **music** and news, but there are also informational and comedy programs.

Besides the state radio network, which operates 16 stations, Syrians frequently listen to Arabic-language foreign programs on British Broadcasting Company, Radio Monte Carlo, and **Egyptian** and even **Israeli** programs.

The two official television channels carry Syrian and Egyptian serials, documentaries on history, folklore, and economic development, and heavily censored news. Syrians who live near **Lebanon** or **Jordan** have more options because they may tune in to radio and television programs from these neighboring countries.

In the 1990s, satellite channels burst state monopolies throughout the Arab world, and in this respect, Syria is no different. Unquestionably, the most popular channel is *al-Jazira*, an all-news outlet based in Qatar. Since its creation in 1996, *al-Jazira* has rapidly attracted a large audience because it offers Arab viewers the liveliest and most candid coverage of regional events. Syrians tune in to watch programs that deal with topics never debated in public forums, including **Islamic fundamentalism**, **human rights**, and democratic reforms. Official television channels have responded with cosmetic changes, but more substantial shifts will only occur if the overall political situation becomes more liberal. In the meantime, under President **Bashar al-Asad**, some programs have ventured to broadcast satires on **corruption** and even the **security forces** (*mukhabarat*). *See also* CENSORSHIP; PRINT MEDIA.

RAILWAYS. *See* **TRANSPORTATION.**

RAQQA, AL-. Located at the point where the **Euphrates** and Balikh Rivers come together, this city is located at a site inhabited since antiquity, called Nikephorion in the Seleucid and **Byzantine** eras. In the **Umayyad** period, its garrison anchored the dynasty's authority in the turbulent **Jazira** region. The **Abbasids** constructed a new, more heavily fortified town, al-Rafiqa, near the older site to strengthen defensive lines against the Byzantines. For a time, the area encompassed by these neighboring towns formed the second largest urban area in the Abbasid Empire, and for a brief spell around 800, they were the imperial capital under **caliph** Harun al-Rashid, who made it the headquarters for annual military campaigns against the Byzantines and for the pilgrimage caravan to Mecca. In spite of the area's proximity to the early Muslim empires' perennial **Christian** adversary, the town's Christian community continued to reside there, as did its **Jewish** inhabitants.

In addition to its political role, al-Raqqa was the site of scientific endeavors, particularly in astronomy, and it acted as an important artistic bridge between the Mediterranean and Persian zones and became renowned for its ceramics. The town came under **Hamdanid** rule in 942, and it quickly declined in population and importance until a period of revival in the 12th and 13th centuries under **Zangid** and **Ayyubid** rulers. The **Mongol** invasions and wars with the **Mamluks** ended al-Raqqa's role as an important military center and resulted in its desertion.

In the late 19th century, the **Ottoman Empire** settled the town with **Circassian** refugees fleeing from Russian expansion in the Caucasus. Since independence, al-Raqqa has become the seat of a governorate and it is now a bustling city of around 175,000. The main impetus for its recent growth was the construction of **Tabqa Dam**, which made it the center of a developing **agricultural** region. The Syrian Department of Antiquities manages an **archaeological** museum displaying Abbasid-era artifacts. The earliest remains date to the Abbasid era and include portions of an eighth-century wall.

RELIGION. Syria has a rich history of coexistence and intermittent tension or conflict between adherents of **Islam**, Christianity, and Judaism. At the time of the Arab conquest, Syria had a largely **Christian** population in addition to several **Jewish** communities residing in the main towns. The Christians were mostly **Greek Orthodox** but there were also **Syrian Orthodox** and **Nestorians**. The majority of the population gradually converted to Islam by the 13th century. Many details of that process are not clear to historians, but the image of forced conversion at swordpoint comes from medieval Christian polemical writings, not from historical accounts. Instead, historians have concluded that a combination of political, fiscal, economic, and social factors brought about conversions in the main towns and that Muslim settlement in the countryside spread Islam to rural areas. Just as Christianity's historical development resulted in the emergence of several distinct denominations, so did Islam's. **Sunni** Muslims have been politically and numerically dominant in the cities but several **Shi`i** sects like the **Druzes**, **Nizaris**, and **Alawis** are firmly anchored in the countryside.

Throughout the centuries of Muslim rule, political authorities derived part of their legitimacy from their public commitment to Islamic ceremonies and symbols. The **Crusades** era was a period of strife between Muslim and Christian powers and of pressure on Christians living under Muslim rule. Otherwise, relations between the two religions were mostly free of strain until the mid-19th century, when Muslim antagonism to European power and the perception that Syrian Christians exploited ties to their coreligionists led to the outbreak of communal riots in **Aleppo** and **Damascus**.

In the 20th century, the **French Mandate** (1920-1946) marked an abrupt break with nearly 1,300 years of Muslim rule (except for coastal areas held by the Franks during the Crusades). During the 1940s, the position of the country's Jews deteriorated as **Arab nationalist** sentiment became inflamed at the prospect of a Jewish state displacing **Palestinian** Arabs. Attacks on Jews and their property shortly before and during the **Palestine War of 1948** prompted many to emigrate. Failure thereafter to resolve the conflict with **Israel** created difficult circumstances for Syrian Jews, and their numbers dwindled as one regime after another imposed harsh conditions and even close surveillance.

In contrast to the deteriorating situation of Jews, the standing of Christians in independent Syria has been as good or better than in other Arab countries. Nevertheless, the place of religion in public life came to the fore in Syrian politics when the **Ba`th Party** seized power in 1963 and pursued secular policies that angered a large segment of the Muslim population. A prolonged struggle between the regime and **Islamic fundamentalist** militants was fueled in part by the conspicuous role in the Ba`th Party of individuals belonging to Muslim sects like the Alawis and the Druzes. Indeed, the head of state since 1970 has been an Alawi, **Hafiz al-Asad**, and then his son **Bashar al-Asad**. The struggle petered out after the 1982 **Hama** uprising and since that time interreligious relations have been calm. Indeed, in the 1990s and first years of the 21st century, Syria is notable among Middle Eastern countries for the secure position of religious minorities with the exception of the Jews, most of whom emigrated in the mid-1990s.

RIDA, MUHAMMAD RASHID (1865-1935). Syrian-born writer who spent most of his life in **Egypt** (from 1897 to 1935). Rida is best known as the publisher of *al-Manar* (*The Lighthouse*), a periodical dedicated to religious reform, which he edited from 1898 until his death in 1935. In addition to issuing what was arguably the most influential Arabic Muslim journal of the 20th century, Rida's essays and articles contributed to the elaboration of thought in the **salafiyya** reform movement, particularly his writings on legal and educational reform. In the early 1920s, he contributed a seminal work on the Islamic state. The timing of this work was significant, as it came out shortly before **Turkey** abolished the **caliphate**, the 1,300-year-old institution representing Muslim political authority. In the arena of Syrian political life, Rida was a critic of the **Committee of Union and Progress**'s policies, perhaps because of their secular bias, and he participated in the **Ottoman Party of Administrative Decentralization**, which supported greater autonomy for the Arab provinces. After **World War I**, Rida returned to Syria, supported the ephemeral regime of Amir **Faysal**, and presided over the **Syrian Congress** of 1920. When **France** crushed Faysal's state, Rida returned to Cairo and in the early years of the **French Mandate** served as vice president of the **Syrian-Palestine Congress** executive committee.

RUWALA. A **bedouin** tribe whose members are concentrated in northwestern **Saudi Arabia** while a smaller number lives in Syria and **Jordan**. In the late 19th and early 20th centuries, their domain from southern Syria to northern Arabia felt the encroachment of expanding forces, the **Ottomans** from the north and the Saudis from the south. At the same time, the modernization of **transportation** ended their economic role as caravaneers for long-distance overland **trade** and forced them to rely exclusively on raising livestock. The demarcation of national boundaries divided Ruwala tribesmen among three countries, so the bonds of tribal affinity were now, in theory, compromised by divergent national loyalties. Because the tribal chief, Nuri Sha`lan, had his summer camp near **Damascus**, he became a Syrian citizen and a member of the Chamber of Deputies in the 1930s. Shaykh Nuri embodied the integration of tribal leaders into the national political system, but friction between tribesmen and national governments reemerged in the 1960s under the **Ba`th Party** regime, and a substantial section permanently resettled in Saudi Arabia.

While the Ruwala tribe's influence on Syrian history has been fairly slight, their experience reflects that of many other nomadic tribes, for whom the establishment of definite international borders forced deep changes in their way of life.

-S-

SA`ADA, ANTUN AL- (1904-1949).** Founder of the **Syrian Social National Party**, he was born to a **Greek Orthodox** Lebanese family. Sa`ada's father emigrated to Brazil during **World War I, and Antun moved there in 1920. While in Brazil, Sa`ada developed his ideas about Syrian nationalism. In 1929, Sa`ada returned to **Lebanon**, and in November

1932 he formed the SSNP, originally called the Syrian National Party. He kept the party secret and initially recruited among students at the American University of Beirut. As party membership grew, Sa`ada decided to compose a party constitution and a manifesto in 1934. When **French Mandate** authorities uncovered the party in November 1935, they arrested Sa`ada on charges of subversive activities and sentenced him to six months' imprisonment. Following his release, he began to recruit members in the Syrian province of **Latakia** and campaigned against **Turkey**'s imminent annexation of **Alexandretta**. Sa`ada left Lebanon in 1938 to organize party cells among Syrian emigrants in Brazil, where he spent the next nine years.

While he was out of the country, SSNP members in Lebanon changed the party's name to the National Party and transformed it into a more conventional Lebanese party focusing on Lebanese political issues. When Sa`ada returned to Lebanon, he ousted the men responsible for this deviation and reestablished his status as the party's sole authority. His relations with the Lebanese government were always fraught with tension as the very essence of his political thought denied the legitimacy of an independent Lebanon. In June 1949, he and his party were charged with plotting to overthrow the government; he then fled to **Damascus**, where he plotted with Syria's military ruler **Husni al-Za`im** to bring down the Lebanese government. In July, Sa`ada's followers launched a few minor attacks on remote police stations in Lebanon. Za`im then betrayed him by arresting and handing him over to the Lebanese on 6 July. The next day a military court tried him for treason and executed him on 8 July. This violent end made him a martyr in many quarters and actually boosted the SSNP's standing in both Syria and Lebanon.

Sa`ada's political thought centered on the idea of the Syrian nation, which in his view had roots in historical and geographical bonds among various ethnic and religious groups. His notion of Syria encompassed **Iraq**, Syria, Lebanon, **Jordan**, **Palestine**, the Sinai Peninsula, and Cyprus. According to Sa`ada, the historical mission of the Syrian nation necessitated its political unity under a secular regime.

SALADIN (c. 1138-1193). In Arabic, Salah al-Din al-Ayyubi. Renowned military hero of the Muslim effort against the **Crusades** and founder of the **Ayyubid** dynasty. Saladin began his rise to power in the service of **Nur al-Din Mahmud**, the **atabeg** who had established unified authority over Syria in 1154. As Nur al-Din's agent in Cairo, Saladin accomplished the termination of the **Fatimid caliphate** and the restoration of nominal

Abbasid authority over **Egypt**. In 1175, one year after Nur al-Din's death, he placed both Syria and Egypt under his own authority. Saladin is best known for his military efforts against the Crusaders, especially the 1187 Battle of Hattin, which led to the Muslim recapture of Jerusalem. By 1189, Saladin had uprooted most of the Latin strongholds along the Syrian coast as far north as **Latakia**. But three years later, a European counterattack, known as the Third Crusade, forced him to retreat from key coastal towns. Nonetheless, at his death on 4 March 1193, Saladin was the first Muslim to rule over both Egypt and most of Syria in nearly two centuries.

SALAFIYYA. This term refers to two distinct trends in modern **Islam**. The earlier one was a 19th- and 20th-century Islamic reform movement whose advocates believed that Muslims became vulnerable to European domination because they had strayed from the correct practice of their religion, so they called for a return to the religious beliefs and practices of the first generation of Muslims (*al-salaf al-salih*). The movement emerged in **Damascus** in the 1890s among a number of **ulama** conversant with reformist tendencies in other Muslim lands. Syrian salafis of the **Ottoman** period, like **Tahir al-Jaza'iri** and **Jamal al-Din al-Qasimi**, strove for reforms in Muslim **education** and law (**shari`a**) to combat the growing influence of secularism in the Ottoman Empire. They also encouraged an Arab cultural revival through their researches on Arab history. Moreover, in the Ottoman political context, the salafis favored the restoration of **constitutional** government that had been suspended by Sultan **Abdulhamid II** in 1878. Their views on cultural and political matters attracted younger Syrians studying in secular schools and informed this rising generation's conceptions of **Arab nationalism**. During the **French Mandate** era, salafis founded religious associations that provided the foundations for the Syrian branch of the **Muslim Brothers**.

The more recent salafi trend emerged in the 1990s outside Syria among militant **Islamic fundamentalists** committed to removing secular Arab regimes in **Egypt** and Algeria and engaged in the conflict to evict from Afghanistan the regime that was backed by the **Soviet Union**. The militant salafis are quite different in aims and methods from the earlier ones but they both use the term "salafi" to legitimize their claim to represent a return to pure Islam.

SALAMIYYA. This is a small town located about halfway between **Homs** and **Hama** on the margins of cultivated land and the steppe. In **Islamic** times, lesser members of the **Abbasid** family settled there, but its historical importance was as the site of decisive developments in the history of **Isma`ili Shi`ism** for which it was a center of religious leadership and propaganda starting in the ninth century. The founder of the **Fatimid** dynasty, Ubayd Allah, was born there and instituted some changes in doctrine that precipitated a split among Isma`ilis and the secession of a faction that became the **Qarmatis**. After Ubayd Allah's departure for North Africa, Salamiyya became the object of struggles among a succession of tribal chieftains and princes of Homs and Hama. In the early **Ottoman** era, it was abandoned. In the mid-19th century, Istanbul allowed Isma`ilis from the **Jabal Ansariyya** to resettle it as part of a campaign to extend control over the steppe. These descendants of the **Nizari** branch of Isma`ili Shi`ism have prospered by developing the area's **agricultural** potential. In addition, they have cultivated strong ties with the spiritual leaders of the Nizaris, the Agha Khans, one of whom is buried in a mausoleum there. The town's population has grown to around 100,000.

SALJUK DYNASTY. The Saljuks were a Turkish clan from Central Asia that in 1055 became the effective power behind the **Abbasid caliphate**. The Saljuk chiefs then took the title of sultan. They opened the way for the mass migration of Turkish nomads into the central lands of the Middle East and laid the foundations for nearly nine centuries of Turkish political and military preeminence in Syria. They first entered northern Syria in 1071, seized **Damascus** in 1078, occupied **Aleppo** in 1086, and drove the **Fatimids** out of the Syrian interior altogether. Unified Saljuk rule lasted but a few years, as after 1092 it quickly fragmented among regional domains divided between various princes, who in turn lost effective power to their tutors or **atabegs** by the early 12th century. In **Iran** and Asia Minor, Saljuk power lasted until the **Mongol** conquests of the early 1200s.

SAN REMO AGREEMENT. In the diplomatic aftermath of **World War I** Great Britain and **France** reached a preliminary accord over the disposition of **Ottoman** territories and resources before formally ending the war in a peace treaty. This accord, signed at San Remo, Italy, on 24 April 1920, included a joint Anglo-French approach to Ottoman Arab lands that they had occupied during the war. They agreed to grant France a mandate over Syria and **Lebanon**, while Great Britain received mandates over **Palestine** and **Iraq**. Two months later, France enforced its claim to Syria by invading the country and ousting the government of Amir **Faysal**.

SARRAJ, ABD AL-HAMID AL- (1925-). Born in **Hama**, Sarraj was part of the growing leftist trend in the officer corps during the 1950s. He served in the national gendarmerie in the **French Mandate** era, then fought alongside other volunteers in the **Palestine War of 1948**. Thereafter he attracted the favorable attention of **Adib al-Shishakli**. In 1954, after Shishakli's fall, he and other officers plotted against the pro-Western cabinet of **Sabri al-Asali**, but the effort was detected in the planning stages, and Sarraj was sent to **France** as an assistant to the military attaché.

He was rehabilitated the following year and in March 1955 promoted to head of military intelligence, in which capacity he presided over the investigation into the April 1955 assassination of Colonel **Adnan al-Malki**, a role that made Sarraj a well-known figure. This task involved the discovery of conspiracies supposedly hatched by **Iraq**, the **Syrian Social National Party**, and Western governments to derail Syria's neutralist stance. Sarraj gained further stature when he uncovered the **conspiracy of 1956** to overthrow the Syrian government. In March 1957, pro-Western officers tried to transfer him to an innocuous post, but his solid backing among junior officers allowed him to resist the order. Two months later Sarraj formed a revolutionary command council of army officers and civilian politicians to keep Syria on its neutral course in **foreign policy**. Along with Major-General **Afif al-Bizri**, Sarraj was now the leading figure in the Syrian military, which since 1949 had dominated the country's politics.

He favored the 1958 merger with **Egypt** to form the **United Arab Republic**, in which he rose to minister of interior, thus acquiring authority over Syria's **security forces**. In this capacity, Sarraj became notorious for introducing police state measures to suppress dissent. In September 1960, Gamal Abd al-Nasir appointed him president of the Syrian Provincial Council, effectively the most powerful position for a Syrian in the UAR. In August the following year, however, Nasir removed him from that post to assume the more ceremonial office of vice president of the UAR. Sarraj resigned on 26 September 1961, two days before the coup that took Syria out of the UAR. The **secessionist regime** arrested him in early October, but in May 1962 he escaped from a military hospital and made his way to Egypt, where he has lived ever since.

SAUDI ARABIA. Even though Syria is a republic and Saudi Arabia is a monarchy, they have usually maintained good relations because of their need to balance pressures from the perennial powers in Arab politics, namely **Egypt** and **Iraq**. During the **French Mandate**, Saudi Arabia's King Abd al-Aziz ibn Saud opposed **Hashemite** influence in Syria through his political ally **Shukri al-Quwwatli**. Ibn Saud's primary concern was to block any move to transform Syria into a monarchy under Amir Abdullah, the ruler of **Transjordan**, or either of his brothers, **Faysal** and Ali. The Saudi-Hashemite rivalry has its roots in their struggle for supremacy in Arabia during the 1920s when the Saudis attacked and defeated the Hashemite kingdom of the Hijaz in 1925. Saudi opposition to Hashemite interests continued during Syria's first years of independence when both **Jordan** and Iraq supported Syrian politicians inclined to form a union with either of those countries. In the inter-Arab struggle for paramount influence in Syria, Saudi Arabia usually cooperated with Egypt against Iraq and Jordan.

Syrian-Saudi relations became strained under the **United Arab Republic** and the first two **Ba'th Party** regimes, which championed the cause of revolution in the Arab world against all forces of "reaction," especially pro-Western monarchies. Since 1970 **Hafiz al-Asad** has cultivated friendlier relations and in return has received large amounts of Saudi financial aid. But relations again became strained during the 1980s because of Syria's support for **Iran** in its war against Iraq. Ties improved in 1990 and 1991 when Asad gave strong support to Saudi Arabia in the wake of Iraq's invasion of Kuwait. In the 1990s, the conservative monarchy and the Ba'th Party regime consistently coordinated positions on various regional issues like the sanctions regime against Iraq and peace talks with **Israel**. They closed a notable gap from the 1980s when Syria helped mend the rift between the Saudis and Iran's **Islamic** Republic. In recent years, Syrian President **Bashar al-Asad** has continued his father's policy of frequent consultation with the Saudis on urgent regional events like the **United States** invasion of Iraq and initiatives to resolve the **Palestinian**-Israeli conflict.

SAYF, RIYAD AL- (c. 1946-). A **Damascus** businessman and independent member of the People's Assembly elected in 1994. Sayf initially focused on efforts to expand the domain of the private commercial sector in Syria's state-dominated **economy**. He rose to prominence in the first year of **Bashar al-Asad**'s rule as a leading establishment voice in the **civil society** movement for ending the state of emergency and restoring democracy. He founded the Movement for Social Peace in a direct challenge to the **Ba`th Party** monopoly on political organization. In particular, he declared the failure of socialist policies to advance Syria's economic fortunes. During the brief spell of political relaxation in Bashar al-Asad's early months, Sayf was a popular figure in Damascus for using his platform in parliament to criticize official **corruption**. When the regime decided to suppress the reform movement in late summer 2001, the authorities arrested Sayf for holding an unauthorized meeting to protest the arrest of another activist, **Riyad al-Turk**. Sayf's trial attracted observers from several European countries and the **United States**. He defended his political activities and statements as within the bounds of a parliamentary deputy. Nevertheless, in April 2002, a court sentenced him to a five-year sentence for subverting the **constitution**.

SAYYADI, ABU AL-HUDA AL- (1850-1909). Religious shaykh who served as adviser to Sultan **Abdulhamid II** and supported the sultan's claim to the **caliphate**. Sayyadi came from a family known as leaders of a small branch of the Rifa`iyya **sufi** order near **Aleppo**. He traveled to Istanbul, where he earned a reputation for his singing of sufi chants and gained entrance to Abdulhamid's entourage. The sultan then made him the head of all Rifa`iyya branches in the **Ottoman Empire**'s Arab provinces. This order had numerous lodges in Syria and **Iraq** and provided a network that channeled propaganda in favor of the sultan to dozens of towns and villages. Abu al-Huda fabricated genealogies to incorporate local sufi orders into the Rifa`iyya order and to grant the status of **ashraf** to minor sufi shaykhs. He also distributed posts, stipends, and medals to his clients. As a result, many who worked in Syrian religious institutions depended on his patronage. Sayyadi also composed many books that supported Abdulhamid's claim to the caliphate and encouraged Muslims to support their ruler.

SECESSIONIST REGIME. This term refers to the series of short-lived governments that emerged following Syria's September 1961 withdrawal from the **United Arab Republic**. Seven cabinets came and went in 17 months of extraordinary instability. The first government restored parliamentary rule and in December held national elections that returned many of the conservative politicians who had dominated politics in the early years of independence. **Khalid al-Azm** won the largest share of votes for his stands in favor of democracy and against union with **Egypt**. On the other hand, **Salah al-Din al-Bitar** and other candidates of the

Ba`th Party** that had brought about the union with Egypt were defeated. Yet **Akram al-Hawrani**, a Ba`thist leader who had criticized UAR policies, and his coalition partners did well. In the new government, **People's Party leaders **Ma`ruf al-Dawalibi** became prime minister and **Nazim al-Qudsi** president. The conservative assembly rescinded the July 1961 **Socialist Decrees** that had nationalized large companies. It also sought to restore civilian authority.

Army officers, however, had grown accustomed to dictating to politicians, and between 28 March and 2 April 1962, three separate attempts at military coups were made. The first was by **Abd al-Karim al-Nahlawi**, who opposed any return to a more liberal regime. Three days later, a group of Nasirist and Ba`thist officers in **Homs** made a clumsy bid for power. Finally, Nasirist officers in **Aleppo** attempted a coup on 2 April. Aside from opposing the restoration of full civilian authority, the officers favored the continuation of **land reform** and the Socialist Decrees. In the wake of these interventions, Dawalibi resigned, Qudsi declared the dissolution of the elected assembly, and **Bashir al-Azma** formed a more progressive cabinet that lasted until September. The Azma government partially restored socialist measures that Dawalibi had rescinded. In September, Qudsi consulted with the army command concerning a cabinet change because of Azma's weakness as prime minister. The army agreed to the appointment of Khalid al-Azm and, to assure the progressive reforms, the retention of Azma as deputy prime minister. Azm continued with gradual implementation of land reform, but his desire to restore a fully democratic government alarmed the officers. His government lasted until the **March 8, 1963 coup** that ended the secessionist regime and brought the Ba`th Party to power.

SECURITY FORCES. One of the mainstays of **Ba`th Party** power since 1963 has been a network of special security units, military intelligence forces, and civilian intelligence agencies that track, intimidate, and suppress groups and individuals critical of the government. Such forces, known in Arabic as *mukhabarat* or information services, have become crucial elements for the stability of most Arab regimes. The security forces are responsible for Syria's abysmal **human rights** record, which includes detention without trial and torture. State Security, also called the General Intelligence Directorate, watches domestic political activity in the universities; Political Security tracks members of political parties; the Bureau of National Security collects information from Ba`th Party members distributed throughout the country. Military Intelligence is one of the two most powerful agencies; it plays a major role in managing Syria's affairs in **Lebanon**. Inside the country, its Palestine Branch maintains surveillance on **Palestinian** camps and organizations. Finally, Air Force Intelligence is a separate entity that seems to specialize in operations abroad. The various military units run their own interrogation centers where torture is reportedly routine.

In addition to these information-collecting bodies, the regime of **Hafiz al-Asad** created special military units that combine intelligence and security functions. The leadership and personnel of these units consist of men whose loyalty to the regime stems from family connection or sectarian, **Alawi**, affinity. The Special Forces, numbering between 10,000 and 15,000, played a critical role in suppressing the protests and insurrection of the late 1970s and early 1980s. This unit also has had a fearful presence in northern Lebanon, carrying out abductions and even executions. A second special military force, the Defense Brigades, was for over a decade the chief institutional prop for **Rif'at al-Asad**. Under his command, the Defense Brigades guarded against coups d'état, but after Rif'at's disgrace in the mid-1980s, President Asad disbanded them. The Presidential Guard (also known as the Republican Guard) is responsible for the head of state's security. In the early 1990s, it served as a power base for Basil al-Asad, the older son of Hafiz al-Asad who died in a 1994 automobile accident.

SELIM I (r. 1512-1520). The **Ottoman** conqueror of Syria (1516) and **Egypt** (1517). His army of **janissaries** routed the **Mamluks** at **Marj Dabiq**, near **Aleppo**, on 24 August 1516. As Sultan Selim led his forces south, the Mamluks fled to Egypt, leaving **Damascus** to fall without a struggle one month later. On 23 January 1517, Ottoman forces easily defeated the Mamluks outside Cairo, thereby ending the Mamluk sultanate. The victorious sultan then organized Ottoman administration over Syria. He appointed a governor over **Aleppo** and its districts, while he designated a Mamluk to preside over Damascus and extensive portions of central and southern Syria. In 1519, he created a new province centered on Tripoli, thereby reducing the scope of the province of Damascus.

SHAHBANDAR, ABD AL-RAHMAN (1880-1940). A prominent Syrian nationalist during the **French Mandate**, he was a leading opponent of compromise with French authority. His devotion to **Arab nationalism** dated to the days of the **Committee of Union and Progress** and its "turkification" policies. He supported the **Arab Revolt** during **World**

War I, and he briefly headed the foreign ministry under Amir **Faysal**. When **France** occupied Syria in July 1920, he fled the country. Shahbandar returned in 1921 and organized the **Iron Hand Society** to agitate against French rule. In April 1922, the French arrested him and other Iron Hand leaders for incitement against their rule. The arrests triggered several days of demonstrations and bloody confrontation between protestors and French forces in **Damascus**. Nonetheless, the French tried Shahbandar for subversive activities and sentenced him to 20 years. After he served a year and a half of his sentence, the French sent him into exile, where he joined the activities of the **Syrian-Palestine Congress** based in Cairo. The French allowed him to return to Syria in 1924. The following year, Shahbandar guided the formation of Syria's first nationalist party, the **People's Party**. He then helped organize the spread of the **Great Revolt** from **Jabal Druze** to the rest of Syria. He eluded the French authorities and moved to Jabal Druze for the duration of the revolt. There he and **Sultan al-Atrash** formed a provisional government. When the revolt collapsed in 1927, Shahbandar fled to **Transjordan** and from there to **Egypt**.

In 1937, a French amnesty allowed him to return from exile, and he directed his supporters to oppose the **Franco-Syrian Treaty** on the grounds that it granted France privileges that detracted from Syrian sovereignty. He also directed a political campaign to discredit the **National Bloc** government and Prime Minister **Jamil Mardam**. During **World War II**, the French considered cooperating with Shahbandar because of his opposition to the National Bloc and because of support for him from Britain and the **Hashemites**. But in June 1940, he was assassinated. The French accused several prominent National Bloc figures, including Jamil Mardam and **Sa`dallah al-Jabiri** of plotting the murder, and they fled to **Iraq**. While Shahbandar was one of Syria's most popular leaders, he never built up an organization that would perpetuate his political legacy.

SHAHRUR, MUHAMMAD (1938-). Author of a modernist interpretation of the Qur'an that generated keen interest and sharp controversy throughout the Arab world. Shahrur's *The Book and the Qur'an: A Contemporary Reading* (1990) is a long, somewhat rambling meditation based in part on his interest in modern linguistics theory. He did not acquire a traditional or even modern **education** in **Islamic** sciences. Rather, he studied civil engineering in the **Soviet Union** and Ireland, then became a professor at **Damascus** University and worked in a private firm.

In his controversial book, Shahrur set out to challenge received idea; about the Qur'an and advanced what he hoped was a more objective and scientific understanding of its meaning. His approach is in line with modernist efforts to reinterpret the Qur'an in the light of current historical circumstances rather than accepting the views of earlier Muslims as final and complete. He explicates a relative conception of knowledge with reference to paradigm shifts in the sciences in modern times and asserts that just as scientific notions about the natural world are susceptible to revision, so are the positions of Muslims on the meaning of the Qur'an. Shahrur applies this relativist epistemology to the sensitive issue of **women**'s status and contends that their exclusion from judgeships and positions of executive authority rests on a historically conditioned reading of the Qur'an, not its eternal meaning.

In other writings, Shahrur has stated that it is imperative to bring the details of Islamic morality and law (**shari`a**) into accord with what he believes to be Islam's general principles, like justice and the free exchange of ideas. At the same time, he retains a believer's certainty that some moral issues are not subject to compromise. Through his sensitivity to historical context and his restriction of eternal rules to those explicitly declared in the Qur'an, Shahrur represents a liberal religious attitude that many Syrian Muslims with modern education find appealing.

SHARA`, FARUQ AL- (1938-    ).** A prominent adviser on **foreign policy** to Presidents **Hafiz** and **Bashar al-Asad**. Shara` is from Dar`a, a town near the **Jordanian border. He attended **Damascus** University and studied English literature. In the late 1970s, he was Syria's ambassador to Italy, and then reached a high post in the foreign ministry in 1980 before becoming foreign minister in 1984 to replace **Abd al-Halim al-Khaddam**. Shara` became familiar to the Western press as head of the Syrian delegation to the 1991 **Madrid Conference**. Throughout the decade, he frequently spoke on behalf of President Asad to Arab and Western audiences. In September 1999, he met American President Bill Clinton in Washington to hammer out a formula for resuming peace talks with **Israel** after a three-year hiatus. After recovering from heart surgery, he led the Syrian team at the 1999-2000 round of peace talks with Israel held in the **United States** and was the highest ranking official of the Syrian government to ever meet an Israeli leader, Prime Minister Ehud Barak. Shara` has retained his post in the transition to the Bashar al-Asad era and represents continuity in the country's key positions on foreign policy.

SHARI`A.** The Arabic term for **Islamic** law, shari`a has been an integral part of Syrian society for more than a thousand years. In Islamic legal theory, there are four sources for Islamic law: (1) the Qur'an, which in Muslim belief is the word of God; (2) the Sunna, or oral traditions of the Prophet Muhammad; (3) the consensus of scholarly opinion; and (4) analogical reasoning. Throughout the Islamic period, experts in Islamic law have been drawn from the **ulama to serve as judges (sing. *qadi*) in religious courts and as jurisconsults (sing. *mufti*) to issue legal opinions. Muslim rulers from the early **caliphate** to the **Ottoman** dynasty legitimized their rule by claiming to abide by and enforce the shari`a.

The status of religious law began to weaken during the **Tanzimat** era of Ottoman history with the introduction of secular legal codes. The first reaction to the tide of secularism issued from the **salafiyya** movement, whose partisans argued for a reinterpretation of shari`a to demonstrate its relevance to the Ottoman project of modernization. Under the **French Mandate**, authorities initially refrained from tampering with the religious courts' remaining jurisdiction over personal status, but in 1928 a French proposal to call for religious equality in a draft **constitution** caused an uproar and the matter had to be abandoned.

On the whole, the shari`a emerged from the colonial period un-scathed, but soon after independence Syria enacted a new civil code that represented a small step away from religious law. On the other hand, the 1953 Law of Personal Status reaffirmed the shari`a's authority over marriage, divorce, and other family matters among Muslims. The place of the shari`a in Syrian society came to the fore in the 1970s and early 1980s when the **Muslim Brothers** led popular demonstrations and a militant insurrection to overthrow the secular **Ba`th Party** regime in order to install an Islamic state that would reestablish the centrality of Islamic law in the **legal system**. The Syrian government suppressed the uprising in 1982, and since that time the confined role of the shari`a in public life has not been challenged.

SHARIF HUSAYN. *See* **HUSAYN IBN ALI.**

SHEPHERDSTOWN. This small American town in West Virginia hosted an intensive phase in the **Syrian-Israeli peace talks** on 3-10 January 2000. They were the first negotiations between the perennial adversaries since a wave of **Palestinian** suicide bombings in **Israel** in February and March 1996 and Syria's refusal to condemn them led Israel to suspend contacts. There followed a three-year freeze while Benjamin Netanyahu was the

Israeli prime minister. Then, in May 1999, Ehud Barak defeated Netanyahu in national elections, and the **United States** helped bring the two sides together with the hope of achieving a peace settlement. Prior to the talks, Israeli Prime Minister Ehud Barak and Syrian Foreign Minister **Faruq al-Shara`** met in Washington. During eight days at Shepherdstown, President Bill Clinton participated on five separate occasions, and Secretary of State Madeleine Albright spent the entire time period with the parties in a strong effort to culminate a deal. Both sides formed special committees to discuss borders, **water**, security, and diplomatic relations, and while the substance of the talks was supposed to be secret, leaks indicated that the atmosphere was positive. Ehud Barak, though, faced a difficult political climate back home because of his narrow majority in the Israeli parliament and popular mistrust of Syria. Likewise, the **Damascus** leadership faced domestic unrest, and there were reports that when the talks were announced in December, the authorities arrested several hundred **Islamic fundamentalist** and leftist figures in the major cities to curtail criticism.

When the talks concluded, it was expected that a second round would begin on 19 January, but a secret American draft agreement leaked out. It embarrassed the Syrians because it indicated that Damascus had yielded on certain issues without gaining Israel's agreement on borders. Syrian President **Hafiz al-Asad** then declared that he would not send Shara` back unless Israel publicly declared it would withdraw to the 4 June 1967 lines. American efforts to restart the talks failed when Clinton traveled to Geneva to meet Asad in March with new proposals and the Syrian president considered them unacceptable. He died just three months later, and in September 2000, a new Palestinian uprising erupted. In retrospect, the Shepherdstown talks represented the high-water mark of diplomatic efforts dating to the 1991 **Madrid Conference**.

SHIHABI, HIKMAT AL- (1931-). One of the most important military figures in **Hafiz al-Asad**'s regime. He was chief of staff of the **armed forces** from 1973 until 1998. Shihabi is a **Sunni** Muslim, and he served the regime in capacities that indicate the confidence and trust that President Asad placed in him. After the **October 1973 War**, he participated in negotiations with the **United States** to achieve a disengagement accord with **Israel** on the **Golan Heights**. During the fall 1983 illness of President Asad, he was part of a committee that managed national affairs while the president recuperated. In December 1994 and June 1995, Shihabi represented Syria in security talks with Israeli counterparts in

Washington. At the time, Asad's dispatch of his chief of staff signaled to the Israelis and the Americans his serious intention to pursue the negotiations. The phase of **Syrian-Israeli peace talks** in which Shihabi participated made little progress in bridging the gap between the Israeli and Syrian positions on the security components of a peace treaty.

His retirement in 1998 sparked speculation that he was in fact forced out to clear the way for **Bashar al-Asad**'s eventual succession. He was followed by Ali Aslan (b. 1938), his deputy chief of staff. Aslan had led the Syrian offensive that initially recovered a large portion of the Golan Heights in the October 1973 War. Shortly before Asad's death in June 2000, Shihabi traveled to the United States amid rumors that he would face prosecution for **corruption** schemes. He returned to **Damascus** the following month, probably after receiving word that he would not face any charges. Observers interpreted the incident to represent substantial continuity in the regime.

SHI`I.** The second largest Muslim sect after the **Sunnis**, the Shi`is are actually divided into several subsects, including the following communities found in Syria: the Twelvers or Imamis, **Isma`ilis**, **Alawis**, and **Nizaris**. The **Druze** religion is an offshoot of Isma`ili Shi`ism. The historical origins of Shi`ism go back to the first generation of **Islam when differences arose concerning the rightful claimant to the **caliphate**. A party of Muslims supported the claims of the Prophet Muhammad's cousin and son-in-law **Ali ibn Abi Talib**, but most Muslims backed other candidates as the first three caliphs. Ali's supporters became known as the "party of Ali," or *shi`at Ali* in Arabic, hence the term Shi`i. Ali gained the caliphate in 656, but his standing was challenged and ultimately he was assassinated in 661. Loyalty to Ali then devolved to his descendants, who were considered the **imams**, the legitimate religious and political leaders of the community. About a century after his death, schisms developed among the Shi`is when they disagreed on the identity of the imam. The various Shi`i sects that evolved during the eighth and ninth centuries arose on the basis of loyalty to different descendants of Ali. *See also* FATIMID; ISLAM; QARMATI; RELIGION.

SHISHAKLI, ADIB AL- (1909-1964). Colonel who launched the third military coup of 1949 in order to thwart any chance of union with **Iraq**. Shishakli was born in **Hama** to a family of rural tax collectors that had become prominent in the early 1800s. He was a longtime associate of his fellow townsman **Akram al-Hawrani**. In the 1930s, Shishakli was attracted to the **Syrian Social National Party**. He played a minor part in **Husni al-Za`im**'s coup of March 1949, but was then forced to retire. **Sami al-Hinnawi** reinstated him, and he then plotted with Hawrani to overthrow Hinnawi. When he deposed Hinnawi on 19 December 1949, he designated civilian politicians to govern Syria. The constituent assembly elected under Hinnawi continued to meet, **Khalid al-Azm** headed a civilian government, and Shishakli retained his post as deputy chief of staff, preferring to wield effective power from behind the scenes.

Shishakli moved to center stage on 28 November 1951, when he removed the **People's Party** from government and arrested its leaders. This event led to the resignation of President **Hashim al-Atasi** and Shishakli's promotion of his associate Colonel **Fawzi Silu** as head of state. He then took a series of steps to shore up his authority. First, he mobilized popular support by establishing the Arab Liberation Movement in August 1952. The movement endorsed improving the standing of **women**, **land reform**, and more progressive **labor** laws. He built up the Syrian **armed forces**, promoted younger officers with training in Western countries, and briefly unified its higher ranks under his control. He also asserted state authority over private and foreign schools. To dampen political opposition, Shishakli closed down political parties and banned members of the civil service and trade unions from political activity.

In July 1953, Shishakli conducted a referendum to approve a new **constitution** under which he was elected president and formed a cabinet of nonentities. That same month, his opponents gathered in **Homs** to plot a revolt that would begin in **Jabal Druze** and include demonstrations in major cities. Iraq also connived at Shishakli's downfall because of his suppression of the People's Party (the pro-Iraqi party) and his alignment with **Saudi Arabia** and **Egypt**. On 25 February 1954, military units in **Aleppo, Dayr al-Zur**, Hama, Homs, and **Latakia** mutinied and called for Shishakli to step down. He resigned and departed for Beirut, and left for Saudi Arabia two days later. In 1960 he moved to Brazil, where a **Druze** gunman assassinated him on 27 September 1964.

SIBA`I, MUSTAFA AL- (1915-1964).** Head of the **Muslim Brothers** in Syria from 1946 until 1957, professor of **Islamic** law (**shari`a), and dean of **Damascus** University's Law Faculty. His family was well-known in Homs for its association with religious learning. Siba`i went to **Egypt** in the early 1930s to study at its prestigious college of Islamic learning, the Azhar. While in Cairo, he joined the Muslim Brothers and participated in anti-British activities that led to his arrest and imprisonment. He returned to Homs in 1941 and established an activist religious group called Muhammad's Youth, modeled on the Muslim Brothers. He was instrumental in the 1946 foundation of the Syrian branch of the Muslim Brothers and became its leader. In addition to his political and religious activism, Siba`i wrote several works that gained influence with **Islamic fundamentalists**. In *Islamic Socialism* he argued that Islam possesses a distinctive economic system that is akin to Western types of socialism. According to Siba`i, Islamic socialism gives the state a guiding role through nationalization of public services.

Siba`i led the Muslim Brothers during the society's heyday of involvement in Syrian politics, between independence and **Adib al-Shishakli**'s ban on the movement in 1952. He formed the Islamic Socialist Front in 1949 to contend in elections to the constituent assembly, and it gained four seats, including one for Siba`i. In the assembly, he was the spokesman for Syrians who favored an article stipulating that Islam would be the state **religion**. Sharp debate in the assembly led to a compromise formula, which stated that the president must be a Muslim and that legislation should be derived from Islamic law. Siba`i remained an outspoken opponent of secular and leftist tendencies and a supporter of a neutralist foreign policy until poor health forced him to retire from politics in 1957.

SILU, FAWZI (1905-1972). Prominent figure in **Adib al-Shishakli**'s regime. Silu had a long career in the military, having joined the **Troupes Spéciales** in 1924. He was the first chief of the **Homs** military academy in independent Syria and led its delegation at the **Armistice of 1949** talks. After Shishakli seized power in December 1949, he forced Silu on Prime Minister **Nazim al-Qudsi** as minister of defense to act as the army's man in the cabinet. When Shishakli established a military dictatorship in December 1951, he gave Silu full executive and legislative powers. Silu was no more than a figurehead as Shishakli set about dismantling the institutions of democratic government. Between June 1952 and July 1953, Silu headed a cabinet, but when Shishakli assumed the presidency, he forced the colonel to retire. A few months later Colonel Silu left Syria and moved to **Saudi Arabia**.

SOCIALIST DECREES. In July 1961, **United Arab Republic** President Gamal Abd al-Nasir announced a set of laws that nationalized **banks**, insurance companies, and three large industrial companies. Because of their unpopularity, the decrees are often cited as a factor in contributing to Syria's **secession** from the UAR two months later. During the tumultuous 18 months following the secession, conservative politicians tried to repeal or at least dilute these measures. As it turned out, they foreshadowed more sweeping measures passed and implemented by the **Ba'th Party** regimes of the 1960s.

SOVIET UNION. In the early 1950s, many Syrians viewed good relations with the USSR as a means to maintain independence from British and American influence. The foundation stone for warm relations was laid on 23 March 1955, when Soviet Foreign Minister Molotov warned **Turkey**, which had massed troops along the border, against threatening Syria to force it into joining the **Baghdad Pact**. This was followed by a series of arms deals over the next three years. In February 1956, Syria negotiated the purchase of weapons from Czechoslovakia; in August, there followed a Soviet-Syrian cultural agreement. Syria then made trade pacts with other communist nations. This notable increase in Soviet influence benefited the **Syrian Communist Party**, which broadcast its ideas to a more sympathetic population. In August 1957, Soviet influence grew further with the signing of yet another economic agreement that included financing for development projects and the purchase of Syrian agricultural exports. Syria's drift toward the Soviets, however, was abruptly halted by the formation of the **United Arab Republic** in 1958 and the subsequent suppression of the SCP.

The conservative regimes that followed Syria's **secession** from the UAR did not pursue better relations with the Soviets, and the first chance for some improvement came after the **March 8, 1963 coup**. Initially, relations with the **Ba'th Party** regime were cool, but they improved in 1964 with the ascendance of more radical members of the party. In April 1966, the Soviets offered to help Syria build a dam on the **Euphrates River**. In the wake of Syria's defeat in the **June 1967 War**, the Soviets resupplied the Syrian **armed forces**.

After **Hafiz al-Asad** came to power in 1970, the Soviets continued to provide military equipment and advisers, and again resupplied Syria after the **October 1973 War**. Syrian-Soviet relations received another boost in 1979 when **Egypt** signed a peace treaty with **Israel** under the auspices of the **United States**. The Soviets reinforced Syria's position against Israel by agreeing to a huge arms deal. Syria indicated its support for the Soviets by refusing to criticize their invasion of Afghanistan at the end of 1979. The peak of Syrian-Soviet relations was reached when the two countries signed the October 1980 Treaty of Friendship and Cooperation. That was followed by another series of large arms transfers in 1982 and 1983, including the Soviet Union's most sophisticated missile defense system (manned by Soviet experts) and long-range surface-to-surface missiles.

At the end of the 1980s, however, Soviet leader Mikhail Gorbachev drew clear limits to his country's willingness to arm Syria when he advised President Asad to seek a negotiated solution to the conflict with Israel. When Gorbachev engineered the Soviet Union's withdrawal from Eastern Europe and rapprochement with the United States in 1989-1990, Syria became alarmed that it would lose the backing of its superpower patron. The end of the Cold War fundamentally altered the geopolitical context of the Arab-Israeli conflict, and President Asad adroitly adjusted to the new context by improving ties with the United States while maintaining good relations with the new Russian state that emerged from the defunct Soviet Union in 1991.

SUFISM. This mystical aspect of Muslim religious practice and belief developed in early **Islamic** times from a movement for greater asceticism and piety. Sufism has long been a widespread phenomenon in all Muslim lands, including Syria. Followers of the mystical way are known as sufis. Sufism concentrates on the individual believer's relationship with *Allah*, the Arabic word for God. Its central concept is that through moral purification and rigorous devotional practice, the believer draws closer to Allah and might eventually attain a mystical union with Him. The characteristic practice of sufism is *dhikr*, the ceremonial remembrance of Allah by an individual or by a group of mystics.

In the 11th century, mystical brotherhoods or sufi orders (sing. *tariqa*) formed on the basis of a particular sufi master's practices and teachings. Groups of sufis gathered at convents called *zawiyas*, which became widespread in Syrian towns during the 11th and 12th centuries under the patronage of the **atabegs** and the **Ayyubid** dynasty. The **Mamluk** sultans added more endowments (sing. **waqf**) for these sufi convents. The best-known early sufi orders in Syria were the Rifa`iyya and Qadiriyya orders, which remained popular well into the 20th century. The Suhrawardiyya and Shadhiliyya orders also had wide followings in medieval times.

The **Ottoman** era saw the spread of two more sufi orders: the Khalwatiyya and Naqshbandiyya. In the 19th century, the latter order became the vanguard of a movement to make sufi practices more rigorously conform to the prescriptions of Islamic law (**shari`a**). This shari`a-minded sufism took root most firmly in **Damascus**, particularly following the arrival of the renowned peripatetic Shaykh Khalid al-Naqshbandi (1780-1827). He founded a branch of the order known as the Mujaddidiyya-Naqshbandiyya, which also gained adherents among high Ottoman officials in Istanbul. Later in the 19th century, this reformist brand of sufism attracted more **ulama** and influenced the early stages of the **salafiyya** reform movement. In the same period, Sultan **Abdulhamid II** and his Syrian adviser **Abu al-Huda al-Sayyadi** supported sufi orders that followed traditional ways, such as the Rifa'iyya.

In the 20th century, Islamic reform groups like the **Muslim Brothers** and secular social movements attracted much of the urban population that historically associated with sufi orders. Nonetheless, the orders continue to provide religious guidance and a milieu for spiritual discipline. The Naqshbandiyya and Rifa'iyya reportedly have the largest followings, but in general the appeal of sufism today is limited.

SULEYMAN I (r. 1520-1566). A great **Ottoman** sultan, known as Suleyman the Magnificent. Upon ascending to the throne, he immediately faced a revolt by the **Mamluk** governor of **Damascus**, Janbardi al-Ghazali, who took over **Homs, Hama**, and Tripoli, but failed in his attempt to seize **Aleppo**. An Ottoman counterattack soon reconquered Tripoli and Damascus. Sultan Suleyman then appointed a Turkish governor for Damascus and separate governors for portions of southern Syria. Ottoman rule over Syria, then, was decisively consolidated during Suleyman's long reign.

SUNNI. The majority Muslim sect, which comprises about 70 percent of the population. In early Islamic history, the Sunnis were those Muslims who accepted the legitimacy of the early **caliphs**, supported **Mu'awiya** in his struggle against **Ali**, and backed the **Umayyad** and **Abbasid** dynasties against various **Shi'i** movements. Sunni political power in Syria faced its most serious challenge during the 10th and 11th centuries when the **Fatimid** dynasty of **Egypt**, the **Hamdanid** dynasty of **Aleppo**, and the **Qarmati** movement dominated most of the country. Sunni authority was restored in the late 11th century by the **Saljuk** dynasty, but **Nizari** strongholds survived in remote parts of Syria and challenged the Saljuks and their **Ayyubid** successors well into the 13th century. During the **Mamluk** sultanate, the last vestiges of Shi'i power were stamped out. Both the Mamluks and the **Ottoman** dynasty legitimized their rule by claiming to uphold Sunni **Islam**.

Sunni preeminence in Syria was firmly established by dynastic tradition, but also by the economic domination of Sunni townsmen over the rural hinterland. In the late 19th century, urban Sunnis came into possession of vast rural estates with hundreds of villages. The political elite of the late Ottoman, **French Mandate**, and early independence eras largely consisted of Sunni absentee landowners. The entry of the **armed forces** into politics through a series of military coups and then the **United Arab Republic**'s **land reform** measures weakened the standing of the Sunni political elite. The final blow to the tradition of Sunni power was struck by the **Ba`th Party** regimes with their concentration of religious **minorities** intent on breaking the power of landlords and promoting a secular identity for Syria. Sunni reaction to the new order took the form of protests and demonstrations in the 1960s, and then an armed insurrection in the 1970s and 1980s that was fiercely repressed by the regime of **Hafiz al-Asad**, himself an **Alawi**. *See also* RELIGION.

SUWAYDA. The capital of **Jabal Druze**. This is a city of 75,000 located 125 kilometers south of **Damascus**. The population is mixed **Druze** and **Greek Orthodox Christians** in a region that still includes **bedouins** raising livestock. In November 2000, there was a sudden outbreak of fighting between Druzes and bedouins in villages near Suwayda that resulted in about 20 deaths. The violence grew from chronic friction over the bedouins' occasional trespassing on the fields of Druze cultivators. The government had to send regular army units to enforce a curfew and quell the clashes.

SYKES-PICOT AGREEMENT. Diplomatic accord of 16 May 1916 between Great Britain and **France** by which they agreed to the disposition of the **Ottoman Empire**'s territories in the event of its defeat in **World War I**. In November 1915 formal negotiations between the two allies had commenced with a view to agreeing on spheres of influence. According to the agreement, which was kept secret for fear of antagonizing Britain's Arab allies, France was to exercise direct control over the Syrian coast and to have a sphere of influence over the Syrian interior, while Britain obtained control over southern **Iraq** and a sphere of influence in southern Syria. In November 1917, the **Soviet Union** disclosed the terms of the Sykes-Picot agreement, and the British sought to minimize its damaging effects by promising its Arab allies that its terms neither contradicted the **Husayn-McMahon Correspondence** nor stipulated the imposition of

French rule over Syria. The postwar settlement, however, followed Sykes-Picot more closely than British promises of Arab independence.

SYRIAN-AMERICAN. Before the late 1880s, very few Syrians immigrated to the **United States**, but their numbers picked up in the 1890s and early 1900s. At that time, the term "Syrian" was applied to inhabitants of both Syria and **Lebanon**, therefore United States immigration records did not distinguish between them, and we do not have exact figures for the number of immigrants from either region. The American authorities' inexact categories included "Turkos," "Asiatic Turks," and Arabs. Almost all of the immigrants were **Christians**, male, young, and unmarried. Many of them dreamed of amassing a fortune in the New World and then going back home. The introduction of conscription in the **Ottoman Empire** in 1908 caused a spike in emigration from the Levant. Syrian immigration to the United States reached a peak of about 6,000 per year in the period before **World War I**. The prewar migration to North America was a small part of a much larger movement of more than 100,000 Syrians to Latin America, Australia, and West Africa. Once in the United States, it seems the typical immigrant worked as an itinerant peddler or an industrial laborer.

After the war, the US Congress passed legislation to establish quotas on immigrants by nationality, and Syrian entries fell to about 100 per year until the rescinding in 1965 of the Immigration Quota Act. There followed a new burst of immigration to the United States by Syrians fleeing political turmoil and seeking economic opportunity. Descendants of the first wave of immigration are thoroughly integrated into American society, in part because their ancestors wished to assimilate and so they frequently adopted anglicized names, such as Thomas for Tuma. The preservation of an ethnic Syrian-American identity has depended in large measure on affiliation with Eastern churches, and distinct communities may be found among larger Arab-American populations in the Detroit and Dearborn, Michigan, areas or as discrete clusters in smaller towns like Allentown and New Castle, Pennsylvania.

SYRIAN ARAB REPUBLIC. The official name of Syria adopted in 1961 after the dissolution of the **United Arab Republic** in September.

SYRIAN CATHOLIC. Former **Syrian Orthodox Christians** who entered communion with Rome beginning in 1783. Their historic homeland was in southern **Turkey** and northern **Iraq**, but in the early 1920s many Syrian

Catholics emigrated to Syria. Their patriarchate is near Beirut. About 30,000 Syrian Catholics live in **Aleppo**, **Damascus**, and **Jazira**.

SYRIAN COMMUNIST PARTY. Established in Syria in 1928 as an extension of the communist Lebanese People's Party that had been founded two years earlier. The SCP grew under the leadership of **Khalid Bakdash**, who became party secretary in 1936. In the next three years its membership increased to 2,000, mostly among students and intellectuals. Then in September 1939, the **French Mandate** authorities banned the party and arrested its leaders. The party was again allowed to openly function from January 1941 until 1948. At the party's national congress of December 1943-January 1944, it adopted a platform that stressed national and democratic principles rather than class struggle and revolution. This position reflected Bakdash's understanding that the party lacked a large proletarian constituency and that it made sense for the party to espouse generally progressive ideas rather than a specific communist platform.

Bakdash's careful formulation of party principles to match the popular mood was sabotaged by the **Soviet Union**'s support for the 1947 **United Nations** resolution to partition **Palestine**. Moscow's position so outraged Syrian opinion that a crowd destroyed the SCP's headquarters in **Damascus** and killed several members. Moreover, the Soviet position angered many members, and large numbers quit the party. At the same time, the Syrian government banned the SCP. Its fortunes revived, however, in the mid-1950s because of growing anti-Western sentiment.

In the campaign for national elections in 1954, party chief Khalid Bakdash ran as an independent because the government refused to lift the ban on the party. He called for a progressive national front against imperialism and for democracy at home. His election in September made him the first communist to gain a seat in an Arab parliament. The SCP then joined forces with the **Ba`th Party** to oppose Syria's joining the **Baghdad Pact** in 1955. An arms deal with Czechoslovakia in February 1956 further bolstered the party's standing. Other developments that helped the SCP included the 1956 Suez war, in which **France**, Great Britain, and **Israel** attacked **Egypt** while the Soviets vigorously supported Egypt, and the crisis in relations with the **United States** in the fall of 1957. Also in 1956 and 1957, the party worked closely with the popular independent politician **Khalid al-Azm**, a powerful member of the cabinet. The phenomenal increase in the SCP's standing by the end of 1957 was a factor in the decision taken by the Ba`th Party leadership and army officers to pursue union with Egypt and the creation of the **United Arab**

Republic in February 1958. The union weakened the SCP in three ways. First, many members favored the union and left the party when Bakdash refused to endorse it; second, Bakdash himself went into exile; and third, all political parties were dissolved and the SCP in particular suffered harsh persecution under Gamal Abd al-Nasir's anti-communist regime.

The SCP has never recovered the influence it enjoyed in the mid-1950s, but in 1972 **Hafiz al-Asad** included it in the National Progressive Front led by the Ba'th Party. That prompted a faction to leave the party. The dissidents formed the Syrian Communist Party-Political Bureau headed by **Riyad al-Turk**. Other splits would occur in subsequent years as members lost patience with Bakdash's high-handed ways and refused to support the mildly liberalizing **economic reforms** of the 1980s. Unlike the nationalist and socialist parties in the National Progressive Front, which is viewed as an instrument of the regime, the communists have managed to maintain a distinct profile and allure for a segment of Syrian society.

SYRIAN CONGRESS. During Amir **Faysal**'s brief rule from October 1918 to July 1920, the Syrian Congress was the closest institution to a nationally elected assembly. In June 1919, members of the Congress were elected under **Ottoman** procedures in the main cities, while local notables chose delegates in other parts of the country. Faysal hoped that it would give his regime greater international legitimacy and strengthen his diplomatic position against **France**'s claim to Syria. In particular, Faysal wanted a representative body to testify to Syrian aspirations before the **King-Crane Commission**, which President Woodrow Wilson sent in order to determine what kind of political arrangements the Syrians desired. A second task of the Congress was to draft a **constitution**. A committee was formed and drew up a document for discussion, but consideration of the draft was interrupted by the French invasion in July 1920.

A minority of radical nationalist members dominated the Congress, and they hampered Faysal's attempts to satisfy France's desire to build up its influence over Syria. To underscore its refusal to countenance any role for the French, in March 1920 the Congress declared Faysal the king of a completely independent Syria. By that time, however, Faysal was more interested in fending off France's aggressive designs than nationalist posturing, yet he needed the Congress to validate his standing in Syria. During the final crisis between Faysal and France, the Congress voted to resist an invasion. The easy victory of French forces at the Battle of **Maysalun** in July 1920 spelled the end of the Syrian Congress.

SYRIAN FLAG. Changes in the official flag reflect Syria's volatile political history. In **Hashemite** Syria, the flag consisted of horizontal bars of green, white, and black to stand for the **Fatimid, Umayyad,** and **Abbasid** dynasties. During the **French Mandate,** in 1932, a new flag added three red stars to the white bar. The stars represented the united provinces of **Aleppo, Damascus,** and **Dayr al-Zur.** Syria kept that flag until it entered the **United Arab Republic** with **Egypt** in 1958. The UAR flag had red, white, and black bars with two green stars representing Syria and Egypt. The 1932 flag was restored after Syria withdrew from the UAR in 1961. When the **Ba`th Party** came to power in 1963, it adopted the UAR flag with three stars, the additional one representing **Iraq** because of hopes for a union of the three states. The current flag has just two stars.

SYRIAN-ISRAELI PEACE TALKS. After the **Madrid Conference** of October-November 1991, **Israel,** Syria, **Jordan, Lebanon,** and a **Palestinian** delegation convened in Washington, D.C., for bilateral talks. Between December 1991 and June 1993, Syria and Israel conducted nine rounds of talks. In the first four rounds until May 1992, the Syrians negotiated with an Israeli delegation appointed by the right-wing Likud government, and the talks made no headway in resolving their dispute. Then in June 1992, Israel's Labor Party headed by Yitzhak Rabin defeated Likud in national elections. When bilateral talks resumed in August, a more civil tone was adopted by both parties, and Syria formally offered a peace treaty in exchange for the **Golan Heights,** which Israel has occupied since the **June 1967 War.** At the same time, Syria also insisted that its peace agreement with Israel be contingent on a comprehensive peace including Jordan, Lebanon, and the Palestinians. Israel rejected that position and insisted that Syria provide specific details on what it meant by normalizing relations that would accompany peace. At the seventh round in October, Israel stated that it would undertake a withdrawal in the Golan Heights but refused to commit itself to a full withdrawal. By the end of the 10th round in June 1993, the parties had not come any closer to agreement.

In August 1993, Israel and the **Palestine Liberation Organization** announced their agreement to exchange mutual recognition and to a process for resolving the Palestinian dimension of the Arab-Israeli conflict under the terms of the Oslo Accords. Syrian President **Hafiz al-**

Asad responded to this stunning development by saying that Syria would neither oppose the accords nor their critics, mainly radical Palestinian factions based in Syria and Lebanon. To indicate his anger at the deal for sabotaging his strategy of negotiating on the basis of a common Arab position, Asad withheld Syrian participation in the 11th round of bilateral talks in September.

While Syrian-Israeli bilateral talks remained suspended, American Secretary of State Warren Christopher undertook shuttle diplomacy throughout 1994 seeking to narrow the differences between Syrian and Israeli positions. His efforts bore no fruit on the Syrian-Israeli track, but he did persuade Jordan to resume bilateral talks in June. This was quickly followed by an agreement to end the state of war between Jordan and Israel in July and a formal peace treaty in October. Once again Asad's desire to maintain a common Arab position was thwarted. Meanwhile, a number of meetings between the Syrian and Israeli ambassadors to the **United States** took place in the second half of 1994. Christopher continued his shuttle diplomacy in 1995 and inched toward bridging the differences in the parties' positions.

After a new round of talks in June 1995 held in Washington, Syria indicated that it would share the Golan's **water** resources if Israel would fully withdraw. The Syrians also accepted Israel's position that demilitarized and limited forces zones would be deeper on the Syrian side of the border than on Israel's because of the latter's shallower strategic depth. The extent of Israel's withdrawal remained the major point of contention because Prime Minister Yitzhak Rabin would not publicly pledge a full withdrawal, perhaps because he had shaky domestic political support for it. Furthermore, Rabin wanted a phased withdrawal over three to five years while Asad insisted it take no longer than one year. Another point of difference was Israel's desire for normal relations, not just a formal peace treaty. Reports about the negotiations described Israel's view of normalization as entailing open borders, **tourism**, **trade**, and bilateral cooperation on **energy** and water projects. Analysts noted that Syrians construed such elements of a peace treaty with suspicion rooted in fear of Israeli economic domination.

An intensive round of talks at the Wye River Plantation in Maryland held between December 1995 and February 1996 was cut short by a wave of Palestinian suicide bombings in Israel, and the Syrian government refused to close the Damascus offices of Palestinian groups opposed to the Oslo Accords. The May 1996 election of Benjamin Netanyahu as Israel's prime minister led to a freeze on talks for the duration of his tenure, but the next prime minister, Ehud Barak, elected in May 1999, revived them and met Syrian Foreign Minister **Faruq al-Shara`** under American auspices in Washington.

The last attempt to resolve the dispute during Asad's tenure took place when the Israeli prime minister and Syrian foreign minister met at **Shepherdstown**, West Virginia, under American auspices in January 2000. The parties formed four special committees to focus on borders, security, water, and normalization. The talks foundered on disagreement over defining "full withdrawal." Israel refused to accede to Syria's demand for access to Lake Tiberias. A large part of the problem was that each side doubted the other's sincerity and intentions. Syrians construed Israel's desire for normal relations as a pretext for establishing economic dominance; Israelis viewed Syria's reluctance to embrace normal relations as evidence of deep-seated hostility. A last-ditch effort by President Bill Clinton to bridge the differences in a meeting with Syrian President Asad in Geneva in March failed. The death of Hafiz al-Asad in June 2000 probably made the prospect of a final settlement more remote because his son and successor, **Bashar al-Asad**, needed time to consolidate his regime. The eruption of violence between Israel and the Palestinian Authority in fall 2000 placed yet another obstacle in the way of a final Israeli-Syrian settlement. The propitious climate of the middle to late 1990s for resolving their 50-year conflict had slipped away.

SYRIAN ORTHODOX. Also known as Jacobite **Christians**. Their origins stem from fifth-century dogmatic disputes over the nature of Christ. One group, the Monophysites, advanced the idea that Christ was purely divine. They became the Copts, the dominant sect in **Egypt**, and in the sixth century they gained a Syrian following largely through the work of Bishop Jacobus Baradaeus. Their **Greek Orthodox** opponents called them followers of Jacobus, or Jacobites. This was the most widely followed Christian sect at the time of the seventh-century Muslim conquest. Like the **Nestorians**, the Jacobites translated Greek scientific and philosophical works into Syriac, from which Arabic translations were made during the early **Islamic** centuries. In the 20th century their patriarchate was first located in **Homs** but then moved in 1957 to **Damascus**. Most Syrian Orthodox Christians live in Damascus, **Aleppo**, the vicinity of **Homs**, and in **Jazira**, especially the towns of **Qamishli** and **al-Hasaka**.

SYRIAN-PALESTINE CONGRESS. Political organization based in Cairo and set up by Syrian exiles at a congress held in Geneva in June 1921.

The Syrian-Palestine Congress strove for the unity of geographical Syria and the end of French and British rule. Its main activities were fundraising and publishing propaganda on behalf of the Syrian nationalist movement, to which it devoted more attention than the **Palestine** cause. The Congress was hampered by personal and political divisions among its leadership. One faction was more secular and looked to the **Hashemites** and Great Britain for support in the struggle against the **French Mandate**. This faction included **Abd al-Rahman Shahbandar**, whose **Iron Hand Society** and **People's Party** depended on funds the Congress raised abroad. The other faction, which laid greater emphasis on Islam, looked more to **Turkey** and **Saudi Arabia** for support. **Shakib Arslan** and **Muhammad Rashid Rida** headed this group. A third faction emerged from members of the **Istiqlal Party**, which was secular, pan-Arab, and anti-British. Its leading figure was **Adil Arslan**.

During the **Great Revolt** of 1925-1927, tensions between the factions mounted as the French negotiated with Shakib Arslan, thereby arousing Shahbandar's jealousy. Furthermore, Istiqlal member **Shukri al-Quwwatli** managed to convince the Saudi ruler Ibn Saud to contribute funds for the revolt. To handle the money, a Jerusalem Committee under Istiqlalist control was established, and when the French gained the upper hand against the revolt in the second half of 1926, the Shahbandar faction accused the Jerusalem Committee of embezzling funds. Mutual recriminations intensified, and by the end of 1927 the Congress formally split into two separate organizations. The personal rivalries that developed in the Syrian-Palestine Congress persisted into the late 1930s in the form of mistrust between Quwwatli, by then a leader in the **National Bloc**, and Shahbandar, who was trying to edge his way back onto the political scene after a decade in exile.

SYRIAN SOCIAL NATIONAL PARTY. Established in **Lebanon** in 1932 by **Antun al-Sa'ada**, this party is devoted to unifying historical Syria, which it defines as the modern states of Cyprus, **Iraq, Israel, Jordan**, Lebanon, and Syria. As an organization, the party emphasizes loyalty to the leader and militaristic discipline. Other key tenets include a firm commitment to secularism and opposition to sectarianism and localism. The party developed a substantial following in Lebanon but held little attraction in Syria until the execution of Sa'ada in 1949 after an alleged plot to overthrow the Lebanese government.

The party then moved its headquarters to **Damascus** under its new leader George Abd al-Masih. Sa'ada's martyrdom elicited a wave of sympathy for the party, and in November 1949 it won nine seats in elections to Syria's constituent assembly, gaining most of its votes from non-**Sunnis** and non-Arabs attracted to its secularism. The party's fortunes seemed to improve when **Adib al-Shishakli** came to power in a military coup in December 1949. The new strongman had briefly belonged to the SSNP during the **French Mandate**, and for a short time after his coup he cultivated the party's backing. But in the campaign for the October 1953 elections to parliament, Shishakli spread insinuations in the press that the SSNP's candidates received funds from the **United States**. The party gained just one seat in the election and it moved into opposition along with the **Ba`th Party**, the **Syrian Communist Party**, and the **Muslim Brothers**.

After Shishakli's fall in February 1954, new parliamentary elections were held in September. Apparently, public sympathy for the SSNP had been exhausted and its fortunes were damaged by swelling sentiment against pro-Western candidates. The party ran 15 candidates and won just two seats. Any potential it might still have had was crushed when a party member assassinated **Adnan al-Malki** in April 1955, after which its supporters in the army and government offices were purged. The party's higher council expelled George Abd al-Masih for his alleged role in plotting Malki's assassination and precipitating the Syrian government's crackdown on the party. Since that time, the SSNP has remained a force in Lebanese politics, but not in Syria.

-T-

TABQA DAM. Located on the **Euphrates River** 200 kilometers east of **Aleppo**, construction began in 1968 and was completed in 1973 with technical and financial assistance from the **Soviet Union**. The Tabqa Dam is five kilometers long and 70 meters high. Its eight turbines have increased Syria's capacity to produce electricity and allowed an expansion of irrigated **agriculture**. An 80-kilometer-long lake behind the dam, called **Lake Asad**, supplies Aleppo's **water** through an underground aqueduct.

Syrian planners originally expected the dam to allow the extension of irrigated agriculture to 640,000 hectares, but this figure has been revised downward several times to 240,000 hectares. By the late 1980s, less than 30,000 hectares had been put under cultivation on state-run farms. The main problem with irrigation systems is the high gypsum content of the soil which allows much water to seep into the earth and makes the irrigation channels susceptible to erosion.

Tabqa was formerly a small village, but the construction of the dam turned it into a provincial center with over 75,000 residents. When the dam was completed, the government renamed Tabqa "Revolution City" (in Arabic, *Madinat al-Thawra*).

TA'IF ACCORD. The October 1989 agreement to restructure **Lebanon**'s political system in a manner that formally ended **Christian** dominance and helped resolve the **Lebanese Civil War**. The immediate background to the accord lay in the stalemated presidential election of 1988, when it proved impossible to elect a successor to Amin Gemayel. President Gemayel designated General Michel Aoun interim prime minister, but the outgoing **Sunni** prime minister Salim al-Hoss refused to recognize Aoun, and for the next two years Lebanon had two contenders for leadership: Michel Aoun and the Hoss cabinet. Heavy fighting broke out in 1988 and the first half of 1989 as General Aoun sought to force the Syrians out of the country. An initiative by the **League of Arab States** to resolve the crisis led to a meeting of the Lebanese parliament at the **Saudi Arabian** resort town of Ta'if in October 1989.

The Ta'if Accord provided for fundamental reform of Lebanon's political system by redistributing power among the president, prime minister, and speaker of the chamber; and by equalizing the Muslim and Christian ratios in parliament. It also called for the restoration of government authority over all of Lebanon, the evacuation of **Israel**'s troops from the south, and the establishment of special ties with Syria.

The accord could not be immediately implemented because of Michel Aoun's opposition on the basis that the withdrawal of foreign forces, Syrian and Israeli, should come first. But the powerful Christian Lebanese Forces decided to support the immediate application of Ta'if, and terrible fighting broke out between Aoun's mostly Christian army and the Lebanese Forces in early 1990. The situation appeared stalemated as Aoun stood his ground and enjoyed open diplomatic and military backing from **Iraq**. The deadlock was broken, however, in the wake of Iraq's invasion of Kuwait in August 1990. Syria supported the **United States** moves against Iraq in the wake of the latter's annexation of Kuwait, and in return the Americans reportedly agreed to a decisive Syrian military move against Aoun, who was forced into exile in **France**. Since then, Syria has consolidated its position as the dominant power in Lebanon and supported the reconstitution of the Lebanese state on the foundation of the Ta'if Accord.

TANZIMAT. This is the term for the reorganization of the **Ottoman Empire's** bureaucratic and military institutions that commenced in 1839 and is usually said to have lasted until 1876. In fact, the process of institutional modernization continued until the end of Ottoman rule in Syria in 1918. The purpose of the Tanzimat was to reestablish imperial control over the provinces, including Syria, and to strengthen the empire against European encroachments. To achieve these goals, Ottoman reformers experimented with new administrative regulations, reformed military practices, overhauled the judicial system, promulgated law codes, invested in **transportation** and communications, and established schools based on European models to train soldiers and officials. The Tanzimat signaled a fundamental change in the purposes of Ottoman rule, which had customarily been limited to providing security and extracting revenues. The authorities now intended to involve the state in **education, trade,** public works, **agriculture,** and relations among the empire's diverse population.

Such an extensive program of change was bound to meet opposition, particularly from provincial groups whose political and economic fortunes might be diminished by a stronger central authority. Another cause of opposition to the Tanzimat lay in its secular thrust, embodied in the 1856 Imperial Rescript guaranteeing equal status between Muslims and non-Muslims. **Christians'** growing prosperity, due in large part to their ties to European traders and consuls, contributed to Muslim resentment and anger in the 1840s and 1850s. In Syria, this anti-Christian sentiment exploded in two violent urban outbursts, the **Aleppo massacre of 1850** and the **July 1860 Damascus massacre.** In both instances the Ottomans firmly suppressed communal violence, displaced the local urban leadership, and elevated a fresh group of individuals to the ranks of provincial leadership. The new urban elite proved more amenable to implementing Tanzimat measures.

The Ottomans applied Tanzimat measures in piecemeal fashion throughout the empire, and they did not take root in Syria until after 1860, when the Ottomans buttressed their authority by increasing the number of imperial troops and undermining the influence of local paramilitary contingents commanded by **aghas.** Over the previous two decades they had experimented with new forms of provincial and urban administration, chiefly councils composed of dignitaries drawn from the religious, civil, and non-Muslim elites. During the 1860s, the scope of the Tanzimat's application in Syria broadened: telegraph lines went up between Syria and Istanbul; provincial gendarmeries supplanted the traditional irregular forces; new criminal, civil, and commercial **legal** codes were enacted; land registration and direct taxation were implemented; and the first state schools opened. The Ottomans improved internal security by stationing larger, better equipped military forces in new barracks and constructing garrisons on the fringes of the desert to control the **bedouin**. By the early 1870s, a new set of local dignitaries that demonstrated loyalty to the Tanzimat Ottoman order was established as the political and economic elite. This provincial nobility and their descendants provided Syria's political leadership and dominated the country's economy for the rest of the Ottoman era, throughout the **French Mandate** era, and in the early years of independence until it was displaced in the 1960s by the regimes of the **Ba`th Party**.

TARTUS. Originally a Phoenician settlement associated with a larger one on the island of Arwad. Located 30 kilometers north of the border with **Lebanon**, Tartus changed hands between Franks and Muslims during the **Crusades**, and it was the last **Christian** stronghold to fall to the **Mamluks** in 1291. In recent years, it has surpassed **Latakia** as the country's leading port. It handles the export of phosphate products and serves as the main transit point for **Iraqi** merchandise. It has also developed into a major site for Syria's cement **industry**.

Many of the 90,000 residents live inside its three ancient walls. Tartus is also the seat of a governorate with a population of 760,000. The region is one of Syria's main olive-growing regions. It also has much potential for **tourism**, therefore it has attracted investment in a beach resort. Furthermore, it makes an attractive base for day excursions to nearby Phoenician and Crusader-era sites. Crusaders called it Tortosa, and they built a formidable fortress and cathedral, "Our Lady of Tortosa," presently preserved as a museum.

TELEVISION. *See* **RADIO AND TELEVISION.**

TERRORISM. Syria has consistently denied supporting terrorist organizations and has claimed that it is itself the victim of antigovernment terrorism sponsored by hostile powers. The crucial episode from Syria's perspective was the uprising launched, primarily by **Islamic fundamentalist** groups, between 1976 and 1982.

The case against the Syrian government, however, is broadly based. The **United States** suspects Syria of complicity in the 1983 suicide bombing of marine barracks in Beirut. Great Britain found evidence of official Syrian involvement in the 1986 **Hindawi affair**. **Turkey** considered Damascus's support for the Kurdistan Workers Party (PKK) a form of involvement with terrorism, and in 1998 threatened to attack Syria if it did not cease harboring PKK leaders. In 2003, the United States included in its roster of terrorist organizations **Hizballah** and the **Palestinian** groups Islamic Jihad, Hamas, and radical **Palestine Liberation Organization** (PLO) factions based in Syria and **Lebanon**. Syria does not deny supporting them, but says it is incorrect to label them terrorist and regards them as forces resisting **Israeli** occupation of Arab lands. No evidence of Syrian support for al-Qa`ida has emerged, and in fact, Syria provided assistance to the American campaign against Usama bin Laden's organization.

THEATER. Syria shares with other Middle Eastern lands a historical tradition of puppet theater known as *karagoz* or shadow theater. Performances often took place in tents near a **coffeehouse**, especially during winter nights and Ramadan. A bright lantern cast puppets' shadows on a screen, and the puppeteer moved the puppets and modulated his voice for the different characters. This popular entertainment occasionally offended conservative sectors because it catered to vulgar tastes with frequent obscene allusions. Political authorities in the **Ottoman** and **French Mandate** eras sometimes kept an eye on performances because they could serve as venues for political criticism.

The modern theatrical tradition began with performances staged in **Damascus** by **Ahmad Abu Khalil al-Qabbani** in the 1860s and 1870s. Conservative circles suppressed the theater in 1881, and it did not reappear until the **Committee of Union and Progress** restored **constitutional** government, and with it a freer cultural climate, in the Ottoman Empire in 1908. In the next few years, progressive young Syrians staged patriotic and historical plays, but once again conservative circles stirred controversy with accusations that theatrical performances violated religious taboos. During the French Mandate era, tours by **Egyptian** companies stimulated the formation of short-lived theatrical clubs for Syrians interested in the **arts**, and they put on amateur performances in public parks, coffeehouses, and **cinemas**. A handful of more lasting theatrical troops in Damascus and **Aleppo** emerged in the 1950s, but it took government support under a Ministry of Culture formed during the

United Arab Republic to create a stable platform for professional theater to evolve. The ministry created a National Theater and paid regular salaries to actors and crews as government employees. Soon, other government-sponsored troupes were set up by the Ministries of Defense, Education, and Information. A growing number of actors, directors, and technical workers studied at European universities. Consequently, productions covered a broad range of the Western theatrical tradition as well as the works of Syrian and other Arab playwrights.

Themes in Syrian scripts tend to focus on regional political issues like the Arab-Israeli conflict, and on social and economic problems, but never directly tackle sensitive domestic political matters. In the late 1960s, **Durayd al-Lahham** and others created a troupe called the Theater of Thorns that satirized **corruption** and bureaucratic inefficiency yet tacitly observed understood, unwritten limits. The country's most renowned playwright was **Sa'dallah al-Wannus**, a pioneer in experimental performances that aimed to make audiences part of the performance. Commercial theatrical performances became more common in the 1980s and drew crowds by staging burlesque, often slapstick routines and by using the colloquial rather than the literary form of Arabic. The spread of **television** in the 1980s and 1990s is said to have hurt attendance at live theater, and a number of actors, directors, and writers shifted to working in television and cinema.

TIMUR LENG (1336-1405). Known in the West as Tamerlane, his name means Timur "the Lame," referring to a limp that resulted from a wound he suffered in his youth. This Central Asian conqueror rose in the service of the Chaghatay **Mongol** ruler of western Central Asia, then rebelled and seized power at Samarkand in 1369. From that point until his death 35 years later, Timur was almost constantly leading devastating military campaigns that struck terror into their victims. Apart from the usual excesses of massacre, rape, and plunder, Timur devised the grotesque practice of constructing towers of human skulls to mark his triumphs.

For 30 years he ravaged **Iran, Iraq**, southern Russia, eastern Asia Minor, and northern India. He briefly threatened Syria in 1387 while his soldiers marauded in Asia Minor. Timur sent an envoy to Cairo to the **Mamluk** Sultan Barquq, who had the envoy murdered and then sought a military alliance with the rising **Ottoman** dynasty of western Asia Minor. Timur pursued other lines of conquest but returned to Syria in 1399, by which time Barquq had died. When the Ottomans proposed an alliance to his successor, the sultan rejected the idea, so the Mamluks faced the onslaught of Timurid forces alone. In the fall of 1400, Timur led an invasion of Syria and drove the Mamluks out of **Aleppo** and **Damascus**. His troops pillaged both cities and Timur ordered the deportation of thousands of skilled craftsmen and laborers to his capital at Samarkand. He left Damascus in March 1401 and headed east to sack Baghdad and then inflicted a devastating defeat on the Ottomans. His departure from Syria, though, gave the Mamluks the opportunity to restore their authority over Syria. Timur's insatiable appetite for conquest then led him to contemplate an invasion of China, but he died as he was planning the campaign. The enormous empire he had conquered over nearly four decades stretched across much of Asia, but it lacked institutional underpinnings and fragmented within two years of his demise.

TLAS, MUSTAFA (1932-). Minister of defense since 1972. Tlas is a **Sunni** Muslim from Rastan, a town near **Homs**. He joined the **Ba`th Party** when he was a schoolboy and attended the Military Academy at Homs, where he became acquainted with another young Ba`thist, **Hafiz al-Asad**. After graduation, Tlas became an officer in a tank unit. He was brought onto the **Military Committee** after the **March 8, 1963 coup**, and in August 1965 Tlas was named to the party's Regional Command. He participated in the **February 23, 1966 coup** by the **neo-Ba`th** against the party's original leadership. When a power struggle developed within the neo-Ba`th between **Salah al-Jadid** and Hafiz al-Asad, Tlas sided with the latter. Asad bolstered his own base of power in the armed forces in February 1968 when he dismissed Ahmad al-Suwaydani as chief of staff and handed the post to Tlas and made him deputy minister of defense. Tlas ensured the loyalty of the **armed forces** to Asad, giving the latter the necessary backing for his seizure of power in the November 1970 **corrective movement**. In 1972, Asad made him minister of defense, and he has held that position ever since.

Few observers consider him a powerful figure in the regime comparable to the commanders of sensitive military units formally under his authority. He is perhaps best known for occasionally making caustic remarks about other Arab leaders and regimes. For example, he once declared that **Palestinian** leader Yasir Arafat betrayed the Palestinians and he accused **Jordan** of blocking **Saudi** military assistance from reaching Syria during the **October 1973 War**.

TOURISM. The advent of steamship navigation in the Mediterranean Sea increased commercial contacts between Europe and Syria and made possible the emergence of tourism. In the 1840s, Syria became a standard part of Americans' and Europeans' journeys to "the Holy Land." A fashion in writing travelogues stimulated not only curiosity about what had seemed a remote land, but also an appetite to see its antiquities. In 1858, the publisher of a popular series of guides issued one for Syria and **Palestine**, and 10 years later, the first organized tour arrived. Because of the lack of European-style tourist amenities at the time, travel in the 1870s and 1880s was more akin to contemporary "adventure" excursions. Throughout the 19th and early 20th centuries, most Western tourists considered Syria a side trip they might take after visiting **Egypt** and Palestine. Moreover, there was no sustained or organized effort in Syria to attract visitors until fairly recently.

Only in the late 1970s did authorities attempt to develop the tourist industry when government economic planners saw the advantages it could bring as a source of foreign **currency** to alleviate balance of payments difficulties, and as a factor in boosting employment. In order to foster the necessary infrastructure, the government has authorized mixed sector companies, ventures that combine private enterprise and **public sector** companies to develop hotels, restaurants, and sightseeing. Since 1986, when the government took some measures to liberalize the **economy**, the tourist sector has grown in response to adjustments to exchange rates, special treatment for imports of capital goods, and tax holidays for investors. The number of visitors increased from around 550,000 per year in the mid-1980s to nearly three million in the mid-1990s. Revenues from the tourist sector reflect the sector's growing contribution to the economy. In 1993, tourism accounted for $700 million and in 1998 that figure grew to nearly $1.2 billion. In the 1990s, about three-quarters of all tourists came from Arab countries, particularly the Gulf. In addition, large numbers of **Iranian** tourists visit religious sites like the shrine of al-Sayyida **Zaynab**. Finally, the rich historical treasures from ancient, classical, and Islamic civilizations make it an attractive destination for curious Western tourists. Their favorite destinations include classical **archaeological** sites like **Palmyra** and Ugarit, early Christians sites like **Ma`lula**, **Crusader**-era castles like **Hisn al-Akrad** (Crac des Chevaliers), and the superb Islamic **architecture** of historic cities like **Damascus**, **Aleppo**, and **Hama**. *See also* ECONOMIC REFORM.

TRADE. Since ancient times, Syria has been a crossroads for commercial traffic between southwest Asia, the Mediterranean, and northern Africa. Its major inland cities—**Damascus** and **Aleppo**—have served as entrepôts for long-distance overland trade. Throughout the centuries of Islamic civilization, goods passed through Syria to and from **Turkey**, Arabia, **Egypt**, **Iraq**, **Iran**, and India. The fortunes of long-distance traders suffered at times of war, plague, and insecurity in the desert, but Syria's central location between centers of production and population ensured that it would always bounce back from hard times and rejuvenate commercial ties with neighboring and more distant lands.

The first significant development in modern times was the increasing volume and value of maritime trade with Europe during the 19th century, particularly from the 1840s with the arrival of steamships in the eastern Mediterranean. By the early 20th century, a substantial share of imports and exports was exchanged with Europe according to a pattern that was common between industrializing economies and primarily agrarian ones. Syria imported European manufactures and exported raw materials and agricultural products. Traditional routes to neighboring lands diminished but did not fall into disuse until the collapse of the **Ottoman Empire** in 1918 and the imposition of national boundaries severed historic trade routes. Thus, Aleppan merchants found themselves cut off from markets in Turkey. The major markets for Syrian crops and textiles during the **French Mandate** period were its Arab neighbors—Iraq, **Palestine**, **Transjordan**—and **France**. Imports came primarily from Western European countries, Japan, and the **United States**. A blow to traditional networks fell on townsmen in **Homs** and **Hama** at independence in 1946 when customary routes to Lebanese ports faced a new international boundary. To compensate for the loss of traditional outlets, Syria has built up two major ports on the Mediterranean at **Tartus** and **Latakia**.

The first decade of independence saw little change in patterns of foreign trade. The bulk of Syria's imports came from **Lebanon**, France, the United Kingdom, West Germany, and the United States. The leading imports were textiles, machinery, minerals, and metals. The main markets for Syrian exports were Arab countries, especially Lebanon, then France and the United Kingdom. Cotton was by far the single largest export, averaging over one-third of the total value. Grain crops, vegetables, and animal products made up the bulk of the remaining exports. The trade picture changed during the mid-1950s when political leaders negotiated deals with the **Soviet Union** to obtain technical assistance and capital for major development projects. These initiatives marked a gradual but dramatic shift in the source and destination for raw materials and manufactures toward the Soviet bloc.

The reorientation of trade received a further boost under **Ba`th Party** regimes that steered the **economy** and **foreign policy** in a socialist direction during the 1960s. It was natural for the Soviet bloc to assume a much larger place in foreign trade, in particular dominating imports in deals that often involved barter terms. In the early 1970s, **Hafiz al-Asad**'s **corrective movement** revived the private sector and Syria received large amounts of financial aid from wealthy Arab Gulf states. One consequence was a brief resurgence of trade with Western Europe. In 1980, Syria and the USSR signed a Friendship Treaty providing for increased trade. Moreover, Syria's ability to trade with Western Europe suffered due to a foreign exchange shortage arising from a combination of falling **petroleum** revenues and declining aid from Gulf states due to low prices and high military expenditures. The close relationship with Moscow enabled Syria to take advantage of barter deals like a 1985 agreement with Yugoslavia that swapped Syrian phosphates for Yugoslav machinery, iron, and medical goods. Between 1980 and 1986, the Soviet bloc's share of Syrian exports rose from 16 percent to 46 percent.

The collapse of the USSR coincided with **economic reform** initiatives, including selective relaxation of foreign exchange transactions to encourage more trade with Western Europe. Consequently, in the 1990s, Syria's main trading partners have been Germany, Italy, and France. Exports to Turkey also became more valuable in that decade. Besides petroleum, Syria exports vegetables, fruit, and textiles. Its chief imports are machinery and manufactured goods. In trade with the United States, Syria exports petroleum products, antiques, and spices, and imports grain, tobacco, and appliances. Most observers agree that for Syria to optimize its potential, the government must dismantle layers of tariffs and red tape that have become instruments for merchants connected to the regime to dominate foreign trade.

TRADE UNIONS. *See* **LABOR MOVEMENT.**

TRANSJORDAN. After **World War I**, Great Britain assumed a League of Nations mandate over **Palestine**, which consisted of southern Syrian lands on both sides of the Jordan River. When the French evicted Amir **Faysal** from Syria, the British decided to install his brother Abdallah as amir of Transjordan, thus founding the one enduring political legacy to Britain's wartime alliance with the **Hashemite** clan.

Abdallah schemed to expand his realm by taking over Syria. To that end he developed good relations with a number of prominent Syrian personalities. Ultimately, Abdallah's territorial ambitions took him westward. In the **Palestine War of 1948** his forces conquered those parts of Palestine that the United Nations had set aside for an Arab state. Since Abdallah's domain was no longer "across the Jordan," he renamed it **Jordan**. *See also* GREATER SYRIA.

TRANSPORTATION. Modern means of transport came to Syria during the reign of Sultan **Abdulhamid II**, who granted concessions to European companies to construct railways. In 1891, a French company completed a line between Beirut, **Damascus**, and the **Hawran**. Two years later a railway linking Damascus and **Aleppo** was finished. In 1911, a foreign company completed work on a railway line between Tripoli and **Homs**. The most important line for Abdulhamid was one to connect Damascus and Mecca in order to ease the difficult journey of the pilgrim caravan from Syria. When it opened in 1908, the Hijaz railway reduced the journey from 40 days to just five.

During the **French Mandate**, there was little further development of rail transport, but paved roads for motor vehicles increased from 700 to 2,900 kilometers by 1939, and a regular motor service between Damascus and Baghdad was begun. The first two decades of independence saw the gradual extension of paved roads to more remote parts of the country. Between 1968 and 1990, paved roads increased from 8,100 to nearly 23,000 kilometers. Over the same period, railway track grew from 850 to more than 2,000 kilometers. The new lines connected **Qamishli** to **Dayr al-Zur**, Aleppo, and **Latakia** to allow easier transport of crops from **Jazira** to major cities and the coast. A second main line was built to link **Tartus** to the existing line from Homs to Aleppo. These rail lines to interior zones have greatly stimulated population growth and economic development around **al-Raqqa**, **Tabqa**, Dayr al-Zur, **al-Hasaka**, and Qamishli.

Before **World War I**, the chief Mediterranean ports for Syria were **Alexandretta**, Tripoli, Beirut, and Haifa, but the post-Ottoman boundaries placed those outlets outside Syria's borders. Syria has developed new ports since independence. Construction on Latakia's port began in 1952; a new port opened at Tartus in 1970, and in the 1980s it surpassed Latakia as Syria's main port. **Baniyas** is a third port that primarily services petroleum exports. In the 1990s, the port at Tartus was expanded so that the volume of merchandise passing through it surpassed Latakia. *See also* ABID, AHMAD IZZAT AL-.

TROUPES SPÉCIALES DU LEVANT. During the **French Mandate**, French authorities set up an **armed force** of Syrians, initially called the Legion Syrienne, then the Troupes Auxiliares, and finally in 1930 the Troupes Spéciales du Levant. The force's numbers grew from 6,500 in 1924 to 14,000 in 1936. To train officers for the Troupes Spéciales, the French established a Military Academy in **Damascus** in 1920, which was moved to **Homs** in 1932. Controversy has swirled over the mandatory authorities' recruitment practices, with Syrian nationalists charging **France** with enlisting disproportionate numbers of non-Arab and non-Muslim **minorities** such as **Armenians**, **Kurds**, and **Circassians**, while others argue that recruiting patterns fluctuated and did not reflect a cynical policy of exploiting and deepening Syria's communal divisions. The issue assumes historiographical and political significance because army officers of minority background have dominated the country's politics since 1963, and some observers explain their ascent by referring to the practices of the country's former colonial power.

TURK, RIYAD AL- (1930-   ). One of Syria's better-known prisoners of conscience during the regime of **Hafiz al-Asad**. Turk first gained prominence as an influential intellectual figure in the **Syrian Communist Party** during the late 1950s. During the **United Arab Republic** and the early **Ba`th Party** regimes, he and other communists spent time in prison and exile. Then Hafiz al-Asad created a coalition of permitted parties in 1972, including the Communist Party, but Turk opposed the decision to participate and left to form his own faction, known as the Communist Party-Political Bureau. The authorities arrested him in 1980 during the height of antigovernment agitation by a spectrum of secular and religious groups. **Human rights** organizations have noted that the severe and frequent torture he underwent during 17 years in prison left him with several chronic ailments. The authorities finally released him in 1998, apparently on condition that he stay out of public life.

Perhaps emboldened by the climate of toleration in **Bashar al-Asad**'s first year as president, Turk spoke out in summer 2001 at so-called **civil society** salons and on the Arabic satellite **television** channel *al-Jazira*. He condemned various aspects of Syria's domestic and **foreign policy**. Shortly afterward, **security forces** rearrested him as part of a broad campaign to suppress the growing movement for democracy. He was sentenced to two-and-a-half years on charges of undermining the **constitution**, but after he served just five months, President Asad pardoned him without a public explanation. The **European Union** had urged his release and Asad's government was in talks with the EU on trade matters, so observers speculate that there was a connection between the two developments.

TURKEY. Relations with the successor state of the **Ottoman Empire** have fluctuated between hostile and cordial. When Syria became independent, just seven years had elapsed since Turkey's annexation of **Alexandretta**. Turkey's recognition of **Israel** further rankled Syrians. Finally, in the 1950s, Turkey joined NATO and openly aligned itself with Western interests in the region. Syria, on the other hand, pursued a neutralist line before seeking economic and military support from the **Soviet Union**. In March 1955, Turkey massed its troops along the border to dissuade the Syrians from signing a defense pact with **Egypt** and **Saudi Arabia**. In the spring and summer of 1957, Turkey again sent troops to the border to signal its disapproval of Syria's economic and weapons deals with the Soviets. Relations did not begin to improve until the 1960s when Turkey sought regional support for its position on Cyprus. In both the **June 1967 War** and the **October 1973 War**, Turkey provided diplomatic and humanitarian support for the Arab side. Moreover, since 1970, **Hafiz al-Asad** actively cultivated better relations, for instance, initiating the frequent exchange of ministerial level missions.

Three outstanding bilateral issues complicate Syrian-Turkish relations. First, there is the 500-kilometer border drawn at the end of **World War I**. The border left many Turks, Syrians, and their respective properties on the wrong side of the new international frontier. This situation most acutely affected families with agricultural properties across the border. The governments have adopted pragmatic policies allowing the other country's nationals to continue cultivating their property. But Syrian **land reforms** and nationalizations disenfranchised Turks with property in Syria. The Turkish government retaliated with seizures of Syrians' property. The second major issue is the sharing of river **waters**, primarily the **Euphrates River**, but also the **Orontes River**. Since the late 1960s, Turkey has been developing a network of dams and hydraulic projects to vastly increase its hydroelectric output and irrigated lands. At the same time, Syria depends on certain levels of the Euphrates for irrigation and electrical generation at the **Tabqa Dam**. The third issue arises from Syrian support for the activities of **Armenian** terrorists and **Kurdish** guerrillas in the Kurdistan Workers Party (PKK).

In 1996, Turkey and Israel secretly concluded a military agreement that permitted Israel's air force to use Turkish air space for exercises. The agreement created a new security dilemma for Syria and rendered it more susceptible to Turkish saber rattling over its assistance to the PKK. In 1998, Ankara declared that Syria must cease harboring PKK leader Abdallah Ocalan. To show they were serious, Turkey's generals put troops stationed along the Syrian border on alert at the same time they sent forces into northern Iraq to pursue PKK rebels. Egyptian President Husni Mubarak and the **Iranian** foreign minister waged intensive diplomacy to defuse the crisis, leading to Syria's decision to expel Ocalan and shut down PKK offices in **Damascus** and bases in Lebanon's Bekaa valley. Since that time, the two main issues are Ankara's warm relations with Israel and water sharing.

TURKOMEN. Non-Arab, **Sunni** Muslim Turks who live in **Jazira** province, along the lower **Euphrates River**, near **Aleppo**, and in villages thinly scattered in central Syria. They are descendants of Turkomen nomadic tribes that entered Syria at various times between the 11th and 17th centuries, often encouraged by dynasties that sought to put the Turkomen's military prowess at their service. The Ottomans established them in central Syria around **Hama** and **Homs** during the 16th century in order to curb **bedouin** depradations and to serve as tax collectors in rural districts.

-U-

ULAMA. The general term for Muslim scholars of **Islamic** sciences, they have held a special status since early Islamic times. In the first Islamic centuries, one acquired religious knowledge by studying under established scholars known for their expertise in particular fields of knowledge. Beginning in the 11th century, religious learning became institutionalized in **madrasas**. In addition to their educational function, ulama staffed the religious law (**shari`a**) courts, served as jurisconsults (*muftis*) interpreting the law, and performed a variety of functions at mosques. The ulama also dominated the administration of endowed properties (sing. **waqf**), for which service they received income. Most ulama pursued private interests in **trade** and manufacture as well.

Ulama comprised a large part of the urban elite until the late 19th century when the **Ottoman**-era **Tanzimat** reforms promoted secular **educational** and **legal** institutions. From that time onward, their significance and status in society began to decline. While most ulama adhered to their traditional ways, a small number advanced an Islamic reform movement, called the **salafiyya**, in a bid to reestablish their centrality and to stave off the tide of secularism. In the 20th century, however, the ulama's prospects and numbers have continued to diminish. The ulama are still central in Islamic religious institutions and education, and some of them have played an important role in modern Islamic movements such as the **Muslim Brothers**.

UMAYYAD DYNASTY. Ruled the Arab Empire from 661 to 750. Its roots are in the clan of Umayya, one of the preeminent clans of Mecca during the life of Muhammad; most clan members bitterly opposed Muhammad, although a few were early converts. The third rightly guided caliph, Uthman (r. 644-656), belonged to this clan and appointed several of his kinsmen to powerful positions in the emergent Arab imperial administration. Uthman was murdered by Muslim opponents, who then proclaimed his rival **Ali ibn Abi Talib** the new caliph. But Uthman's Umayyad clansmen demanded revenge for his murder and refused to recognize Ali as caliph until they were satisfied. There ensued a Muslim civil war between forces loyal to Ali and the Umayyads, headed by the governor of Syria, **Mu`awiya**. The military confrontation fizzled into arbitration, and before a resolution of the matter, Ali was assassinated by a disgruntled former partisan, thus opening the way for Mu`awiya's unchallenged ascent to the **caliphate**.

Under the Umayyads, Arab military expeditions reached India and China in the east and Spain in the west, pushing the bounds of the Arab Empire to their greatest extent. They consolidated Arab rule over much of Central Asia, leading to the eventual conversion of that region's peoples to **Islam**. In the later 740s, Umayyad rule weakened because of rivalry between factions within the ruling family and increasing discontent among the empire's growing number of non-Arab converts to Islam, who continued to receive the treatment of conquered subjects. In 749, a revolutionary movement led by the **Abbasid** clan took advantage of the Umayyads' vulnerability and swept them out of power. The last Umayyad caliph was hunted down and killed in **Egypt** in 750, but a handful of survivors fled to North Africa, then to Spain, where they established a new line of Muslim rulers that lasted into the 11th century.

UMAYYAD MOSQUE. The major Islamic monument in **Damascus**. Originally an Arameaen temple to Baal-Hadad, then successively a Roman temple to Jupiter, and a **Christian** church dedicated to John the Baptist. For 70 years after the Arab conquest of Damascus, the new Muslim rulers left the church alone. Then the **Umayyad** caliph al-Walid

(r. 705-715) turned the church into a mosque and built a splendid new structure that blended the older Christian **architecture** with newer Islamic elements. He leveled the Church of St. John, preserving only the four towers at the corners. One of the mosque's most unusual features is the extensive **Byzantine**-style mosaic ornamentation on the façade of the courtyard. It contains perhaps the oldest extant specimen of Islamic carving in marble in a geometric pattern. The mosque has been burned three times, in 1069 during fighting between townsfolk and the **Fatimid** garrison, in 1400 when **Timur Leng** sacked the city, and by accident in 1893.

UNIATE. Any eastern church that has entered into union with the Roman **Catholic** Church. These include the **Greek Catholic, Syrian Catholic, Chaldaean Catholic**, and **Armenian Catholic** churches. They acknowledge papal authority in dogma yet retain their distinctive liturgies.

UNITED ARAB REPUBLIC (UAR). Political union of Syria and **Egypt** that formed on 1 February 1958 and lasted until 28 September 1961. It came about largely due to the initiative of members of the **Ba`th Party** in the Syrian government. Army officers also tended to favor union as a way to secure their dominance in Syrian politics. In the new republic, Egypt and Syria were referred to as the northern and southern regions, respectively, and Cairo became the capital. Egyptian President Gamal Abd al-Nasir completely dominated the UAR's politics by insisting on the dissolution of all Syrian political parties, including the Ba`th, as a condition for forming the union. He also sent Egyptian security services to stamp out any dissent.

The first UAR government counted three Syrians in the cabinet, including Ba`th Party leaders **Salah al-Din al-Bitar** and **Akram al-Hawrani**. In addition, the Ba`th was given three ministries in the provincial Syrian cabinet. Nonetheless, Nasir allotted little authority to the ministries, and the Ba`thists became disenchanted with union. In December 1959, Ba`th Party leaders resigned from the UAR government that they had brought about. A few months later, three more Syrians resigned their central government posts as well. Nasir then purged the Syrian officer corps of any individuals whose loyalty could be questioned and reduced by half the number of Syrian officers; at the same time, he sent more than 2,000 Egyptian officers to Syria. In addition to Egypt's political domination of the UAR, it dominated the union's **economy** through preferential treatment for Egyptian **industries** and **banks** and restrictions on Syria's foreign **trade**.

By the beginning of 1961, most Syrians' enthusiasm for the union had dissipated and their disenchantment deepened with the announcement in July 1961 of **Socialist Decrees** nationalizing broad sectors of the economy. Perhaps the final straw for Syrians came in August 1961 when Nasir proposed to decentralize administration. This would have divided Syria into several provinces, each governed by an individual appointed by Nasir. **Damascus** would no longer serve as an effective capital even of the UAR's northern region. On 28 September 1961, disaffected Syrian officers and politicians seized power and dissolved the union.

After the **March 8, 1963 coup** brought to power a pro-union regime, Egyptian and Syrian leaders held talks for reviving an enlarged UAR that would add **Iraq**, where a Ba'thist regime had come to power in February, to the union. The talks lasted for one month, but mutual mistrust clouded the chances for agreement on a formula that would achieve unity, yet respect the distinct conditions in each country.

UNITED NATIONS. Syria is a founding member of the United Nations. It signed the United Nations declaration in April 1945 and sent a delegation to the San Francisco Conference in October 1945. A handful of UN bodies have played prominent roles in Syria. The most important is the United Nations Relief and Works Agency (UNRWA), which provides basic **education** and **health** care to over 400,000 **Palestinian** refugees. Since 1974, the **United Nations Disengagement Observer Force** has patrolled a buffer zone on the **Golan Heights** to preserve calm between Syria and **Israel**. A third body, the United Nations Educational, Scientific, and Cultural Organization (UNESCO) has assisted in the preservation of historical and **archaeological** sites.

Syria and other Arab countries frequently use the United Nations to exert pressure on Israel to return land it conquered in the **June 1967 War**, to refrain from annexing Palestinian land in the West Bank and Gaza, and to treat Palestinians under Israeli occupation less harshly. In October 2002, Syria was elected to a rotating seat on the UN Security Council for a two-year term as one of 10 nonpermanent members. That diplomatic opportunity came at a moment of regional crisis because the **United States** was seeking Security Council authorization for the use of force against **Iraq** for failure to comply with previous UN resolutions dating to its 1990 invasion of Kuwait. In November, Syria voted for Resolution 1441, which required Iraq to allow weapons inspectors back into the country and to voluntarily dismantle weapons of mass destruction. When the United States lobbied for a second resolution in early 2003, Syria did not have to resist authorizing the use of force because **France** and Russia threatened to veto such a motion.

UNITED NATIONS DISENGAGEMENT OBSERVER FORCE. After the **October 1973 War,** American Secretary of State Henry Kissinger mediated an agreement between Syria and **Israel** to disengage their forces on the **Golan Heights.** They concluded a disengagement accord on 31 May 1974, and on the basis of UN Resolution 350, the **United Nations** created the UN Disengagement Observer Force (UNDOF) to oversee implementation. The accord created three distinct zones. The buffer zone, termed the "area of separation," is about 80 kilometers long and two to nine kilometers wide. UNDOF patrols it and neither country may place armed forces there. On either side of the buffer there are two more zones where the Israelis and Syrians observe limits on arms and forces. The UN forces number about 1,000 men. Their base is on the Syrian side of the zone and their administrative offices operate in **Damascus.** UNDOF has worked with the Syrians and the Israelis to maintain quiet on the Golan Heights for 30 years.

UNITED NATIONS RESOLUTION 242. At the conclusion of the **June 1967 War,** the United Nations Security Council passed this resolution calling for the withdrawal of **Israel**'s forces from territories it occupied during the war: the **Golan Heights,** the Sinai Peninsula, Gaza, and the West Bank. The resolution also called for an end to the state of war and for the establishment of peace in the region. Syria's **neo-Ba`th** regime rejected the resolution, but after the **October 1973 War** the regime of **Hafiz al-Asad** accepted it. Ever since then, Syria has regarded UN Resolution 242 as the basis for peace with Israel because the Syrians believe that its implementation will bring about the recovery of the Golan Heights.

UNITED NATIONS RESOLUTION 338. At the end of the **October 1973 War,** the United Nations Security Council passed this resolution calling for implementation of Resolution 242, including the withdrawal of **Israel**'s forces from the occupied territories. Syria accepted the resolution in the hope that a diplomatic approach would bring about an Israeli withdrawal from the **Golan Heights.**

UNITED STATES. During the Cold War, the chief concern of American policy makers was to bring Syria into the region's pro-Western camp. Syria's primary **foreign policy** concerns, however, were regional ones, particularly the conflict with **Israel** and ties with other Arab nations. The United States supported the military coup of **Husni al-Za`im** in March 1949 in the hope that he would reach an agreement with Israel. The US also had good relations with **Adib al-Shishakli** and tried to persuade him to enter into an anticommunist military alliance in 1951, but he had to contend with the popular neutralist campaign of the **Ba`th Party**, the **Arab Socialist Party**, and the Islamic Socialist Front. Following Shishakli's overthrow in 1954, Syria continued to elude American and British attempts to bring it into pro-Western alliances, such as the **Baghdad Pact**. As the leftist trend in Syrian politics gained strength, the Eisenhower administration became alarmed and decided to try to overthrow the government. On 12 August 1957, the Syrian government expelled three American diplomats for plotting a coup d'état. The Americans had contacted several army officers, but the plot was quickly detected and aborted. Washington then orchestrated a public campaign criticizing Syria for falling into the orbit of the **Soviet Union**. It dispatched a State Department official to confer with leaders of **Turkey**, **Iraq**, **Lebanon**, and **Jordan** about the "Syria problem." By October the crisis in American-Syrian relations was smoothed over by the diplomatic efforts of **Saudi Arabia**, but the threat it posed accelerated Syria's rush into union with **Egypt**'s Gamal Abd al-Nasir and the formation of the **United Arab Republic.**

There followed a long period of poor relations that reached their nadir when Syria severed diplomatic relations after the **June 1967 War.** Six years later, after the **October 1973 War**, the Syrians accepted American mediation for a disengagement of forces on the **Golan Heights**. The two countries restored diplomatic relations in June 1974, and the US provided limited assistance for economic development projects. The following year, however, the US mediated an Egyptian-Israeli agreement that revived President **Hafiz al-Asad**'s distrust for the US.

Relations continued to deteriorate in the early 1980s, particularly over Israel's invasion of Lebanon in 1982 and the American attempt to secure diplomatic gains for Israel in the form of a security agreement with Lebanon. The US decided to give full support to Lebanese President Amin Gemayel's bid to establish his government's authority over the country. Syria responded by rallying Lebanese opposition to Gemayel and his American backers. Washington accused the Syrians of plotting the suicide truck bomb that demolished the marine barracks and killed over 200 Americans in Beirut in October 1983. American naval and air forces bombarded Lebanese militias allied with Syria, and in December 1983, Syrian forces shot down two American warplanes. Two months later, the US withdrew its forces from Lebanon. In the next few years, relations remained strained as the US pursued the Reagan Plan for a peace settlement between Jordan and Israel.

The administration of George H. W. Bush (1989-1993) moved to improve relations with Syria by cooperating in Lebanon, and Syria was seeking to repair relations with the US at a time when Soviet power was clearly on the wane. Then, Iraq's invasion of Kuwait created an opening for a greater degree of cooperation with the US. Asad seized the opportunity by agreeing to send Syrian forces to participate in Operation Desert Shield to protect Saudi Arabia from a possible Iraqi attack. In return, the US apparently acquiesced to a Syrian attack on its nemesis in Lebanon, General Michel Aoun, to pave the way for an end to the **Lebanese Civil War** on Damascus's terms, including implementation of the **Ta'if Accord**. Throughout the crisis leading up to the 1991 war between Iraq and the American-led coalition, Syria provided valuable political support for the US and its Arab allies. After the conclusion of "Desert Storm," the US pushed harder for a comprehensive settlement to the Arab-Israeli conflict that addressed Syria's desire to recover the Golan Heights. The Syrians agreed to attend the **Madrid Conference** in October-November 1991 largely because of a desire to maintain better relations with the US.

Between 1993 and 2000, President Bill Clinton and his secretaries of state Warren Christopher and Madeleine Albright expended much effort to bring the **Syrian-Israeli peace talks** to a successful conclusion. In that pursuit, Washington and Damascus frequently consulted, and Clinton became the first president to visit Damascus in 20 years when he stopped there in October 1994 after attending the signing of the Israeli-Jordanian peace treaty. Five years later, Clinton gave strong backing to Israeli Prime Minister Ehud Barak's bid for a final deal with the ailing President Asad in December 1999-January 2000. Talks at **Shepherdstown**, West Virginia, saw the most intensive American engagement in Syrian-Israeli diplomacy so far, but they failed. Clinton tried one last time to bridge the gaps by meeting with Asad at Geneva on 26 March 2000, but the meeting proved fruitless and a high point in American-Syrian relations had passed.

While Washington and Damascus worked toward a regional peace agreement, bilateral tensions simmered. The US considered Syrian support for militant resistance to Israel in Lebanon and the Palestinian territories to be state-sponsored **terrorism**. Washington also criticized Damascus for pursuing **nonconventional weapons** and violating its citizens' **human rights**. Moreover, American congresspeople found it convenient to sanction Syria to attract support from pro-Israel political groups. The collapse of peace talks with Israel, the death of Hafiz al-Asad, and the arrival in 2001 of a more aggressive American administration under President George W. Bush all contributed to a worsening of relations. Initially, the second Bush administration tried to persuade **Bashar al-Asad** to respect **United Nations** sanctions on **trade** with Iraq that Syria was clearly violating. That issue receded after the 11 September 2001 attacks on the US, and Damascus offered assistance in the campaign against Usama bin Laden's al-Qa'ida organization. But after the US overthrew the Taliban in Afghanistan, it turned its attention to Saddam Husayn's regime in Iraq. While Syria had a track record of bad relations with Saddam, it did not wish to see a pro-American regime installed in Baghdad. During the spring 2003 American war in Iraq, Syria sent some military equipment and permitted volunteers to enter Iraq to fight against the Americans. The US expressed its unwillingness to tolerate support for Saddam, and the Syrians backed off. At the end of the year, Washington stepped up pressure on Damascus by enacting the Syrian Accountability and Lebanese Sovereignty Restoration Act, which authorized President Bush to impose new sanctions if the Syrians did not satisfy American demands on a range of issues, including proliferation of nonconventional weapons, support for terrorism, and withdrawal from Lebanon. Given the low level of US-Syrian trade, observers consider the threat of sanctions more symbolic than substantial, but the proximity of American troops across the Iraqi border certainly causes the Syrians some concern.

With American troops in Iraq and unfriendly neighbors in Turkey and Israel, Syria is in a more vulnerable position than any time in recent decades. The Soviet Union is not around to balance American domination. The Arab countries are divided between clearly pro-American regimes like Egypt and Jordan and those like Syria trying to maintain correct relations without accepting American dictates regarding domestic and foreign policies. On the other hand, the US has its hands full in Iraq and tracking down al-Qa'ida, so it may prefer to continue the tactics of persuasion and light pressure while Syria tries to persuade Washington to assume a balanced approach to Arab-Israeli diplomacy.

-W-

WAHHABI MOVEMENT. A religious reform movement that arose in central Arabia during the second half of the 18th century inspired by the teachings of Muhammad ibn Abd al-Wahhab. Around 1745, Muhammad ibn Sa`ud, the ruler of a small oasis town, lent the movement his support and he in turn received its blessing for a campaign to expand his realm. Since that time, the Saudis' political fortunes and the Wahhabi teachings have been inextricably connected. Ibn Abd al-Wahhab advanced a rigorous interpretation of Islamic belief and practice, and his followers regarded **Ottoman** rule as illegitimate because it countenanced religious practices that they, the Wahhabis, deemed idolatrous.

The Wahhabis impinged on Syrian history in the 1790s by raiding villages south of **Damascus**. Then in 1803 they seized Mecca and forced the return of the pilgrim caravan from Damascus. This amounted to a direct challenge to Ottoman authority because the governors of Damascus were responsible for the safe conduct of the pilgrimage. Between 1803 and 1813, the Wahhabis restricted access to Mecca and occasionally blocked Syrian **trade**. In 1807, the governor of Damascus, Abd Allah Pasha **al-Azm**, attempted to conduct the annual pilgrimage by force, but the Wahhabis turned him back before he reached Medina. The pilgrimage of the following year was also turned back, and to add insult to injury, **bedouin** plundered the retreating caravan. Three years later the Wahhabis raided villages in the **Hawran**. Then, in 1811, the Ottomans persuaded the powerful governor of **Egypt**, **Muhammad Ali**, to invade Arabia and evict the Wahhabis from the holy cities.

In addition to applying military pressure on Syria, the Wahhabis tried to attract Muslims to their reformist teachings by corresponding with the Ottoman governor and the **ulama** of Damascus, urging them to suppress prostitution, card playing, tobacco, storytelling in **coffeehouses**, and **music**. The ulama admitted the presence of sinners, but asserted that their religious practice was perfectly proper and that it was the Wahhabis who needed instruction in religion and that they must cease all violence against fellow Muslims. Nonetheless, Wahhabi propaganda did have effects in Damascus, as when the Ottoman governor decreed that **Christians** had to wear black garments and **Jews** had to don red clothes. In the end, Wahhabi propaganda made no real inroads in Syria. The movement did revive in Arabia, though, and at the beginning of the 20th century, Wahhabi fervor played a central part in the foundation of the modern nation of **Saudi Arabia**. The teachings of Muhammad ibn Abd al-

Wahhab are the foundation for that country's interpretation and application of Islamic law (**shari`a**).

WANNUS, SA`DALLAH AL- (**1941-1997**). He was the country's foremost contemporary playwright and a prominent theorist of Arab drama. Wannus first made his mark with a play entitled *Evening Party for the 5th of June*, a furious condemnation of the Arab political and social order that he and other Arabs held responsible for their stunning defeat in the **June 1967 War**. The play was first performed in **Damascus** in 1971, shortly after **Hafiz al-Asad** seized power from the **neo-Ba`th** regime that had led Syria to defeat in 1967. In this and later plays, Wannus strove to instill a critically engaged political consciousness in his audiences by placing actors among the audience and by using Syrian dialect, improvisational dialogue, and other techniques borrowed from Western avant-garde theater. Until his untimely death, Wannus was a leading figure in Syrian **theater**, which is one of the liveliest in the Arab world.

WAQF. This is an institution that under Islamic law (**shari`a**) provides for dedicating revenue from endowed property to a charitable purpose. For centuries, Muslim donors created these permanent endowments to support the construction and maintenance of mosques, fountains for prayer ablutions, **madrasas**, and hospitals (**bimaristans**). The endowed properties included bathhouses, workshops, warehouses, shops, **coffeehouses**, gardens, orchards, and crops. The waqf appeared in early Islamic times and it is richly documented for the **Ottoman** era, when hundreds of urban and rural properties became dedicated to the public good. Administration of waqf properties, supervision of the disbursement of revenues, and legal oversight of both were typically handled by experts in religious law, the **ulama**.

WATER. Syria's population depends on water for household consumption, **agricultural** production, electricity generation, and **industrial** use. Most of the countryside is either arid or semiarid, but the northwestern region and the western interior regularly receive enough precipitation to nurture large expanses of rain-fed cultivation. The second major source of water is the country's rivers: the **Euphrates**, **Orontes**, **Khabur**, **Yarmuk**, and **Afrin**. The Euphrates River alone accounts for nearly 90 percent of the country's supply of river water. Syria has constructed over 140 dams to manage water for irrigation and electric generation. The **Tabqa Dam** on the Euphrates River is the largest one followed by the Rastan and

Muharda Dams on the Orontes. Agriculture uses nearly 95 percent of Syria's water supply, followed by household and industrial use. The most important state agency in managing water resources is the Ministry of Irrigation, followed by the Ministry of Agriculture and the Ministry of Housing and Public Services. Syria's rapid rate of population growth is exerting pressure on the balance between water supply and demand. Shortages in **Aleppo** and **Damascus** are endemic, particularly during summer months, so that the authorities have resorted to rationing that cuts water to households for up to 15 hours per day.

Water is a sensitive factor in Syria's **foreign policy**, particularly with **Turkey** and **Israel**. In view of increasing demand from a young population and a thirsty agricultural sector, Syria needs to reach a definitive water sharing agreement on the Euphrates River with Turkey and **Iraq** and to develop efficient conservation methods. With respect to Israel, water is an issue in the **Syrian-Israeli peace talks** because Syria wishes to recover the **Golan Heights** and to draw the international boundary in a way that would give it a small foothold on the shore of Lake Tiberias. In the event of a peace treaty, Israel wants assurances that Syria would not interrupt the flow of the **Baniyas River**, a tributary of the upper Jordan River. As for Lake Tiberias, it is Israel's main source of freshwater and consequently the Israelis have rejected Syria's proposed boundary. *See also* ENERGY.

WEAPONS OF MASS DESTRUCTION. *See* **NONCONVENTIONAL WEAPONS.**

WOMEN. In recent years, scholars have produced studies on the historical and contemporary circumstances of women, paying close attention to their social status, economic roles, and legal and political rights. These studies have revealed both profound changes in Syrian society in modern times and significant variation according to setting (rural or urban) and social class. It appears that the provisions of Islamic law (**shari`a**) have enabled urban women of the middle and upper classes to exercise control over personal wealth and property even though the same law gives male heirs a larger portion of inheritance than females. Historical research indicates that urban women inherited and managed residential and commercial property and engaged in moneylending. They also had control over agricultural properties surrounding some of the major towns.

Like other Arab countries in the early 20th century, Syria had magazines published by women addressing a female readership and calling for women's rights in all spheres. Various women's organizations have striven for equal access to **education** and improved public **health**. Over the long term, these publishing and organizing efforts have borne fruit. Educated urban women have participated in Syrian political endeavors ranging from resistance against the imposition of French rule to demonstrations on labor issues. Suffrage was first debated in the **Syrian Congress** under Amir **Faysal** in 1920, and it was granted in September 1949. Nowadays Syria is one of those countries where a very small number of women have reached high positions, such as the former Minister of Culture Najah al-Attar, and hold a small number of elected seats in the national assembly, but in fact women have no influence on policy.

Ba`th Party regimes have created more opportunities for women in education and the paid **labor force**. In 1967, the party created the General Union of Syrian Women to promote education and child care programs. Government efforts to raise literacy rates for girls have yielded significant results. The female literacy rate has risen to 60 percent largely because of compulsory elementary education for all children. Another indication of efforts to equalize girls' access to education is that girls comprise almost half of pupils in primary and secondary schools. The percentage of women university graduates is more than one-third. Women's participation in the labor force is difficult to gauge with exactitude because of the informal division of labor in **agriculture** where much work is unpaid and thus not counted. Since the 1960s, the ratio of women in the urban work force has grown to about one-fifth and now includes professions as well as unskilled labor.

Syria is like most other Arab countries in preserving a traditional **legal** framework for matters like marriage, divorce, custody, and inheritance. The minimum marriage age is 17 years old. A Muslim man may have as many as four wives at a time but a woman may specify the marriage contract to require the man to obtain her permission to take an additional wife. Men also have an easier time obtaining a divorce than do women, who must have specific grounds like abandonment or insanity. The mother has presumptive custody for boys until age nine and for girls until age 11. Outside the legal sphere, conservative customs in rural areas, and to a lesser extent in the cities, maintain the notion that any behavior that compromises a woman's moral purity reflects on her family. As in other Arab countries, there are still honor killings, in which a male relative puts to death a female relative for even the suspicion of sexual misconduct. On the other hand, in some circles, norms are changing, as indicated by the recognition that domestic violence against women is a social problem, not a matter of custom.

WORLD WAR I. On 14 November 1914, the **Ottoman Empire** entered the war on the side of Germany against Great Britain, **France**, and Russia. Syria suffered tremendous hardship during the war because the Ottomans stripped the provinces of food and labor to support the military effort. Furthermore, the Ottomans subjected Syria to a strict political regime under **Jamal Pasha**, who ordered the executions of several **Arab nationalists**. Nonetheless, public sentiment generally favored the Ottomans and no general uprising for independence took place in Syria.

During the war, Ottoman atrocities and deportation orders drove thousands of **Armenians** from central and eastern Anatolia into northern Syria. From these tragic events stem modern Syria's substantial Armenian population. Toward the end of the war, a British offensive launched from **Egypt** in December 1917 occupied southern **Palestine** and Jerusalem. Then in September 1918, **Hashemite** forces advanced through **Transjordan** while an allied column marched toward **Damascus**. On 30 September, the Ottoman army withdrew from Damascus and the same evening saw the arrival of Arab troops. The following day an Arab government under Amir **Faysal** was proclaimed, bringing to an end more than four centuries of Ottoman rule. A few weeks later, **Aleppo** fell to Anglo-Arab forces on 26 October.

WORLD WAR II. At the outbreak of the war, Syria had been under the rule of the **French Mandate** for nearly two decades during which the movement for independence had gained widespread support. Nonetheless, the various nationalist parties and organizations all declared their support for **France** in its wartime efforts. When France fell to German forces in June 1940, the Vichy regime appointed General Henri Dentz high commissioner for Syria. But in June-July 1941, Great Britain and Free French forces under Charles de Gaulle launched an invasion of Syria and **Lebanon** from **Palestine** that removed the Vichy regime and placed Syria under a Free French administration. At the start of the invasion, the commanding French officer issued a proclamation pledging France's commitment to granting Syria its independence. The preponderance of British forces in Syria meant that Britain could push the French to make good on their promise, but De Gaulle intended to postpone a final withdrawal, and he suspected that Britain's interest in Syrian independence masked a desire to exploit France's weakness in order to achieve hegemony in the Levant. Nonetheless, Syrian independence was no longer in question; rather, it was a matter of timing.

Pressures from Britain and Syrian nationalists induced the French to announce national elections for July 1943. **Shukri al-Quwwatli** headed the **National Party** list, which triumphed at the polls, and Quwwatli became the president. There followed a prolonged stalemate between the Syrian and French governments over the terms by which France would leave the country. The French insisted on a treaty before evacuating, while the Syrians argued that a treaty should be negotiated afterward. The main sticking point was control over the **Troupes Spéciales**. In May 1945, anti-French demonstrations erupted throughout Syria. France responded by launching air attacks and shelling on **Damascus** on 29 and 30 May, killing 400 Syrians. Britain intervened by having its troops take control, and international opinion condemned France. In July, the French agreed to cede control over the Troupes Spéciales to the Syrian authorities. On 17 April 1946, nearly a year after the end of the war in Europe, French troops withdrew from independent Syria.

-Y-

YARMUK, BATTLE OF. In 636, the **Byzantine** Emperor Heraclius responded to the first wave of Arab invasions into southern and central Syria by sending a huge army to regain the lost territories. The Arabs evacuated **Homs** and **Damascus**, which they had only recently occupied, and withdrew southward. Byzantine and Muslim forces gathered near the **Yarmuk River** in the summer of 636. That August they fought the largest battle in the Arab conquest of Syria. The Arabs routed the Byzantines, thus paving the way for the consolidation of Arab control over Syria without any further serious military resistance.

YARMUK RIVER. The main tributary for the Jordan River and the watershed for a portion of Syria's border with **Jordan**. The Yarmuk River rises in Syria and has a 40-kilometer course before forming the international boundary. Jordan and Syria formally agreed on sharing the river's **waters** in 1955, so this has not aggravated bilateral relations. In the 1980s and 1990s, Syria constructed a series of dams along *wadis* (dry flood channels) that flow into the Yarmuk to divert water for irrigation. In 1987, Syrian and Jordanian water experts conceived the Unity Dam (255 cubic meter capacity) project to build a dam that would alleviate Jordan's endemic water shortage.

YAZIDI. About 12,000 of these non-Muslim **Kurds** live in Jabal Sim`an west of **Aleppo**, in Jabal Akrad north of Aleppo, and in **Jazira**. The Yazidis, who account for less than five percent of all Kurds, came from **Iraq** in the 15th and 16th centuries. There used to be a larger Yazidi community in Syria, but their numbers dwindled under the impact of **Ottoman** persecution. Their religion is a vestige of the ancient Kurdish religion, Yazdani, or the cult of the angels. They believe in a Universal Spirit that created all spiritual existence, including seven angels. One of those angels, the Peacock Angel, is venerated for having created the material world. The Yazidis also believe in avatars of the Universal Spirit, and they celebrate Shaykh Adi as such an avatar.

-Z-

ZA`IM, HUSNI AL-** (1894-1949). Born in **Aleppo**, he served in the **Ottoman** army during **World War I**. In the **French Mandate** era, Za`im was an officer in the **Troupes Spéciales. As chief of staff, Colonel Za`im led Syria's first military coup on 30 March 1949. The coup sprang from widespread discontent in the army with the government, particularly regarding criticism of the army's performance in the **Palestine War of 1948**. Za`im arrested President **Shukri al-Quwwatli** and Prime Minister **Khalid al-Azm** in a bloodless coup. In the next few days, Za`im tried to convince a number of prominent politicians to form a provisional cabinet, but they turned him down. So on 3 April, he disbanded parliament and promised elections under a new **constitution**. He also pledged to enfranchise **women** and distribute state lands to peasants. While Za`im promised to restore democracy, he banned political parties, barred civil servants from political activities, and suppressed dozens of newspapers. One of the more ominous steps Za`im took was to end the interior ministry's control over the gendarmerie and place it under the defense ministry, thereby giving the military a formal role in domestic affairs. Unable to obtain cooperation from political leaders, Za`im formed a cabinet in which he held the offices of prime minister, minister of interior, and minister of defense.

In **foreign policy** Za`im first pursued closer economic and military relations with **Iraq**, but **Saudi Arabia** and **Egypt** persuaded him to reject unity with the **Hashemites**. A more pressing problem brewed along the 1949 cease-fire lines. Za`im sent a team of army officers to conduct **armistice** negotiations (12 April to 20 July) with **Israel**. At one point, he offered to absorb 300,000 **Palestinian** refugees and to reach a peace treaty with Israel in return for border adjustments in Syria's favor. Israel rejected his offer because of its desire to control **water** resources along the frontier with Syria.

By August, the roster of Za`im's opponents included partisans of the **Syrian Social National Party** upset at Za`im's betrayal of their leader **Antun al-Sa`ada, Druze** officers who distrusted the colonel's deployment of troops in **Jabal Druze**, and the Iraqi government. More generally, his growing arrogance and pomposity deeply offended public opinion. On 14 August 1949, Colonel **Sami al-Hinnawi** led a military coup to depose Za`im. A Druze lieutenant and partisan of the SSNP arrested Za`im at his residence and carried out the order to execute him and his civilian associate Muhsin al-Barazi.

ZANGI, IMAD AL-DIN AL- (1087-1146). Atabeg for the **Saljuk** prince of Mosul, Zangi ruled **Aleppo** from 1128 until 1146. After taking over Aleppo, he resolved to extend his rule to the rest of Muslim Syria, leaving the coast under **Crusader** rule. This ambition involved him in several campaigns that eventually brought **Hama** and **Homs** under his rule, but the atabegs of **Damascus** defied him. In Muslim annals, Zangi is best known for his 1144 conquest of the County of Edessa, the first Frankish state to fall to Muslim reconquest.

ZANGID. A line of 12th-century Muslim rulers in Syria and northern **Iraq** descended from the **atabeg Imad al-Din al-Zangi.** The most prominent figure in this illustrious line was **Nur al-Din Mahmud**, the ruler who reunified most of Syria after three centuries of fragmentation. The other Zangid rulers of Iraq and Syria helped pave the way for an era of urban efflorescence marked by construction of public buildings and patronage of **Sunni** institutions.

ZAYNAB BINT ALI. Known as "Sitt Zaynab," she was the daughter of **Ali ibn Abi Talib** and Fatima, the Muslim prophet Muhammad's daughter. Thus, she was his granddaughter and a member of **Shi`ism**'s Holy Family. Her more famous brothers Hasan and Husayn are Shi`ism's second and third **imams**. According to Shi`i lore, she was present at the battle of Karbala in 680, when **Umayyad** forces martyred her brother Husayn. She is reported to have rescued his only son, Ali Zayn al-`Abidin, from execution at the hands of an Umayyad governor. Her captors transported her to **Damascus**, where she is supposed to have been the first person to conduct the ritual of lamenting Husayn. In the Shi`i tradition, Zaynab expresses unvanquished defiance of illegitimate Umayyad tyranny. Her splendid mausoleum outside Damascus is a pilgrimage destination for Shi`i Muslims from **Iran, Lebanon**, Pakistan, and Afghanistan. In recent years, it has drawn 100,000 Iranian pilgrims annually. In accordance with the Shi`i belief in the powers of Ali's family to possess powers of intercession, pilgrims customarily recite a salutation to Zaynab to obtain her blessing, especially for **women** seeking to have children or to heal ailments.

ZAYZUN DAM. In 1996, Syria added a new dam to its network of hydraulic projects designed to draw on the **Orontes River** to irrigate thirsty fields. Just six years later, in June 2002, the Zayzun Dam burst. In the ensuing flood, Zayzun village was destroyed but its 1,000 inhabitants were spared because cracks in the dam had been noticed and the local **imam** broadcast an evacuation order from the mosque just an hour before the dam broke. Villagers living farther along the path of the flood had no warning, and more than 20 people perished. The disaster inundated 10,000 acres, including cultivated fields, so it ruined crops for thousands of farmers. Four villages downstream in the Idlib governorate suffered extensive damage to buildings and fields. The dam was only six years old, but the **public sector** companies that operated it had failed to carry out regular inspection and maintenance. Furthermore, villagers reported that the dam's managers had allowed it to fill beyond capacity in order to extract a higher price for water. The authorities took the drastic step of arresting a former minister of irrigation and manager of the company that had constructed the dam. In the eyes of many Syrians, the disaster was a symptom of the sort of bureaucratic ineptitude and public sector **corruption** that the country's leaders were failing to address.

ZU`AYYIN, YUSUF AL- (1931- ).** Medical doctor and member of the **neo-Ba`th regime of 1966 to 1970. **Salah al-Jadid** had appointed Zu`ayyin, a **Sunni** from the **Euphrates River** town of Abu Kamal, prime minister in the first Ba`thist regime in August 1965. He retained the post in the neo-Ba`th regime from 1966 until **Hafiz al-Asad** forced his resignation in October 1968. After Asad came to power in November 1970, he had Zu`ayyin imprisoned until 1981 when he was allowed to leave the country and settle in Hungary.

ZU`BI, MAHMUD AL- (1938-2000).** Prime minister of Syria from October 1987 to March 2000. Zu`bi had been speaker of the People's Assembly and was a veteran member of the **Ba`th Party. He assumed office at a time of deep economic problems marked by **inflation**, electricity cuts, shortages in essential commodities, and a foreign exchange crisis. His government proceeded with cautious implementation of a policy called "relaxation," a term intended to distinguish Syria's economic liberalization from the more thorough campaign undertaken in **Egypt** and other Arab countries since the 1970s. The economic crisis gradually subsided and Zu`bi remained in office longer than any prime minister under **Hafiz al-Asad**.

Zu`bi's term came to a sudden and ignominious end in March 2000. Shortly after his dismissal, he became the target of an investigation on embezzlement charges. He was the highest-ranking government or Ba`th Party official to face **corruption** charges in a campaign headed by Asad's son **Bashar al-Asad**. Two months later, Zu`bi was expelled from the Ba`th Party National Command. On 21 May, he reportedly committed suicide, but observers speculate that the government had killed him to prevent him from exposing widespread corruption in the highest levels of the regime.

BIBLIOGRAPHY

INTRODUCTION

Before World War II, 20th-century scholarship on Syria was predominantly the work of French orientalists, so works by the most prominent early French authors have been included. In the postwar era, a new generation of French scholars has continued the distinguished tradition of their predecessors, while American and British scholars have produced a vast corpus on Syria. Consequently, this bibliography includes more English-language works and, for reasons of space, adopts a more selective approach to recent French-language publications. Naturally, there is a vast amount of Arabic-language literature on all aspects of Syria, but because this is a general reference for Western readers, Arabic works are not included. There is also an enormous amount of literature on archaeology in Syria and nearby lands, but in view of this work's more recent focus, I have selected just a few general works on the country's prehistoric and ancient heritage.

The only comprehensive historical survey of Syria from ancient times to the 20th century is Philip Hitti's classic, though somewhat dated, *History of Syria*. Detailed treatment of individual topics is found in various articles in *The Encyclopaedia of Islam*, second edition. More recent surveys of modern history (since 1800) include A. L. Tibawi's *A Modern History of Syria* and Tabitha Petran's *Syria*. Kamal Salibi's *Syria under Islam* covers the first Islamic centuries; the Crusades are comprehensively treated in Kenneth Setton's five-volume *History of the Crusades*; for the Mamluk era, one should consult *Muslim Cities in the Later Middle Ages* by Ira Lapidus.

Much recent historical scholarship has focused on the Ottoman era, but no single work covers the entire four centuries. Notable monographs on the early Ottoman period are Adnan Bakhit's *The Ottoman Province of Damascus in the Sixteenth Century*, Karl Barbir's *Ottoman Rule in Damascus, 1708-1758*, Abraham Marcus's *The Middle East on the Eve of Modernity: Aleppo in the Eighteenth Century*, and Bruce Masters's *The Origins of Western Economic Dominance in the Middle East: Mercantilism and the Islamic Economy in Aleppo, 1600-1750*. For the 19th century one should consult *An Occasion for War: Civil Conflict in Lebanon and Damascus in 1860* by Leila Fawaz and *Families in Politics: Damascene Factions and Estates of the 18th and 19th*

Centuries by Linda Schatkowski Schilcher.

For social and economic history in the 18th and 19th centuries, the works of Abdul Karim Rafeq and James Reilly are essential reading. Monographs that represent efforts by scholars to explore the history of women and the family include *The Kin Who Count: Family and Society in Ottoman Aleppo, 1770-1840* by Margaret Meriwether and *In the House of Law: Gender and Islamic Law in Ottoman Syria and Palestine* by Judith Tucker. The rise of Arab nationalism in the late Ottoman period is the subject of Ernest Dawn's *From Ottomanism to Arabism: Essays on the Origins of Arab Nationalism*, Philip Khoury's *Urban Notables and Arab Nationalism: The Politics of Damascus, 1860-1920*, and a fine collection of essays, *The Origins of Arab Nationalism*, edited by Rashid Khalidi. The most sophisticated study of nationalism in Syria is *Divided Loyalties: Nationalism and Mass Politics in Syria at the Close of Empire*, James Gelvin's conceptually rich exploration of its elite and popular forms during the brief span of Amir Faysal's rule after World War I.

Syria's first bid for independence is the subject of Malcolm Russell's careful study *The First Modern Arab State: Syria under Faysal, 1918-1920*. For the Mandate era Philip Khoury's *Syria and the French Mandate: The Politics of Arab Nationalism, 1920-1945* is the outstanding work on political dynamics. A study on the role of gender in the same period is *Colonial Citizens: Republican Rights, Paternal Privilege, and Gender in French Syria and Syria* by Elizabeth Thompson. Two classic studies remain the best sources on the first decade of independence: Patrick Seale's *The Struggle for Syria: A Study of Postwar Arab Politics, 1945-1958* examines Syrian developments in a regional context, while Gordon Torrey's *Syrian Politics and the Military, 1945-1958* treats domestic developments in greater detail. The definitive study of the Ba'th Party's early development is John Devlin's *The Ba'th Party: A History from Its Origins to 1966*; a more specific work on the first Ba'thist regime is *Syria under the Baath, 1963-1966: The Army-Party Symbiosis* by Itamar Rabinovich. For the unity experiment with Egypt and the Syrian Ba'th's relations with Egypt, Malcolm Kerr's *The Arab Cold War, 1958-1970* is a model of elegant conciseness. Malik Mufti presents a convincing interpretation of attempts at Arab unity in *Sovereign Creations: Pan-Arabism and Political Order in Syria and Iraq*.

A number of valuable studies by political scientists provide thorough analyses. Raymond Hinnebusch published a number of specialized studies, of which *Authoritarian Power and State Formation in Ba'thist Syria: Army, Party, and Peasant* is the most accessible to the general reader. Patrick Seale's *Asad of Syria: The Struggle for the Middle East* gives a more journalistic treatment that is sympathetic to the official Syrian perspective. Two works that place Syria's political economy in comparative context are Steve Heyde-mann's *Authoritarianism in Syria: Institutions and Conflict, 1946-1970* and David Waldner's *State Building and Late Development*.

There is no single work that surveys the conflict with Israel; instead the reader must consult general works on the Arab-Israeli wars. Mention should be made, however, of Aryeh Shalev's *The Israel-Syria Armistice Regime, 1949-1955*. A review of Syria's terms for a settlement with Israel is in Alasdair Drysdale and Raymond Hinnebusch's *Syria and the Middle East Peace Process*. Syrian foreign policy is considered in Seale's two monographs and Kerr's study as well in the following works: Adeed Dawisha, *Syria and the Lebanese Crisis*; Yair Evron, *War and Intervention in Lebanon: The Israeli-Syrian Deterrence Dialogue*; Eberhard Kienle, *Ba`th v. Ba`th: The Conflict between Syria and Iraq*; and Pedro Ramet, *The Syrian-Soviet Relationship since 1955: A Troubled Alliance*.

There are few general studies on the economy. In 1955, the International Bank for Reconstruction and Development published *The Economic Development of Syria*, an overview of Syria's economy in the early years of independence that serves as a sound baseline for later works. Two decades later, E. Kanovsky surveyed developments in a monograph also entitled *The Economic Development of Syria*. For a review of the results of land reform and state domination of manufacturing, trade, and finance, one should refer to Volker Perthes's *The Political Economy of Syria under Asad*. The best current sources for specific and general aspects of the economy are international organizations like the World Bank and the United Nations (see the websites below).

The flavor of everyday life is elegantly captured by Andrea Rugh's study of a Syrian family, *Within the Circle: Parents and Children in an Arab Village*. Laurence Deonna's *Syrians: A Travelogue* offers glimpses of Syrians from different religious and ethnic groups and sketches of some prominent personalities in the arts, entertainment, and politics. Readers interested in portraits of women's lives will find a compelling account in *Both Right and Left-Handed: Arab Women Talk about their Lives* by Bouthaina Shaaban. Perhaps the keenest insights into Syrian life would come from reading the growing volume of fiction translated into English. Ulfat Idilbi's novel *Sabriya* depicts facets of conservative Muslim customs in Damascus while Hanna Mina's *Fragments of Memory* portrays vignettes of rural life. Muhammad al-Maghut's poetry in *The Fan of Swords* conveys the alienation of rural migrants to the city and the pervasive fear of living in the shadow of intrusive security forces.

To stay abreast of current scholarship, the quarterly bibliography *Index Islamicus* is indispensable. For those seeking a synopsis of recent developments, there is an annual review in each year's *The Middle East and North Africa*, published by Europa Publications Limited; and the *Middle East Journal* contains a quarterly chronology in each issue.

The World Wide Web is a realm of treasures and pitfalls for students and researchers. Statistical data from international organizations like the United Nations and the World Bank were formerly available only in library reference collections, but one may now easily access such information with a computer and a modem. Current news reports from around the world are also readily available. The pitfalls of the "Web" are twofold. The first is the ephemeral character of websites. One might bookmark a useful website and then find that it has moved or no longer exists just a few months later. The second pitfall is its unmediated or unfiltered character. Anyone can post a website and broadcast distortions and tendentious assertions. The discriminating web surfer, however, will find three dependable kinds of websites: academic societies and libraries, Internet directories, and official bodies such as international organizations and government sites.

The Middle East Studies Association of North America is the professional society of regional specialists in various disciplines. Its website maintains links to major academic institutions: fp.arizona.edu/mesassoc/. The Syrian Studies Association for scholars, graduate students, and researchers maintains a website: www.ou.edu/ssa/index.html. Elissa Slotkin has compiled and annotated a General Research Guide: www.sipa.columbia.edu/REGIONAL/mei/syria.doc. Lawrence Joffe's guide posted on the site of MERIA, an online journal, is also very useful: meria.idc.ac.il/research-g/syria.html.

There are now several fairly well-tested Internet directories for Syria with many links to sites on the arts, culture, travel, business, and news: www.syriaonline.com/index.htm; www.syriagate.com/index.htm; www.syria-net.com/. For a directory of businesses and cities, see www.made-in-syria.com/index.htm. This site for chat rooms, jokes, magazine articles, and society apparently appeals to Syrians living overseas: www.souria.com/home.asp. Al-Bab is an Internet directory for Arab countries. Its Syria page has many links for news, books, history, economy, and government websites: www.al-bab.com/arab/countries/syria.htm. Syria Report, begun in November 2002, offers current economic and business news on a monthly basis: www.syria-report.com/. One may find two English-language Syrian newspapers: www.teshreen.com/syriatimes/ and www.thawra.com/english/english-.htm. The Syrian government has begun to maintain websites. The Ministry of Tourism site is www.syriatourism.org/new/index.html; the Ministry of Economy and Foreign Trade site is www.syrecon.org/ main_frame.html.

The human rights situation in Syria is monitored and updated by various groups. The Syrian Human Rights Committee posts its reports and petitions as well as links to international organizations at www.shrc.org/english/index.shtml. Human Rights Watch on Middle East and North Africa has a site at www.hrw.org/mideast/index.php. Economic and social data is maintained by international organizations. The United Nations Relief and Works Agency has data on Palestinian refugees at www.un.org/unrwa/. The World Bank website is a vast storehouse of reports, charts, and statistics: www.worldbank.org/. The United Nations Development Program has reports on political and social developments pertaining to rule of law, civil society, and the status of women: www.undp-pogar.org/countries/syria/index.html.

The bibliography is divided into the following sections:

1. BIBLIOGRAPHIES

Bleaney, C. H. *Modern Syria: An Introduction to the Literature.* Durham: University of Durham, 1979.

Bloomfield, B. C., and Edmond Y. Asfour (eds.). *A Cumulation of a Selected and Annotated Bibliography of Economic Literature on the Arabic Speaking Countries of the Middle East, 1938-1960.* Boston: G. K. Hall, 1967.

Bybee, Howard C., and Conrad E. L'Heureux. *Bibliography of Syrian Archaeological Sites to 1980.* Lewiston, N.Y.: Edwin Mellen Press, 1994.

Cahen, Claude. *Introduction à l'histoire du monde musulman médiéval, VIIe-XVe siècle: méthodologie et éléments de bibliographie.* Paris: Librairie Amérique et d'Orient, 1983.

Middle East Journal. Washington, D.C. Quarterly. 1947-

Patai, Raphael. *Jordan, Lebanon, Syria: An Annotated Bibliography.* Westport, Conn.: Greenwood Press, 1975.

Pearson, J. D. (ed.). *Index Islamicus, 1906-1955. A Catalogue of Articles on Islamic Subjects in Periodicals and Other Collective Publications.* Cambridge: W. Heffer, 1958; Supplements: 1: 1956-1960. Cambridge: W. Heffer, 1962; 2: 1961-1965. Cambridge: W. Heffer, 1967; 3: 1966-1970. London: Mansell, 1972; 4: 1971-1975. London: Mansell, 1975.

———. *The Quarterly Index Islamicus: Current Books, Articles and Papers on Islamic Studies.* London: Mansell, 1977-.

Quilliam, Neil. *Syria.* Santa Barbara, Calif.: ABC-Clio, 1999. Rev. ed.

Sauvaget, Jean. *Introduction to the History of the Muslim East: A Bibliographical Guide.* Berkeley: University of California Press, 1965.

Seccombe, Ian J. *Syria.* Oxford: Clio Press, 1987.

Zahlan, A. B. (ed.). *Agricultural Bibliography of Syria to 1983.* London: Ithaca Press, 1984.

2. PERIODICALS

Ancient History

Les Annales Archéologiques Arabes Syriennes. Revue d'Archéologie et d'Histoire. Damascus. Annual. 1950-

Biblical Archaeologist

Studi Eblaiti. Rome. Annual. 1979-

Syria. Revue d'art oriental et d'archéologie. Paris. Annual. 1923-

Syro-Mesopotamian Studies. Malibu, Calif. Quarterly. 1977-

Ugarit-Forschungen. Neukirchener, Germany. Annual. 1969-

History and Politics

Arab Studies Quarterly
Bulletin of the School of Oriental and African Studies
International Journal of Middle East Studies
Der Islam
Journal of the American Oriental Society
Journal of Asian and African Studies
Journal of Semitic Studies
Journal of the Social and Economic History of the Orient
Journal of South Asian and Middle East Studies
Maghreb/Machrek
Middle East Journal
Middle East Report
Middle East Research and Information Project
Middle East Review of International Affairs (http://meria.idc.ac.il/)
Middle Eastern Studies
Muslim World
Peuples Méditerrannéens
Revue des Etudes Islamiques
Revue du Monde Musulman
Revue du Monde Musulman et de la Méditerrannée
Studia Islamica
Die Welt des Islams

Economics

Arab Report and Record/MEED Arab Report. London. Fortnightly. 1966-
    1979.
Middle East Economic Digest. London. Weekly. 1957-
Middle East Economic Survey. Nicosia. Weekly. 1957-
Quarterly Economic Review: Syria, Jordan. London. 1978-1986.
Quarterly Economic Review of Syria, Lebanon, and Cyprus. London. 1968-
    1978.
Quarterly Economic Review of Syria, Lebanon, Jordan. London. 1956-1967.

3. ARCHIVES AND LIBRARIES

De Jong, Fred. "Arabic Periodicals Published in Syria before 1946: The
    Holdings of Zahiriyya Library in Damascus," *Bibliotheca Orientalis*, 36
    (1979): 292-300.

Lentin, Jerome. "La bibliothèque de l'Institut Français d'Etudes Arabes de Damas," *L'Arabisant*, 18-19 (1981-1982): 2-10.

Mandaville, Jon E. "The Ottoman Court Records of Syria and Jordan," *Journal of the American Oriental Society*, 86 (1966): 311-318.

4. STATISTICAL REFERENCES

Brom, Shlomo, and Yiftah Shapir (eds.). *Middle East Military Balance, 2001-2002*. Cambridge, Mass.: MIT Press, 2002.

Demographic Yearbook. New York: United Nations. Annual. 1948-

International Financial Statistics Yearbook. Washington, D.C.: International Monetary Fund. Annual. 1974-

McCarthy, Justin. *The Arab World, Turkey, and the Balkans (1878-1914): A Handbook of Historical Statistics*. Boston: G. K. Hall, 1982.

Statistical Abstract of Syria. Damascus: Central Bureau of Statistics. Annual. 1947-

UNESCO Statistical Yearbook. Paris: UNESCO. Annual. 1963-

United Nations Statistical Yearbook. New York: United Nations. Annual. 1948.

UNRWA Statistical Yearbook. Vienna: UNRWA. Annual. 1964-

Wilson, Rodney. *The Arab World: An International Statistical Directory*. Brighton, UK: Wheatsheaf Books, 1984.

Women and Men in the Syrian Arab Republic: A Statistical Portrait. New York: United Nations, 2001.

5. GENERAL REFERENCES

Encyclopaedia of Islam. 1st ed. M. T. Houtsma et al. (eds.). Leiden: E. J. Brill, 1913-1942. 4 vols.

Encyclopaedia of Islam. 2d ed. H. A. R. Gibb et al. (eds.). Leiden: E. J. Brill, 1954-

Hurewitz, J. C. (ed.). *The Middle East and North Africa in World Politics: A Documentary Record*. New Haven, Conn.: Yale University Press, 1975, 1979. 2 vols. Volume 1 (1535-1914), Volume 2 (1914-1945).

The Middle East and North Africa. London: Europa Publications Limited, Annual. 1955-

Nyrop, Richard F. *Syria: A Country Study*. Washington, D.C.: The American University, 1979. 3d ed.

Sinai, Anne, and Allen Pollack (eds.). *The Syrian Arab Republic*. New York: American Academic Association for Peace in the Middle East, 1976.

Somel, Selcuk Aksin. *The Historical Dictionary of the Ottoman Empire*.

Lanham, Md.: Scarecrow Press, 2003.

6. TRAVEL GUIDES

Ball, Warwick. *Syria*. New York: Interlink, 1998.
Beattie, Andrew, and Timothy Pepper. *The Rough Guide to Syria*. London: Rough Guides, 2001.
Burns, Ross. *Monuments of Syria: An Historical Guide*. London: I. B. Tauris, 1999.
Davis, Scott C. *The Road from Damascus: A Journey through Syria*. Seattle: Cune Press, 2000.
Deonna, Laurence. *Syrians, A Travelogue (1992-1994)*. Christopher Snow (trans.). Pueblo, Colo.: Passeggiata Press, 1996.
Fedden, Robin. *Syria and Lebanon*. London: John Murray, 1965. 3d ed.
Humphreys, Andrew, and Damien Simonis. *Syria*. London: Lonely Planet, 1999.
Joris, Lieve. *The Gates of Damascus*. Oakland, Calif.: Lonely Planet, 1996.
Keenan, Brigid. *Damascus: Hidden Treasures of the Old City*. New York: Thames & Hudson, 2000.
King, Anthony. *Syria Revealed: A Comprehensive Guide to the Country*. London: Boxer, 1995.
Lewis, Peter, *Syria: Land of Contrasts*. London: Namara Publications, 1980.
Pillement, Georges. *Liban, Syrie et Chypre Inconnus: Itinéraires Archéologiques*. Paris: Editions Albin Michel, 1971.
Rihawi, Abdulqader. *Damascus: Its History, Development, and Artistic Heritage*. Damascus: Rihawi, 1977.
Simonis, Damien, and Hugh Finlay. *Jordan and Syria: A Lonely Planet Travel Survival Kit*. Berkeley: Lonely Planet, 1997.
South, Coleman. *Culture Shock! Syria*. Portland, Ore.: Graphic Arts Center, 2001.

7. GEOLOGY

Burdon, David J., and Chafic Safadi. "The Karst Groundwater of Syria," *Journal of Hydrology*, 2 (1964): 324-347.
————. "Ras-el-Ain: The Great Karst Spring of Mesopotamia; an Hydrogeological Study," *Journal of Hydrology*, 1 (1963): 58-93.
Khouri, J. "Hydrogeology of the Syrian Steppe and Adjoining Arid Areas," *Quarterly Journal of Engineering Geology*, 15 (1982): 35-54.
Wolfart, Reinhard. *Geologie von Syrien und dem Libanon*. Berlin: Gebruder Borntrager, 1967.

8. FLORA AND FAUNA

Baumgart, Wolfgang, Max Kasparek, and Stephan Burkhard. *Birds of Syria.* Bedfordshire, UK: Ornithological Society of the Middle East, 2003.

Bouloumoy, Louis. *Flore du Liban et de la Syrie.* Paris: Vigot Frères, 1930.

Harrison, David L. *The Mammals of Arabia.* London: Ernest Benn, 1964-1972. 3 vols.

Joger, Ulrich. *The Venomous Snakes of the Near and Middle East.* Wiesbaden: Ludwig Reichart, 1984.

Mouterde, Paul S. *Nouvelle Flore du Liban et de la Syrie.* Beirut: Dar el-Machreq, 1966-1979. 6 vols.

Thiebaut, J. *Flore Libano-syrienne.* Cairo: Institut d'Egypte, 1936, 1940; Paris: Centre National de la Recherche Scientifique, 1953. 3 vols.

Zohary, Michael. *Geobotanical Foundations of the Middle East.* Stuttgart: Gustav Fischer, 1973; Amsterdam: Swets & Zeitlinger. 2 vols.

9. GEOGRAPHY

Beaumont, Peter, Gerald H. Blake, and J. Malcolm Wagstaff. *The Middle East: A Geographical Study.* New York: Halsted Press, 1978. 2d ed.

Bianquis, Anne-Marie. "Damas et la Ghouta." In André Raymond (ed.). *La Syrie d'aujourd'hui.* Paris: Editions de CNRS, 1980.

Boghossian, Roupen. *La Haute-Djezireh.* Aleppo: Imprimerie Chiras, 1952.

David, Jean-Claude. "Alep." In André Raymond (ed.). *La Syrie d'aujourd'hui.* Paris: Editions du CNRS, 1980.

———. "Alep, dégradation et tentatives actuelles de réadaptation des structures urbaines traditionnelles," *Bulletin d'Etudes Orientales*, 28 (1975): 19-50.

———. "Les quartiers anciens dans la croissance moderne de la ville d'Alep." In Dominique Chevallier (ed.). *Espace social de la ville arabe.* Paris: G.-P. Maisonneuve & Larose, 1979.

Fisher, William B. *The Middle East: A Physical, Social, and Regional Geography.* London: Methuen, 1978. 7th ed.

Kolars, John, and William A. Mitchell. *The Euphrates River and the Southeast Anatolia Development Project.* Carbondale: Southern Illinois University Press, 1991.

Sauvaget, Jean, and Jacques Weulersse. *Damas et la Syrie Sud.* Damascus: Office Touristique de la République Syrienne, 1936.

Thoumin, Richard. *Géographie humaine de la Syrie centrale.* Paris: Librairie Ernest Leroux, 1936.

———. "Damas. Notes sur la répartition de la population par origine et par religion," *Revue de Géographie Alpine*, 25 (1937): 633-697.

————. "Deux quartiers de Damas. Le quartier chrétien de Bab Musalla et le quartier kurde," *Bulletin d'Etudes Orientales*, 1 (1931): 99-135.

————. "Le Ghab," *Revue de Géographie Alpine*, 24 (1936): 467-538.

United States Board on Geographic Names. *Syria, Official Standard Names*. Washington, D.C.: Office of Geography, Department of the Interior, 1967.

Weulersse, Jacques. *L'Oronte, étude du fleuve*. Paris: Institut Français de Damas, 1940.

————. *Le Pays des Alaouites*. Tours: Institut Français de Damas, 1940. 2 vols.

————. "Antioch, essai de géographie urbaine," *Bulletin d'Etudes Orientales*, 4 (1934): 27-79.

Wirth, Eugen. *Syrien. Eine Geographische Landeskunde*. Darmstadt: Wissenschaftliche Buchges., 1971.

10. TRAVELERS' ACCOUNTS

Abassi, Ali Bey el- (Domingo Badia y Leblich). *Travels of Ali Bey in Morocco, Tripoli, Cyprus, Egypt, Arabia, Syria and Turkey, between the years 1803 and 1807*. Farnborough, UK: Gregg International, 1970. Rep. ed. 2 vols.

Addison, Charles G. *Damascus and Palmyra: A Journey to the East. With a Sketch of the State of Prospects of Syria under Ibrahim Pasha*. New York: Arno Press, 1973. Rep. ed.

Barker, Edward B. *Syria and Egypt under the Last Five Sultans of Turkey: Being Experiences, during Fifty Years, of Mr. Consul-General Barker, Chiefly from his Letters and Journals*. New York: Arno Press, 1973. Rep. ed. 2 vols.

Bell, Gertrude. *Amurath to Amurath*. London: Macmillan, 1924. 2d ed.

————. *Syria: The Desert and the Sown*. London: Darf, 1985. Rep. ed.

Berchet, Jean-Claude. *Le Voyage en Orient. Anthologie des Voyageurs Français dans le Levant au XIXe Siècle*. Paris: Robert Laffont, 1985.

Grant, Christina P. *The Syrian Desert. Caravans, Travel, and Exploration*. London: A. C. Black, 1937.

Hachico, Mohamad Ali. "English Travel Books about the Arab Near East in the Eighteenth Century," *Die Welt des Islams*, 9 (1964): 1-26.

Lewis, W. H. *Levantine Adventurer: The Travels and Missions of the Chevalier D'Arvieux, 1653-1697*. New York: Harcourt, Brace & World, 1962.

Maundrell, Henry. *A Journey from Aleppo to Jerusalem in 1697*. Beirut: Khayats, 1963.

Musil, Alois. *Arabia Deserta: A Topographical Itinerary.* New York: American Geographical Society, 1927.

―――. *Palmyrena: A Topographical Itinerary.* New York: American Geographical Society, 1928.

Russell, Alexander. *The Natural History of Aleppo.* London: G. G. Robinson, 1794. 2d ed. 2 vols.

Sim, Katherine. *Desert Traveller: The Life of Jean Louis Burckhardt.* London: Victor Gollancz, 1969.

Stark, Freya. *Letters from Syria.* London: John Murray, 1942.

Volney, Constantin-Francois, Comte de. *Travels through Syria and Egypt in the Years 1783, 1784 and 1785.* Farnborough, UK: Gregg International, 1972. Rep. ed. 2 vols.

11. GENERAL HISTORY

Devlin, John F. *Syria: Modern State in an Ancient Land.* Boulder, Colo.: Westview Press, 1983.

Hitti, Philip. *History of Syria, including Lebanon and Palestine.* New York: Macmillan, 1951.

Lewis, Norman N. *Nomads and Settlers in Syria and Jordan, 1800-1980.* Cambridge: Cambridge University Press, 1987.

Petran, Tabitha. *Syria.* London: Ernest Benn, 1972.

Philipp, Thomas. *The Syrians in Egypt, 1775-1975.* Berlin: Franz Steiner, 1985.

Raymond, André (ed.). *La Syrie d'aujourd'hui.* Paris: Editions du Centre National de la Recherche, 1980.

Sauvaget, Jean. *Alep. Essai sur le développement d'une grande ville syrienne des origines au milieu du XIXe siècle.* 2 vols. Paris: Paul Geuthner, 1941.

―――. "Esquisse d'une histoire de la ville de Damas," *Revue des Etudes Islamiques*, 8 (1934): 421-480.

Thubron, Colin. *Mirror to Damascus.* London: Heinemann, 1967.

Tibawi, A. L. *A Modern History of Syria, including Lebanon and Palestine.* London: St. Martin's Press, 1969.

Ziadeh, Nicola A. *Syria and Lebanon.* Beirut: Librairie du Liban, 1968.

12. HISTORY TO 634

Balty, Jean C. "Apamea in Syria in the Second and Third Centuries A.D.," *Journal of Roman Studies*, 78 (1988): 91-104.

Batto, Bernard Frank. *Studies on Women at Mari.* Baltimore: Johns Hopkins University Press, 1974.

Bermont, Chaim, and Michael Weitzman. *Ebla: An Archaeological Enigma.* London: Weidenfeld & Nicolson, 1979.

Bonatz, Dominik, Hartmut Kuhne, and As'ad Mahmoud. *Rivers and Steppes: Cultural Heritage and Environment of the Syria Jezireh: Catalogue to the Museum of Deir ez-Zor.* Damascus: Ministry of Culture, Directorate-General of Antiquities and Museums, 1998.

Browning, Iain. *Palmyra.* London: Chatto & Windus, 1979.

Colledge, Malcolm A. R. *The Art of Palmyra.* London: Thames & Hudson, 1976.

Curtis, Adrian. *Ugarit (Ras Shamra).* Grand Rapids, Mich.: Eerdmans Publications, 1985.

Downey, Glanville. *A History of Antioch in Syria from Seleucus to the Arab Conquest.* Princeton, N.J.: Princeton University Press, 1961.

Drijvers, H. J. W. *The Religion of Palmyra.* Leiden: E. J. Brill, 1976.

Grabar, Oleg, Renata Holod, James Knustad, and William Trousdale. *City in the Desert: Qasr al-Hayr East.* 2 vols. Cambridge, Mass.: Harvard University Press, 1978.

Heltzer, Michael. *Goods, Prices and the Organisation of Trade in Ugarit.* Wiesbaden: Ludwig Reichart, 1978.

———. *The Internal Organization of the Kingdom of Ugarit.* Wiesbaden: Ludwig Reichart, 1982.

———. *The Rural Community in Ancient Ugarit.* Wiesbaden: Ludwig Reichart, 1976.

Hopkins, Clarke, and Bernard Goldman (eds.). *The Discovery of Dura-Europos.* New Haven, Conn.: Yale University Press, 1979.

Kaizer, Ted. *The Religious Life of Palmyra: A Study of the Social Patterns of Worship in the Roman Period.* Stuttgart: Franz Steiner, 2000.

Klengel, Horst. *Syria, 3000 BC to 300 BC: A Handbook of Political History.* Berlin: Akademie Verlag, 1992.

Liebeschuetz, J. H. *Antioch: City and Imperial Administration in the Later Roman Empire.* Oxford: Oxford University Press, 1972.

Matthiae, Paolo. *Ebla: An Empire Rediscovered.* London: Hodder & Stoughton, 1980.

Michalowski, Kazimierz. *Palmyra.* London: Pall Mall Press, 1970.

Moore, A. M. T., Gordon C. Hillman, and A. J. Legge. *Village on the Euphrates: From Foraging to Farming at Abu Hureyra.* London: Oxford University Press, 2000.

Perkins, Ann. *The Art of Dura-Europos.* London: Oxford University Press, 1973.

Peters, F. E. *The Harvest of Hellenism: A History of the Near East from Alexander the Great to the Triumph of Christianity.* London: Allen &

Unwin, 1972.

———. "Byzantium and the Arabs of Syria," *Annales Archéologiques Arabes Syriennes*, 27-28 (1977-78): 97-113.

Pettinato, Giovanni. *The Archives of Ebla: An Empire Inscribed in Clay*. New York: Doubleday, 1981.

Schaeffer, Claude F. A. (ed.). *Le Palais Royal d'Ugarit*. Paris: Imprimerie Nationale, 1955-1970. 6 vols.

Schwartz, Glenn M., and Peter M. M. G. Akkermans. *The Archaeology of Syria*. Cambridge: Cambridge University Press, 2003.

Weiss, Harvey. "Archaeology in Syria," *American Journal of Archaeology*, 95 (1991): 683-740.

Young, Gordon D. (ed.). *Ugarit in Retrospect: Fifty Years of Ugarit and Ugaritic*. Winona Lake, Ind.: Eisenbrauns, 1981.

13. HISTORY, 634-1517

Allouche, Adel. "A Study of Ibn Battutah's Account of his AD 1326 Journey through Syria and Arabia," *Journal of Semitic Studies*, 35 (1990): 283-299.

Ashtor, Eliyahu. *Levant Trade in the Later Middle Ages*. Princeton, N.J.: Princeton University Press, 1983.

———. "Migrations de l'Irak vers les pays méditerrannéens. Un mouvement migratoire au haut Moyen-Age," *Annales: Economies, Sociétés et Civilisations*, 27 (1972): 185-214.

Assaad, Sadik A. *The Reign of Al-Hakim Bi Amr Allah*. Beirut: The Arab Institute for Research and Publishing, 1974.

Ayalon, David. "Aspects of the Mamluk Phenomenon: Ayyubids, Kurds, and Turks," *Der Islam*, 54 (1974): 1-32.

Bianquis, Thierry. *Damas et la Syrie sous la domination fatimide (359-468/969-1076). Essai d'interprétation des chroniques arabes médiévales*. 2 vols. Damascus: Institut Français de Damas, 1986-1989.

Brinner, William M. "The Banu Sasra: A Study on the Transmission of a Scholarly Tradition," *Arabica*, 7 (1960): 167-195.

———. "The Significance of the Harafish and Their Sultan," *Journal of the Social and Economic History of the Orient*, 6 (1963): 190-215.

Cahen, Claude. *Mouvements populaires et autonomisme urbain dans l'Asie musulmane du moyen âge*. Leiden: E. J. Brill, 1959. First published in *Arabica*, 5 (1958): 225-250; 6 (1959): 25-56, 233-265.

———. *La Syrie du nord à l'époque des Croisades et la principauté Franque d'Antioch*. Paris: P. Geuthner, 1940.

———. "L'évolution de l'iqta` du IXe au XIIIe siècle: Contribution à une histoire comparée des sociétés médiévales," *Annales: Economies, Sociétés, Civilisations*, 8 (1953): 25-52.

Chamberlain, Michael. *Knowledge and Social Practice in Medieval Damascus, 1190-1350*. Cambridge: Cambridge University Press, 1994.

Cobb, Paul. *White Banners: Contention in Abbasid Syria, 750-880*. Albany: State University of New York Press, 2001.

Crusader Syria in the Thirteenth Century: The Rothelin Continuation of the History of William of Tyre. Brookfield, Vt.: Ashgate, 1999.

Dixon, `Abd al-Ameer. *The Umayyad Caliphate, 665-86/684-705: A Political Study*. London: Luzac, 1971.

Donner, Fred. *The Early Islamic Conquests*. Princeton, N.J.: Princeton University Press, 1981.

Eddé, Anne-Marie. *La Principauté Ayyoubide d'Alep (579/1183-658/1260)*. Stuttgart: Franz Steiner, 1999.

Ehrenkreutz, Andrew S. *Saladin*. Albany: State University of New York Press, 1972.

El-Azhar, Taef Kamal. *The Saljuqs of Syria: During the Crusades, 463-549 A.H./1070-1154 A.D.* Berlin: Schwarz, 1997.

Elisséef, Nikita. *Nur al-Din: Un grand prince musulman de Syrie au temps des croisades (511-569 AH/118-1174)*. 3 vols. Damascus: Institut Français de Damas, 1967.

―――. "Damas à la lumière des théories de Jean Sauvaget." In Albert Hourani and S. M. Stern (eds.). *The Islamic City: A Colloquium*. Oxford: Cassirer, 1970.

―――. "Les Monuments de Nur al-Din," *Bulletin d'Etudes Orientales*, 13 (1949-1951): 5-43.

Farsag, W. "The Aleppo Question: A Byzantine-Fatimid Conflict of Interests in Northern Syria in the Later 10th Century A.D.," *Byzantine and Modern Greek Studies*, 14 (1990): 44-60.

Gabrieli, Francesco (ed.). *Arab Historians of the Crusades*. London: Routledge & Kegan Paul, 1969.

Gibb, H. A. R. *The Damascus Chronicle of the Crusades*. Mineola, N.Y.: Dover Publications, 2002.

―――. *The Life of Saladin*. Oxford: Clarendon, 1973.

Gilbert, Joan. "Institutionalization of Muslim Scholarship and Professionalization of the `Ulama' in Medieval Damascus," *Studia Islamica*, 52 (1980): 105-135.

Goussous, Nayef G. *Umayyad Coinage of Bilad al-Sham*. Amman: Arab Bank, 1996.

Haarmann, Ulrich. "Arabic in Speech, Turkish in Lineage: Mamluks and their Sons in the Intellectual Life of Fourteenth-Century Egypt and Syria,"

Journal of Semitic Studies, 33 (1988): 81-114.

Havemann, Axel. "The Vizier and the Ra'is in Saljuq Syria: The Struggle for Urban Self-Representation," *International Journal of Middle East Studies*, 21 (1989): 233-242.

Hitti, Philip. *An Arab-Syrian Gentleman and Warrior in the Period of the Crusades: Memoirs of Usamah Ibn-Munqidh*. Princeton, N.J.: Princeton University Press, 1987. Rep. ed.

Hodgson, Marshall G. S. "Al-Darazi and Hamza in the Origin of the Druze Religion," *Journal of the American Oriental Society*, 82 (1962): 5-20.

Holt, P. M. *The Age of the Crusades in the Near East from the Eleventh Century to 1517*. London: Longman, 1986.

————. *The Memoirs of a Syrian Prince: Abul-Fida, Sultan of Hamah (672-732/1273-1330)*. Wiesbaden: Franz Steiner, 1983.

————. "The Structure of Government in the Mamluk Sultanate." In P. M. Holt (ed.). *The Eastern Mediterranean Lands in the Time of the Crusades*. Forest Grove, Ore.: Aris & Phillips, 1977.

Humphreys, R. Stephen. *From Saladin to the Mongols: The Ayyubids of Damascus, 1193-1260*. Albany: State University of New York Press, 1977.

————. "The Emergence of the Mamluk Army," *Studia Islamica*, 45 (1977): 67-99, 147-182.

————. "Politics and Architectural Patronage in Ayyubid Damascus." In C. E. Bosworth et al. (eds.). *The Islamic World from Classical to Modern Times: Essays in Honor of Bernard Lewis*. Princeton, N.J.: Darwin Press, 1989.

Ibn Shaddad, Baha' al-Din Yusuf ibn Rafi`. *The Rare and Excellent History of Saladin*. D. S. Richards (trans.). Burlington, Vt.: Ashgate, 2001.

Irwin, Robert. *The Middle East in the Middle Ages: The Early Mamluk Sultanate, 1250-1382*. London: Croom Helm, 1986.

Kaegi, Walter. *Byzantium and the Early Islamic Conquests*. Cambridge: Cambridge University Press, 1992.

Kennedy, Hugh. "From Polis to Madina: Urban Change in Late Antique and Early Islamic Syria," *Past and Present*, 106 (1985): 3-27.

Lapidus, Ira. *Muslim Cities in the Later Middle Ages*. Cambridge, Mass.: Harvard University Press, 1967.

Leiser, Gary. "The Endowment of the al-Zahiriyya in Damascus," *Journal of the Economic and Social History of the Orient*, 27 (1983): 33-55.

Lewis, Bernard. *The Assassins: A Radical Sect in Islam*. New York: Oxford University Press, 1987. Rep. ed.

Lyons, Malcolm Cameron, and D. E. P. Jackson. *Saladin: The Politics of the Holy War*. Cambridge: Cambridge University Press, 1982.

Morray, D. W. *An Ayyubid Notable and His World: Ibn al-'Adim and Aleppo as Portrayed in His Biographical Dictionary of People Associated with the City.* Leiden: E. J. Brill, 1994.

Newby, P. H. *Saladin in His Time.* Boston: Faber & Faber, 1983.

Nicolle, David. *Yarmuk, 636 AD: The Muslim Conquest of Syria.* London: Osprey, 1994.

Popper, William. *Egypt and Syria under the Circassian Sultans, 1382-1468 AD. Systematic Notes to Ibn Taghri Birdi's Chronicles of Egypt.* Berkeley: University of California Press, 1955-1958. 2 vols.

Pouzet, Louis. *Damas au VIIe/XIIIe siècle. Vie et structures religieuses d'une metropole islamique.* Beirut: Dar el-Machreq, 1988.

Rabbat, Nasser O. "The Ideological Significance of the *Dar al-'Adl* in the Medieval Islamic Orient," *International Journal of Middle East Studies,* 27 (1995): 3-28.

Salibi, Kamal S. *Syria under Islam.* Delmar, N.Y.: Caravan Press, 1977.

———. "The Banu Jama'a: A Dynasty of Shafi'i Jurists in the Mamluk Period," *Studia Islamica,* 9 (1958): 97-109.

Setton, Kenneth M. (gen. ed.). *A History of the Crusades.* Madison: University of Wisconsin Press, 1969. 2d ed. 5 vols.

Shatzmiller, Maya (ed.). *Crusaders and Muslims in Twelfth Century Syria.* Leiden: E. J. Brill, 1993.

Sourdel, Dominique. "Les professeurs de madrasa à Alep aux XIIe-XIIIe siècles d'après Ibn Shaddad," *Bulletin d'Etudes Orientales,* 13 (1949-1951): 85-115.

Sourdel, Dominique, and Janine Sourdel-Thomine. "Nouveaux documents sur l'histoire religieuse et sociale de Damas au Moyen-Age," *Revue des Etudes Islamiques,* 32 (1964): 1-25.

Von Sivers, Peter. "Military, Merchants and Nomads: The Social Evolution of the Syrian Cities and Countryside during the Classical Period, 780-969/164-358," *Der Islam,* 56 (1979): 212-244.

Wellhausen, Julius. *The Arab Kingdom and Its Fall.* Beirut: Khayats, 1963. Rep. ed.

Yunini, Musa ibn Muhammad. *Early Mamluk Syrian Historiography: Al-Yunini's Dhayl Mir'at al-Zaman.* Li Guo (trans.). Leiden: E. J. Brill, 1998.

Yusuf, Muhsin D. *Economic Survey of Syria during the Tenth and Eleventh Centuries.* Berlin: Klaus Schwarz, 1985.

Ziadeh, Nicola A. *Damascus under the Mamluks.* Norman: University of Oklahoma Press, 1964.

———. *Urban Life in Syria under the Early Mamluks.* Westport, Conn.: Greenwood Press, 1970. Rep. ed.

Zukkar, Suhayl. *The Emirate of Aleppo, 994-1094.* Beirut: Dar al-Amanah, 1971.

14. HISTORY, 1517-1918

Abdel-Nour, Antoine. *Introduction à l'histoire urbaine de la Syrie Ottomane (XVIe-XVIIIe siècles).* Beirut: Imprimerie Catholique, 1982.

Abu-Manneh, Butrus. "The Establishment and Dismantling of the Province of Syria." In John Spagnolo (ed.). *Problems of the Modern Middle East in Historical Perspective: Essays in Honour of Albert Hourani.* Reading, UK: Ithaca Press, 1992.

————. "The Naqshbandiyya-Mujaddidiyya in the Ottoman Lands in the Early 19th Century," *Die Welt des Islams,* 22 (1982): 1-36.

————. "Sultan Abdulhamid II and Shaikh Abulhuda al-Sayyadi," *Middle Eastern Studies,* 15 (1979): 131-153.

Akarli, Engin. "Abdulhamid II's Attempts to Integrate the Arabs into the Ottoman System." In David Kushner (ed.). *Palestine in the Late Ottoman Period: Political, Social, and Economic Transformation.* Leiden: E. J. Brill, and Jerusalem: Yad Izhak Ben Zvi, 1986.

Antonius, George. *The Arab Awakening.* New York: G. P. Putnam, 1979. Rep. ed.

Baer, Gabriel. "The Evolution of Private Landownership in Egypt and the Fertile Crescent." In Charles Issawi (ed.). *The Economic History of the Middle East, 1800-1914.* Chicago: University of Chicago Press, 1966.

————. "Village and City in Egypt and Syria: 1500-1914." In Abraham Udovitch (ed.). *The Islamic Middle East, 700-1900.* Princeton, N.J.: Darwin Press, 1981.

Bakhit, Muhammad Adnan. *The Ottoman Province of Damascus in the Sixteenth Century.* Beirut: Librairie du Liban, 1982.

Barbir, Karl. *Ottoman Rule in Damascus, 1708-1758.* Princeton, N.J.: Princeton University Press, 1980.

————. "From Pasha to Effendi: The Assimilation of Ottomans into Damascene Society, 1516-1783," *International Journal of Turkish Studies,* 1 (1979-1980): 68-83.

Bodman, Herbert L. *Political Factions in Aleppo, 1760-1826.* Chapel Hill: University of North Carolina Press, 1963.

Braude, Benjamin, and Bernard Lewis (eds.). *Christians and Jews in the Ottoman Empire.* Vol. 2: *The Arabic-Speaking Lands.* New York: Holmes & Meier, 1982. 2 vols.

Chevallier, Dominique (ed.). *Villes et travail en Syrie du XIXe au XXe siècles.* Paris: G.-P. Maisonneuve & Larose, 1982.

————. "A Damas, production et société à la fin du XIXe siècle," *Annales: Economies, Sociétés, Civilisations*, 19 (1964): 966-972.

————. "De la production lente à l'économie dynamique en Syrie," *Annales: Economies, Sociétés, Civilisations*, 21 (1966): 59-70.

————. "Un exemple de résistance technique de l'artisanat Syrien aux 19e et 20e siècles. Les tissus ikates d'Alep et de Damas," *Syria*, 39 (1962): 300-324.

————. "Techniques et société en Syrie: Le filage de la soie et du coton à Alep et à Damas," *Bulletin d'Etudes Orientales*, 18 (1963-1964): 85-93.

————. "Western Development and Eastern Crisis in the Mid-Nineteenth Century: Syria Confronted with the European Economy." In William R. Polk and Richard L. Chambers (eds.). *The Beginnings of Modernization in the Middle East: The Nineteenth Century*. Chicago: University of Chicago Press, 1968.

Cioeta, Donald J. "Ottoman Censorship in Lebanon and Syria, 1876-1908," *International Journal of Middle East Studies*, 10 (1979): 167-181.

Commins, David Dean. *Islamic Reform: Politics and Social Change in Late Ottoman Syria*. New York: Oxford University Press, 1990.

Cuno, Kenneth M. "Was the Land of Ottoman Syria *Miri* or *Milk*? An Examination of Juridical Differences within the Hanafi School," *Studia Islamica*, 81 (1995): 121-152.

Davis, Ralph. *Aleppo and Devonshire Square: English Traders in the Levant in the Eighteenth Century*. London: Macmillan, 1967.

Dawn, C. Ernest. *From Ottomanism to Arabism: Essays on the Origin of Arab Nationalism*. Urbana: University of Illinois Press, 1973.

————. "Ottoman Affinities of 20th Century Regimes in Syria." In David Kushner (ed.). *Palestine in the Late Ottoman Period: Political, Social, and Economic Transformation*. Jerusalem: Yad Izhak Ben-Zvi, 1986.

————. "The Rise of Arabism in Syria," *Middle East Journal*, 16 (1962): 145-168.

Deguilhem, Randi. "Centralised Authority and Local Decisional Power: Management of Endowments in Late Ottoman Damascus." In J. Hanssen, T. Philipp, and S. Weber (eds.). *The Empire in the City: Arab Provincial Capitals in the Late Ottoman Empire*. Beirut: Orient-Institut, 2002.

————. "La réorganisation du waqf dans les provinces Syriennes Ottomanes," *Arab Historical Review for Ottoman Studies*, 5-6 (1992): 31-38.

Djemal Pasha. *Memories of a Turkish Statesman, 1913-1919*. London: Hutchinson, 1922.

Doumani, Beshara. "Endowing Family: Waqf, Property Devolution, and Gender in Greater Syria, 1800 to 1860," *Comparative Studies in Society and History*, 40 (1998): 3-41.

Douwes, Dick. *The Ottomans in Syria: A History of Justice and Oppression*. New York: I. B. Tauris, 2000.

Douwes, Dick, and Norman N. Lewis. "The Trials of Syrian Isma'ilis in the First Decade of the 20th Century," *International Journal of Middle East Studies*, 21 (1989): 215-232.

Emerit, Marcel. "La Crise syrienne et l'expansion économique française en 1860," *Revue Historique*, 207 (1952): 211-232.

Escovitz, Joseph. "He Was the Muhammad 'Abduh of Syria: A Study of Tahir al-Jaza'iri and His Influence," *International Journal of Middle East Studies*, 18 (1986): 293-310.

Establet, Colette, and Jean-Paul Pascual. "Damascene Probate Inventories of the 17th and 18th Centuries: Some Preliminary Approaches and Results," *International Journal of Middle East Studies*, 24 (1992): 373-393.

Farah, Caesar E. "Censorship and Freedom of Expression in Ottoman Syria and Egypt." In William W. Haddad and William Ochsenwald (eds.). *Nationalism in a Non-National State: The Dissolution of the Ottoman Empire*. Columbus: Ohio State University Press, 1977.

———. "Necip Pasha and the British in Syria, 1841-1842," *Archivium Ottomanicum*, 2 (1970): 115-153.

———. "Protestantism and British Diplomacy in Syria," *International Journal of Middle East Studies*, 7 (1976): 321-344.

———. "The Quadruple Alliance and Proposed Ottoman Reforms in Syria, 1839-1841," *International Journal of Turkish Studies*, 2 (1981): 101-130.

Fawaz, Leila Tarazi. *An Occasion for War: Civil Conflict in Lebanon and Damascus in 1860*. Berkeley: University of California Press, 1994.

Frankel, Jonathan. *The Damascus Affair: "Ritual Murder," Politics and the Jews in 1840*. Cambridge: Cambridge University Press, 1997.

Gerber, Haim, and Nachum T. Gross. "Inflation and Deflation in Nineteenth Century Syria and Palestine," *Journal of Economic History*, 40 (1980): 351-371.

Grehan, James. "Street Violence and Social Imagination in Late-Mamluk and Ottoman Damascus (ca. 1500-1800)," *International Journal of Middle East Studies*, 35 (2003): 215-236.

Haddad, Mahmoud. "The Rise of Arab Nationalism Reconsidered," *International Journal of Middle East Studies*, 26 (1994): 201-222.

Haddad, Robert. "Constantinople over Antioch, 1516-1724: Patriarchal Politics in the Ottoman Era," *Journal of Ecclesiastical History*, 41 (1990): 217-238.

Haim, Sylvia. *Arab Nationalism: An Anthology*. Berkeley: University of California Press, 1962.

Hofman, Yitzhak. "The Administration of Syria and Palestine under Egyptian

Rule (1831-1840)." In Moshe Maoz (ed.). *Studies on Palestine during the Ottoman Period.* Jerusalem: Magnes, 1975.

Holt, P. M. *Egypt and the Fertile Crescent, 1516-1922: A Political History.* Ithaca, N.Y.: Cornell University Press, 1966.

Hopwood, Derek. *The Russian Presence in Syria and Palestine, 1843-1914: Church and Politics in the Near East.* Oxford: Clarendon Press, 1969.

Hourani, Albert H. "The Fertile Crescent in the Eighteenth Century." In Albert Hourani. *A Vision of History.* Beirut: Khayats, 1961.

————. "Ottoman Reform and the Politics of the Notables." In William R. Polk and Richard L. Chambers (eds.). *The Beginnings of Modernization in the Middle East: The Nineteenth Century.* Chicago: University of Chicago Press, 1968.

————. "Shaykh Khalid and the Naqshbandi Order." In S. M. Stern, A. Hourani, and V. Brown (eds.). *Islamic Philosophy and the Classical Tradition: Essays Presented to R. Walzer.* Columbia: University of South Carolina Press, 1972.

Issawi, Charles (ed.). *The Fertile Crescent, 1800-1914. A Documentary Economic History.* New York: Oxford University Press, 1988.

Kayali, Hasan. *Arabs and Young Turks: Ottomanism, Arabism, and Islamism in the Ottoman Empire, 1908-1918.* Berkeley: University of California Press, 1997.

Kedourie, Elie. *Arabic Political Memoirs and Other Studies.* London: Cass, 1974.

————. "The Capture of Damascus, 1 October 1918," *Middle Eastern Studies,* 1 (1964): 66-83.

————. "The Impact of the Young Turk Revolution in the Arabic-Speaking Provinces of the Ottoman Empire." In Elie Kedourie. *Arabic Political Memoirs and Other Studies.* London: Cass, 1974.

Khalidi, Rashid. *British Policy towards Syria and Palestine, 1906-1914: A Study of the Antecedents of the Hussein-McMahon Correspondence, the Sykes-Picot Agreement, and the Balfour Declaration.* London: Ithaca Press, 1980.

————. "Arab Nationalism in Syria: The Formative Years." In William W. Haddad and William Ochsenwald (eds.). *Nationalism in a Non-National State: The Dissolution of the Ottoman Empire.* Columbus: Ohio State University Press, 1977.

————. "The 1912 Election Campaign in the Cities of *bilad al-Sham*," *International Journal of Middle East Studies,* 16 (1984): 461-474.

————. "Social Factors in the Rise of the Arab Movement in Syria." In Said Arjomand (ed.). *From Nationalism to Revolutionary Islam.* Albany: State University of New York Press, 1986.

————. "Society and Ideology in Late Ottoman Syria: Class, Education, Profession, and Confession." In John P. Spagnolo (ed.). *Problems of the Modern Middle East in Historical Perspective: Essays in Honour of Albert Hourani*. Reading, UK: Ithaca Press, 1992.

Khalidi, Rashid (ed.). *The Origins of Arab Nationalism*. New York: Columbia University Press, 1991.

Khoury, Philip S. *Urban Notables and Arab Nationalism: The Politics of Damascus, 1860-1920*. Cambridge: Cambridge University Press, 1983.

Kurd `Ali, Muhammad. *Memoirs of Muhammad Kurd `Ali, A Selection*. Khalil Totah (trans.). Washington, D.C.: American Council of Learned Societies, 1954.

Landau, Jacob. "An Arab Anti-Turk Handbill, 1881," *Turcica*, 9 (1977): 215-270.

Lawson, Fred. "Economic and Social Foundations of Egyptian Expansionism: The Invasion of Syria in 1831," *International History Review*, 10 (1988): 378-404.

Leeuwen, Richard van. *Waqfs and Urban Structures: The Case of Ottoman Damascus*. Leiden: E. J. Brill, 1999.

Lewis, Bernard. "Ottoman Land Tenure and Taxation in Syria," *Studia Islamica*, 50 (1979): 109-124.

Maoz, Moshe. *Ottoman Reform in Syria and Palestine, 1840-1861: The Impact of the Tanzimat on Politics and Society*. Oxford: Clarendon Press, 1968.

————. "Communal Conflict in Ottoman Syria during the Reform Era: The Role of Political and Economic Factors." In Benjamin Braude and Bernard Lewis (eds.). *Christians and Jews in the Ottoman Empire*. Vol. 2: *The Arabic-Speaking Lands*. New York: Holmes & Meier, 1982.

————. "The Impact of Modernization on Syrian Politics and Society during the Early Tanzimat Period." In William R. Polk and Richard L. Chambers (eds.). *The Beginnings of Modernization in the Middle East*. Chicago: University of Chicago Press, 1968.

————. "Syrian Urban Politics in the Tanzimat Period between 1840 and 1861," *Bulletin of the School of Oriental and African Studies*, 29 (1966): 277-301.

————. "The 'Ulama' and the Process of Modernization in Syria during the Mid-Nineteenth Century," *Asian and African Studies*, 7 (1971): 77-88.

Marcus, Abraham. *The Middle East on the Eve of Modernity: Aleppo in the Eighteenth Century*. New York: Columbia University Press, 1989.

————. "Men, Women, and Property: Dealers in Real Estate in Eighteenth-Century Aleppo," *Journal of the Social and Economic History of the Orient*, 26 (1983): 137-163.

————. "Privacy in Eighteenth-Century Aleppo: The Limits of Cultural Ideals," *International Journal of Middle East Studies*, 18 (1986): 165-183.

Masters, Bruce. *Christians and Jews in the Ottoman Arab World: The Roots of Sectarianism*. Cambridge: Cambridge University Press, 2001.

————. *The Origins of Western Economic Dominance in the Middle East: Mercantilism and the Islamic Economy in Aleppo, 1600-1750*. New York: New York University Press, 1988.

————. "The 1850 'Events' in Aleppo: An Aftershock of Syria's Incorporation in the Capitalist World System," *International Journal of Middle East Studies*, 22 (1990): 3-20.

————. "Patterns of Migration to Ottoman Aleppo in the 17th and 18th Centuries," *International Journal of Turkish Studies*, 4 (1987): 75-89.

————. "Power and Society in Aleppo in the 18th and 19th Centuries," *Revue du Monde Musulman et de la Méditerrannée*, 62 (1992): 151-158.

————. "The Sultan's Entrepreneurs: The *Avrupa Tuccaris* and the *Hayriye Tuccaris* in Syria," *International Journal of Middle East Studies*, 24 (1992): 579-597.

————. "Trading Diasporas and 'Nations': The Formulation of National Identities in Ottoman Aleppo," *International History Review*, 9 (1987): 345-367.

————. "The View from the Province: Syrian Chronicles of the Eighteenth Century," *Journal of the American Oriental Society*, 114 (1994): 353-362.

Meriwether, Margaret L. *The Kin Who Count: Family and Society in Ottoman Aleppo, 1770-1840*. Austin: University of Texas Press, 1999.

Musa, Suleiman. "The Role of Syrians and Iraqis in the Arab Revolt," *Middle East Forum*, 43 (1967): 5-18.

Nevakiki, Jukka. *Britain, France, and the Arab Middle East, 1914-1922*. London: Athlone Press, 1969.

Ochsenwald, William. *The Hijaz Railroad*. Charlottesville: University of Virginia Press, 1980.

————. "The Vilayet of Syria, 1901-1914: A Reexamination of Diplomatic Documents as Sources," *Middle East Journal*, 22 (1968): 73-87.

Pascual, Jean-Paul. "The Janissaries and the Damascus Countryside at the Beginning of the Seventeenth Century according to the Archives of the City's Military Tribunal." In Tarif Khalidi (ed.). *Land Tenure and Social Transformation in the Middle East*. Beirut: American University of Beirut, 1984.

Philipp, Thomas (ed.). *The Syrian Land in the 18th and 19th Century: The Common and the Specific in the Historical Experience*. Stuttgart: Franz Steiner, 1992.

————. "Class, Community, and Arab Historiography in the Early 19th Century: The Dawn of the New Era," *International Journal of Middle East Studies*, 16 (1984): 161-175.

————. "The Farhi Family and the Changing Position of the Jews in Syria, 1750-1860," *Middle Eastern Studies*, 20 (1984): 37-52.

Philipp, Thomas, and Birgit Schaebler (eds.). *The Syrian Land: Processes of Integration and Fragmentation: Bilad al-Sham from the 18th to the 20th Century.* Stuttgart: Franz Steiner, 1998.

Polk, William R. "Rural Syria in 1845," *Middle East Journal*, 16 (1962): 508-514.

Polk, William R., and Richard L. Chambers (eds.). *The Beginnings of Modernization in the Middle East: The Nineteenth Century.* Chicago: University of Chicago Press, 1968.

Qattan, Najwa al-. "Dhimmis in the Muslim Court: Legal Autonomy and Religious Discrimination," *International Journal of Middle East Studies*, 31 (1999): 429-444.

Rafeq, Abdul-Karim. *The Province of Damascus, 1723-1783.* Beirut: Khayats, 1966.

————. "Changes in the Relationship between the Ottoman Central Administration and the Syrian Provinces from the Sixteenth to the Eighteenth Centuries." In Thomas Naff and E. Roger Owen (eds.). *Studies in Eighteenth Century Islamic History.* Carbondale: Southern Illinois University Press, 1977.

————. "Craft Organization, Work Ethics, and the Strains of Change in Ottoman Syria," *Journal of the American Oriental Society*, 111 (1991): 495-511.

————. "Economic Relations between Damascus and the Dependent Countryside, 1743-1771." In Abraham Udovitch (ed.). *The Islamic Middle East, 700-1900.* Princeton, N.J.: Darwin Press, 1981.

————. "The Impact of Europe on a Traditional Economy: The Case of Damascus, 1840-1870." In Jean-Louis Bacque-Grammont and Paul Dumont (eds.). *Economie et sociétés dans l'Empire Ottoman.* Paris: Editions de CNRS, 1983.

————. "Land Tenure Problems and Their Social Impact in Syria around the Middle of the Nineteenth Century." In Tarif Khalidi (ed.). *Land Tenure and Social Transformation in the Middle East.* Beirut: American University of Beirut, 1984.

————. "The Law Court Registers and Their Importance for a Socio-Economic and Urban Study of Ottoman Syria." In Dominique Chevallier (ed.). *L'Espace social de la ville arabe.* Paris: G.-P. Maisonneuve et Larose, 1979.

————. "The Law-Court Registers of Damascus, with Special Reference to Craft Corporations during the First Half of the 19th Century." In Jacques Berque and Dominique Chevallier (eds.). *Les Arabes par leurs archives (XVI-XX siècles)*. Paris: Editions de CNRS, 1976.

————. "The Local Forces in Syria in the Seventeenth and Eighteenth Centuries." In V. J. Parry and M. E. Yapp (eds.). *War, Technology, and Society in the Middle East*. London: Oxford University Press, 1975.

————. "New Light on the 1860 Riots in Ottoman Damascus," *Die Welt des Islams*, 28 (1988): 412-430.

————. "The Social and Economic Structure of Bab al-Musalla (al-Midan), Damascus, 1825-1875." In George N. Atiyeh and Ibrahim M. Oweiss (eds.). *Arab Civilization: Challenges, and Responses. Studies in Honor of Constantine K. Zurayk*. Albany: State University of New York Press, 1988.

Raymond, André. *The Great Arab Cities in the 16th-18th Centuries: An Introduction*. New York: New York University Press, 1984.

Reid, Donald M. *The Odyssey of Farah Antun: A Syrian Christian's Quest for Secularism*. Minneapolis, Minn.: Bibliotheca Islamica, 1975.

————. "The Syrian Christians and Early Socialism in the Arab World," *International Journal of Middle East Studies*, 5 (1974): 177-193.

————. "Syrian Christians, the Rags-to-Riches Story, and Free Enterprise," *International Journal of Middle East Studies*, 1 (1970): 358-367.

Reilly, James A. *A Small Town in Syria: Ottoman Hama in the Eighteenth and Nineteenth Centuries*. Bern: Peter Lang, 2002.

————. "Damascus Merchants and Trade in the Transition to Capitalism,"*Canadian Journal of History*, 27 (1992): 1-27.

————. "From Workshops to Sweatshops: Damascus Textiles and the World Economy in the Last Ottoman Century," *Review*, 16 (1993): 199-213.

————. "Past and Present in Local Histories of the Ottoman Period from Syria and Lebanon," *Middle Eastern Studies*, 35 (1999): 45-65.

————. "Property, Status, and Class in Ottoman Damascus: Case Studies from the 19th Century," *Journal of the American Oriental Society*, 112 (1992): 9-21.

————. "Shari`a Court Registers and Land Tenure around 19th-Century Damascus," *Middle East Studies Association Bulletin*, 21 (1987): 155-169.

————. "Status Groups and Property Holding in the Damascus Hinterland, 1828-1880," *International Journal of Middle East Studies*, 21 (1989): 517-539.

————. "Women in the Economic Life of Late-Ottoman Damascus," *Arabica*, 42 (1995): 79-106.

Roded, Ruth. "Great Mosques, Zawiyas and Neighborhood Mosques: Popular Beneficiaries of Waqf Endowments in Eighteenth- and Nineteenth-Century Aleppo," *Journal of the American Oriental Society*, 110 (1990): 32-38.

———. "Ottoman Service as a Vehicle for the Rise of New Upstarts among the Urban Elite Families of Syria in the Last Decades of Ottoman Rule." In Gabriel R. Warburg and Gad G. Gilbar (eds.). *Studies in Islamic Society: Contributions in Memory of Gabriel Baer*. Haifa: Haifa University Press, 1984.

Rustum, Asad Jabrail. "Syria under Mehemet Ali," *American Journal of Semitic Languages and Literature*, 41 (1924-1925): 34-57, 183-191.

Saliba, Najib. "The Achievements of Midhat Pasha as Governor of the Province of Syria," *International Journal of Middle East Studies*, 9 (1978): 307-323.

Salibi, Kamal S. "The 1860 Upheaval in Damascus as Seen by al-Sayyid Muhammad Abu'l Su'ud al-Hasibi, Notable and Later *Naqib al-Ashraf* of the City." In William R. Polk and Richard L. Chambers (eds.). *The Beginnings of Modernization in the Middle East: The Nineteenth Century*. Chicago: University of Chicago Press, 1968.

Salibi, Kamal S., and Yusuf Q. Khuri. *The Missionary Herald: Reports from Ottoman Syria, 1819-1870*. Amman: Royal Institute for Inter-Faith Studies, 1995.

Salih, Shakeeb. "The British-Druze Connection and the Druze Rising of 1896 in the Hawran," *Middle Eastern Studies*, 13 (1977): 251-257.

Sanjian, Avedis K. *The Armenian Communities in Syria under Ottoman Rule*. Cambridge, Mass.: Harvard University Press, 1965.

Sauvaget, Jean, and Robert Mantran. *Règlements fiscaux ottomans. Les Provinces Syriennes*. Beirut: Institut Français de Damas, 1951.

Schilcher, Linda Schatkowski. *Families in Politics: Damascene Factions and Estates of the 18th and 19th Centuries*. Stuttgart: Franz Steiner, 1985.

———. "The Famine of 1915-1918 in Greater Syria." In John P. Spagnolo (ed.). *Problems of the Modern Middle East in Historical Perspective: Essays in Honour of Albert Hourani*. Reading, UK: Ithaca Press, 1992.

———. "The Hauran Conflict of the 1860s: A Chapter in the Rural History of Modern Syria," *International Journal of Middle East Studies*, 13 (1981): 159-179.

———. "Violence in Rural Syria in the 1880s and 1890s: State Centralization, Rural Integration, and the World Market." In Farhad Kazemi and John Waterbury (eds.). *Peasants and Politics in the Modern Middle East*. Miami: Florida International University Press, 1991.

Schlict, Alfred. *Frankreich und die syrischen Christen, 1799-1861:*

Minoritäten und Europäischer Imperialismus im Vorderen Orient. Berlin: Klaus Schwarz, 1981.

―――. "The Role of Foreign Powers in the History of Lebanon and Syria from 1799 to 1861," *Journal of Asian History,* 14 (1980): 97-126.

Seikaly, Samir. "Damascus Intellectual Life in the Opening Years of the 20th Century: Muhammad Kurd `Ali and *al-Muqtabas.*" In Marwan R. Buheiry (ed.). *Intellectual Life in the Arab East, 1890-1939.* Beirut: American University of Beirut, 1981.

Shamir, Shimon. "As`ad Pasha al-`Azm and Ottoman Rule in Damascus (1743-1758)," *Bulletin of the School of Oriental and African Studies,* 26 (1963): 1-28.

―――. "Midhat Pasha and Anti-Turkish Agitation in Syria," *Middle Eastern Studies,* 10 (1974): 115-141.

―――. "The Modernization of Syria: Problems and Solutions in the Early Period of Abdulhamid." In William R. Polk and Richard L. Chambers (eds.). *The Beginnings of Modernization in the Middle East: The Nineteenth Century.* Chicago: University of Chicago, 1968.

Shorrock, William I. *French Imperialism in the Middle East: The Failure of French Policy in Syria and Lebanon, 1900-1914.* Madison: University of Wisconsin Press, 1976.

Sluglett, Peter, and Marion Farouk-Sluglett. "The Application of the 1858 Land Code in Greater Syria: Some Preliminary Observations." In Tarif Khalidi (ed.). *Land Tenure and Social Transformation in the Middle East.* Beirut: American University of Beirut, 1984.

Smilianskaya, I. M. "The Disintegration of Feudal Relations in Syria and Lebanon in the Middle of the Nineteenth Century." In Charles Issawi (ed.). *The Economic History of the Middle East, 1800-1914.* Chicago: University of Chicago Press, 1966.

Spagnolo, J. P. "French Influence in Syria prior to World War I: The Functional Weakness of Imperialism," *Middle East Journal,* 23 (1969): 45-62.

Tamari, Steve. "Ottoman Madrasas: The Multiple Lives of Educational Institutions in Eighteenth-Century Syria," *Journal of Early Modern History,* 5 (2001): 99-127.

Thieck, Jean-Pierre. "Décentralisation ottomane et affirmation urbaine à Alep à la fin du XVIIIe siècle." In Jean-Pierre Thieck. *Passion d'Orient.* Paris: Editions Karthala, 1992.

Thompson, Elizabeth. "Ottoman Political Reform in the Provinces: The Damascus Advisory Council in 1844-1845," *International Journal of Middle East Studies,* 25 (1993): 457-475.

Tibawi, A. L. *American Interests in Syria, 1800-1901.* Oxford: Clarendon

Press, 1966.

―――. "Russian Cultural Penetration of Syria and Palestine in the 19th Century," *Royal Central Asian Journal*, 53 (1966): 166-182.

―――. "Syria in War Time Agreements," *Islamic Quarterly*, 12 (1968): 22-57.

Tresse, Rene. "Histoire de la route de Beyrouth à Damas, 1857-1892," *La Géographie*, 65 (1936): 227-252.

Tucker, Judith. *In the House of Law: Gender and Islamic Law in Ottoman Syria and Palestine*. Berkeley: University of California Press, 1998.

Vatter, Sherry. "Journeymen Textile Weavers in Nineteenth-Century Damascus: A Collective Biography." In Edmund Burke III (ed.). *Struggle and Survival in the Modern Middle East*. Berkeley: University of California Press, 1993.

―――. "Militant Journeymen in Nineteenth-Century Damascus: Implications for the Middle Eastern Labor History Agenda." In Zachary Lockman (ed.). *Workers and Working Classes in the Middle East*. Albany: State University of New York Press, 1994.

Venzke, Margaret L. "Aleppo's *Malikane-Divani* System," *Journal of the American Oriental Society*, 106 (1986): 451-469.

Vincent, Andrew. "Western Travellers to Southern Syria and the Hawran in the Nineteenth Century: A Changing Perspective," *Asian Affairs*, 24 (1993): 164-169.

Voll, John. "The Non-Wahhabi Hanbalis of Eighteenth-Century Syria," *Der Islam*, 49 (1972): 277-291.

―――. "Old Ulama Families and Ottoman Influence in Eighteenth-Century Damascus," *American Journal of Arabic Studies*, 3 (1975): 48-59.

Weismann, Itzchak. *Taste of Modernity: Sufism, Salafiyya, and Arabism in Late Ottoman Damascus*. Leiden: E. J. Brill, 2001.

Wood, Alfred C. *A History of the Levant Company*. New York: Barnes & Noble, 1964.

Zeine, Zeine. *Arab-Turkish Relations and the Emergence of Arab Nationalism*. Beirut: Khayats, 1958.

15. HISTORY, 1918-1946

Amadouny, V. M. "The Formation of the Transjordan-Syria Boundary, 1915-32," *Middle Eastern Studies*, 31 (1995): 533-549.

Bou-Nacklie, N. E. "The 1941 Invasion of Syria and Lebanon: The Role of the Local Paramilitary," *Middle Eastern Studies*, 30 (1994): 512-529.

―――. "Les Troupes Spéciales: Religious and Ethnic Recruitment, 1916-1946," *International Journal of Middle East Studies*, 25 (1993): 645-660.

————. "Tumult in Syria's Hama in 1925: The Failure of a Revolt," *Journal of Contemporary History*, 33 (1998): 273-290.

Burke, Edmund. "A Comparative View of French Native Policy in Morocco and Syria, 1912-1925," *Middle Eastern Studies*, 9 (1973): 175-186.

Chevallier, Dominique. "Lyon et la Syrie en 1919. Les bases d'une intervention," *Revue Historique*, 224 (1960): 275-320.

Cleveland, William. *Islam against the West: Shakib Arslan and the Campaign for Islamic Nationalism*. Austin: University of Texas Press, 1985.

————. *The Making of an Arab Nationalist: Ottomanism and Arabism in the Life and Thought of Sati` al-Husri*. Princeton, N.J.: Princeton University Press, 1971.

Deguilhem, Randi. "Turning Syrians into Frenchmen: The Cultural Politics of a French Non-governmental Organization in Mandate Syria (1920-1967)—the French Secular Mission Schools," *Islam and Christian-Muslim Relations*, 13 (2002): 449-460.

Dillemann, Louis. "Les Français en Haute-Djezireh (1919-1939)," *Revue Française d'Histoire d'Outre-Mer*, 66 (1979): 33-58.

Dodge, Bayard. "The Settlement of the Assyrians on the Khabur," *Journal of the Royal Central Asian Society*, 27 (1940): 301-320.

Eldar, Dan. "France in Syria: The Abolition of the Sharifian Government, April-July 1920," *Middle Eastern Studies*, 29 (1993): 487-504.

Garfinkle, Adam. *War, Water, and Negotiation in the Middle East: The Case of the Palestine-Syria Border, 1916-1923*. Tel Aviv: Tel Aviv University, Moshe Dayan Center for Middle Eastern and African Studies, 1994.

Gelvin, James. *Divided Loyalties: Nationalism and Mass Politics in Syria at the Close of Empire*. Berkeley: University of California Press, 1999.

————. "Demonstrating Communities in Post-Ottoman Syria," *Journal of Interdisciplinary History*, 25 (1994): 23-49.

Gil-Har, Yitzhak. "French Policy in Syria and Zionism: Proposal for a Zionist Settlement," *Middle Eastern Studies*, 30 (1994): 155-165.

Heald, Stephen (ed.). "The Hatay (Sanjak of Alexandretta)." *Documents on International Affairs, 1937*. London: Oxford University Press, 1939.

————. "Treaty of Friendship and Alliance between France and Syria, September 9, 1936." *Documents on International Affairs, 1937*. London: Oxford University Press, 1939.

Hourani, Albert. *Syria and Lebanon: A Political Essay*. London: Oxford University Press, 1954.

Howard, Harry N. *The King-Crane Commission: An American Inquiry in the Middle East*. Beirut: Khayats, 1963.

al-Husri, Sati. *The Day of Maysalun. A Page from the Modern History of the Arabs*. Washington, D.C.: Middle East Institute, 1966.

Kedourie, Elie. *In the Anglo-Arab Labyrinth: The Hussein-McMahon Correspondence and Its Interpretations, 1914-1939.* Cambridge: Cambridge University Press, 1976.

Khadduri, Majid. "The Alexandretta Dispute," *American Journal of International Law*, 39 (1945): 406-425.

Khoury, Philip S. *Syria and the French Mandate: The Politics of Arab Nationalism, 1920-1945.* Princeton, N.J.: Princeton University Press, 1989.

————. "Continuity and Change in Syrian Political Life: The Nineteenth and Twentieth Centuries," *American Historical Review*, 96 (1991): 1374-1395.

————. "Divided Loyalties? Syria and the Question of Palestine, 1919-1939," *Middle Eastern Studies*, 21 (1985): 324-348.

————. "Factionalism among Syrian Nationalists during the French Mandate," *International Journal of Middle East Studies* 13 (1981): 441-469.

————. "A Reinterpretation of the Origins and Aims of the Great Syrian Revolt, 1925-1927." In George N. Atiyeh and Ibrahim M. Oweiss (eds.). *Arab Civilization: Challenges and Responses. Studies in Honor of Constantine K. Zurayk.* Albany: State University of New York Press, 1988.

————. "Syrian Urban Politics in Transition: The Quarters of Damascus during the French Mandate," *International Journal of Middle East Studies*, 16 (1984): 507-540.

————. "The Tribal Shaykh, French Tribal Policy, and the National Movement in Syria between the Two World Wars," *Middle Eastern Studies*, 18 (1982): 180-193.

Longrigg, Stephen H. *Syria and Lebanon under French Mandate.* London: Oxford University Press, 1958.

Lust-Okar, Ellen Marie. "Failure of Collaboration: Armenian Refugees in Syria," *Middle Eastern Studies*, 32 (1996): 53-68.

Mardam Bey, Salma. *Syria's Quest for Independence, 1939-1945.* Reading, UK: Ithaca Press, 1994.

Melki, James A. "Syria and the State Department, 1937-1947," *Middle Eastern Studies*, 33 (1997): 92-106.

Mickelsen, Martin L. "Another Fashoda: The Anglo-Free French Conflict over the Levant, May-September 1941," *Revue Français d'Histoire d'Outre-Mer*, 63 (1976): 75-99.

Miller, Joyce Laverty. "The Syrian Revolt of 1925," *International Journal of Middle East Studies*, 8 (1977): 545-563.

Mockler, Anthony. *Our Enemies the French. Being an Account of the War Fought between the French and the British, Syria 1941.* London: Leo

Cooper, 1976.

Montagne, Robert. "French Policy in North Africa and Syria," *International Affairs*, 16 (1937): 263-279.

————. "Le traité franco-syrien," *Politique Etrangère*, 5 (1936): 34-54.

Olmert, Yossi. "A False Dilemma? Syria and Lebanon's Independence during the Mandatory Period," *Middle Eastern Studies*, 32 (1996): 41-73.

Rabinovich, Itamar. "The Compact Minorities and the Syrian State, 1918-1945," *Journal of Contemporary History*, 14 (1979): 693-712.

————. "Germany and the Syrian Political Scene in the Late 1930s." In Jehuda L. Wallach (ed.). *Germany and the Middle East, 1835-1939*. Tel Aviv: Tel Aviv University, 1975.

Russell, Malcolm B. *The First Modern Arab State: Syria under Faysal, 1918-1920*. Minneapolis: Bibliotheca Islamica, 1985.

Sanjian, Avedis K. "The Sanjak of Alexandretta (Hatay): Its Impact on Turkish-Syrian Relations (1939-1956)," *Middle East Journal*, 6 (1956): 379-384.

Satloff, Robert B. "Prelude to Conflict: Communal Interdependence in the Sanjak of Alexandretta, 1920-1936," *Middle Eastern Studies*, 22 (1986): 147-180.

Seurat, Michel. "Le rôle de Lyon dans l'installation du mandat français en Syrie: intérêts économiques et culturels, luttes d'opinion (1915-1925)," *Bulletin d'Etudes Orientales*, 31 (1979): 131-164.

Shambrook, Peter A. *French Imperialism in Syria, 1927-1936*. Reading, UK: Ithaca Press, 1998.

Shimizu, Hiroshi. "The Mandatory Power and Japan's Trade Expansion into Syria in the Inter-War Period," *Middle Eastern Studies*, 21 (1985): 152-171.

Sluglett, Peter. "Urban Dissidence in Mandatory Syria: Aleppo, 1918-1936." In Kenneth Brown (ed.). *Etat, ville et mouvements sociaux au Maghreb et au Moyen-Orient*. Paris: L'Harmattan, 1989.

Spears, Sir Edward. *Fulfilment of a Mission: The Spears Mission to Syria and Lebanon 1941-1944*. Hamden, Conn.: Archon Books, 1977.

Tauber, Eliezer. *The Formation of Modern Syria and Iraq*. London: Frank Cass, 1995.

————. "Rashid Rida and Faysal's Kingdom in Syria," *Muslim World*, 85 (1995): 235-245.

————. "The Struggle for Dayr al-Zur: The Determination of the Borders between Syria and Iraq," *International Journal of Middle East Studies*, 23 (1991): 361-385.

Thobie, Jacques. "Le nouveau cours des relations franco-turques et l'affaire Sandjak d'Alexandrette, 1929-1939," *Relations Internationales*, 19

(1979): 355-374.

Thomas, Martin C. "French Intelligence-Gathering in the Syrian Mandate," *Middle Eastern Studies*, 38 (2002): 1-32.

Thompson, Elizabeth. *Colonial Citizens: Republican Rights, Paternal Privilege, and Gender in French Syria and Lebanon.* New York: Columbia University Press, 2000.

Tibawi, A. L. "Syria from the Peace Conference to the Fall of Damascus," *Islamic Quarterly*, 1 (1967): 77-122.

Velud, Christian. "Syrie: État mandataire, mouvement national et tribus (1920-1936)," *Monde arab Maghreb-Mashrek*, 147 (1995): 48-71.

Warner, Geoffrey. *Iraq and Syria, 1941.* London: Davis-Poynter, 1974.

Watenpaugh, Keith D. "'Creating Phantoms': Zaki al-Arsuzi, the Alexandretta Crisis, and the Formation of Modern Arab Nationalism in Syria," *International Journal of Middle East Studies*, 28 (1996): 363-389.

————. "Middle-Class Modernity and the Persistence of the Politics of Notables in Inter-war Syria," *International Journal of Middle East Studies*, 35 (2003): 257-286.

Winder, Bayly. "Syrian Deputies and Cabinet Ministers, 1919-1959," *Middle East Journal*, 16 (1962): 407-429; 17 (1962-1963): 35-54.

Yaffe, Gitta. "Suleiman al-Murshid: Beginnings of an Alawi Leader," *Middle Eastern Studies*, 29 (1993): 624-640.

Yaffe-Schatzmann, Gitta. "Alawi Separatists and Unionists: The Events of 25 February 1936," *Middle Eastern Studies*, 31 (1995): 28-38.

Zamir, Meir. "Faisal and the Lebanese Question, 1918-1920," *Middle Eastern Studies*, 27 (1991): 404-426.

Zeine, Zeine. *The Struggle for Arab Independence: Western Diplomacy and the Rise and Fall of Faisal's Kingdom in Syria.* Beirut: Khayats, 1966. 2d ed.

16. HISTORY SINCE 1946

Abu Jaber, Kamel S. *The Arab Ba'th Socialist Party: History, Ideology, and Organization.* Syracuse, N.Y.: Syracuse University Press, 1966.

Antoun, Richard T., and Donald Quataert (eds.). *Syria: Society, Culture, and Polity.* Albany: State University of New York Press, 1991.

Batatu, Hanna. *Syria's Peasantry, the Descendants of Its Lesser Rural Notables, and Their Politics.* Princeton, N.J.: Princeton University Press, 1999.

Choueiri, Youssef M. (ed.). *State and Society in Syria and Lebanon.* New York: St. Martin's Press, 1993.

Devlin, John F. *The Ba'th Party: A History from Its Origins to 1966.* Stanford,

Calif.: Hoover Institution Press, 1976.

————. "The Baath Party: Rise and Metamorphosis," *American Historical Review*, 96 (1991): 1396-1407.

Hopwood, Derek. *Syria, 1945-1986: Politics and Society.* London: Unwin Hymans, 1988.

Ismael, Tareq Y., and Jacqueline S. Ismael, *The Communist Movement in Syria and Lebanon.* Gainesville: University Press of Florida, 1998.

Jankowski, James. *Nasser's Egypt, Arab Nationalism, and the United Arab Republic.* Boulder, Colo.: Lynne Rienner, 2002.

Kaylani, Nabil. "The Rise of the Syrian Ba'th, 1940-1958: Political Success, Party Failure," *International Journal of Middle East Studies*, 3 (1972): 3-23.

Kerr, Malcolm. *The Arab Cold War, 1958-1970: Gamal Abd al-Nasir and His Rivals.* London: Oxford University Press, 1971.

Kienle, Eberhard. "Arab Unity Schemes Revisited: Interest, Identity, and Policy in Syria and Egypt," *International Journal of Middle East Studies*, 27 (1995): 53-71.

Landis, Joshua. "Syria and the Palestine War: Fighting King 'Abdullah's 'Greater Syria' Plan." In Eugene L. Rogan and Avi Shlaim (eds.). *The War for Palestine: Rewriting the History of 1948.* Cambridge: Cambridge University Press, 2001.

Lesch, David. *Syria and the United States: Eisenhower's Cold War in the Middle East.* Boulder, Colo.: Westview Press, 1992.

Little, Douglas. "Cold War and Covert Action: The United States and Syria: 1945-1958," *Middle East Journal*, 44 (1990): 51-75.

Moubayed, Sami M. *Damascus between Democracy and Dictatorship.* Lanham, Md.: University Press of America, 2000.

————. *Steel and Silk: Women and Men Who Shaped Syria, 1900-2000.* Seattle: Cune Press, 2003.

Neff, Donald. "Israel-Syria: Conflict at the Jordan River, 1949-1967," *Journal of Palestine Studies*, 23 (1994): 26-40.

Olson, Robert. *The Ba'th and Syria, 1947 to 1982. The Evolution of Ideology, Party and State from the French Mandate to the Era of Hafiz al-Asad.* Princeton, N.J.: Kingston Press, 1982.

Picard, Elisabeth. "Retour au Sandjak," *Maghreb-Machrek*, 99 (1983): 47-64.

Pipes, Daniel. *Greater Syria: The History of an Ambition.* New York: Oxford University Press, 1990.

Podeh, Elie. *The Decline of Arab Unity: The Rise and Fall of the United Arab Republic.* Brighton, UK: Sussex Academic Press, 1999.

Rabinovich, Itamar. *The Road Not Taken: Early Arab-Israeli Negotiations.* New York: Oxford University Press, 1991.

————. *Syria under the Baath, 1963-1966: The Army-Party Symbiosis.* New York: Halstead Press, 1972.

Rathmell, Andrew. *Secret War in the Middle East: The Covert Struggle for Syria, 1949-1961.* London: Tauris Academic Studies, 1995.

Salem-Babikian, Norma. "Michel `Aflaq: A Biographic Outline," *Arab Studies Quarterly*, 2 (1980): 162-179.

Seale, Patrick. *The Struggle for Syria: A Study of Postwar Arab Politics, 1945-1958.* New Haven, Conn.: Yale University Press, 1986.

Torrey, Gordon. *Syrian Politics and the Military, 1945-1958.* Columbus: Ohio State University Press, 1964.

Zisser, Eyal. "June 1967: Israel's Capture of the Golan Heights," *Israel Studies*, 7 (2002): 168-194.

17. POLITICS

Abdallah, Umar. *The Islamic Struggle in Syria.* Berkeley: Mizan Press, 1983.

`Aflaq, Michel. "L'idéologie du parti socialiste de la résurrection arabe," *Orient* (Paris), 29 (1964): 151-172; 30 (1964): 103-112.

————. "Le socialisme dans la doctrine du parti Ba`th," *Orient* (Paris), 26 (1963): 161-166; 28 (1963): 185-195.

Amnesty International. *Report from Amnesty International to the Government of the Syrian Arab Republic.* London: Amnesty International, 1983.

————. *Syria: Indefinite Political Imprisonment.* London: Amnesty International, 1992.

————. *Syria: Repression and Impunity: The Forgotten Victims.* New York: Amnesty International, 1995.

————. *Syria: Torture by the Security Forces.* London: Amnesty International, 1987.

————. *Syria: Torture, Despair, and Dehumanization in Tadmur Military Prison.* London: International Secretariat, 2001.

Batatu, Hanna. "Some Observations on the Social Roots of Syria's Ruling Military Group and the Causes of Its Dominance," *Middle East Journal*, 35 (1981): 331-344.

————. "Syria's Muslim Brethren," *Merip Reports*, 110 (1982): 12-20, 34.

Beshara, Adel. *Syrian Nationalism: An Inquiry into the Political Philosophy of Antun Sa`adeh.* Beirut: Bissan, 1995.

Brand, Laurie A. "Economics and Shifting Alliances: Jordan's Relations with Syria and Iraq, 1975-1981," *International Journal of Middle East Studies*, 26 (1994): 393-413.

————. "Palestinians in Syria: The Politics of Integration," *Middle East Journal*, 42 (1988): 621-637.

Dam, Nikolaos Van. *The Struggle for Power in Syria: Sectarianism, Regionalism, and Tribalism in Politics, 1961-1980.* London: Croom Helm, 1981. 2d ed.

————. "Middle Eastern Political Cliches: 'Takriti' and 'Sunni' Rule in Iraq; 'Alawi' Rule in Syria. A Critical Approach," *Orient* (Oplanden), 21 (1980): 42-57.

Davis, Uri. "Citizenship Legislation in the Syrian Arab Republic," *Arab Studies Quarterly*, 18 (1996): 29-47.

Diab, M. Zuhair. "Syria's Chemical and Biological Weapons: Assessing Capabilities and Motivations," *Nonproliferation Review*, 4 (1997): 104-111.

Drysdale, Alasdair. "Ethnicity in the Syrian Officer Corps: A Conceptualization," *Civilizations*, 29 (1979): 359-374.

————. "The Syrian Armed Forces in National Politics." In Roman Kolkowicz and Andrzej Korbonski (eds.). *Soldiers, Peasants, and Bureaucrats.* London: George Allen & Unwin, 1982.

————. "The Syrian Political Elite, 1966-1976: A Spatial and Social Analysis," *Middle Eastern Studies*, 17 (1981): 3-30.

George, Alan. *Syria: Neither Bread nor Freedom.* London: Zed Books, 2003.

Ghadbian, Najib. "The New Asad: Dynamics of Continuity and Change in Syria," *Middle East Journal*, 5 (2001): 624-641.

Haddad, George. *Revolutions and Military Rule in the Middle East.* Volume 2, Part 1: *The Arab States.* New York: Robert Speller, 1971.

Hanna, Sami A., and George H. Gardner. *Arab Socialism: A Documentary Survey.* Salt Lake City: University of Utah Press, 1969.

Heydemann, Steven. *Authoritarianism in Syria: Institutions and Social Conflict, 1946-1970,* Ithaca, N.Y.: Cornell University Press, 1999.

Hinnebusch, Raymond. *Authoritarian Power and State Formation in Ba'thist Syria: Army, Party, and Peasant.* Boulder, Colo.: Westview, 1990.

————. *Party and Peasant in Syria: Rural Politics and Social Change under the Ba'th.* Cairo: American University of Cairo, 1979.

————. *Peasant and Bureaucracy in Ba'thist Syria: The Political Economy of Rural Development.* Boulder, Colo.: Westview, 1989.

————. *Syria: Revolution from Above.* New York: Routledge, 2001.

————. "The Islamic Movement in Syria: Sectarian Conflict and Urban Rebellion in an Authoritarian-Populist Regime." In Ali E. Hillal Dessouki (ed.). *Islamic Resurgence in the Arab World.* New York: Praeger, 1982.

————. "Local Politics in Syria: Organization and Mobilization in Four Village Cases," *Middle East Journal*, 30 (1976): 1-24.

————. "Political Recruitment and Socialization in Syria: The Case of the Revolutionary Youth Federation," *International Journal of Middle East*

Studies, 11 (1982): 143-174.

———. "Rural Politics in Ba'thist Syria: A Case Study in the Role of the Countryside in the Political Development of Arab Societies," *Review of Politics*, 44 (1982): 110-130.

———. "Syria under the Ba'th: State Formation in a Fragmented Society," *Arab Studies Quarterly*, 4 (1982): 177-199.

Human Rights Watch. *Syria Unmasked: The Suppression of Human Rights by the Asad Regime*. New Haven, Conn.: Yale University Press, 1991.

Kedar, Mordechai. *Asad in Search of Legitimacy: Messages and Rhetoric in the Syrian Press, 1970-2000*. Portland, Ore.: Sussex Academic Press, 2002.

Kerr, Malcolm. "Hafiz Assad and the Changing Patterns of Syrian Politics," *International Journal*, 28 (1975): 689-706.

Khalidi, Tarif. "A Critical Study of the Political Ideas of Michel Aflaq," *Middle East Forum*, 42 (1966): 55-67.

Kienle, Eberhard (ed.). *Contemporary Syria: Liberalization between Cold War and Cold Peace*. New York: St. Martin's Press, 1994.

Koszinowski, Thomas. "Rif at al-Asad," *Orient* (Oplanden), 25 (1984): 465-470.

Lawson, Fred. "Domestic Transformation and Foreign Steadfastness in Contemporary Syria," *Middle East Journal*, 48 (1994): 47-64.

———. "From Neo-Ba'th to Ba'th Nouveau," *Journal of South Asian and Middle Eastern Studies*, 14 (1990): 1-21.

———. "Social Bases for the Hamah Revolt," *MERIP Reports*, 12 (1982): 24-28.

Lesch, David. "Is Syria Ready for Peace? Obstacles to Integration in the Global Economy," *Middle East Policy*, 6 (1999): 93-111.

Macintyre, Ronald R. "Syrian Political Age Differentials, 1958-1966," *Middle East Journal*, 29 (1975): 207-213.

Maoz, Moshe. *Asad: The Sphinx of Damascus*. London: Weidenfeld & Nicolson, 1988.

Moaddel, Mansoor. "The Social Bases and Discursive Context of the Rise of Islamic Fundamentalism: The Cases of Iran and Syria," *Sociological Inquiry*, 66 (1996): 330-355.

Mufti, Malik. *Sovereign Creations: Pan-Arabism and Political Order in Syria and Iraq*. Ithaca, N.Y.: Cornell University Press, 1996.

Omar, Saleh. "Philosophical Origins of the Arab Ba'th Party: The Work of Zaki al-Arsuzi," *Arab Studies Quarterly*, 18 (1996): 23-37.

Perthes, Volker. *The Political Economy of Syria under Asad*. London: I. B. Tauris, 1995.

Pipes, Daniel. "The Alawi Capture of Power in Syria," *Middle Eastern*

Studies, 25 (1989): 429-450.

Quilliam, Neil. *Syria and the New World Order*. Reading, UK: Ithaca Press, 1999.

Reissner, Johannes. *Ideologie und Politik der Muslimbruder Syriens*. Freiburg: Klaus Schwarz, 1980.

Roy, Delwin A., and Thomas Naff. "Ba'thist Ideology, Economic Development, and Educational Strategy," *Middle Eastern Studies*, 25 (1989): 451-479.

Sadowski, Yahya. "Ba'thist Ethics and Spirit of State Capitalism: Patronage and the Party in Contemporary Syria." In P. J. Chelkowski and R. J. Pranger (eds.). *Ideology and Power in the Middle East: Studies in Honour of George Lenczowski*. Durham, N.C.: Duke University Press, 1988.

————. "Cadres, Guns, and Money: The Eighth Regional Congress of the Syrian Ba'th," *MERIP Reports*, 15 (1985): 3-8.

————. "Patronage and the Ba'th: Corruption and Control in Contemporary Syria," *Arab Studies Quarterly*, 9 (1987): 442-461.

Saqr, Naomi, et al. *Walls of Silence: Media and Censorship in Syria*. London: Article 19, 1998.

Seale, Patrick. *Asad of Syria: The Struggle for the Middle East*. Berkeley: University of California Press, 1988.

Sherry, Virginia N. *Syria: The Price of Dissent*. New York: Human Rights Watch/Middle East, 1995.

————. *Syria: The Silenced Kurds*. New York: Human Rights Watch/Middle East, 1996.

————. *Syria's Tadmor Prison*. New York: Human Rights Watch/Middle East, 1996.

Springborg, Robert. "Baathism in Practice: Agriculture, Politics, and Political Culture in Syria and Iraq," *Middle Eastern Studies*, 17 (1981): 191-209.

Van Dusen, Michael H. "Political Integration and Regionalism in Syria," *Middle East Journal*, 26 (1972): 123-136.

————. "Syria: Downfall of a Traditional Elite." In Frank Tachau (ed.). *Political Elites and Political Development in the Middle East*. Cambridge, Mass.: Schenkman, 1975.

Waldner, David. *State Building and Late Development*. Ithaca, N.Y.: Cornell University Press, 1999.

Wedeen, Lisa. *Ambiguities of Domination: Politics, Rhetoric, and Symbols in Contemporary Syria*. Chicago: University of Chicago Press, 1999.

Weismann, Itzchak. "Sa'id Hawwa and Islamic Revivalism in Ba'thist Syria," *Studia Islamica*, 85 (1997): 131-154.

————. "Sa'id Hawwa: The Making of a Radical Muslim Thinker in Modern

Syria," *Middle Eastern Studies*, 29 (1993): 601-623.

Winder, R. Bayly. "Islam as a State Religion: A Muslim Brotherhood View in Syria," *Muslim World*, 44 (1954): 215-226.

Yamak, Labib Zuwiyya. *The Syrian Social Nationalist Party: An Ideological Analysis*. Cambridge, Mass.: Harvard University Press, 1966.

Zisser, Eyal. *Asad's Legacy: Syria in Transition*. London: Hurst, 2001.

18. FOREIGN RELATIONS

Agha, Husayn, and Ahmad Samih Khalidi. *Syria and Iran: Rivalry and Cooperation*. London: Royal Institute of International Affairs, 1995.

Avi-Ran, Reuven. *The Syrian Involvement in Lebanon since 1975*. Boulder, Colo.: Westview Press, 1991.

Cobban, Helena. *The Israeli-Syrian Peace Talks: 1991-1996 and Beyond*. Washington, D.C.: United States Institute of Peace, 1999.

Davis, Uri. *The Golan Heights under Israeli Occupation, 1967-1981*. Durham, UK: University of Durham, 1983.

Dawisha, Adeed I. *Syria and the Lebanese Crisis*. London: Macmillan, 1980.

Ehteshami, Anoushiravan, and Raymond A. Hinnebusch. *Syria and Iran: Middle Powers in a Penetrated Regional System*. London: Routledge, 1997.

Eppel, Michael. "Syrian-Iraqi Relations during the 1948 Palestine War," *Middle Eastern Studies*, 32 (1996): 74-91.

Evron, Yair. *War and Intervention in Lebanon: The Israeli-Syrian Deterrence Dialogue*. Baltimore: Johns Hopkins University Press, 1987.

Ginat, Rami. "The Soviet Union and the Syrian Ba'th Regime: From Hesitation to Rapprochement," *Middle Eastern Studies*, 36 (2000): 150-171.

Golan, Galia, and Itamar Rabinovich. "The Soviet Union and Syria: The Limits of Cooperation." In Yacov Ro'i (ed.). *The Limits to Power: Soviet Policy in the Middle East*. London: Croom Helm, 1979.

Gresh, Alain. "Turkish-Israeli-Syrian Relations and Their Impact on the Middle East," *Middle East Journal*, 55 (1998): 188-203.

Hanna, John P. *At Arms Length: Soviet-Syrian Relations in the Gorbachev Era*. Washington, D.C.: Washington Institute for Near East Policy, 1989.

Harris, William W. *Taking Root: Israeli Settlement in the West Bank, the Golan and Gaza-Sinai, 1967-1980*. New York: John Wiley, 1980.

Hinnebusch, Raymond. "Revisionist Dreams, Realist Strategies: The Foreign Policy of Syria." In Bahgat Korany and Ali E. Hillal Dessouki (eds.). *The Foreign Policies of Arab States*. Boulder, Colo.: Westview Press, 1984.

Hof, Fredric. *Line of Battle, Border of Peace? The Line of June 4, 1967*. Washington, D.C.: Middle East Insight, 1999.

————. "A Practical Line: The Line of Withdrawal from Lebanon and Its Potential Applicability to the Golan Heights," *Middle East Journal*, 55 (2001): 25-42.

Human Rights Watch. *Syria/Lebanon: An Alliance beyond the Law: Enforced Disappearances in Lebanon.* New York: Human Rights Watch, 1997.

Karsh, Efraim. *The Soviet Union and Syria: The Asad Years.* London: Routledge, 1988.

Kaufman, Asher. "Who Owns the Shebaa Farms?" *Middle East Journal*, 56 (2002): 576-596.

Kienle, Eberhard. *Ba`th v. Ba`th: The Conflict between Syria and Iraq, 1968-1989.* London: I. B. Tauris, 1990.

Knudsen, Erik L. "The Syrian-Israeli Political Impasse: A Study in Conflict, War and Mistrust," *Diplomacy & Statecraft*, 12 (2001): 213-234.

————. "United States-Syrian Diplomatic Relations: The Downward Spiral of Mutual Political Hostility," *Journal of South Asian and Middle Eastern Studies*, 19 (1996): 55-77.

Lawson, Fred. *Why Syria Goes to War: Thirty Years of Confrontation.* Ithaca, N.Y.: Cornell University Press, 1996.

Lesch, Ann Mosely. "Contrasting Reactions to the Persian Gulf Crisis: Egypt, Syria, Jordan, and the Palestinians," *Middle East Journal*, 45 (1991): 30-50.

Maoz, Moshe. *Syria and Israel: From War to Peacemaking.* Oxford: Clarendon Press, 1995.

————. "From Conflict to Peace: Israel's Relations with Syria and the Palestinians," *Middle East Journal*, 53 (1999): 393-416.

Maoz, Moshe, and Avner Yaniv (eds). *Syria under Assad: Domestic Constraints and Regional Risks.* New York: St. Martin's Press, 1986.

Miller, R. Reuben. "The Israeli-Syrian Negotiations," *Mediterranean Quarterly*, 11 (2000): 117-139.

Muslih, Muhammad Y. *The Golan: The Road to Occupation.* Washington, D.C.: Institute for Palestine Studies, 1999.

————. "The Golan: Israel, Syria, and Strategic Calculations," *Middle East Journal*, 47 (1993): 611-632.

O'Ballance, Edgar. *No Victor, No Vanquished: The Yom Kippur War.* London: Barrie & Jenkins, 1979.

Perthes, Volker. "Syrian Regional Policy under Bashar al-Asad: Realignment or Economic Rationalization?" *Middle East Report*, 220 (2001): 36-41.

Rabil, Robert. *Embattled Neighbors: Syria, Israel, and Lebanon.* Boulder, Colo.: Lynne Rienner, 2003.

————. "The Ineffective Role of the US in the US-Israeli-Syrian Relationship," *Middle East Journal*, 55 (2001): 415-438.

Rabinovich, Itamar. *The Brink of Peace: The Israeli-Syrian Negotiations.* Princeton, N.J.: Princeton University Press, 1998.

Ramet, Pedro. *The Syrian-Soviet Relationship since 1955: A Troubled Alliance.* Boulder, Colo.: Westview Press, 1990.

Shalev, Aryeh. *Israel and Syria: Peace and Security on the Golan.* Tel Aviv: Jaffee Center for Strategic Studies, 1994.

————. *The Israel-Syria Armistice Regime.* Boulder, Colo.: Westview, 1994.

Shapland, Greg. *Rivers of Discord: International Water Disputes in the Middle East.* New York: St. Martin's Press, 1997.

Strindberg, Anders. "The Damascus-Based Alliance of Palestinian Forces: A Primer," *Journal of Palestine Studies,* 29 (2000): 60-76.

Usher, Graham. "Hizballah, Syria, and the Lebanese Elections," *Journal of Palestine Studies,* 26 (1997): 59-67.

Weinberger, Naomi J. *Syrian Intervention in Lebanon.* New York: Oxford University Press, 1986.

Zisser, Eyal. "The Israel-Syria Negotiations: What Went Wrong?" *Orient,* 42 (June 2001): 225-252.

19. POPULATION

David, Jean-Claude. "L'urbanisation en Syrie," *Maghreb-Machreq,* 81 (1978): 40-49.

Dewdney, J. C. "Syria's Patterns of Population Distribution." In J. I. Clarke and W. B. Fisher (eds.). *Population of the Middle East and North Africa: A Geographical Approach.* London: University of London Press, 1972.

Karpat, Kemal H. *Ottoman Population, 1830-1914: Demographic and Social Characteristics.* Madison: University of Wisconsin Press, 1985.

McCarthy, Justin. "The Population of Ottoman Syria and Iraq, 1878-1914," *Asian and African Studies,* 15 (1981): 3-44.

Proust-Tournier, J. M. "La population de Damas," *Hannon. Revue Libanaise de Géographie,* 5 (1970): 129-145.

Rabbath, Edmond. "Esquisse sur les populations syriennes," *Revue Internationale de Sociologie,* 46 (1938): 443-525.

Raymond, André. "The Population of Aleppo in the Sixteenth and Seventeenth Centuries according to Ottoman Census Documents," *International Journal of Middle East Studies,* 16 (1984): 447-460.

Samman, Mouna L. *La Population de la Syrie. Etude géo-démographique.* Paris: Editions de l'Office de la Recherche Scientifique et Technique Outre-Mer, 1978.

————. "Dimension de la famille et attitude des femmes syriennes à l'égard de la contraception," *Population* (Paris), 32 (1977): 1267-1276.

————. "Le recensement syrien de 1981," *Population* (Paris), 38 (1983): 184-188.

————. "La situation démographique de la Syrie," *Population* (Paris), 31 (1976): 1253-1287.

Shorter, Frederic C. "Croissance et inégalités au recensement de Damas," *Population* (Paris), 34 (1979): 1067-1086.

Syria Fertility Survey 1978: Principal Report. London: World Fertility Survey, 1982. 2 vols.

United Nations Economic Commission for Western Asia. *The Population Situation in the ECWA Region: Syrian Arab Republic.* Beirut: UNECWA, 1980.

Winckler, Onn. *Demographic Developments and Population Policies in Ba'athist Syria.* Portland, Ore.: Sussex Academic Press, 1999.

20. ECONOMY

Ahsan, Syed Aziz al-. "Economic Policy and Class Structure in Syria: 1958-1980," *International Journal of Middle East Studies*, 16 (1984): 301-323.

Asfour, Edmond. *Syria: Development and Monetary Policy.* Cambridge, Mass.: Harvard University Press, 1959.

Carr, David W. "Capital Flows and Development in Syria," *Middle East Journal*, 34 (1980): 455-467.

Clawson, Patrick. *Unaffordable Ambitions: Syria's Military Buildup and Economic Crisis.* Washington, D.C.: The Washington Institute for Near East Policy, 1989.

Elefteriades, Eleuthere. *Les chemins de fer en Syrie et au Liban. Etude historique financière et économique.* Beirut, 1944.

Gray, Matthew. "The Political Economy of Tourism in Syria: State, Society, and Economic Liberalization," *Arab Studies Quarterly*, 19 (1997): 57-73.

Guine, Antoine. *Les Communications en Syrie.* Damascus: Office Arabe de Presse et de Documentation, 1968.

Helbaoui, Youssef. *La Syrie. Mise en valeur d'un pays sous-développé.* Paris: Librairie Générale de Droit et de Jurisprudence, 1956.

————. "Major Trends in Syria's Foreign Trade, 1951-1962," *Middle East Economic Papers*, (1964): 1-24.

Heydemann, Steven. "The Political Logic of Economic Rationality: Selective Stabilization in Syria." In Henri J. Barkey (ed.). *The Politics of Economic Reform in the Middle East.* New York: St. Martin's Press, 1992.

————. "Taxation without Representation: Authoritarianism and Economic Liberalization in Syria." In Ellis Goldberg, Resat Kasaba, and Joel Migdal (eds.). *Rules and Rights in the Middle East: Society, Law, and*

Democracy. Seattle: University of Washington Press, 1993.

Hilan, Rizkallah. *Culture et développement en Syrie et dans les pays retardés.* Paris: Editions Anthropos, 1969.

Hinnebusch, Raymond. "The Political Economy of Economic Liberalization in Syria," *International Journal of Middle East Studies,* 27 (1995): 305-320.

International Bank for Reconstruction and Development. *The Economic Development of Syria.* Baltimore: Johns Hopkins University Press, 1955.

Kanovsky, E. *The Economic Development of Syria.* Tel Aviv: University Publishing Projects, 1977.

Keilany, Ziad. "Socialism and Economic Change in Syria," *Middle Eastern Studies,* 9 (1973): 51-72.

Makdisi, Samir. "Fixed Capital Formation in Syria, 1936-1957," *Middle East Economic Papers* (1963): 95-112.

————. "Syria: Rate of Economic Growth and Fixed Capital Formation, 1936-1958," *Middle East Journal,* 25 (1971): 157-179.

Park, Se-Hark. "Investment Planning and the Macroeconomic Constraints in Developing Countries: The Case of the Syrian Arab Republic," *World Development,* 13 (1985): 837-853.

Perthes, Volker. "The Private Sector, Economic Liberalization, and the Prospects of Democratization: The Case of Syria and Some Other Arab Countries." In Ghassan Salame (ed.). *Democracy without Democrats? The Renewal of Politics in the Muslim World.* New York: St. Martin's Press, London: I. B. Tauris, 1994.

————. "The Syrian Economy in the 1980s," *Middle East Journal,* 46 (1992): 37-58.

Sullivan, Paul. "Globalization: Trade and Investment in Egypt, Jordan, and Syria since 1980," *Arab Studies Quarterly,* 21 (1999): 35-72.

21. AGRICULTURE AND RURAL CONDITIONS

Ashram, M. al-. *The Agricultural System of the Syrian Arab Republic.* Aleppo: Aleppo University, 1985.

————. *Public Agricultural Sector in the Syrian Arab Republic.* Aleppo: Aleppo University, 1985.

Bianquis, Anne-Marie. "Les coopératives agricoles en Syrie; l'exemple de l'oasis de Damas," *Revue de Géographie de Lyon,* 54 (1979): 289-303.

————. "Le marché en gros des fruits et légumes à Damas," *Revue de Géographie de Lyon,* 53 (1978): 195-209.

Bourgey, A. "Le Barrage de Tabqa et l'aménagement du bassin de l'Euphrate en Syrie," *Revue de Géographie de Lyon,* 54 (1979): 434-454.

Dabbagh, Salah M. "Agrarian Reform in Syria," *Middle East Economic Papers*, (1962): 1-15.

Garzouzi, Eva. "Land Reform in Syria," *Middle East Journal*, 17 (1963): 83-90.

Hannoyer, Jean. "Essai d'histoire socio-économique des villages de la basse vallée de l'Euphrate," *Revue de Géographie de Lyon*, 54 (1979): 271-282.

———. "Le monde rural avant les réformes." In André Raymond (ed.). *La Syrie d'aujourd'hui*. Paris: Editions de CNRS, 1980.

Hannoyer, Jean, and Jean-Pierre Thieck. "Observations sur l'élevage et le commerce du mouton dans la région de Raqqa en Syrie," *Production Pastorale et Société*, 14 (1984): 47-63.

Hinnebusch, Raymond. "Bureaucracy and Development in Syria: The Case of Agriculture," *Journal of Asian and African Studies*, 24 (1989): 79-93.

Keilany, Ziad. "Land Reform in Syria," *Middle Eastern Studies*, 16 (1980): 209-224.

Khader, Bichara. *La Question agraire dans les pays arabes. Le Cas de la Syrie*. Louvain-la-Neuve, Belgium: CIACO Editeur, 1984.

———. "Propriété agricole et réforme agraire en Syrie," *Civilisations*, 25 (1975): 62-83.

———. "Réforme agraire en Syrie," *Revue Français d'Etudes Politiques Méditerrannéenes*, 7-8 (1978): 74-86.

———. "Structures et réformes agraires en Syrie," *Maghreb-Machrek*, 65 (1974): 45-55.

Klat, Paul. "Musha Holdings and Landownership in Syria," *Middle East Economic Papers* (1957): 12-23.

———. "The Origins of Landownership in Syria," *Middle East Economic Papers* (1958): 51-66.

Latron, André. *La Vie rurale en Syrie et au Liban. Etudes d'économie sociale*. Beirut: Imprimerie Catholique, 1936.

———. "En Syrie et au Liban: Village communautaire et structure sociale," *Annales d'histoire économique et sociale*, 4 (1934): 224-234.

Mahouk, Adnan. "Recent Agricultural Development and Bedouin Settlement in Syria," *Middle East Journal*, 10 (1956): 167-176.

Manners, Ian R., and Tagi Sagafi-Nejad. "Agricultural Development in Syria." In Peter Beaumont and Keith McLachlan (eds.). *Agricultural Development in the Middle East*. London: John Wiley, 1985.

Meliczek, Hans. "Land Settlement in the Euphrates Basin of Syria," *Ekistics*, 53 (1986): 202-212.

Metral, Francoise. "Land Tenure and Irrigation Projects in Syria: 1948-1982." In Tarif Khalidi (ed.). *Land Tenure and Social Transformation in the*

Middle East. Beirut: American University of Beirut, 1984.

———. "Le Monde rural syrien à l'ère des réformes, 1958-1978." In André Raymond (ed.). *La Syrie d'aujourd'hui.* Paris: Editions de CNRS, 1980.

———. "State and Peasants in Syria: A Local View of a Government Irrigation Project," *Peasant Studies,* 11 (1984): 69-90.

Metral, Francoise, and Paul Sanlaville. "L'eau, la terre et les hommes dans les campagnes syriennes," *Revue de Géographie de Lyon,* 54 (1979): 229-237.

Thoumin, Richard. "Notes sur l'aménagement et la distribution des eaux à Damas et dans sa Ghouta," *Bulletin d'Etudes Orientales,* 4 (1934): 1-26.

Tresse, Rene. "L'irrigation dans la Ghouta de Damas," *Revue des Etudes Islamiques,* 3 (1929): 459-573.

Warriner, Doreen. *Land Reform and Development in the Middle East: A Study of Egypt, Syria, and Iraq.* London: Oxford University Press, 1962. 2d ed.

Weulersse, Jacques. *Paysans de Syrie et du Proche-Orient.* Paris: Gallimard, 1946.

22. INDUSTRY AND LABOR

Allouni, Abdel Aziz. "The Labour Movement in Syria," *Middle East Journal,* 13 (1959): 64-76.

Atasi, Nadr. "Minimum Wage Fixing and Wage Structure in Syria," *International Labour Review,* 98 (1968): 337-353.

"Conditions of Work in Syria and Lebanon under the French Mandate," *International Labour Review,* 39 (1939): 513-526.

Gaulmier, Jean. "Notes sur le mouvement syndicaliste à Hama," *Revue des Etudes Islamiques,* 6 (1932): 95-126.

Guine, Antoine. *Etude sur l'Industrie Syrienne.* Damascus: Office Arabe de Presse et de Documentation, 1973.

Hannoyer, Jean, and Michel Seurat. *Etat et secteur public industriel en Syrie.* Beirut: Centre d'Etudes et de Recherches sur le Moyen-Orient Contemporain, 1979.

Imam, Chafiq, Malak Issa-Abayad, Francoise Metral, Jean Metral, and Rabah Naffakh. "L'artisanat du verre à Damas," *Bulletin d'Etudes Orientales,* 27 (1974): 141-181.

Kubursi, A. A., D. W. Butterfield, and Se Hark Park. *Syrian Manufacturing Activity: Past Performance and Future Prospects.* Hamilton, Ontario: McMaster University, 1981.

Longuenesse, Elisabeth. "L'industrialisation et sa significance sociale." In André Raymond (ed.). *La Syrie d'aujourd'hui.* Paris: Editions de CNRS, 1980.

————. "Labor in Syria: The Emergence of New Identities." In Ellis Goldberg (ed.). *The Social History of Labor in the Middle East.* Boulder, Colo.: Westview Press, 1996.

————. "The Syrian Working Class Today," *MERIP Reports*, 15 (1985): 17-25.

————. "Travail et rapports de production en Syrie. Une enquête sur les travailleurs de la bonneterie à Damas," *Bulletin d'Etudes Orientales*, 32-33 (1980-1981): 161-200.

Massignon, Louis. "La structure du travail à Damas en 1927," *Cahiers Internationaux de Sociologie*, 15 (1953): 34-52.

Perthes, Volker. "The Syrian Private Industrial and Commercial Sectors and the State," *International Journal of Middle East Studies*, 24 (1992): 207-230.

"Working Conditions in Handicrafts and Modern Industry in Syria," *International Labour Review*, 29 (1934): 407-411.

23. ANTHROPOLOGY

Boucheman, Albert de. *Matériel de la vie bédouine, recueilli dans la désert de Syrie.* Damascus: Institut Francais de Damas, 1935.

————. "Note sur la rivalité de deux tribus moutonnières de Syrie, les 'Mawali' et les 'Hadidiyn'?" *Revue des Etudes Islamiques*, 8 (1934): 11-58.

Charles, Henri S. "Quelques travaux des femmes chez les nomades moutonnières de la région de Homs-Hama: étude ethnographique et dialectale," *Bulletin d'Etudes Orientales*, 7-8 (1937-1938): 195-213.

————. *Tribus moutonnières du Moyen-Euphrate.* Beirut: Institut Francais de Damas, 1939.

Chatila, Khaled. *Le mariage chez les musulmans en Syrie, étude de sociologie.* Paris: Paul Geuthner, 1934.

Gerbino, Virginia Jerro, and Philip M. Kayal. *A Taste of Syria.* New York: Gazelle, 2002.

Kamp, Kathryn A. "Towards an Archaeology of Architecture: Clues from a Modern Syrian Village," *Journal of Anthropological Research*, 49 (1993): 293-317.

Khalaf, Sulayman N. "Settlement of Violence in Bedouin Society," *Ethnology*, 29 (1990): 225-242.

Rabo, Annika. *Change on the Euphrates.* Stockholm: Studies in Social Anthropology, 1986.

Rugh, Andrea B. *Within the Circle: Parents and Children in an Arab Village.* New York: Columbia University Press, 1997.

Seeden, Helga. "Aspects of Pre-history in the Present World: Observations Gathered in Syrian Villages from 1980 to 1985," *World Archaeology*, 17 (1985): 289-303.

Seeden, Helga, and Muhammad Kaddour. "Space, Structures, and Land in Shams ad-Din Tannira on the Euphrates: An Ethnoarchaeological Perspective." In Tarif Khalidi (ed.). *Land Tenure and Social Transformation in the Middle East.* Beirut: American University of Beirut, 1984.

Shaaban, Bouthaina. *Both Right and Left-Handed: Arab Women Talk about Their Lives.* Bloomington: Indiana University Press, 1988.

————."Persisting Contradictions: Muslim Women in Syria." In Herbert L. Bodman and Nayereh Tohidi (eds.). *Women in Muslim Societies.* Boulder, Colo.: Lynne Rienner, 1998.

Sweet, Louise. *Tell Toqaan: A Syrian Village.* Ann Arbor: University of Michigan Press, 1960.

Tresse, Rene. "L'évolution du costume des citadins en Syrie depuis le XIXe siècle," *La Géographie*, 71 (1939): 257-271; 72 (1939): 29-40.

————. "L'évolution du costume des citadins syro-libanais depuis un siècle," *La Géographie*, 70 (1938): 1-76.

24. MINORITIES

Abu-Izzeddin, Nejla M. *The Druzes: A New Study of Their History, Faith, and Society.* Leiden: E. J. Brill, 1984.

Bakhit, Adnan. "The Christian Population of the Province of Damascus in the 16th Century." In Benjamin Braude and Bernard Lewis (eds.). *Christians and Jews in the Ottoman Empire: The Functioning of a Plural Society.* Vol. 2: *The Arabic-Speaking Lands.* New York: Holmes & Meier, 1982.

Berard, Maurice. "Installing the Assyrians in the Orontes Valley," *Royal Central Asian Society Journal*, 23 (1936): 477-485.

Betts, Robert Brenton. *Christians in the Arab East: A Political Study.* Atlanta: John Knox Press, 1978. Rev. ed.

————. *The Druze.* New Haven, Conn.: Yale University Press, 1988.

Fakhsh, Mahmud. "The Alawi Community of Syria: A New Dominant Political Force," *Middle Eastern Studies*, 20 (1984): 133-153.

Firro, Kais. *A History of the Druzes.* Leiden: E. J. Brill, 1992.

Greenshields, Thomas H. "The Settlement of Armenian Refugees in Syria and Lebanon, 1915-1939." In John I. Clarke and Howard Bowen-Jones (eds.). *Change and Development in the Middle East.* London: Methuen, 1981.

Gubser, Peter. "Minorities in Isolation: The Druzes of Lebanon and Syria." In R. D. McLaurin (ed.). *The Political Role of Minority Groups in the Middle East.* New York: Praeger, 1979.

———. "Minorities in Power: The Alawites of Syria." In R. D. McLaurin (ed.). *The Political Role of Minority Groups in the Middle East.* New York: Praeger, 1979.

Haddad, Robert. *Syrian Christians in Muslim Society: An Interpretation.* Princeton, N.J.: Princeton University Press, 1970.

Hourani, Albert. *Minorities in the Arab World.* London: Oxford University Press, 1947.

Khuri, Fuad I. "The Alawis of Syria: Religious Ideology and Organization." In Richard T. Antoun and Donald Quataert (eds.). *Syria: Society, Culture, and Polity.* Albany: State University of New York Press, 1991.

Lewis, Norman N. "The Isma`ilis of Syria Today," *Royal Central Asian Society Journal,* 39 (1952): 69-77.

Maoz, Moshe. "Alawi Officers in Syrian Politics, 1966-1974." In H. Z. Schiffrin (ed.). *The Military and State in Modern Asia.* Jerusalem: Academic Press, 1976.

Michaud, Gerard. "Caste, confession et société en Syrie," *Peuples Méditerrannéens,* 16 (1981): 119-130.

Nieger, Colonel. "Choix de documents sur le Territoire des Alaouites (Pays des Noseiris)," *Revue du Monde Musulman,* 49 (1922): 1-69.

Picard, Elizabeth. "Y a-t-il un problème communautaire en Syrie?" *Maghreb-Machrek,* 87 (1980): 7-21.

Schaebler, Birgit. "State(s) Power and the Druzes: Integration and the Struggle for Social Control (1838-1949)." In Thomas Philipp and B. Schaebler (eds.). *The Syrian Land: Processes of Integration and Fragmentation.* Stuttgart: Franz Steiner, 1998.

Thomas, David. *Syrian Christians under Islam: The First Thousand Years.* Leiden: E. J. Brill, 2001.

Weulersse, Jacques. "Un peuple minoritaire d'orient, les Alaouites," *La France Méditerrannéene et Afrique,* 1 (1938): 41-61.

Zenner, Walter P. "Jews in Late Ottoman Syria: Community, Family, and Religion." In Shlomo Deshen and Walter P. Zenner (eds.). *Jewish Societies in the Middle East: Community, Culture, and Authority.* Washington, D.C.: University Press of America, 1982.

———. "Jews in Late Ottoman Syria: External Relations." In Shlomo Deshen and Walter P. Zenner (eds.). *Jewish Societies in the Middle East: Community, Culture, and Authority.* Washington, D.C.: University Press of America, 1982.

———. "Syrian Jews in Three Social Settings," *Jewish Journal of Sociology,* 10 (1968): 101-120.

25. RELIGION

Bryer, David. "The Origins of the Druze Religion," *Der Islam*, 52 (1975): 47-84; 53 (1976): 4-27.

Clark, Peter. "The Shahrur Phenomenon: A Liberal Islamic Voice from Syria," *Islam and Christian-Muslim Relations*, 7 (1996): 337-341.

Daftary, Farhad. *The Isma'ilis: Their History and Doctrines*. Cambridge: Cambridge University Press, 1990.

Kramer, Martin. "Syria's Alawis and Shi'ism." In Martin Kramer (ed.). *Shi'ism, Resistance, and Revolution*. Boulder, Colo.: Westview Press, 1987.

Laoust, Henri. *Essai sur les doctrines sociales et politiques de Taki-al-Din Ahmad ibn Taimiya*. Cairo: L'Institut Français d'Archéologie Orientale, 1939.

Little, Donald. "Did Ibn Taymiyya Have a Screw Loose?" *Studia Islamica*, 41 (1975): 93-111.

—. "The Historical and Historiographical Significance of the Detention of Ibn Taymiyya," *International Journal of Middle East Studies*, 4 (1973): 311-327.

Makarem, Sami. *The Druze Faith*. Delmar, N.Y.: Caravan Books, 1974.

Makdisi, George. "Ibn Taymiya: A Sufi of the Qadiriya Order," *American Journal of Arabic Studies*, 1 (1973): 118-130.

Memon, Muhammad Umar. *Ibn Taymiya's Struggle against Popular Religion*. The Hague: Mouton, 1976.

Meri, Josef W. *The Cult of Saints among Muslims and Jews in Medieval Syria*. Oxford: Oxford University Press, 2002.

Mirza, Nasseh Ahmad. *Syrian Ismailism: The Ever Living Line of the Imamate, AD 1100-1260*. Richmond, Surrey, UK: Curzon, 1997.

Moosa, Matti. *The Extremist Shiites: The Ghulat Sects*. Syracuse, N.Y.: Syracuse University Press, 1988.

Najjar, Abdallah. *The Druze: Millennium Scrolls Revealed*. Fred Massey (trans.). Atlanta: American Druze Society, 1973.

26. EMIGRATION

Hamui-Halabe, Liz. "Re-Creating Community: Christians from Lebanon and Jews from Syria in Mexico, 1900-1938," *Immigrants & Minorities*, 16 (1997): 125-145.

Hitti, Philip K. *The Syrians in America*. New York: George H. Doran, 1924.

Nicholls, David. "No Hawkers and Peddlers: Levantines in the Caribbean," *Ethnic and Racial Studies*, 4 (1981): 415-431.

Plummer, B. G. "Race, Nationality, and Trade in the Caribbean: The Syrians in Haiti, 1903-1934," *International History Review*, 3 (1981): 517-539.

Sales, Mary E. *International Migration Project Country Case Study: Syrian Arab Republic*. Durham, UK: University of Durham, 1978.

Saliba, Najib E. "Emigration from Syria," *Arab Studies Quarterly*, 3 (1981): 56-67.

Samman, Mouna L. "Aperçu sur les mouvements migratoires récents de la population en Syrie," *Revue de Géographie de Lyon*, 53 (1978): 211-228.

Zenner, Walter P. *A Global Community: The Jews from Aleppo, Syria*. Detroit: Wayne State University Press, 2000.

27. HEALTH AND EDUCATION

Cioeta, Donald J. "Islamic Benevolent Societies and Public Education in Ottoman Syria, 1875-1882," *Islamic Quarterly*, 26 (1982): 40-55.

Diab, Henry, and Lars Wahlin. "The Geography of Education in Syria. With a Translation of 'Education in Syria' by Shahin Makarius, 1883," *Geografiska Annaler*, 658 (1983): 105-128.

Drysdale, Alasdair. "The Regional Equalization of Health Care and Education in Syria since the Ba`thi Revolution," *International Journal of Middle East Studies*, 13 (1981): 93-111.

Gaulmier, Jean. "Note sur l'état présent de l'enseignement traditionnel à Alep," *Bulletin d'Etudes Orientales*, 9 (1942-1943): 1-33.

Goichon, A. M. "Oeuvres de bienfaisance et oeuvres sociales en Syrie," *Orient* (Paris), 12 (1959): 95-127; 13 (1960): 53-77; 14 (1960): 73-84, 217-237.

Sanagustin, Floreal. "Contribution à l'étude de la matière médicale traditionnelle chez les herboristes d'Alep," *Bulletin d'Etudes Orientales*, 35 (1983): 65-112.

Sharabi, Hisham. "The Syrian University," *Middle Eastern Affairs*, 6 (1955): 152-156.

28. LEGAL SYSTEM

Anderson, J. N. D. "The Syrian Law of Personal Status," *Bulletin of the School of Oriental and African Studies*, 17 (1955): 34-49.

Berger, Maurits S. "The Legal System of Family Law in Syria," *Bulletin d'Etudes Orientales*, 49 (1997): 115-127.

Botiveau, Bernard. "Le mouvement de rationalisation du droit en Syrie au cours de la première moitié du XXe siècle," *Bulletin d'Etudes Orientales*, 35 (1985): 123-135.

"The Electoral Law of Syria," *Middle East Journal*, 4 (1950): 476-481.

Heller, Peter B. "The Permanent Syrian Constitution of March 13, 1973," *Middle East Journal*, 28 (1974): 53-66.

Khadduri, Majid. "Constitutional Development in Syria with Emphasis on the Constitution of 1950," *Middle East Journal*, 5 (1951): 137-160.

Khairallah, Ibrahim A. *The Law of Inheritance in the Republics of Syria and Lebanon*. Beirut: American University of Beirut, 1941.

Manley, Mary Louise. "The Syrian Constitution of 1953," *Middle East Journal*, 7 (1953): 520-538.

Marayati, Abid A. al-. *Middle East Constitutions and Electoral Laws*. New York: Praeger, 1968.

29. LITERATURE

Adwan, Mamdouh. *The Old Man and the Land*. Damascus: Al-Tawjih Press, 1971.

Allen, Roger. "Arabic Drama in Theory and Practice: The Writings of Sa'dallah Wannus," *Journal of Arabic Literature*, 15 (1984): 94-113.

―――. "The Mature Arabic Novel outside Egypt." In M. M. Badawi (ed.). *Modern Arabic Literature*. Cambridge: Cambridge University Press, 1992.

Altoma, Salih J. "The Emancipation of Women in Contemporary Syrian Literature." In Richard T. Antoun and Donald Quataert (eds.). *Syria: Society, Culture, and Polity*. Albany: State University of New York Press, 1991.

Asfour, J. "Adonis and Muhammad al-Maghut: Two Voices in a Burning Land," *Journal of Arabic Literature*, 20 (1989): 20-30.

Attar, Samar. *The House on 'Arnus Square*. Pueblo, Colo.: Passeggiata Press, 1998.

―――. *Lina: A Portrait of a Damascene Girl*. Boulder, Colo.: Lynne Rienner, 1994.

Awwad, Hanan Ahmad. *Arab Causes in the Fiction of Ghadah al-Samman (1961-1975)*. Sherbrook, Quebec: Naaman, 1983.

Azrak, Michel (trans.). *Modern Syrian Short Stories*. Washington, D.C.: Three Continents Press, 1988.

Boullata, Issa J. (ed.). *Modern Arab Poets, 1950-1975*. London: Heinemann, 1976.

Boullata, Kamal (ed.). *Women of the Fertile Crescent: An Anthology of Modern Poetry by Arab Women*. Washington, D.C.: Three Continents Press, 1978.

Cooke, Miriam. "Ghassan al-Jaba'i: Prison Literature in Syria after 1980,"

World Literature Today, 75 (Spring 2001): 237-245.

Dahan, Sami. "The Origin and Development of the Local Histories of Syria." In Bernard Lewis and P. M. Holt (eds.). *Historians of the Middle East*. London: Oxford University Press, 1962.

Farzat, Ali. *A Pen of Damascus Steel*. Seattle: Cune Press, 2003.

Gabay, Z. "Nizar Qabbani: The Poet and His Poetry," *Middle Eastern Studies*, 9 (1973): 208-222.

Gabrieli, Francesco. "The Arabic Historiography of the Crusades." In Bernard Lewis and P. M. Holt (eds.). *Historians of the Middle East*. London: Oxford University Press, 1962.

Hafez, Sabry. "The Novel, Politics, and Islam," *New Left Review*, 5 (2000): 117-141.

Hazo, Samuel (ed. and trans.). *The Blood of Adonis*. Pittsburgh: University of Pittsburgh Press, 1971.

Idilbi, Ulfat. *Sabriya: Damascus Bitter Sweet*. Peter Clark (trans.). New York: Interlink Books, 1997.

Kahf, Mohja. "Politics and Erotics in Nizar Kabbani's Poetry: From the Sultan's Wife to the Lady Friend," *World Literature Today*, 74 (Winter 2000): 44-52.

Maghut, Muhammad. *The Fan of Swords*. May Jayyusi and Naomi Shihab Nye (trans.). Salma Khadra Jayyusi (ed.). Washington, D.C.: Three Continents Press, 1991.

Mina, Hanna. *Fragments of Memory*. O. Kenny and L. Kenny (trans.). Austin: Center for Middle Eastern Studies at the University of Texas, 1993.

Rayhanova, Baian. "Mythological and Folkloric Motifs in Syrian Prose: The Short Stories of Zakariyya Tamir," *Journal of Arabic and Islamic Studies*, 5 (2003): 1-12.

Schami, Rafik. *Damascus Nights*. Philip Boehm (trans.). New York: Scribner, 1995.

Tergeman, Siham. *Daughter of Damascus*. Austin: Center for Middle Eastern Studies at the University of Texas, 1994.

Wannous, Sa`dallah, and Nadim Mohammed. "Syria." In Don Rubin (ed.). *World Encyclopedia of Contemporary Theatre*, Vol. 4. London: Routledge, 1996.

Young, M. J. L. "`Abd al-Salam al-Ujayli and His Maqamat," *Middle Eastern Studies*, 14 (1978): 205-210.

30. MEDIA AND PUBLISHING

Dehni, Salah. "History of the Syrian Cinema 1918-1962." In G. Sadoul (ed.). *The Cinema in the Arab Countries*. Beirut: Interarab Centre of Cinema and Television, 1966.

Douglas, Allen, and Fedwa Malti-Douglas. *Arab Comic Strips*. Bloomington: Indiana University Press, 1994.

Ghadbian, Najib. "Contesting the State Media Monopoly: Syria on al-Jazira Television," *MERIA Journal*, 5:2 (2001).

31. ART AND ARCHITECTURE

Ali, Wijdan. *Modern Islamic Art*. Gainesville: University of Florida Press, 1997.

"Les arts en Syrie," *L'Oeil: Revue d'Art Mensuelle*, 37 (1983): 1-108.

Bahnassi, Afif. "Aleppo." In R. B. Serjeant (ed.). *The Islamic City*. Paris: UNESCO, 1980.

————. "Contemporary Art and Artistic Life in Syria," *Cultures*, 4 (1977): 167-186.

Butler, Howard Crosby. *Early Churches in Syria: Fourth to Eleventh Centuries*. Princeton, N.J.: Princeton University Press, 1929.

Cantacuzino, Sherban. "Aleppo," *Architectural Review*, 944 (1975): 241-250.

Copeland, Paul W. "Beehive Villages of North Syria," *Antiquity*, 29 (1955): 21-24.

Degeorge, Gerard. *Syrie: Art, histoire, architecture*. Paris: Hermann, 1983.

Dodd, Erica. *The Frescoes of Mar Musa al-Habashi: A Study in Medieval Painting in Syria*. Toronto: Pontifical Institute of Mediaeval Studies, 2001.

Dussaud, Rene, P. Deschamps, and H. Seyrig. *La Syrie antique et médiévale illustrée*. Paris: Librairie Orientaliste, 1931.

Favieres, Jacques de Moussion de. "Note sur les bains de Damas," *Bulletin d'Etudes Orientales*, 17 (1961-1962): 121-131.

Flood, Finbarr Barry. *The Great Mosque of Damascus: Studies on the Makings of an Umayyad Visual Culture*. Leiden: E. J. Brill, 2001.

Gaulmier, Jean. "Notes sur les toiles imprimées de Hama," *Bulletin d'Etudes Orientales*, 7-8 (1937-1938): 265-279.

Herzfeld, Ernst. *Inscriptions et monuments d'Alep*. Cairo, 1954-1956. 2 vols.

————. "Damascus: Studies in Architecture," *Ars Islamica*, 9 (1942): 1-53; 10 (1943): 13-70; 11 (1944): 1-71; 12 (1945): 118-138.

Hillenbrand, Robert. "*La Dolce Vita* in Early Islamic Syria: The Evidence of Later Umayyad Palaces," *Art History*, 5 (1982): 1-35.

Nassar, N. "Saljuq or Byzantine: Two Related Styles of Jaziran Miniature Painting." In Julian Raby (ed.). *The Art of Syria and the Jazira, 1100-1250*. Oxford: Oxford University Press, 1985.

Sauvaget, Jean. *Les monuments historiques de Damas*. Beirut: Imprimerie

Catholique, 1932.

———. "L'architecture musulmane en Syrie," *Revue des Arts Asiatiques*, 8 (1934): 19-54.

———. "Caravansérails syriens du moyen-âge," *Ars Islamica*, 6 (1939): 48-55.

———. "Inventaire des monuments musulmans de la ville d'Alep," *Revue des Etudes Islamiques*, 5 (1931): 59-114.

Sauvaget, Jean, and Michel Ecochard. *Les monuments Ayyoubides de Damas*. Paris: E. de Boccard, 1938-1950. 4 vols.

Tabbaa, Yasser. *Constructions of Power and Piety in Medieval Aleppo*. University Park: Pennsylvania State University Press, 1997.

Thoumin, Richard. *La maison syrienne dans la plaine hauranaise, le bassin du Barada et sur les plateaux du Qalamoun*. Paris: Ernest Leroux, 1932.

ABOUT THE AUTHOR

David Commins (A.B., University of California, Berkeley; Ph.D., University of Michigan) lived in Syria for two years in the early 1980s, first as a student at Damascus University, then as recipient of a Fulbright-Hays doctoral dissertation research grant to study Muslim religious reformers in the late Ottoman period. In 2001-2002, he received a Fulbright grant to support his residence as a guest scholar at the King Faisal Center for Research and Islamic Studies in Riyadh, Saudi Arabia, where he studied the history of Wahhabism in the 19th century. He is the author of *Islamic Reform: Politics and Social Change in Late Ottoman Syria* as well as articles on modern Islamic thought and Wahhabism. He is professor of history at Dickinson College in Carlisle, Pennsylvania.